CONF

# CONFRONTING DESIRE

## PSYCHOANALYSIS AND INTERNATIONAL DEVELOPMENT

## ILAN KAPOOR

CORNELL UNIVERSITY PRESS
*Ithaca and London*

First published 2020 by Cornell University Press

Library of Congress Cataloging-in-Publication Data

Names: Kapoor, Ilan, author.
Title: Confronting desire : psychoanalysis and interna-
   tional development / Ilan Kapoor.
Description: Ithaca [New York] : Cornell University Press,
   2020. | Includes bibliographical references and index.
Identifiers: LCCN 2020009151 (print) | LCCN 2020009152
   (ebook) | ISBN 9781501751721 (hardcover) |
   ISBN 9781501751752 (paperback) |
   ISBN 9781501751738 (pdf) | ISBN 9781501751745 (epub)
Subjects: LCSH: Social sciences and psychoanalysis. |
   Economic development. | Neoliberalism. |
   Postcolonialism. | Psychoanalytic interpretation.
Classification: LCC BF175.4.S65 K37 2020 (print) |
   LCC BF175.4.S65 (ebook) | DDC 150.19/5—dc23
LC record available at https://lccn.loc.gov/2020009151
LC ebook record available at https://lccn.loc.
   gov/2020009152

*To Anish and Roy*
*and*
*to Kent, as always*

# Contents

# Acknowledgments

I am extremely grateful to the three anonymous reviewers for their thorough, incisive, and engaging comments. Many thanks to the following for their helpful questions and remarks on one or more of the chapters in this book: Anna Agathangelou, Maria Eriksson Baaz, Sheila Cavanagh, Sara de Jong, Pieter de Vries, Anup Dhar, Arturo Escobar, Robert Fletcher, Gavin Fridell, Andil Gosine, Jason Glynos, Mary Hawkesworth, Naeem Inayatullah, Paul Kingsbury, Tereza Kuldova, Yahya Madra, Nivi Manchanda, Aysem Mert, Kent Murnaghan, Ceren Ozselcuk, Mustapha Pasha, Randy Persaud, Jesse Proudfoot, Joel Pruce, Lisa Ann Richey, Chizu Sato, Anna Secor, Maureen Sioh, Erik Swyngedouw, Gautam Basu Thakur, Japhy Wilson, Zahi Zalloua, and Aram Ziai. Any errors, gaps, and exclusions are mine alone.

My editor, Jim Lance, has been as supportive, helpful, and efficient as one could possibly ask for, as have the production and marketing teams at Cornell University Press. Thank you so much!

Immense gratitude to my dear friends for their always warm and invaluable company and support: Michael Bach, Nigel Barriffe, Anne-Marie Cwikowski, Leesa Fawcett, Honor Ford-Smith, Liette Gilbert, Rob Gill, Shubhra Gururani, Sherdil Hussain, James Ingram, Kate Irvine, Kajri Jain, Zamil Janmohamed, Alok Johri, Mohamed Khaki, Prabha Khosla, Stefan Kipfer, Jennifer and Kevin Knelman, Terry Maccagno, Patricia Messica, Radhika Mongia, Justin Podur, Usha Rangan, Nicola Short, Vasanthi Srinivasan, Aparna Sundar, Gert ter Voorde, Cyril Thivollet, Geeta Uppal, Karen Wirsig, Paul Yee, and Anna Zalik.

I owe to my family more than I can say: Kent, Anish, Roy, Michele, Sophie, Devon, Alba, Ben, Ishan, and Habiba. Special thanks to Jodi and Charlie for their always enthusiastic encouragement, and to the Murnaghans.

I gratefully acknowledge the following research funding, which helped support research for this book: Social Sciences and Humanities Research Council (Canada) Insight Grant, York University Faculty Association Sabbatical Leave Fellowship, and Faculty of Environmental Studies Small Research Grant.

The following chapters have been slightly revised from their original publication in the journals *Human Geography* and *Third World Quarterly*, and they are reprinted by permission of the publishers, *Human Geography* and Taylor & Francis Limited.

Chapter 4: "What 'Drives' Capitalist Development?" *Human Geography* 8 (3) (2015): 66–78.

Chapter 10: "The Queer Third World." *Third World Quarterly* 36 (9) (2015): 1611–1628.

Chapter 2: "Cold Critique, Faint Passion, Bleak Future: Post-Development's Surrender to Global Capitalism." *Third World Quarterly* 38 (12) (2017): 2664–2683.

# PREFACE

## A Novel Approach

This book offers a novel way of analyzing the problems, challenges, and potentialities of international development: psychoanalysis. Indeed, over the last decade or so, there has been a revitalization of the psychoanalytic perspective—particularly the Lacanian one—spearheaded mainly by Slavoj Žižek, but including notable others such as Joan Copjec, Alenka Zupančič, Mladen Dolar, and Todd McGowan, and spurring renewed interest in postcolonial pyschoanalytic thinkers such as Frantz Fanon, Ashis Nandy, Homi Bhabha, and Kalpana Seshadri-Crooks. This book draws on this perspective to analyze how development's unconscious desires "speak out," most often in excessive and unpredictable ways that contradict its outwardly rational declarations but also constitute the grounds for a radical politics.

Tellingly, international development (and social science more generally) has tended to disavow the unconscious. Yet, the theory and practice of development are replete with unacknowledged memories (racism, [neo]colonialism, gender discrimination) and traumatic prohibitions (economic recession, poverty), which show up in fantasies (the exoticized Third World, structural adjustment as universal panacea), obsessions (economic growth, "wars" on poverty or terror), or stereotypes (denigration, infantilization, sexualization, or feminization of the Third World Other). Psychoanalysis aims precisely at teasing out these unconscious processes. It can help explain the gap between development's scientific commitments (e.g., belief in progress, neutrality, objectivity, rationality) and its "irrational" practices (e.g., the seductive draw of narrow capitalistic growth, the fatal pull to aggressive racism, or the blind conformity to bureaucratic procedures or ethnic/religious identities). It can help us understand that development is not only a socioeconomic construction, but also an ideological construction intent on effacing its various internal traumas and contradictions—for example, the way in which development is "naturally" equated with neoliberal growth and liberal democracy, concealing the reality of rapacious capitalism, growing global inequalities and unevenness, and diminishing avenues for political contestation.

The novelty of the psychoanalytic perspective, as this book explains, lies not simply in its ideology critique, but also in opening up possibilities for radical political change. The unconscious, in other words, is to be seen as not only a basis upon which ideology is constructed, but also a political resource: its excess may well be unpredictable, yet such unpredictability can also be enabling, providing the subject with a means to break through the global capitalist status quo.

This view stands in contrast to Foucauldian discourse analysis, which has tended to dominate critical thinking in Development Studies over the last few decades. While discourse analysis is useful in focusing on power/knowledge dynamics in development, it ignores the fact that such power is able to take hold, expand and, crucially, persist only through unconscious libidinal attachments (e.g., desires, enjoyment). As this book suggests, this neglect leaves discourse analysis with few resources beyond localized resistance to address the structural challenges of global capitalism, depriving it of the radical political possibilities brought to light by psychoanalysis. I suggest, in fact, that local resistance is not only unthreatening to, and tolerated by, the global capitalist order but also psychoanalytically revealing for being an implicit acceptance of this order, often preventing the Left from imagining or struggling for a postcapitalist alternative.

But while Foucauldian-inspired development theorizing constitutes the main intellectual adversary in this book (see chapters 2, 7, 8, and 12), it is not the only one. I also take social construction to task, including its Butlerian performative variant (chapter 8), for yielding to a timid and fragmented feminist politics that may help reproduce the patriarchal capitalist status quo. Moreover, while partial to Marxist political economy for its uncompromising opposition to global capitalism and inequality, I highlight its neglect of the unconscious (chapters 1, 4, 5, and 12), which causes it to underestimate the power and stubbornness of neoliberal development. Instead, I suggest that complementing political economy with "libidinal economy" can not only help better understand how global capitalism reproduces itself, but also bring to the fore the passionate underpinnings (e.g., excess, drive) of any anticapitalist politics.

## Book Structure and Cross-Cutting Themes

The book has a relatively unique structure: the first section is composed of two chapters aimed at introducing the topic (the Lacanian psychoanalytic perspective and what it can contribute to Development Studies) and putting it into context (how the psychoanalytic perspective differs from, and innovates politically, the Foucauldian-inspired Post-Development perspective that has tended to dominate critical analysis in international development over the last few decades). The second section, "Keywords/Essays," is a collection of ten chapters applying key psychoanalytic concepts (antagonism, drive, envy, fetish, gaze, gender/sex, etc.) to the field of international development. These chapters are ordered alphabetically according to psychoanalytic keyword, dictionary-like, and used to examine a variety of arguments, examples, and case studies in development (e.g., Eurocentrism, universalism, capitalist accumulation/growth, structural adjustment, poverty, inequality, participation, technology, corruption, revolution, "race," LGBTI politics, etc.).

This structure is inspired by the influential edited volume *The Development Dictionary: A Guide to Knowledge as Power* (Sachs 1992), also organized in dictionary-like form; although unlike the latter, which is a collection of essays investigating key concepts in *development* from a Post-Development perspective ("development," "environment," "economy," "helping," "market," etc.), the idea here is to forefront important *psychoanalytic* concepts to help us better understand the politics of development.

The latter structure, it should be noted, is what helps explain the choice of subtitle for this book—it is not "A Psychoanalysis of International Development" but "Psychoanalysis and International Development," underscoring psychoanalysis as a well-established field with a range of analytic lenses and concepts that Development Studies would (arguably) do well to take seriously. In other words, while this book does indeed attempt to psychoanalyze development, the idea is also to decenter development (a typically psychoanalytic move!) by foregrounding a Lacanian understanding of the unconscious.

This unconventional structure implies two points. First, the book aims not so much at providing an overarching psychoanalytic argument as introducing some important psychoanalytic concepts—"keywords"—as a way of investigating a variety of problems in international development. The thread that does run through these keywords and essays is the thread of psychoanalysis itself: investigating the unconscious (of international development), that is, the multiple ways in which desire manifests, through processes of displacement, disavowal, envy, fetishism, and so forth. What emerges is how subjects of development do not necessarily seek their own good and often act against their stated intentions. Their unconscious desires are, in this sense, a barrier to their self-identity, impelling them to act contrary to their conscious wishes, obeying a logic of enjoyability, excess, and self-destruction rather than rationality, effectiveness, or humanitarianism.

Second, the book does not aim at comprehensiveness in relation to psychoanalysis (or indeed international development). It is a collection of essays on psychoanalytic concepts that, drawing on the recent Lacanian psychoanalytic literature, I see as important, fully acknowledging that other concepts are missing (e.g., aggression, delusion, madness, paranoia, psychosis, sublimation, etc.). Noteworthy in this regard is the fact that there are no exclusive chapter treatments of perhaps the most important Lacanian notions—enjoyment (*jouissance*), fantasy/ideology, and the Real. This is because they are dealt with in a variety of ways in multiple chapters, and in that sense are crucial cross-cutting themes in the book.

Enjoyment, which denotes not simply pleasure, but excess, to the point of being painful and counterproductive, is integral to almost every chapter. It is a central Lacanian/Žižekian concept that helps elucidate development's many "irrationalities": why people are seduced by capitalist development in spite of its production of inequalities and environmental ills (chapters 1, 2, 4, and 6), why racism endures despite decades of antiracist education (chapters 1, 7, and 11), or why the follies and excesses of development might themselves be the grounds for derailing and transgressing politics as usual (chapters 2, 4, 5, 8, 9, 10, and 12). An important dimension that I elaborate in the book (chapters 2, 7, and 12) is what I call "institutional enjoyment": in contrast to (idealized) Weberian conceptions of the state, which seek to ensure a rational and "neutral" functioning of bureaucracies, institutional enjoyment points to the unconscious processes as a result of which the civil service, as much as development nongovernmental organizations (NGOs), derive satisfaction from routine, red tape, and spectacle (e.g., of development interventions in crises such as famines, earthquakes, or war). In several instances, I point out how such satisfaction takes the form of sadomasochistic pleasure—lording bureaucratic power over the poor or sometimes instrumentalizing or even scapegoating them. This helps explain, in my view, not only why institutional power can veer toward the irrational and the authoritarian, but also why red tape—and in our mediatic age, spectacle—persists and grows in spite of repeated attempts at improving efficiency, slashing programs, or better "serving the poor." My claim is that the development institutional machine is a wellspring of pleasure and excess that defies rationality, objectivity, or humanitarianism.

"Fantasy" and "the Real," for their part, are also key notions highlighted throughout this book, the former underlining ways in which development is an ideological construction that attempts to efface its unconscious underpinnings (chapters 1, 2, 3, 6, 7, 10, and 12), the latter pointing to the inherent ruptures and contradictions of ideological formations which threaten to erupt at any moment (chapters 1, 2, 3, 4, 7, 8, 10, and 12). What is crucial about the former, I claim, is that ideological fantasies function at the level not simply of dreams or ideas but of institutional practices: desires and fantasies are externalized and materialized in the form of actions and institutional policy-making. This is another way of saying that all material or institutional practices—whether in international development or otherwise—are psychically charged, that is, they are constructed around, and respond to, various forms of trauma (the Real). It is also a way of conveying that the power, seduction, and rigidity of development practice lies in the disavowed desires that support it. And the wager in the book is that it is because such desires remain unconscious that ideological constructions are so difficult to dismantle. Ideology critique involves, then, not just deconstructing dominant discourses (identifying their gaps, exclusions, etc.), but unearthing and confronting their unconscious processes, as well as our own unconscious investments in them.

But if ideology's endurance and pervasiveness are made possible by its unconscious supports, these same supports are its Achilles's heel. This is to say that the material-discursive apparatus that is development is replete with gaps, excesses, and antagonisms (the Real), which render it insecure and unpredictable, thereby making possible a destabilizing politics. The book makes it a point to take up several of these (radical) political possibilities: ideology critique (chapters 1, 2, 3, 6, 8, and 12), aimed not only at dismantling neoliberalism but, as described above, also at facing up to our own libidinal expenditures in it; the strategy of subaltern mimicry, which strives to hijack state or corporate power and resources for subaltern purposes (chapter 7); a psychoanalytic antiracist politics, that struggles to challenge and recast dominant fantasies (chapter 11); a queer or hysterical Left politics, which attempts to inhabit drive's derailed excess to resist the seductions of neoliberalism and remain uncompromising on the Left desire for a post-capitalist alternative (chapters 4, 9, 10, and 12); and most importantly, a (negative) universal politics (chapters 3, 8, and 12) that bids to bring together a range of actors, based not on their particular identities as workers, women, or queers—which most often divide people along and across North-South lines—but their shared trauma (i.e., the inequalities and dispossession wrought by global capitalism). For, it will surely require nothing less than a series of coordinated and collective assaults, small and large, to (even begin to attempt to) destabilize the ever-changing and revolutionary global order that is capitalism.

Of course, such a panoply of (complementary) psychoanalytically informed political maneuvers is neither definitive nor sufficient, and comes without guarantees. As I emphasize repeatedly throughout the book, each would require tremendous determination and courage, not only to be able to "traverse the fantasy" of capitalist development, but also to fail (and perhaps fail again) while trying. But in any case, as Žižek reminds us (2018), we should not fall into the trap of always having to follow up a negative critique with an uplifting political alternative: for the latter may serve as pretext to avoid the true traumas of our times. There is the distinct prospect that, in our current historical conjuncture, no discernible way out can be found, so that assuming the "courage of hopelessness" means neither despairing nor grasping for easy solutions, but rather better confronting the deadlocks of our age, with the hope that something new might emerge. Psychoanalysis may well help point up the political resources available to us in a particular historical-spatial conjuncture, but this does not necessarily mean they are the appropriate resources, that is, that we have meaningfully identified and confronted the conjunctural antagonism, or that we have the collective commitment, courage, and wherewithal to do so.

## References

Sachs, Wolfgang, ed. 1992. *The Development Dictionary: A Guide to Knowledge as Power.* London: Zed.

Žižek, Slavoj. 2018. *The Courage of Hopelessness: Chronicles of a Year of Acting Dangerously.* London: Penguin.

# PART ONE

## *Introduction and Context*

# CHAPTER 1

# Psychoanalysis and International Development

## Introduction

When the indigenous leader confronts the development economist, accusing him of promoting a project that would mean the loss of livelihoods, the economist vehemently denies it, asserting:

- first, that the project *will* be beneficial for the community;
- second, that the project *may be* damaging but only because of community resistance to it; and
- third, that the project *may well be* damaging for the local community, but it will be good for broader national development!

This quip is meant to be humorous, but like all jokes it has a ring of truth to it, describing quite accurately how, for example, many recent megadevelopment projects—the Three Gorges and Narmada hydroelectric dams, the Trans-Anatolian Gas Pipeline, the Guinea Simandou mining project, and so on—have been justified in the face of local resistance (see De Wet 2006; Sovacool and Cooper 2013). The humor of the joke lies in what can be called the "kettle defense," the one evoked in Freud's famous joke in *The Interpretation of Dreams* (1955, 143–144; see also Žižek 2004, 1): "the defence put forward by the man who was charged by one of his neighbours with having given him back a borrowed kettle in a damaged condition. The defendant asserted first, that he had given it back undamaged; secondly, that the kettle had a hole in it when he borrowed it; and thirdly, that he had never borrowed a kettle from his neighbour at all." Taken individually, the denials are a plausible justification, yet strung together, they are contradictory, confirming precisely what they are trying to deny: that the defendant returned a broken kettle, or in our case that the development project will indeed be damaging to the local indigenous community. What psychoanalysis helps reveal here, even (or perhaps especially) through a joke, is the disavowed desire of development, its attempts at camouflaging and justifying its institutional power.

Yet international development—by which I mean the socioeconomic and discursive/institutional practices that structure relationships between the West and the Third World[1]—has tended to ignore psychoanalysis. In Development Studies, for example, there has been relative silence on the topic.[2] Partly, such neglect is attributable to the belief by social science disciplines (and Western modernity more generally) in the rational and empirical, taking seriously only that which is logical, measurable, and quantifiable, while disparaging the emotional, qualitative, unpredictable, or indeed humorous.

But partly I would venture to say that development's relative silence on psychoanalysis is itself psychoanalytically telling: it betrays a suspicion of human/social passions, which threaten to destabilize and alienate the subject, divide social identity, and thus endanger development's projects, intentions, aspirations. Yet, such resistance is revealing precisely of development's unconscious, of its inability or unwillingness to confront the antagonisms of its desires. The theory and practice of development, in this sense, are replete with unconscious social passions, which, as we shall see below, exactly because they remain unacknowledged can result in "irrational" behaviors. Thus, the function of psychoanalysis is to better understand the role of the unconscious, to help us identify and come to terms with our attachments and disavowed passions.

Accordingly, this chapter examines the contributions of psychoanalysis to international development, illustrating ways in which thinking and practice in this field are psychoanalytically structured. Drawing mainly on the work of Lacan and Žižek, I will emphasize three key points: (1) psychoanalysis can help uncover the unconscious of development—its gaps, dislocations, blind spots—thereby elucidating the latter's contradictory and seemingly "irrational" practices; (2) the important psychoanalytic notion of *jouissance* (enjoyment) can help explain why development discourse endures, that is, why it has such sustained appeal, and why we continue to invest in it despite its many problems; and (3) psychoanalysis can serve as an important tool for ideology critique, helping to expose the socioeconomic contradictions and antagonisms that development persistently disavows (e.g., inequality, domination, sweatshop labor). But while partial to Lacan/Žižek, I will also reflect on the limits of psychoanalysis—the extent to which it is gendered and, given its Western origins, universalizable.

## What Psychoanalysis Can Contribute to International Development

Freud is often considered to have discovered a new "continent"—the unconscious—that domain of repressed desires that disrupts and distorts our conscious lives yet remains inaccessible to us. His pioneering psychoanalytic insights see childhood development and family relationships as key to the formation of selfhood and the unconscious. According to him, the infant's separation from the maternal body is traumatic (resulting in painful loss and repression, which inaugurates the unconscious), as is the child's relationship to its father (resulting in rejection and the rise of the "Oedipus complex," crucial to the construction of sexual and gender identity). But in making these claims, Freud tends toward biological essentialism, famously attributing gender difference, for example, to the presence or absence of the penis, or affirming an innate human sexual drive or libido.[3]

Lacan takes up Freud's insights but reinterprets them linguistically. That is, he averts biological essentialism by constructing trauma around, not biological drives or anatomy, but symbolic processes.[4] Thus, the "Phallus" is not a bodily member but a symbol of fraudulent authority; the "castration complex" traumatizes, not because "we" don't have a penis, but because we experience a fundamental lack (the cutting off of one's enjoyment, rooted in our emergence from nature into culture); and sexual difference is based, not on physiological characteristics, but on the gap in structures of representation (see chapter 8).

Lacan draws on structural linguistics to argue that our horizons of meaning are thoroughly linguistic, so that we can make sense of the world only through language. The fundamental issue for him is that language is nothing but a string of signifiers, with each signifier deriving meaning purely relative to other signifiers (Lacan 1977, 105). The color blue, for instance, makes sense only in relation to the series red, green, black, white, yellow, brown, and so on; thus, the "blue" of the sky inheres not in some intrinsic "blueness" but in the linguistic relationship of blue to the other colors in the series.

Two important implications follow. The first is that there are no master signifiers or ultimate reference points: since each signifier depends on others, our signifying systems are incomplete and unstable, never able to express any definitive meaning or justification and never able to fully capture the thing being described. Master signifiers (e.g., freedom, democracy, God, beauty), and for that matter meanings, are fixed only by such factors as social convention, habit, acts of authority, and/or leaps of faith.

The second implication is that, once we (as human animals) enter language, we are thoroughly denaturalized. That is, we are unable to relate to the world directly any more, since it is always mediated by and through language. Psychoanalytically speaking, this means that we are cut off (i.e., symbolically castrated) from our "instincts." Our biological "needs," in the sense of pure and unmediated instincts, are accessible only through language, thus becoming what Lacan calls "desires" (2017, 203).[5] The problem is that, while an instinctual need such as thirst can be satisfied, desire never can be, because it is mediated by a signifying system that is always imprecise and lacking. There is, therefore, a gap between desire and need, as a result of which we often desire what we don't need. So, for example, the global North doesn't need to engage in overconsumption, but many of us who live there desire to nonetheless; or we don't need to eat fatty or sweet foods, but we often desire them (Eisenstein and McGowan 2012, 12). The related, more general, point here is that because we are linguistic beings and the symbolic order is lacking, so are *we* lacking, always divided and alienated (from the world, from our own biological instincts).

Lacan articulates many of the above ideas by positing three interrelated registers, which make possible our interpsychic life: the Imaginary (the order of seductive images and meanings, which often provide the illusion of wholeness and clarity); the Symbolic (the order of language, the result of historical, intersubjective, and collective practice);[6] and the Real (the order of traumas, antagonisms, and contradictions that undermine reality but also constitute its conditions of possibility) (see Homer 2004, 10; Lacan 2016, 11–12; Žižek and Daly 2004, 65).[7] For Lacan, we are positioned, and create ourselves, in all three registers, with the Symbolic and Imaginary helping to make the fabrics of our reality (however incompletely), and the Real tearing them apart.

One last point before we tease out the implications of all of this for development: to say that we are linguistic beings does not mean that we create the material world. Lacan is not positing an idealist ontology here. Rather, the view is that our signifying systems frame reality, laying down the structures and parameters for our understanding of it (in this sense, the Lacanian standpoint is quite consistent with discourse theory). In fact, Joan Copjec (1994, 7–8) claims that Lacan is a materialist:

[Suggesting that] something cannot be claimed to exist unless it can first be stated, articulated in language—is no mere tautology; it is a materialist argument parallel to the rule of science which states that no object can be legitimately posited unless one can also specify the technical means of locating it. The existence of a thing materially depends on its being articulated in language, for only in this case can it be said to have an objective—that is to say, a verifiable—existence, one that can be debated by others.

In other words, materiality cannot be apprehended without immateriality (the Symbolic), and each is meaningless without the other, a claim that aligns well with modern physics (e.g., quantum mechanics, wave theory) (see Žižek 2013, 905ff.).

Žižek pushes this "dialectical materialism" further to argue that human consciousness emerges from material reality itself, or more precisely as a result of the gap (the Real) or lack in reality. No wonder that our own subjectivity mirrors this same lack; a lack, as we shall see below, that we are constantly trying to avoid and disavow even as we try to apprehend reality. Listen to Žižek on this point:

> We cannot pass directly from nature to culture. Something goes terribly wrong in nature: nature produces an unnatural monstrosity and I claim that it is in order to cope with, to domesticate, this monstrosity that we symbolize. Taking Freud's fort/da example as model: something is primordially broken (the absence of the mother and so on) and symbolization functions as a way of living with that kind of trauma. (Žižek and Daly 2004, 65; see also Žižek 2014, 29; Zupančič 2017, 121)

So on the one hand, materiality is meaningless in the absence of a gap or negativity; it is sustained only by its inability to complete itself. And on the other, subjectivity emerges as a consequence of the self-alienation of materiality, becoming, as it were, the embodiment of reality's antagonism (see chapter 8).

## Development's Unconscious: Uncovering Gaps, Slips, Blind Spots

The unconscious is not, as is commonly held, some discrete, hidden domain of wild and unpredictable drives; rather, it is a linguistic site in which desire reveals itself. As explained above, from the point of view of Lacanian psychoanalysis, our language is always marked by holes, gaps, erasures: these gaps are precisely the unconscious. In this regard, Lacan famously states that "the unconscious is structured like a language" (1998a, 48; 1998b, 203). That is, it is integral to language but is an excess or remainder to it. It comes about because of a mismatch between language and reality (i.e., a "cut" in materiality itself, as we saw earlier) and the inability of meaning to be fixed, thereby obeying a logic and grammar that psychoanalysis attempts to decipher (Homer 2004, 69). Thus, as linguistic subjects, our everyday lives are replete with unconscious acts, which, because they are *unconscious*, are inaccessible to us; nonetheless, they manifest themselves in the form of slips, miscommunications, confusion, mistakes, blind spots.

It is important to note that the unconscious is conceived intersubjectively here. Lacan is deliberately depsychologizing the concept, in the sense of wresting it from any notion of a separate, individual mind. Rather, because the unconscious is intrinsic to language, it is part and parcel of a shared (albeit unstable) horizon of meaning. It is therefore broadly sociocultural, and hence transindividual. It becomes a vital part of our subjectivity without residing "inside" us. In fact, for Lacan, the unconscious is decidedly outside. In this connection, he writes, "the unconscious is the discourse of the Other" (1998b, 131), underlining how language always precedes us, so that we form our subjecthood and desires through the Other.[8]

It should be clearer now why Lacanian psychoanalysis lends itself to the task of uncovering *development*'s unconscious. Because psychoanalysis is primarily a cultural and linguistic practice, it can be used to analyze development's texts—be these written or institutional, social or economic, academic or policy-oriented—to reveal their gaps and blind spots. Or to put it another way: that development is a linguistic/discursive/institutional/socioeconomic construction is proof that it is replete with unconscious desires that "speak." In fact, following Lacan's thinking, to identify the unconscious thusly helps underline that trauma is not an "inner" condition to development and its subjects, but is externalized and materialized in development institutions. Our symbolic world, after all, is not some theoretical entity; in the way that Lacanians conceive it, we understand, desire, act, and interact only through it. No wonder that its gaps show up in everything we do, and hence that it is possible to say that the unconscious is present as much in family circles as our work environments, shopping malls as much as universities, and discursive politics as much as development's institutional policies and programs.

There are likely innumerable ways of pointing to development's unconscious, but I want to focus on two sets of examples. The first is what might be called *development's "slips of the tongue."* As stated above, while the unconscious cannot be fully apprehended, it does reveal itself in a number of ways, one of which is slips of the tongue. I use that expression broadly to refer to verbal tics, and institutional stumbles and confusion. For a start, what comes to mind here are commonly used development concepts, each of which betrays itself:

- *Population control*: this refers to neo-Malthusian programs aimed at better managing rapid population growth in developing countries (e.g., India, China, Peru, especially during the period from the 1970s to the 1990s), which resulted in such widespread excesses as forced sterilization, including vasectomies for men and tubal sterilization of women, as well as the sterilization of people with disabilities, and the medical abuse of transgender people, practices that continue to some extent even today (see Eager 2004; Fletcher, Breitling, and Puleo 2014). "Population control" is thus precisely that—a technology aimed at controlling the population (what Foucault calls "biopower").
- *Sustainable development*: this is meant to convey the limits that our biosphere imposes on capitalist growth, but has come to mean exactly the opposite—the sustenance of capitalist growth—which is, in fact, the literal meaning of the term. Sustainable development (or "sustainability") is now very much part of the mainstream lexicon, which sees business, governments, and NGOs alike conceptualize the environment not as a problem / limit, but as a business opportunity (i.e., "greenwashing" or "green capitalism").
- *Foreign aid*: ostensibly referring to Western "gifts" to the Third World, much Official Development Assistance (ODA) is in fact tied (to foreign-policy or security objectives, or the purchase of goods and services from the donor country) and conditional (on the recipient fulfilling certain ideological conditions, in the form of neoliberal structural adjustment programs, for example). From the point of view of the recipient, then, foreign aid is often about receiving *foreign* gifts, that is, strange or poisoned gifts, which in many ways primarily *aid* the foreigner—materially and ideologically, as suggested above, but also symbolically, because they make the donor look and feel good (see Kapoor 2008, chap. 5).

What is interesting about these terms is that their unconscious desires reveal themselves retroactively. Each term is first conceived and uttered, often constructed to signify more than its literal meaning (and in the case of "sustainable development," the precise opposite of its literal meaning). But then, once it is discursively deployed and institutionally practiced, its unconscious content reveals itself to be the literal meaning that had been staring at us in the first place. More often than not, the unconscious is plainly evident from the start, but only retroactively discovered (more on this below).

It is also worth mentioning the myriad verbal gaffes or "bloopers" in development, which so often divulge unspoken intentions or prejudices:

- Ronald Reagan's notorious slips, including, "The United States has much to offer the Third World War" (instead of just "Third World," an error repeated nine times during the same speech) (quoted in Cornelius 2001, 176), as if confirming his government's impending bellicose politics and close ties to the military-industrial complex;
- George W. Bush's equally notorious gaffes, including, "I think the best way to attack—to handle—the attacks of September the 11th is to fight fear with friendship,"[9] presaging his regime's "attack" on (and precisely not friendship with) Iraq and Afghanistan;
- Bob Geldof's Live Aid statement, "Something must be done, anything must be done, whether it works or not" (quoted in Glennie 2008, 9), betraying that what really matters for humanitarian celebrities such as him is the publicity, that is, *being seen* to be doing something, whether it works or not;
- the 2013 corporate PR executive's tweet, written as she boarded a flight from London to South Africa, "Going to Africa. Hope I don't get AIDS. Just Kidding. I'm White!" (BBC 2013), which discloses the not uncommon Western racist anxiety (cloaked as humor) about Africa and Africans; and
- the 2018 tweet by the United Kingdom's then Conservative Minister of State for International Development, Penny Mordaunt, announcing her new private investment policy to "irradiate extreme global poverty" (instead of irradicate/eradicate), which echoes frequent references to "wars" on poverty/terror, while also inadvertently expressing the not uncommon *leftist* equation of capitalism with ("extreme") violence.[10]

One of the more significant slips of the tongue though is that of Lawrence Summers, who as chief economist and vice president of the World Bank in 1991, writes an infamous memo to Brazil's then secretary of the environment: "Just between you and me, shouldn't the World Bank be encouraging MORE migration of the dirty industries to the LDCs [Least Developed Countries]?" The memo goes on to argue that the "poor" have short lives, Africa is "vastly UNDER-polluted," and rich people value clean air and water more than the poor (quoted in Pellow 2007, 9; see also Korten 1992).[11]

The memo is remarkable in terms of both its content and form. Its content reveals a callous (if not racist) disregard for the poor / Third World, which is characterized as a (potential) toxic dumping ground for First World industries. But its form is telling as well: while it was leaked, it was clearly not meant to be (the "Just between you and me" is an important detail), which points up precisely its unconscious (or "dirty"!) underside. Thus, the *form* of the memo is what makes its content embarrassing, doubly so in fact: not only does its secretive intent help strip bare the pretense that the World Bank works on behalf of the Third World (as partly implied by the memo, the Bank is controlled by, and primarily serves the economic interests of, the First World), but it also casts doubt on the "scientific" and "rational" construction of development economics, which in its neoclassical guise here is being used as nothing but an ideological rationalization of free market economics. Summers goes so far as to assert that "I think the economic logic behind dumping a load of toxic waste in the lowest-wage country is impeccable and we should face up to that" (quoted in Pellow 2007, 9). But is it logical or *ideo*logical to assert that improving the human welfare of the rich justifies poisoning the poor and the Third World? And perhaps more importantly for our present purpose, how "impeccable" can this economic logic be if it can only be uttered in a *secret* memo?

Summers's memo, in this sense, is revealing of not just his personal prejudices but the Bank's unconscious. Speaking from a powerful leadership position as the Bank's chief economist and vice president, his words are indicative of a shared Bank culture (belief in free market economics, the assumption of the Bank as global development authority, etc.) and its attendant desires (domination of the poor and the Third World to facilitate free trade and the mobility of Western capital). And while free market ideology can be (and is) loudly promoted within and beyond the walls of the Bank, its accompanying (unconscious) supremacist desires can be uttered only in camera. Embarrassment ensues precisely when these "private" desires become public, exposing the callousness and irrationality of the "free market" economics the Bank continues to defend.

A second way of illustrating development's unconscious is by focusing on its *blind spots*. Once again, there are likely multiple examples available, but to mention just a few: the persistent failure by such mainstream economic indicators as gross domestic product or the Human Development Index to count women's household work or subtract environmental destruction (they both tally deforestation, for example, as a gain), which reveals the priority given to what is considered "productive growth" under global capitalism, to the exclusion of gender or environmental concerns (see chapter 6); the frequent treatment by development organizations of those they serve (e.g., those affected by war or climate change) as passive victims, underlining the deep and longstanding paternalism that pervades development (see Baaz 2008); and the overwhelming tendency of global (liberal) human rights discourse to focus on individual civil and political rights (e.g., free speech, rule of law), to the exclusion of collective rights (e.g., indigenous peoples' rights, communal biodiversity, and intellectual property rights) and socioeconomic rights (e.g., land claims, workers' rights, living wages).

The blind spot on which I would like to dwell a little though is the continuing neglect of colonialism in mainstream development discourse. This neglect coincides with the very "invention" of international development in the period after the Second World War: aid to "underdeveloped" areas became vital to containing what the United States and other Western powers saw as Soviet expansionism. No wonder that Modernization Theory—which pioneered development as an academic field, and has anchored Western foreign policy and development institutions ever since—bears the strong imprint of such Cold War politics. As several analysts have argued (e.g., Escobar 1995, 14–15; Frank 1967; Valenzuela and Valenzuela 1998),[12] Modernization tends to take a decidedly post–Second World War view of history, thus avoiding the history of Western colonialism. For instance, Walt Rostow's *The Stages of Economic Growth*—so influential in economic and foreign policy circles—fails to deal with colonial rule in any meaningful way. It's not that Rostow doesn't mention colonialism at all; he does, but its significance is notably downplayed. In a short section on "colonialism," he goes so far as to state that colonies were founded for "oblique reasons" and colonial subjects "looked kindly" on the colonizer's efforts to organize "suitable political frameworks" (1960, 110).

But such disavowal continues in various guises even today. It is visible in World Bank/International Monetary Fund structural adjustment programs, which make no mention of, or allowances for, the fact that the West's colonial plunder might have something to do with the recipient's current socioeconomic conditions. And it is evident in World Trade Organization trade deals, which so often assume a global economic level playing field in their pursuit of "free" trade, amounting to trade "freed" of any past colonial entanglements. Robert Fletcher (2012) calls such persistent sanitization of colonialism "imperialist amnesia." He analyzes the work of several development/globalization pundits to drive home the point: *New York Times* columnist Thomas Freidman, former World Bank economist Paul Collier, and economist and UN advisor Jeffrey Sachs, all of whom treat wealth accumulation in the global North or poverty in the global South by omitting consideration of the imperialist extraction of Third World resources. In *The End of Poverty* (2005, 208), for example, Sachs claims that "the combination of Africa's adverse geography and its extreme poverty creates the worst poverty trap in the world." Vandana Shiva, struck by the glaring blind spot, takes Sachs to task, declaring:

> This is a totally false history of poverty. . . . The wealth accumulated by Europe and North America is largely based on riches taken from Asia, Africa and Latin America. Without the destruction of India's rich textile industry, without the takeover of the spice trade, without the genocide of the Native American tribes [sic], without African slavery, the Industrial Revolution would not have resulted in new riches for Europe or North America. It was this violent takeover of Third World resources and markets that created wealth in the North and poverty in the South. (2005)

What this recurring blind spot reveals is the tendency to deny the West's complicity (and one's own complicity as Westerner) in the plight of the Third World. It is a tendency that, as many postcolonial[13] critics have suggested (e.g., Bhabha 1994; Spivak 1999), is rife within the history of Western thought, which so often represses the barbarism (colonialism, racism, violence against the subaltern and women) that founds modernity. And it is a tendency, as underlined above, that equally inaugurates the field of Development Studies, since Cold War politics demanded the construction of a strong and irreproachable West, cleansed of any suggestion of complicity in Third World "underdevelopment." Thus, the discourse of Modernization (in its postwar *and* contemporary forms) can be seen as receiving back its own message to the Third World in inverted form: it is as if it is saying "you *need* to be backward, irrational, poor, terroristic, weak, exotic, fundamentalist, passive, etc., since that is my way of reassuring myself that I am civilized, rational, scientific, rich, strong, secular, active, etc." What psychoanalysis adds to the postmodern understanding of binary construction is the dimension of the Real, which shows up here in the form of the blind spot—the element of self-limitation that one cannot really come to terms with, so one averts it by (unconsciously) projecting it onto the Other.

To conclude this section, let me underline again how psychoanalysis can help uncover the unconscious of development discourse, pointing to the latter's desires and traumas, which so often "speak" when things go wrong (e.g., in the form of slips and blind spots). Thus, in the example discussed above, the mastery, credibility, and neutrality of the World Bank are tripped up by the "Summers memo," revealing the Bank's desire for free market economics, even if this means First World domination of the Third World; and the traumatic inability of Modernization to face its limitations and complicities shows up in its disavowal of Western colonialism.

Note that both these illustrations exemplify what is known in psychoanalysis as the "return of the repressed": mainstream development's construction of itself as rational, scientific, and authoritative implies precisely the evacuation of certain desires and traumas, which "speak" nonetheless, sometimes at the most inopportune moments. Note as well that, even though development's slips and stumbles may appear "irrational" (e.g., the "irrational" implications of free market economic logic), such irrationality is the product of the excess of reason (e.g., development's prioritization of positivist economics and science), that is, development's inability to come to terms with its conflicting desires (e.g., its desire to appear pure, yet its past yearnings for colonial plunder). Irrationality, in this sense, is integral to the very construction of a rational and scientific development discourse (in the same way that, for Lacan, the unconscious is integral to the very construction of language). Finally, note the emphasis on surface rather than depth when it comes to the unconscious: Lacanian psychoanalysis is not a "depth psychology" meant to excavate unconscious desires from the recesses of the individual mind. Rather than going below the surface, the point is to glean the unconscious *hidden in plain view*. The unconscious is thus immanent to language / discourse, visible topologically. This is why *how* the Summers memo is presented (its secretive form) is more important, psychoanalytically speaking, than what is uttered in it. This is also why the slips contained in "population control" and "sustainable development" are outwardly visible from the start, although as pointed out earlier, they are gleaned only retroactively, in light of the institutional machinations that stem from each.

## Enjoying Development: Understanding Why Development Discourse Endures

The Lacanian concept of *jouissance* (enjoyment) refers not to the pleasure we derive from things but, rather, the excessive satisfaction or kick we get from doing something transgressive, irrational, or even wrong. It has been called "the thrill of the [R]eal" (Kay 2003, 4; see also Žižek 2006a, 79), and helps explain, for example, such self-destructive pursuits as smoking and binge drinking, or such "extreme sports" as bungee jumping and freediving. People do them not *despite* the fact that they are dangerous, but *because* they are (i.e., even when there is physical addiction, it is infused with enjoyment). *Jouissance* thus involves the intense pleasure taken from pain, a kind of idiotic stupor that often makes us ask for more even though we well know the risks.

According to Lacan, *jouissance* is the outcome of the child's separation from the primordial (m)Other and entry into the symbolic order. This is a traumatic separation that results in deep loss (of enjoyment), a loss that we are never able to forget. The tragedy is that the loss is actually a fiction (no real primordial fullness ever existed in the first place), yet it always remains with us. We repeatedly assume fullness exists but constantly remain dissatisfied, thus turning "nothing into something" (Homer 2004, 90; see also Lacan 2006, 45–46). The promise of enjoyment is always deferred, with the result that we continuously miss our goal, yet keep coming back for more.

One of Žižek's significant contributions to political theory has been to make the notion of *jouissance* a political factor, showing how it is a crucial ingredient in the formation of political community and identity (see 1989; 2002). For example, the deep comfort people may get from following rituals (bureaucratic or religious), or the enjoyment and thrill that may bind us together against an external enemy, help explain why institutions, nations, or groups often do "irrational" things—in this case, obstinately defending bureaucratic red tape or religious identity, or engaging in aggressive racism or nationalism. *Jouissance* elucidates why people become so attached to cultural values and sociopolitical systems, and why power can turn out to be so intractable, persistent, and enduring. One has trouble giving up such things as racism, materialism, sexism, or religious fundamentalism because one *enjoys* them; they give one a certain sense of stability and fulfillment, despite (and sometimes *because* of) the fact that one may well know they can be pernicious and cruel. As Stavrakakis points out, "by taking into account emotion, affect [and enjoyment] . . . one may be able to reach a more thorough understanding of 'what sticks': both what fuels identification processes and what creates fixity" (2007, 165).

Let me provide the following three illustrations. The first concerns the emphatically capitalist orientation of development. Despite the fact that capitalism has been severely criticized—it results in socioeconomic inequality, global unevenness, and ecological destruction—it is very much in the ascendancy; arguably, it constitutes the only available economic horizon today, whether in the global North or South. From a Žižekian perspective, one of the key reasons for such tremendous success is *jouissance*. That is to say, people *enjoy* capitalism (see chapters 2, 5, 6, 12). We are libidinally bound to it because we get so much from it—cars, TVs, houses, nice clothes, cheap fast food, iPhones, and so on. And capitalism, especially in its latest neoliberal phase, has been very effective in appealing to our passions. It is able to exploit what Lacanians see as our deep-seated sense of lack/loss, enabling us to fill such lack through consumerism and materialism. This means that we cannot easily postpone capitalism, since it promises to heal our ontological wound.

Late capitalism's productive engine thus *depends* on enjoyment-as-excess; its strength and success hinges on the extent to which it can elevate *jouissance* "into the very principle of social life" (Žižek 2006b, 297). This is why late cap-italist societies (whether in the West or Third World) are characterized by the normalization of excess—the desire for the best, biggest, tallest, richest, most original; the pervasiveness of "supersized" everything, from dams and build-ings to coffee and art; the orgiastic show of wealth; the rise of sexual promis-cuity and "extreme" sports; or the overabundance of "choice," whether in TV channels, music, restaurants, or university programs (see chapter 5).

The problem, however, is that although capitalist development promises enjoyment, it never quite delivers: a Coke doesn't quite quench, more wealth is still never enough, and supersized fast food sickens rather than satisfies. But such failure is written into the very logic of capitalism. For, if an end to dis-satisfaction were possible, that would spell the end of the global capitalist sys-tem. Instead, the aim of the system is always to solicit and activate desire, but never allow it to be satiated; this is what enables ever-increasing growth, profit, or market share. Capitalist development, in this sense, is driven by insatiable lack, so that try as we may to satisfy our enjoyment, we always miss our mark. As Todd McGowan states, "the problem with the society of enjoyment is not that we suffer from too much enjoyment, but that we don't have enough" (2004, 8).

A second illustration of *jouissance* involves nationalism. Indeed, little else has been more enduring than national identifications in the development con-text. Appeals to national bonds were of course crucial during independence struggles across the former colonies, but they have also been a key ingredient in postindependence national politics to help unify the nation on key political issues (land reform, industrialization or liberalization strategies, pet or pres-tige development projects, emergencies, humanitarian disasters, wars, antimi-nority or antirefugee/immigration policies, etc.). What is notable is that these appeals have invariably relied, not so much on rational arguments as on social passions. Nationalism operates at the libidinal level (i.e., at the level of our "guts," hearts, affect), engaging our sense of belonging, community, and pride. It relies on the (fantasmatic) promise of full enjoyment, which once again helps to explain the secret of its persistence.

The problem is that, while nationalism may be able to deliver on a few of its development goals, it often leads to irrationalities and excesses. We are all too aware of stories about excessive government spending on the military or costly prestige projects (megadams, space programs, state-of-the-art hospitals, etc.) at the expense of, say, basic health care and education. It is precisely this that Frantz Fanon warned about in his scathing critique of the national bour-geoisie, which he famously accused of pandering to nationalist sentiment as a pretext for continuing elite wealth accumulation and "racket" (1963, 150).

But there is also a more sinister dimension to nationalism: its tendency to scapegoat, visible for example in the current neopopulist nationalist politics of Duterte, Bolsonaro, Modi, Erdoğan, Orbán, or Trump. This is a tendency that arises as part of the very formation of national identity. To construct the nation is to appeal to what makes "us" unique (our customs, culture, landscapes, food, dress, festivals, etc.). It is this uniqueness that provides people with an ecstatic sense of unity and togetherness (i.e., *jouissance*). Yet, as Lacanians are quick to point out, such togetherness is a fiction, masking the lack and instability at the heart of any identity. And so, usually when things go wrong and this sense of national togetherness is threatened (e.g., by economic crises, recessions, or internal political instability), a scapegoat is constructed—fundamentalists who terrorize us, the poor who threaten our security or environment, immigrants who steal our jobs or menace our women, the Jews/Indians/Chinese who plot to rule the world. Žižek underlines how such scapegoating allows the nation to avoid confronting its own inadequacies or contradictions by projecting them onto a stereotypical Other (Žižek 1989, 96–97, 124ff.; see also Stavrakakis 2002, 100–101).

My third, related example is about racism (developed further in chapter 11). Since colonial times, not only has Western domination of the Third World been exercised in the socioeconomic and political spheres, but also when it comes to "race." As Fanon claims, the "White man" has become the universal subject or master signifier, so that being Black (or a person of color) is meaningful only in relation to whiteness (1967; see also Fuss 1995, 143). From the Lacanian standpoint, this implies that whiteness has been constructed as the promise of being less lacking, that is, more human and more whole. There is thus, as Kalpana Seshadri-Crooks argues (2000, 7–9), a kernel of *jouissance* in the construction of "race"/racism, with people of color (and white people themselves) *desiring* whiteness, something which, it must be noted, fits neatly with the preponderant idealization of the West in development discourse. No wonder once again that, despite the fact that people decry racism, it so obstinately remains with us. Skin bleaching ("lactification"), the denigration of local culture in favor of all things Euro–North American, racial profiling (in policing, immigration), the resurgence of white supremacist movements, all speak to the *jouissance* inherent in racism and to persistent forms of "internalized whiteness," whether in the global South or North.

Žižek often associates racist enjoyment with envy (see chapter 5), claiming that our enjoyment is always imbricated with the Other's enjoyment, so that we can never enjoy on our own; we most often enjoy by envying the Other's enjoyment, too (Žižek 2010, 366; see also Homer 2004, 60; Stavrakakis 2007, 197–198). The creation of a scapegoat, according to him, is accompanied by the anxiety about the "theft of enjoyment": we cannot properly enjoy because the Other—terrorists who are threatening our security, foreigners who are taking our jobs—has stolen our enjoyment or is enjoying more than us; hence, only by eliminating the Other can we recover our lost enjoyment and really enjoy (of course, no such real enjoyment exists). Such a perspective would help explain why extreme forms of racism result in the Other's extermination (e.g., the Rwandan and Armenian genocides, Bosnian ethnic cleansing, the massacre of indigenous peoples in Guatemala, Nazi concentration camps, etc.). But it also helps explain more subtle or everyday forms of racism. For example, the neighbor declaring she likes family X living next door, but there's something about them that bothers her (their noisy music, their entrepreneurialism, their body odor, their cooking smells, etc.). What bothers her is (her construction of) *their* excess, *their* particular mode of enjoyment.

An illustration of this in the development context is the recent discourse on HIV/AIDS. As Kalpana Wilson contends (2012, 97ff.), despite the fact that the AIDS pandemic has much to do with political economy, the crisis is most often explained or rationalized (e.g., by Western aid agencies) in terms of "risk behaviors" among "Africans." Wilson shows that weakened immune systems are the result not merely of the spread of a virus, but of people living in poverty, and the lack of access to cheap generic retroviral drugs (blocked by the big pharmaceuticals with the support of Western governments). That people live in poverty is the product of neoliberal structural adjustment policies across sub-Saharan Africa, which has seen reduced access to educational and health services for the poorest (especially women) and high unemployment, particularly among the ranks of former civil servants, teachers, and health workers (several of whom live with HIV/AIDS). Yet, the HIV/AIDS discourse tends toward a racialized stereotype on sexual behavior: Africans lack sexual control, or African men and women are promiscuous. The consequence, according to Wilson, is a tendency on the part of Western aid agencies to target not the socioeconomic causes of the pandemic, but "African culture" (by behavioral modification, changes in values, etc.).

The stereotype of the hypersexual African is an old colonial one that Fanon (1967, 141ff.) famously seized upon. He claimed, from a psychoanalytic point of view, that it displayed a certain paranoid anxiety on the part of the colonizer about "African" sexual prowess. That is, white racist repulsion was accompanied by its opposite—desire for, or sexual attraction to, Black people. And the same applies to the contemporary AIDS-related stereotype about the oversexed African. To put it in Lacanian terms, it betrays a Western racist envy of the Other's excess or enjoyment. The "African" is constructed as possessing something we lack, which is what bothers us. But of course, what such racist constructions do is blind us to our own contradictions and deficiencies, which in this case have to do, as Wilson underlines, with Western complicities in the HIV/AIDS pandemic (support to the big pharmaceuticals on restricting cheaper generic drugs, imposition of structural adjustment programs, etc.).

Consequently, Lacanian psychoanalysis helps us glean how such an unconscious social passion as enjoyment is so intertwined with development. Enjoyment provides for a (false) sense of satisfaction, stability, and togetherness (as illustrated in the examples of neoliberal capitalism, nationalism, and racism), but the excess it represents can also give way to irrational conduct (over-indulgent materialism, scapegoating, and so on). Yet, whether in its positive or its negative form (and often in both forms simultaneously), the notion of *jouissance* helps explain why things stick, why people hold on to sociocultural identifications, why such social ills as racism or rabid nationalism so obdurately persist.

## Development as Fantasy: Doing Ideology Critique

It is Žižek who has almost single-handedly renewed current interest in ideology. Given the Lacanian position that reality is always ruptured by gaps and contradictions (i.e., the Real), ideology according to Žižek is that which attempts to cover up these contradictions, to obscure the Real (1989, 45). In this sense, social reality is thoroughly ideological, with ideology serving as a way for the social to escape its traumatic core and ideology critique constantly trying to focus attention back on this trauma. Thus, in the case of (the ideology of) nationalist-populist racism discussed above, we saw how a scapegoat is produced to cover up, and divert attention away from, the nation's internal troubles (the Real). Here, the underlying ideological fantasy is that once the scapegoat is removed or eliminated, the nation will recover its (impossible) harmony.

Note that Žižek's position on ideology differs from the classical Marxist one, which implies a privileged, neutral point from which one can distinguish between "objective reality" and "false consciousness." For Žižek, we are all ideologically produced, so there is no question of being outside ideology. Rather, what we *can* do in terms of ideology critique is to try and detect, in the manner of the psychoanalyst, the gaps of ideologically constructed reality, gaps which, as we have seen, show up as slips, blind spots, symptoms, irrationalities. Ideology critique is therefore possible only from within the belly of the beast, so to speak.

Note as well that ideological fantasies secure our consent and compliance through desire (and enjoyment) (Kay 2003, 5).[14] In fact, as Žižek points out, fantasy is the mise-en-scène for desire: it helps make reality smooth, coherent, and harmonious, protecting us from trauma/lack, gentrifying turbulence or negativity, and promising a world that is more bearable, attractive, and enjoyable. Fantasy thus animates and manages desire; it teaches us *how to* desire (Žižek 1989, 44). But just as fantasy can never live up to its promises (because no fullness exists), so desire is never satisfied; it is condemned to repetition and failure in search of the missing object.

Let me illustrate by examining a couple of development's ideological fantasies. To begin, the very discourse of "poverty," upon which development centers, is ideological (see also chapter 12). Indeed, poverty discourse typically constructs the Third World as underdeveloped and backward, as though such "underdevelopment" is a fait accompli. By so isolating underdevelopment/poverty, the discourse mystifies the close relationship between surplus extraction and impoverishment, wherein wealth in some parts of the world (i.e., the affluent centers of the global North and South) is the historical result of the pauperization of others (Frank 1967; see Wallerstein 2004). Hence poverty discourse simplifies and dehistoricizes inequality by privileging the "now" of poverty, thus eliding the Real—in this case, continuing forms of elite domination, particularly the West's (neo)colonial immiseration of the Third World. (Note that this is the same traumatic Real that, as was pointed out earlier, Modernization tries to escape by disavowing Western colonial history.)

It is worth reflecting on the desires elicited by such an ideological fantasy. A typical response to the mise-en-scène of (Third World) poverty is to blame this "backwardness" on individuals and values—rogue civil servants, corrupt leaders, uneducated or irresponsible mothers, "ethnic" or "traditional" practices—so that the solution becomes the need/desire for better (i.e., modern, Western-style) leadership, norms, and codes of conduct. A distinct moral righteousness pervades such a discourse, with experts and elites standing as arbiters of the "right" values and "good" governance. Ideologies and moralizing discourses such as that of poverty are most successful when they are able to depoliticize desires, precisely in order to avoid coming too close to the Real. It would be risky—and traumatic—for the discourse of poverty to be staged in terms of *inequality*, for this would likely animate the desire to problematize (if not eliminate) the relationship between wealth accumulation and pauperization. This is likely why it is the discourse of poverty, not inequality, that is so hegemonic in development, reflecting elites' desires to maintain the status quo.

A second prevalent ideological fantasy is neoliberalism, with which, for all intents and purposes, mainstream capitalist development is closely associated these days. Neoliberalism proposes that market mechanisms maximize human

PSYCHOANALYSIS AND INTERNATIONAL DEVELOPMENT        21

well-being and are ideal for addressing social and political problems. It promises that everyone wins, and anyone can "make it" (see Dean 2008). We have already examined how such an ideological system binds people to it by seducing them (through *jouissance*); it creates a series of lacks, and through a cycle of satisfaction–disappointment (and hence postponement) is able to endlessly stimulate and redirect our desires (for consumption, wealth, jobs, etc.).

But in pledging to eliminate our ontological loss, in vowing to make us whole, the neoliberal fantasy conceals a lot. It hides the rapaciousness of markets, which have led to global ecological crisis and growing inequalities and unevenness (see Harvey 2006). It disavows the large reserve army of (sweatshop) labor upon which the smooth functioning of global capital depends (see chapter 12). And it ignores how the neoliberal gutting of state social programs has hit hardest those most in need (women, the unemployed, migrants, racialized minorities). Neoliberal capitalism is founded on the gentrification of, and inability to acknowledge, its contradictions and deficiencies.

What can be gleaned from the above is that Žižekian ideology critique involves two complementary steps (Žižek 1989, 125). The first is about examining how an ideological fantasy is constructed and what it is trying to hide or disavow. Often, this means identifying the fantasy's master signifiers, taken-for-granteds, or "sublime objects" (in the above two examples: "poverty," "corruption," "free market," "growth"). Moreover, this means locating the ideology's Real, that is, what it is trying to render invisible or unutterable (e.g., inequality, the relationship between poverty and wealth accumulation, sweatshop labor).

But detecting the holes and traumas within our knowledge systems is not nearly enough. This is because of what Žižek calls the *fetishistic disavowal*, according to which we can know, but still continue to do (1989, 18, 32–33). The problem is evident in, say, global hedge fund managers mocking or making fun of the industrial layoffs caused by their own financial speculation, while continuing their business as usual; or critical TV audience members decrying product advertising but still engaging in consumerism. The strength of ideology, according to Žižek, lies in allowing us a certain ironic distance, which makes us think we know better and can rise above ideology (see chapters 2, 3, 6, 9). In contrast to those who maintain that having the information and "exposing the facts" are sufficient to undermine power, Žižek argues emphatically that most often, it is not a lack of knowledge that is the problem, but our unconscious commands and passions that bind us to ideology despite a critical distance.

Acknowledging and tracking the desires / enjoyment we invest in ideology, then, is a crucial second procedure for ideology critique. It means "articulating the way in which . . . an ideology implies, manipulates, produces a pre-ideological enjoyment structured in fantasy" (Žižek 1989, 125). This is precisely why I have been arguing for the importance of psychoanalysis in development: to better identify and come to terms with our libidinal attachments and the lure of development's many sublime objects and fantasies. Psychoanalysis tells those of us who work in this field that we do not necessarily know our interests. Our libidinal attachments so often circumscribe our thinking and actions. This is why, despite the fact that we may be critical or despondent about development, we buy into such development fantasies as "doing good" or "free markets," which often screen our lacks and anxieties (about social injustice, inequality, or our own complicities as Westernized elites) and sets off our desires (e.g., to help, to save the Other, to donate money to charity, or to call for the privatization of public services).

## The Limits of Psychoanalysis?

There are two main critiques that must be taken into account to help determine the limits (and limitations) of psychoanalysis. The first is the feminist critique: French feminist theorists—Irigaray (1985), Cixous (1976), and Kristeva (1984)—have, each in their own way, warned against psychoanalysis's repression of the feminine. Irigaray, for example, shows how both the oedipal and phallic narratives are privileged in psychoanalysis, thereby naturalizing patriarchy and relegating the feminine to the margins. Women thus tend to be defined negatively in relation to men, lacking voice and agency. Along the same lines, queer theorists (e.g., Butler 1990; Grosz 1994) have emphasized the heteronormativity of psychoanalysis, pointing to its normalization of heterosexual practices and treatment of homosexuality as abnormal (see chapter 10).

Much of the critique here is directed toward Freud, more than Lacan, targeting the former's biologism and fetishization of anatomy (as pointed out earlier). But Lacan is not spared: even if he insists that the Phallus represents a certain social authority and not anatomy, the metaphor still remains, as Iginla points out (1992, 32), with patriarchal law seen as universal (although it must be noted that for Lacan, ultimately, the Phallus is a symbol of lack and failure; see chapter 8). McClintock (2013, 192–193) accuses Lacan of portraying women as victims, so that even when they do speak or act, it is through patriarchic desire.

Yet, many of these same feminist critics find in Lacan the resources for a thoroughgoing critique of patriarchic culture and institutions, some of them taking his implied (hetero)sexism as descriptive rather than prescriptive, and others rethinking his work to retrieve women's agency. In the former case, for example, Juliet Mitchell suggests that "psychoanalysis is not a recommendation *for* a patriarchal society, but an analysis *of* one," and goes on to analyze ways in which women can be marginalized by semiotic, social, and familial inequalities and power relations (1974, xii, italics in original; see also Mitchell and Rose 1982). In the latter case, Irigaray, Cixous, and Kristeva (often labeled Post-Lacanian Feminists) all attempt to valorize the feminine, with Irigaray (1985) arguing for a "feminine imaginary," Cixous (1976) a disruptive and plural "feminine libidinal economy," and Kristeva (1984) a potentially subversive "feminine semiotic." Ironically though, while trying to retrieve a feminism of *différance*, these French Post-Lacanians have themselves been accused of biologistic and semiotic essentialism (see Cornell 1991; Flax 1990). The point to retain nonetheless is that, despite tendencies toward the marginalization of women and queer people, the Lacanian psychoanalytic tradition is highly amenable to, and offers plenty of resources for, a critique of patriarchy and heteronormativity *and* the retrieval of subaltern voices (see chapters 5–12).

A second important critique of psychoanalysis concerns its universalizability. Fanon was one of the first to question the relevance of the Oedipus complex to the colonial world, arguing that, for the Black child, it is not entry into the family but the White world that is traumatic; it is the process of racialization, through which the child discovers the social meaning and stigma of blackness, that is crucial to subject formation (1967, 151–154). This would suggest the limited universalizability of the oedipal model of subjecthood.

Taking their cue from Fanon, several postcolonial critics make a broader critique by underlining the colonial backdrop to the development of psychoanalysis as a discipline. Indeed, Freud wrote at a time when the European civilizing mission needed an "uncivilized" Other. Ranjana Khanna states in this regard that Europe's national-colonial self thus "situated itself, with fascination, in opposition to its repressed, concealed, and mysterious 'dark continents': colonial Africa, women, and the primitive" (2003, 6; see also Doane 1991, 11, 210–211; Greedharry 2008; Iginla 1992, 32; Seshadri-Crooks 1994; Spivak 1994). Not surprisingly, some of Freud's work pathologized colonial subjects, characterizing them as "savages" and "primitive peoples" in order to distinguish them from their European counterparts (1950, 3). The human psyche that Freud promulgated thus grew out of a particular time and place, but was made to stand as universal; or as Mary Ann Doane puts it, psychoanalysis became a kind of "ethnography," a "writing of the ethnicity of the white western psyche" (1991, 11).

Once again though, these critiques are addressed more to Freud than Lacan. Yet, even if Lacan averts Freud's universalizing essentialism through a linguistic model, there is still the thorny issue of upholding this very linguistic model as universal. Let me tackle the problem in two ways. First, the point is that, for all intents and purposes, the Western symbolic order has become the de facto global symbolic order. Through processes of globalization and (neo) colonialism, the West's dominant representational and knowledge systems are all-pervasive (although not unchallenged). As Ashis Nandy, another psychoanalytically inclined postcolonial critic, contends, "colonialism colonizes minds in addition to bodies and it releases forces within the colonized societies to alter their cultural priorities once and for all. . . . The West is now everywhere, within the West and outside; in structures and in minds" (1983, 11).[15] As a result, "psychoanalysis works in non-European cultures, not because of the universalism of the categories of the mind but precisely because of colonial history, which has had the effect of imposing Western structures."[16] This argument is particularly relevant to international development, since development discourses have been dominated by the West, with development workers, professionals, and academics hailing from predominantly Western educated and/or Western(ized) elites, whether in the global North or South. Hence my present contention concerning the applicability of psychoanalysis to development.

Second, even putting aside this historically constructed/imposed universalism, the Lacanian viewpoint manifestly underscores the particular and the contextual, through what might be called a "negative" or "contingent" universalism. Thus, while Lacan does emphasize the dominance of patriarchic desire, especially within the family context, his main argument reveals the structures of authority to which we must succumb if we are to emerge from nature into culture; so there is no necessary reason for the oedipal to manifest itself in the same way everywhere, or even for it to be restricted to the nuclear family. In this sense, the Lacanian position is quite consistent with those feminists who insist on the different ways in which patriarchy can be lived, embodied, and resisted in different sociocultural contexts, and with those like Fanon who insist that, in colonial Africa, it is not patriarchic but racialized authority that is primary. In fact, by rooting the oedipal in the broader social/ racialized milieu of colonial Africa, Fanon can be said to be contextualizing, and indeed extending, Lacanian psychoanalytic thought.[17]

But while the symbolic order can and does manifest itself differently in space and time, resulting from particular social and historical practices, this is not to say it is purely contingent. On the contrary, every symbolic order is undone by the Real, which as we have seen is the negative form of a universal (see also chapter 3). As Eisenstein and McGowan put it, "[t]here are no transcendent principles that every society shares, but there is a constitutive failure that marks every society" (2012, 69). The Real is, therefore, not some unchanging and transcendental substance, but is immanent to every social order, reflecting each order's inability to fully constitute itself. It is in this sense that Lacanian psychoanalysis can be seen as contingently/negatively universal—sensitive to sociohistorical specificities (e.g., to the different manifestations of patriarchy across the Third World, or the predominance of racial over patriarchic law in certain contexts), while pointing up the self-division of every social order. That is, even if Western(ized) development discourse is hegemonic today, even if racialized politics does dominate in, say, postapartheid South Africa, these are always already unraveling by way of gaps, slips, or blind spots.[18]

## Conclusion

I have argued for taking psychoanalysis seriously in development. For, without considering the unconscious, mainstream development is unable to explain its gaps and blind spots—from its longstanding neglect of gender and ecological issues to its disavowal of colonial history. And without attention to the human/social passions, it cannot adequately account for the inconsistencies between its scientific declarations (e.g., belief in reason, progress, objectivity) and its irrational practices (e.g., the pernicious draw of narrow economic growth, the fatal attraction to aggressive nationalism, or the blind conformity to red tape). The Lacanian concept of *jouissance*, as we have seen, is key to helping us understand, not just why development politics can be irrational and dangerous, but also how such problems as inequality, racism, and patriarchy persist (see chapters 5–8, 11). It is *jouissance* that illuminates why people buy into ideologies (neoliberalism, racism, poverty), despite knowing better. Ideology critique in development requires, then, not just the deconstruction of development discourse, but the identification of its (unconscious) libidinal attachments.

Two brief closing notes: while I have claimed that development constructs a rational and scientific discourse that denies social passions and often results in a kind of "return of the repressed" in the form of slips or irrationalities, this is not to say that psychoanalysis is simply about focusing on the passions embedded in development. The Lacanian standpoint is not a mere reversal of the reason–passion binary. On the contrary, what it points up is, on the one hand, the co-dependence of the two, that is, the impossibility of constructing the one (reason) without at the same time implicating the other (passion), and, on the other hand, the self-division and instability of both, so that neither a truly scientific development nor a purely passionate politics is possible, the former obfuscating its traumas, the latter unable to ever satisfy its lack.

And second, while the Lacanian take on psychoanalysis is decidedly cultural, relying on a linguistic model, it lends itself very well to political economy (as we will see in chapters 4–6, 12). This is because, as pointed out earlier, its culturalism is materially grounded, the symbolic order emerging from nature's turbulence and closely tied to material/institutional practices. Žižek, in fact, makes political economy central to his project, claiming that capital is so hegemonic today that it has made it very difficult to imagine anything beyond it. This is why doing ideology critique and politicizing capital are such crucial tasks, no more so than in development, where neoliberal capitalist growth is so taken for granted.

## Notes

1. I use the term Third World in this book well aware of its current pejorative meanings. But given that the mainstream discourse of development and its accompanying terminology is so problematic, I find the term the least of evils (marginally better, in my view, than "global South," which tends to be the current politically correct *academic* term, but a term I will nonetheless also employ in the book). I prefer "Third World" because of its antihegemonic connotations and origins—it became popular after the 1955 Bandung meeting of nonaligned countries, at which Third World leaders attempted to chart an alternative course to either the capitalist West or the communist Soviet Bloc. See chapter 10 for details.

2. Only recently has there been some research into the psychoanalytic dimensions of development: see for example, de Vries (2007), Edkins (2000), Fletcher (2012), Fridell (2013), Kapoor (2005), Kingsbury (2011), Sato (2006), Sioh (2010), the subtheme issue of *Third World Quarterly* on "Psychoanalysis and Development" (see Kapoor 2014), Kapoor (2018), Kingsbury and Pile (2014), and Wilson (2014).

3. Freud has been roundly criticized for this biological essentialism, particularly by feminists (see for example, Irigaray 1985). More on this in the section on "The Limits of Psychoanalysis?" later in this chapter.

4. Note that Lacanian psychoanalysis is critical of essentialism not just in Freudian psychoanalysis, but also in Object Relations Theory, the third main strand of psychoanalytic thinking. This is because Object Relations, according to Lacanians, tends to conceptualize objects as "real things" which are needed by the child (the mother, the parent's face, etc.). It thus misses the important linguistic dimension of psychoanalysis, according to which our biological needs are always linguistically mediated, so that objects are never unmediated things but discursively constructed and riven with antagonisms (see Lacan 1977, 30ff., 251–252; Mitchell and Rose 1982; Žižek 1989, 194).

5. Note that there are two ways in which human animals deal with primordial loss—desire and drive (see McGowan 2011, 10–11). Desire is based on the belief that enjoyment can be regained through a lost object, while drive is based on the belief that enjoyment lies in the repetition of loss. See chapter 4.

6. The Symbolic is sometimes referred to as the "big Other," although the latter usually refers to our complex networks of social authority and rules.

7. The Real creates the conditions of possibility for reality because, as is pointed out two paragraphs below, the latter cannot be, and is not, apprehended without symbolization, which emerges as a consequence of turmoil.

8. This is why it is not an uncommon practice for psychoanalytically informed writers to use the pronoun "we" when referring to the subject (as opposed to "I" or an impersonal pronoun), a convention I adhere to throughout this book: "we" indicates that we are all subjects *of* language, so that even though each subject interiorizes language/desire, language (the big Other) also speaks us. It is such transindividuality that makes it possible to psychoanalyze culture and society, although we have to be vigilant not to overgeneralize, since social pluralism and antagonism are always in our midst.

9. Bush (2001) also subsequently referred to the war in Afghanistan as a "crusade."

10. Tweet by Penny Mordaunt, former Minister of State for International Development, https://twitter.com/PennyMordaunt/status/1049616553405308928?s=20, 9 October 2018. My thanks to @Robbie_Watt for alerting me to this tweet.

11. Thanks to Anna Zalik for reminding me about this "Summers Memo" controversy.

12. Note that, although Dependency did mount a vehement critique of Modernization for ignoring colonialism, arguing that colonial ties are fundamental to understanding modernity, the latter is very much a minority analysis in Development Studies, and certainly in the broader, mainstream development discourse.

13. In this book, I am distinguishing between "postcolonial" and "post-colonial," the first term referring to the critical literary field, the second to the historical period following the formal end of colonial rule.

14. Note that, according to Lacan, desire and enjoyment (*jouissance*) are related but not the same: *jouissance* is closely associated with drive, often setting off desire. Like desire, *jouissance* is the result of a (false) sense of loss (from one's separation from the (m)Other). But *jouissance* is continuous and never ending, while desire moves from object to object in search of (impossible) satisfaction and plenitude. As Homer (2004, 90) puts it, "Lacan opposed *jouissance* to desire and suggested that desire seeks satisfaction in the consistency of *jouissance*." See chapter 4 for details.

15. See also Spivak (1985, 9), who claims that there is no escaping colonial discourse, so that one cannot retrieve any "pure" precolonial narrative.

16. This is a quote from Young (2004, 184), summarizing the argument of Deleuze and Guattari's book *Anti-Oedipus* (1972), but the idea is directly pertinent here.

17. This is what Fanon suggests he was doing anyway (1967, 152n14). It should also be mentioned that, although Fanon may have an important point to make regarding the primacy of racialized power in the colonial African context, he has been taken to task for neglecting patriarchy and, in fact, for the sexist (and homophobic) undertones of some of his writing: for example, for having very little to say about African women, and then too, speaking about them disparagingly. See Fuss (1995, 160) and Greedharry (2008, 38ff.).

18. This is different from the contingent universalism advocated by the likes of Laclau and Mouffe (e.g., in *Hegemony and Socialist Strategy*, 1985), who argue that, through a logic of equivalence, a social movement's claims can undergo change as they

are articulated with other movements' claims. But what Laclau and Mouffe miss, according to Eisenstein and McGowan (2012, 68), is the dimension of the Real: "There is no need to construct a universal . . . because antagonism or what we call rupture is already universal." See chapter 3 on this important point.

# References

Baaz, Maria Eriksson. 2008. *The Paternalism of Partnership: A Postcolonial Reading of Identity in Development Aid*. London: Zed.
BBC. 2013. "Racist Tweet Costs PR Officer Job." BBC News, US and Canada, December 22. https://www.bbc.com/news/world-us-canada-25484537.
Bhabha, Homi K. 1994. *The Location of Culture*. London: Routledge.
Bush, George W. 2001. "Message to the Congress Transmitting a Report of the Railroad Retirement." United States Government Records and Documents. http://www.govrecords.org/pd29oc01-message-to-the-congress-transmitting-a-report-of-10.html.
Butler, Judith. 1990. *Gender Trouble: Feminism and the Subversion of Identity*. New York: Routledge.
Cixous, Hélène. 1976. "The Laugh of the Medusa." *Signs* 1 (4): 875–893.
Copjec, Joan. 1994. *Read My Desire: Lacan against the Historicists*. London: Verso.
Cornelius, Judson K. 2001. *Political Humour*. Bombay: Better Yourself.
Cornell, Drucilla. 1991. *Beyond Accommodation: Ethical Feminism, Deconstruction, and the Law*. New York: Routledge.
Dean, Jodi. 2008. "Enjoying Neoliberalism." *Cultural Politics* 4 (1): 47–72.
De Wet, Chris J., ed. 2006. *Development-Induced Displacement: Problems, Policies and People*. New York: Berghahn.
de Vries, Pieter. 2007. "Don't Compromise Your Desire for Development! A Lacanian/Deleuzian Rethinking of the Anti-Politics Machine." *Third World Quarterly* 28 (1): 25–43.
Doane, Mary Ann. 1991. *Femmes Fatales: Feminism, Film Theory, Psychoanalysis*. London: Routledge.
Eager, Paige Whaley. 2004. *Global Population Policy: From Population Control to Reproductive Rights*. Aldershot: Ashgate.
Edkins, Jenny. 2000. *Whose Hunger? Concepts of Famine, Practices of Aid*. Minneapolis: University Of Minnesota Press.
Eisenstein, Paul, and Todd McGowan. 2012. *Rupture: On the Emergence of the Political*. Evanston, IL: Northwestern University Press.
Escobar, Arturo. 1995. *Encountering Development: The Making and Unmaking of the Third World*. Princeton, NJ: Princeton University Press.
Fanon, Frantz. 1963. *The Wretched of the Earth*. Translated by Richard Philcox. New York: Grove.
———. 1967. *Black Skin, White Masks*. Translated by Charles Markmann. New York: Grove.
Flax, Jane. 1990. *Thinking Fragments: Psychoanalysis, Feminism, and Postmodernism in the Contemporary West*. Berkeley: University of California Press.

Fletcher, Robert. 2012. "The Art of Forgetting: Imperialist Amnesia and Public Secrecy." *Third World Quarterly* 33 (3): 423–439.

Fletcher, Robert, Jan Breitling, and Valerie Puleo. 2014. "Barbarian Hordes: The Overpopulation Scapegoat in International Development Discourse." *Third World Quarterly* 35 (7): 1195–1215.

Frank, Andre Gunder. 1967. *Capitalism and Underdevelopment in Latin America.* New York: Monthly Review.

Freud, Sigmund. 1950. *Totem and Taboo: Some Points of Agreement between the Mental Lives of Savages and Neurotics.* London: Routledge and Kegan Paul.

——. 1955. *The Interpretation of Dreams.* Translated by James Strachey. New York: Basic Books.

Fridell, Gavin. 2013. "Debt Politics and the Free Trade 'Package': The Case of the Caribbean." *Third World Quarterly* 34 (4): 613–629.

Fuss, Diana. 1995. *Identification Papers.* New York: Routledge.

Glennie, Jonathan. 2008. *The Trouble with Aid: Why Less Could Mean More for Africa.* London: Zed.

Greedharry, Mrinalini. 2008. *Postcolonial Theory and Psychoanalysis: From Uneasy Engagements to Effective Critique.* Basingstoke: Palgrave Macmillan.

Grosz, Elizabeth A. 1994. *Volatile Bodies: Toward a Corporeal Feminism.* Bloomington: Indiana University Press.

Harvey, David. 2006. *Spaces of Global Capitalism.* London: Verso.

Homer, Sean. 2004. *Jacques Lacan.* London: Routledge.

Iginla, Biodun. 1992. "Black Feminist Critique of Psychoanalysis." In *Feminism and Psychoanalysis: A Critical Dictionary*, edited by Elizabeth Wright, 31–33. Cambridge, MA: Blackwell.

Irigaray, Luce. 1985. *This Sex Which Is Not One.* Ithaca, NY: Cornell University Press.

Kapoor, Ilan. 2005. "Participatory Development, Complicity and Desire." *Third World Quarterly* 26 (8): 1203–1220.

——. 2008. *The Postcolonial Politics of Development.* London: Routledge.

——. 2014. "Psychoanalysis and Development: An Introduction." *Third World Quarterly* 35 (7): 1117–1119.

——, ed. 2018. *Psychoanalysis and the GlObal.* Lincoln: University of Nebraska Press.

Kay, Sarah. 2003. *Žižek: A Critical Introduction.* Cambridge: Polity.

Khanna, Ranjana. 2003. *Dark Continents: Psychoanalysis and Colonialism.* Durham, NC: Duke University Press.

Kingsbury, Paul. 2011. "Sociospatial Sublimation: The Human Resources of Love in Sandals Resorts International, Jamaica." *Annals of the Association of American Geographers* 101 (3): 650–669.

Kingsbury, Paul, and Steve Pile, eds. 2014. *Psychoanalytic Geographies.* Farnham: Ashgate.

Korten, David. 1992. "To Improve Human Welfare, Poison the Poor: The Logic of a Free Market Economist." Living Economies Forum. https://davidkorten.org /29korten/.

Kristeva, Julia. 1984. *Revolution in Poetic Language.* New York: Columbia University Press.

Lacan, Jacques. 1977. *Écrits: A Selection.* Translated by Alan Sheridan. New York: Norton.

——. 1998a. *Encore. On Feminine Sexuality, the Limits of Love and Knowledge: The Seminar of Jacques Lacan, Book XX*. Edited by Jacques-Alain Miller. Translated by Bruce Fink. New York: Norton.

——. 1998b. *The Four Fundamental Concepts of Psychoanalysis: The Seminar of Jacques Lacan, Book XI*. Edited by Jacques-Alain Miller. New York: Norton.

——. 2006. *The Other Side of Psychoanalysis: The Seminar of Jacques Lacan, Book XVII*. Edited by Jacques-Alain Miller. New York: Norton.

——. 2016. *The Sinthome: The Seminar of Jacques Lacan, Book XXIII*. Cambridge: Polity.

——. 2017. *Formations of the Unconscious: The Seminar of Jacques Lacan, Book V*. Edited by Jacques-Alain Miller. Translated by Russell Grigg. Cambridge: Polity.

McClintock, Anne. 2013. *Imperial Leather: Race, Gender, and Sexuality in the Colonial Contest*. New York: Routledge.

McGowan, Todd. 2004. *The End of Dissatisfaction? Jacques Lacan and the Emerging Society of Enjoyment*. Albany: SUNY Press.

——. 2011. *Out of Time: Desire in Atemporal Cinema*. Minneapolis: University of Minnesota Press.

Mitchell, Juliet. 1974. *Psychoanalysis and Feminism*. New York: Vintage.

Mitchell, Juliet, and Jacqueline Rose, eds. 1982. *Feminine Sexuality: Jacques Lacan and the École Freudienne*. New York: Norton.

Nandy, Ashis. 1983. *The Intimate Enemy: Loss and Recovery of Self under Colonialism*. Delhi: Oxford University Press.

Pellow, David N. 2007. *Resisting Global Toxics: Transnational Movements for Environmental Justice*. Cambridge, MA: MIT Press.

Rostow, Walt W. 1960. *The Stages of Economic Growth: A Non-Communist Manifesto*. Cambridge: Cambridge University Press.

Sachs, Jeffrey D. 2005. *The End of Poverty: Economic Possibilities for Our Time*. New York: Penguin.

Sato, Chizu. 2006. "Subjectivity, Enjoyment, and Development: Preliminary Thoughts on a New Approach to Postdevelopment." *Rethinking Marxism* 18 (2): 273–288.

Seshadri-Crooks, Kalpana. 1994. "The Primitive as Analyst: Postcolonial Feminism's Access to Psychoanalysis." *Cultural Critique* 28: 175–218.

——. 2000. *Desiring Whiteness: A Lacanian Analysis of Race*. London: Routledge.

Shiva, Vandana. 2005. "Two Myths that Keep the World Poor." *Ode Magazine*, November 1, 2005. http://my2.ewb.ca/posts/8895/print/

Sioh, Maureen. 2010. "The Hollow Within: Anxiety and Performing Postcolonial Financial Policies." *Third World Quarterly* 31 (4): 581–597.

Sovacool, Benjamin, and Christopher Cooper. 2013. *The Governance of Energy Megaprojects*. Cheltenham: Edward Elgar.

Spivak, Gayatri Chakravorty. 1985. "Strategies of Vigilance: An Interview with Gayatri Chakravorty Spivak." *Block* 10: 5–9.

——. 1994. "Psychoanalysis in Left Field and Fieldworking: Examples to Fit the Title." In *Speculations after Freud*, edited by Sonu Shamdasani and Michael Munchow, 41–75. London: Routledge.

——. 1999. *A Critique of Postcolonial Reason: Toward a History of the Vanishing Present*. Cambridge, MA: Harvard University Press.

Stavrakakis, Yannis. 2002. *Lacan and the Political*. London: Routledge.
——. 2007. *The Lacanian Left: Essays on Psychoanalysis and Politics*. Albany: SUNY Press.
Valenzuela, J. Samuel, and Arturo Valenzuela. 1998. "Modernization and Dependency: Alternative Perspectives in the Study of Latin American Underdevelopment." In *Development and Underdevelopment: The Political Economy of Global Inequality*, edited by Mitchell A. Seligson and John T. Passé-Smith, 343–382. 2nd ed. Boulder, CO: Lynne Rienner.
Wallerstein, Immanuel Maurice. 2004. *World-Systems Analysis: An Introduction*. Durham, NC: Duke University Press.
Wilson, Japhy. 2014. "Fantasy Machine: Philanthrocapitalism as an Ideological Formation." *Third World Quarterly* 35 (7): 1144–1161.
Wilson, Kalpana. 2012. *Racism and Development: Interrogating History, Discourse and Practice*. London: Zed.
Young, Robert J. C. 2004. *White Mythologies: Writing History and the West*. London: Routledge.
Žižek, Slavoj. 1989. *The Sublime Object of Ideology*. London: Verso.
——. 2002. *For They Know Not What They Do: Enjoyment as a Political Factor*. London: Verso.
——. 2004. *Iraq: The Borrowed Kettle*. London: Verso.
——. 2006a. *How to Read Lacan*. London: Granta.
——. 2006b. *The Parallax View*. Cambridge, MA: MIT Press.
——. 2010. *Interrogating the Real*. Edited by Rex Butler and Scott Stephens. London: Continuum.
——. 2013. *Less than Nothing: Hegel and the Shadow of Dialectical Materialism*. London: Verso.
——. 2014. *Absolute Recoil: Towards a New Foundation of Dialectical Materialism*. London: Verso.
Žižek, Slavoj, and Glyn Daly. 2004. *Conversations with Žižek*. Cambridge: Polity.
Zupančič, Alenka. 2017. *What Is Sex?* Cambridge, MA: MIT Press.

CHAPTER 2

# Post-Development's Surrender to Global Capitalism

## A Psychoanalytic Critique

## Introduction

In *The Anti-Politics Machine*, while making the case for a Foucauldian discourse analysis, James Ferguson declares that "the most important political effects of a planned intervention may occur *unconsciously*, behind the backs or against the wills of the 'planners' who may seem to be running the show" (1990, 20, italics added). He proceeds to demonstrate how development interventions in Lesotho have unintended consequences, which end up advancing institutional authority and control. But he stops short of analyzing precisely the role of the *unconscious* in such interventions, preferring to stick to his nonpsychoanalytic, Foucauldian predispositions.[1]

Similarly, in *Territories of Difference* (2008), Arturo Escobar reflects on Pieter de Vries's psychoanalytic work on the place of desire in development (see de Vries 2007). Escobar readily admits to the Foucauldian weakness of treating development only discursively: when development is seen simply as an apparatus of power, it ends up disavowing people's subjectivity, that is, it fails to acknowledge that "development is a desiring machine . . . not only an apparatus of governmentality" (2008, 175). He goes on to examine how development can be used to cultivate subjects of alternate developments/modernities—an enduring preoccupation of his—but like Ferguson, he fails to take up the psychoanalytic challenge.

This chapter treads where Ferguson and Escobar fear to. It carries out a psychoanalytic critique of Post-Development, arguing that the latter's inattention to the unconscious underpinnings of power not only leaves it unable to explain why development discourse persists, but also deprives it of a deviant or radical politics, resulting in a surrender to global capitalism.[2] Drawing mainly on the work of Escobar and Ferguson, but also of Gustavo Esteva, the chapter valorizes Post-Development's important insights on the production of development discourse and its attendant power mechanisms. But using a Lacanian lens, it also probes Post-Development's failure to address how power is mediated at the level of the subject: in maintaining that (capitalist) development is produced discursively in a cold, impersonal way (like an "anti-politics machine"), Post-Development ignores the fact that such power is able to take hold, expand and, crucially, persist only through unconscious libidinal attachments (e.g., desires, enjoyment). This failure leaves Post-Development with few resources—beyond localized resistance (Escobar, Esteva) or the call for a universal basic income (Ferguson)—to address the structural challenges of global capitalism. Psychoanalytically speaking, such a (Left) position appears to manifest a secret desire that nothing too much must change: Post-Development may well criticize the disciplinary mechanisms of neoliberal development, but ultimately it engages in an unconscious acceptance of capitalism. Thus, to turn Ferguson's above-mentioned words against themselves: the most important political effects of *Post-Development* occur unconsciously, behind the backs or against the intentions of its exponents.

It should be noted that I focus on Escobar, Ferguson, and Esteva primarily because they, more than other Post-Development analysts, draw on Foucauldian discourse analysis. As we shall see, Escobar and Ferguson ground their arguments theoretically, taking a more complex view of discursivity.[3] Esteva, on the other hand, is less theoretically inclined, employing what some have called an "impoverished" notion of discourse[4] and drawing more eclectically on "postmodernism" and social movement politics, especially the Zapatista movement.[5] Nonetheless, all three analysts share Foucault's predilections toward discursive productivity, which as I hope to demonstrate, ignores at its own peril the important issue of libidinal desire and agency.

## Post-Development's Foucauldian Underpinnings

One of Post-Development's notable contributions is to have brought discourse analysis to Development Studies. As is now well known, Foucault defines discourse not simply as a collection of words or utterances but as a set of "practices which systematically form the objects of which they speak" (2002, 49). For him, discourse constructs objects of knowledge, so that statements and socioinstitutional practices centered on, say, madness, homosexuality, or medicine prescribe what is sayable (and not sayable) about "mad" people, "homosexuals," or doctors. Post-Development's ingenuity is to have applied such thinking to the field of development. Thus, Escobar sees development discourse as allowing the West to "manage and control and, in many ways, even create the Third World politically, economically, sociologically and culturally" (1984, 384; see also 1995, 9, 11).[6] For him, as for Ferguson and Esteva,[7] the construction of knowledge systems in development is coterminous with a will to power and domination. As a result, much Post-Development writing is devoted to challenging the epistemological assumptions and categories of development discourse. Escobar and Esteva are critical, in particular, of the scientific and economistic thinking that dominates development (e.g., its fixation with technological and narrow economic growth-oriented solutions), as well as its Eurocentric and paternalistic assumptions (Escobar 1995, 215; Esteva 1992; see also Ziai 2015, 846). In response, they express interest in local culture and knowledge systems, with Esteva echoing Foucault by advocating for the "insurrection of subordinated knowledges" (1987, 146; see also Esteva, Babones, and Babcicky 2013, 105; Foucault 1980, 81).

An important way in which discourse plays out in development, for Escobar and Ferguson especially, is through "governmentality." This is the Foucauldian notion that fuses "governance" with "mentality" (or modes of thought) to underline the co-constitution of knowledge and power. Thus, when an institution identifies and defines a "problem," it is at the same time creating and rationalizing the corresponding strategies (and technologies of power) for addressing it (see Foucault 1991, 87ff.). Escobar examines, for example, how the categorization of the Third World as "abnormal," "underdeveloped," or "illiterate" yields a host of institutional practices—from field work and the collection of dossiers to the establishment of academic disciplines (e.g., Development Studies, Development Economics) and experts (e.g., food specialists, educators, business trainers, and anthropologists). He shows that such institutionalization opens up new sites not only of expertise but also of power: it ends up regulating and disciplining Third World populations (peasants, children, indigenous people, etc.) and producing "biopolitical" subjects (e.g., neoliberal entrepreneurial subjects) (Escobar 1984, 387–388; 1995, 17, 21ff.; 2000; 2008, 69ff.; see also Esteva, Babones, and Babcicky 2013, 115).

Similarly, Ferguson demonstrates how the classification of Lesotho as "aboriginal" or "agricultural" constructs the country as a "generic 'LDC' [Least Developed Country]—a country with all the right deficiencies, the sort that 'development' institutions can easily and productively latch on to" (1990, 70). He underlines how knowledge about the country is accordingly simplified and depoliticized, resulting in the aggrandizement of institutional authority, so much so that, even when development projects fail, they help expand bureaucratic power.

These three commentators' discursive analysis therefore cedes to a biting critique of development. Given what they see as the latter's many failings—the way in which development discourse represents the Third World, its use of hierarchic and Eurocentric categorization, its implied professionalization and institutionalization, its biopolitical production of development subjects—they question not only how development is done but its very framing, indeed our very need for it (Esteva 1992, 6, 16). No wonder that they seek out, as we shall see later, radical alternatives.

## Where Are the Passions?

The problem, however, is that this is a cold critique, devoid of human passion. Indeed, the Post-Development writers even admit as much. Ferguson sees his Foucauldian analysis as a "cold-blooded operation," characterizing Lesotho's development apparatus as an "anonymous," "anti-politics machine" (1990, xvi, xv, 275). Likewise, Escobar describes discourse analysis as allowing for the possibility of standing "detached" from development in order to examine its social and cultural dimensions (1995, 6). Accordingly, both the subject and the object of enquiry, the discourse analyst as much as the development worker or bureaucrat, are caught in an inescapable, impersonal power-ridden network. This is certainly Foucault's import when he declares that power does not operate over and above the subject, but is a *"machine* in which everyone is caught, those who exercise power as much as those over whom it is exercised. . . . It becomes a machinery that no one owns" (1980, 156, italics added).

Now contrast this viewpoint with the psychoanalytic one. Lacanian psychoanalysis is quite consistent with Foucault's conception of power/knowledge and how these discipline bodies, produce subjects, and shape such modern institutions as asylums, prisons, hospitals, schools, and indeed psychoanalysis itself. But while Lacan deploys a similar notion of discourse, he stresses not peoples' inescapable anonymity and detachment in the power/knowledge network, but on the contrary their unavoidable libidinal engagement in it. As we saw in chapter 1, for him our entry into language (i.e., the infant's separation from the (m)Other) is accompanied by traumatic loss or lack (from a false sense of plenitude). Desire, then, is the psychic remainder that occurs when we enter the symbolic world—an unconscious desire engaged in a futile quest to fill the lack, to regain once again the impossible fullness (Lacan 1977, 287; see also Homer 2004, 71–72). The libidinal is thus the complement to discourse, so that power is never impersonal; it is always passionately invested.

Yet, the problem is that Foucault assumes that power produces the body without any mediation, that is, without any process of interiorization. As Joan Copjec argues, quoting Foucault against himself, in "Foucault's work the techniques of disciplinary power (of the construction of the subject) are conceived as capable of 'materially penetrat[ing] the body in depth without depending even on the mediation of the subject's own representations. If power takes hold on the body, this isn't through its having first to be interiorized into people's consciousness'" (1994, 19).

True, Foucault does have a notion of "desire," but for him it is positively produced, not repressed. In his *History of Sexuality* (1979, 15ff., 129–130), for example, he argues that European discourses of sexuality arose in the nineteenth century as a result of social practices (medicine, psychoanalysis), which meant that far from being repressed, sexuality was spoken about a lot.[8] But as Copjec and others point out, such discursive productivism makes social reality "realtight" (1994, 14; see also Vighi and Feldner 2007, 18–23; Žižek 1992, 81). That is, by refusing any type of negation, gap, or excess (what Lacan calls the "Real"), discourse is reduced to the field of its effects without remainder. The problem with Foucault, then, is his refusal of any type of transcendence: his historicist discursivism ends up reducing society to power-knowledge relationships. But because power is always immanent for Foucault, his is a discursivism which can neither account for itself (how does one apprehend power/discourse if one is always within it?) nor explain how social orders persist or can be changed. If there is no gap between the discursive space and its positive content or effect, then Foucault is at pains to explain either his own role as discourse analyst or how the subject becomes an agent of social transformation. (This Lacanian critique, it should be noted, echoes feminist critiques of Foucault, which take him to task for reducing people to docile bodies and objects of power.)[9]

For Lacanians, it is precisely desire that fixes the subject (however precariously and contingently), explaining how we both (mis)perceive power and become libidinally invested in it. And such desire is not discursively produced, as Foucault would have it, but as noted above is an inherent excess (the Real)[10] to any discourse; it is the result of the insubstantial loss that arises the moment we enter language. Discourse therefore simultaneously implies an unconscious gap or leftover. And it is on the basis of such libidinal excess that

Lacanians envisage the possibility of agency and social change (see chapters 3, 8–10, and 12). Our passions may well bind us to the world (through intense attachments), but their excess may also help us liberate ourselves (more on this below).

## Rejecting Development or Enjoying It?

What this implies for Post-Development is that it fails to confront the psychic inclinations that support development discourse. This can be seen, in particular, in Escobar's and Esteva's black-and-white argumentation: because they depict development discourse as a form of Western domination of Third World subjects, they assume the latter will reject development, ignoring that many may not be psychically inclined. Both analysts have been roundly criticized, as we know, for homogenizing development discourse and painting development subjects with too broad a brush (see Kiely 1999, 30). To wit, Escobar calls for "alternatives to development," presuming that people are either for or against it (1995, 215, 226). And Esteva often portrays development subjects as "victims," comparing development to an "unburied corpse," "doomed to extinction" (1992, 6; see also Ziai 2004, 1048).

The glitch is that both analysts provide little to no evidence of any overwhelming disillusionment with, or indeed demise of, development across the global South. In fact, to date, the record is just the opposite. Critics of Post-Development point out that many communities have often fought *for* development (e.g., more jobs, even if they are low-paid, and better access to health, education, etc.) (Kiely 1999; Storey 2000, 42; Ziai 2015, 839). Jonathan Rigg contends, for example, that in Southeast Asia many groups have "climbed aboard the modernisation bandwagon, whether they be for or against it" (1997, 36). Similarly, Ray Kiely (1999, 44) submits that peasant communities are far from uninterested in accumulation, with many already well integrated into the global capitalist agricultural sector. And on the consumer front, development subjects—whether rural farming communities or urban transnational classes—often appear to be yearning for consumer goods. Thus, while Esteva asserts that "people at the grassroots [in the global South] . . . are learning to simply say 'no' to Coke" (Esteva and Prakash 1998, 25), precisely the contrary is true. If anything, it is people in the global North who are saying "No" and those in the South "Yes": carbonated drink consumption has been steadily declining in North America and Western Europe over the last two decades, with for example a 25 percent drop in the United States between 1998 and 2014. In contrast, soft drink consumption in Mexico (precisely where Esteva grounds his work) has been steadily increasing, with per capita consumption currently one of the highest in the world (CSPI 2016).

I want to suggest that it is because Escobar and Esteva's Foucauldianism does not explicate how power is libidinally mediated at the level of the subject that it fails to grapple with why people so often acquiesce in development discourse and neoliberal capitalism. The two analysts miss that development subjects may actually desire—nay even *enjoy*—development. To be sure, as explained in chapter 1, enjoyment (*jouissance*) in the Lacanian lexicon denotes not simply pleasure, but overwhelming or excessive (unconscious) gratification, so much so that despite knowing better, the subject may make irrational or counterproductive choices. In the same vein, it appears that development subjects (and many of us, for that matter) not only like what development has on offer, but (unconsciously) *love* it: given their above-noted record of embracing development, they are evidently seduced by development's fantasies of wealth, technology, and progress, and thrilled by iPhones, cars, and cola drinks. More pertinent is that even those subjects who may have doubts about development (on account of, say, its social inequities or negative environmental effects), may nonetheless buy into it. This is what Žižek terms "fetishistic disavowal" (1989, 18, 32–33), as discussed in chapter 1: one knows something is bad or wrong, but one desires it anyway (because one is so libidinally captivated by it). The upshot is that by ignoring people's psychic inclinations, the proponents of Post-Development underestimate the hold and charms of development discourse.

Post-Development may not be wrong in desiring an "alternative to development," but it errs in believing that people can be easily diverted from the mainstream. By neglecting the subject's unconscious desires, it is unable to explain why development discourse endures or indeed how people can be so invested in it. By the same token, it fails to appreciate the complex libidinal economy at work in development: for example, those who buy wholesale into development, those who buy into it reluctantly (fetishistic disavowal), and those who manage to come to terms with their unconscious desires and direct them elsewhere (see chapters 3, 9, 10, and 12). It is the last who may perhaps be able to work toward an "alternative to development," but the important point is that reaching such an alternative requires working through a complex economy of desire. In other words, radical transformation in development requires more than changing the discourse or the power/knowledge frame, as Foucault, Escobar, and Esteva would have it; it requires, critically, also attending to people's libidinal attachments.

## Bureaucratic Power: A Question of Intent or Enjoyment?

But let us not forget Ferguson's neglect of the libidinal as well, evident in his approach to governmentality. He repeatedly emphasizes the Foucauldian point that power circulates, so that the expansion of state power in Lesotho is "subjectless," the result of "unintended," "unforeseen," and "unlikely" state bureaucratic interventions (1990, 19–21, 254–255). According to him,

> the outcomes of planned social interventions can end up coming together into powerful constellations of control that were never intended and in some cases never recognized. . . . [It is this] unauthored resultant constellation that I call "the anti-politics machine." (1990, 19, 21)

Yet again, in following Foucault, Ferguson ignores how power is mediated subjectively. Reading him one gets the unmistakable impression that the development bureaucrat is a quasi-robotic body on (and through) which power is written and exercised. This seems vague and unpersuasive, in my view. It not only erases any meaningful subjectivity on the part of bureaucrats but appears to allow them to avoid any responsibility by portraying their decision-making process as faceless and somehow disinterested (or at least dispassionate).

Ferguson fails to recognize the important role of unconscious desire and enjoyment in bureaucratic politics: for instance, the ways in which development administrators or workers may obtain a certain reassurance and stability from following and applying bureaucratic procedures and rules; that they may enjoy disbursing (state) funds for "good" causes and programs, or get a kick out of the prestige (and in the development context, benevolence) of their bureaucratic position and the discretionary power that comes with it. There may even be, as I argue in chapters 7 and 12 (see also Kapoor 2013, 34; Wilson 2015), a sadomasochistic dimension to bureaucratic *jouissance*, especially across the global North-South divide: for example, relishing one's position of privilege relative to the Third World "poor" (i.e., enjoying inequality), or deriving an (unspeakable) satisfaction from siting a toxic environmental project far away from "us," for instance in a "remote" area where indigenous people live (i.e., enjoying environmental racism or "NIMBY"). Here, one luxuriates not despite the recklessness of one's decisions or positioning, but *because* of it.

Ferguson looks off the mark, then, when he insists that institutional decisions are subjectless or unintended. They may not be consciously intentional, but they are unconsciously invested and interested on the part of bureaucratic subjects. In other words, there is no such thing as "pure" lack of intention of the subjects of which he speaks. By reducing the bureaucratic space to the power-knowledge relationships within it, he misses the disavowed desires, dirty secrets, and tainted unspoken enjoyments that affect bureaucrats' choices and strategies.

No wonder that development bureaucracies engage in what Ferguson calls expanding "symbiotic networks of experts, offices, and salaries" (1990, 269).[11] While bureaucrats may well be blinded by (their own) discursive straightjacketing, it is the dimension of the unconscious that explains more adequately why institutional power is able to sustain itself and multiply: the latter is not only produced discursively in an almost impersonal and anonymous way (i.e., an anti-politics machine), but is able to take hold and expand through libidinal attachments. Or to put it differently, institutional growth is not simply about the circulation and congealment of power, but about how that power is savored and passionately charged by bureaucratic subjects. There is not-to-be-missed enjoyment, then, in the dissemination of power.[12]

Moreover, what Ferguson sees as "failure" of projects (which nonetheless result in bureaucratic expansion) can be seen as "success" from the perspective of unconscious desire. Such outward "failure" is less the "unintended" outcome or "side effect" of conscious decision making than the unavoidable other side of rationality—its dirty, secretive, excessive, sometimes even sadomasochistic underside which ensures institutional growth no matter whether projects succeed or fail. The "failure" of projects and the resulting aggrandizement of bureaucratic power are thus the symptoms of the institutional excess and enjoyment; they are proof of the success of unconscious desire.

Finally, from the psychoanalytic perspective, the development bureaucracy appears to be less a "machine" than a dysfunctional cyborg: intelligent perhaps, but complexly divided; making "rational" decisions, but being overwhelmed and undermined by the excesses of desire and enjoyment; and deploying knowledge and power in the service of development, but doing so passionately, woundedly, or possibly sadomasochistically, but not coldly, automatically, or altogether impersonally.

## Insecure Responses: Surrendering to Global Capitalism

As already emphasized, Foucault's reliance on an immanent notion of power leaves little room for social change and agency. This poses a significant conundrum for Post-Development, doubly so given its stinging critique of development and desire for a radical alternative. Following Foucault, Escobar and Esteva turn to localized forms of resistance, while Ferguson counts on a reworking of governmentality. Yet both responses, I will argue, are unpersuasive if not insecure, ultimately representing an (unconscious) acceptance of the status quo.

## Championing Social Movements and Local Autonomy: Anxious Defense?

As is now well known, rather than "agency," which he sees as relying too much on the Enlightenment myth of the rational subject, Foucault offers up "resistance." "[T]here are no relations of power without resistances," he famously pens, envisaging not "total revolution" but specific and localized struggles to resist the multiple capillaries of power (1980, 142, 99).

True to form, Escobar and Esteva adhere to this Foucauldian logic, calling for the need to "resist development interventions" (Escobar 1995, 11, 215, 218) and defending grassroots movements and local autonomy. Thus, Escobar writes, "To the multiplicity of forms of power, we must respond with a multiplicity of localised resistances and counteroffensives" (1984, 377; see also Alavarez, Dagnino, and Escobar 1998; Escobar and Alvarez 1992). Esteva, for his part, appears to give up on the (development) state, characterizing it as "naturally . . . unjust and arbitrary" (1999, 165; see also Esteva and Prakash 1998, 161). The goal instead is to build decentralized, autonomous spaces as counterpowers to the state.[13] He sees the Zapatista movement as embodying this "radical democratic" struggle, focusing not on "seizing State power" but creating local, autonomous spaces that can create "new political relations" (1999, 173).

The trouble is that Escobar's and Esteva's arguments are overconfident, with little evidence to back them up. There is, first, the issue of whether smaller, localized power struggles can (and do) significantly affect broader structural transformations. Esteva appears to answer in the affirmative: "a world struggle against GATT or the World Bank, at their headquarters . . . seems to be useless. . . . [Instead] an accumulation of local struggles may well produce the formulation of a new set of arrangements" (Esteva and Prakash 1998, 31, 34). But he supplies no corroborating data. There are indeed many cases across the global South of local (and transnational) social movements successfully blocking specific development projects (mining, oil, dams, etc.) backed by, say, the Bank or multinational corporations (MNCs), but to date there is little to show that such action has significantly undermined the latter's broader global operations—for example, reversing Western powers' control of the Bank or the Bank's commitments to neoliberal economic policy; or seriously threatening global MNC profits or the goal of capitalist accumulation.[14] Escobar admits as much, appearing to contradict his earlier defense of the local: "social movements are unlikely to radically transform large structures of domination or dramatically expand elite democracies" (Escobar and Alvarez 1992, 325–326; see also Escobar 1995, 226).

Post-Development's championing of popular movements is further undermined by the fact that many of these movements' issues have been co-opted by the mainstream. As the last three decades have shown, liberal democratic capitalism can so often blunt these movements' effectiveness by culturalizing and commodifying their demands (see chapters 8, 10, and 12). Thus, multiculturalism, while providing civil rights protection and cultural recognition, has often tamed or ignored key socioeconomic demands (e.g., indigenous land claims, economic equality, labor rights). And corporate capitalism has successfully exploited social movement causes by niche-marketing products for the likes of LGBTI groups, young women, "ethnic" communities, organic food lovers, and so forth (Della Porta 2015; Žižek 1999, 355).

But the glaring glitch in this Post-Development universe is the absence of the state. Escobar barely gives it any place in his work, while Esteva, as pointed out above, is so critical of it that he appears to ignore it altogether in his proposals for a radical democratic alternative. Yet in the absence of a state, what is the authority for coordinating, controlling, or protecting against political claims and power? How would locally autonomous spaces withstand the forces of globalization, particularly capital? What is most glaring, in fact, is that the Post-Development alternative *needs and assumes the state*. A complex network of material, legal, and institutional conditions must exist and be maintained in order for "autonomous" spaces (and social movements, for that matter) *to* function (see Žižek 2012, 179). Decentralization, equitable land tenure, cultural autonomy, and democracy itself would be meaningless without a state that provides safety, security, justice, education, health care, and the like. So Post-Development might well be highly critical of governmentality and the development state, but it provides no substitute for such a state, all the while surreptitiously (i.e., unconsciously) requiring one.

Given the above gaps—a weak theoretical basis for social transformation (i.e., resistance rather than agency) and a lack of adequate evidence and argumentation for a radical alternative to development—Post-Development ends up resorting to inflated claims. I want to suggest in fact that, psychoanalytically speaking, such inflation is an anxious defense against these shaky foundations. To be sure, for Lacan, anxiety is closely connected to a lack or gap; it is a way of sustaining desire—in this case the desire for a credible alternative—despite an absence (2014, 16ff., 157ff.).

Post-Development's first anxious defense is the tendency to romanticize the local. This is a well-known critique that I need not rehearse here. Suffice it to say that critics point to Post-Development's inclination to conflate the "global" and the "state" with everything bad, and "social movements" and the "local" with everything good (an inclination we noted earlier in relation to "development," which it similarly rejects outright) (see Hart 2001, 655; Kiely 1999; Pieterse 2000; Storey 2000; Ziai 2015). Accordingly, Ray Kiely (1999, 46) sees Post-Development as the "last refuge of the noble savage," emphasizing how it celebrates the local while downplaying such problems as internal disagreements, gender violence, exploitation, or inequality. Esteva is to be especially singled out in this regard: his published work on the Zapatistas and other indigenous movements is mostly a paean to them; he barely has anything negative to say about them and hardly mentions their weaknesses or internal conflicts (1999, 2001; Esteva and Prakash 1998). Such romanticization, such black-and-white construction, it seems to me, is camouflage; it is a remedy— an anxious compensation—against weak arguments. It is also, as I have contended elsewhere (Kapoor 2008, 51–53), a way of consolidating the Self: the desire for the Other as hero is at the same time an anxious desire for the intellectual to appear benevolent or progressive, to ingratiate himself to his audience (or critics).

A second anxious defense is Post-Development's moralistic and inflated rhetoric. This is likely more a question of style and tone than content, although it points once again to an ardent desire for a "worthy" alternative. In Escobar it is evident in repeated calls for the need to resist, of which here is a sampling: "localized resistances . . . *must* be of a radical and uncompromising character . . . the strategy *must* be aimed at developing a network of struggles, points of resistance, and popular bases."[15] This "ought," this appeal to act "radically," it seems to me, has no discursive grounding; rather, contrary to Foucauldian logic, it is an *extradiscursive* moral exhortation that Escobar is obliged to resort to precisely because of the weak basis for resistance. Indeed, Foucault has himself been taken to task for too simply linking resistance to power without providing an ethicopolitical basis for which people *would* resist (see Harstock 1990, 170). No wonder, then, that in Escobar this translates into an anxious recourse to a categorical imperative.

The problem is even more pronounced in Esteva's work. His style and tone tend to be rhetorical, if not polemical, with many of his publications written like political manifestos (his coauthored 2013 book is subtitled, *A Radical Manifesto*[16]). Like Escobar, his writing is littered with moral imperatives (e.g., "It is time to stop the dominant insanity," or "It is essential that Mexicans adopt new political forms"):[17] but more than Escobar, he engages in exaggeration, if not hyperbole (e.g., "The Zapatistas activated millions of discontents . . . with one single word: Enough [Basta]!" or "An epic is unfolding at the grassroots").[18] Here, it is not just the bravura but its relative intensity and pervasiveness that are psychoanalytically telling: Esteva's insistent repetition is about anxiously searching for the lost object (a radical, alternate politics of development) yet never being able to find it (given, among other things, shaky theoretical grounds and evidence). The result is more—and more insistent—bravura.

Finally, Esteva's moralistic stance is reflected perhaps nowhere better than in the very movement that he most champions—the Zapatistas (EZLN).[19] This is a movement that, at least at its origins in 1994, appeared subversive, instigating a "revolution" and declaring "war" against the Mexican state. But since then, it has gradually traded in its uncompromising stance for a more transactional position, mixing negotiation with the state with unilateral declarations of autonomy for Chiapas. It has become notably media savvy and celebrity conscious, relying until recently on its ubiquitous spokesman, the masked Subcomandante Marcos, to issue a series of calls for social justice and "declarations" in favor of alternative democratic elections, women's rights, and indigenous cultural and political autonomy (see Esteva 1999). It has thus begun to play moral authority, challenging the state and global capitalism mainly symbolically, and being embraced more and more by the mainstream (i.e., political elites, corporate media, advertising, etc.). In this sense, it has become, as Žižek claims, not a counterforce to the state but its "shadowy double" (2012, 177): the EZLN's moralistic protest now places it in an increasingly unthreatening, symbiotic relationship with the state (and capital). In hindsight, as a result of this ultimately placid and conscientious politics, the EZLN could even be seen, not as posing a threat to NAFTA[20]—the movement's main objective at NAFTA's inauguration in 1994—but as helping facilitate NAFTA's integration. This is certainly Žižek's view:

> with Zapatista help, Mexico got the first post-revolutionary government, a government that cut the last links with the historical heritage of Zapata and fully endorsed Mexico's integration into the neo-liberal New World Order. (2012, 178)

This is not to disparage the notable struggles of the Zapatista movement or to take away from its successes in gaining a degree of local autonomy. But these local successes have done little to transform wider sociopolitical power.[21] The movement certainly appears to have failed in reaching its initial goals of defeating the Mexican state and dismantling NAFTA. If anything, the EZLN's increasingly unthreatening moralistic stance has let the Mexican state off the hook, allowing the latter to concede a degree of local autonomy to Chiapas but at the same time substantially increase Mexico's integration into NAFTA/ USMCA (of which the recent constitutional privatization of much of the country's energy sector is a sobering reminder).

The Zapatistas thus illustrate Post-Development's inherent political problem—having to rely on an ineffectual moralistic position to compensate for an equally ineffectual local politics of resistance (at least in terms of effecting broader structural change). Escobar's and Esteva's search for a radical alternative to development may be laudable, but their hype, admonitions, and rhapsodic tone appear as little more than an anxious cover for a lack of adequate political resources to muster this alternative.

## Universal Basic Income: More Welfarism?

If the state is absent in Escobar's and Esteva's politics, it is very much present in Ferguson's broader conception of governmentality. His earlier work on bureaucratic politics, as we saw, was highly critical; but his most recent work (especially his 2015 book, *Give a Man a Fish*) is a more hopeful reworking of governmentality, which he characterizes as a new Left "mechanism" or "art" of government intended to rethink contemporary capitalism and "conceive of real political alternatives in these neoliberal times" (2010, 173; 2015, 32, xiii). He sees neoliberalism as a field of governmental techniques that can be "repurposed" and "put to work in the service of political projects very different from those usually associated with that word" (2010, 183).

The "real political alternatives" he has in mind are universal basic income programs, which are increasingly being discussed and instituted around the world (e.g., in Brazil, Alaska, Finland, and other parts of Europe, most recently in Switzerland, where it was put to a 2016 referendum and defeated). Ferguson's focus is southern Africa, but he writes that the programs are "happening in several African countries . . . [and] in a great many [other] postcolonial states . . . where leftist and rightist regimes alike have seen fit to introduce policies that transfer cash directly into the hands of the poor" (2010, 173). Thus, a basic income grant (BIG) in South Africa and Namibia is provided to all citizens (with payments to high-income earners recouped through progressive taxes). Grants are unconditional—recipients can choose whether or not to engage in productive labor—and sufficient to cover minimal expenses for such items as food, housing, health care, and education (Ferguson 2015, 15, 17).

For Ferguson, these programs are not charity or social assistance but a "rightful share." Citizens become rightful owners of the national wealth, "of which they have been unjustly deprived." Thus, the "most basic citizenship right is . . . understood not as a right to vote but as a right 'to partake in the wealth of the nation'" (2015, 24, 26, 56).

Admittedly, there is much to extol in these programs. They are distributive in allowing the poorest sections of society, in particular, to spend more on social goods (nutrition, housing, etc.) and turn down unacceptable or poorly paid jobs. They also help jettison the welfarist and productivist assumptions of mainstream government assistance schemes, which as Ferguson underlines are so often accompanied by moral opprobrium (e.g., treating recipients as "welfare bums" or "parasites") and strict conditions (e.g., obliging people to undergo skills training and to seek market employment). Ferguson's Foucauldian loyalties come through in his critique of the surveillance and paternalistic dimensions of traditional "nanny state" programs, which he contrasts with the BIG program's enablement of the poor to actively choose whether and how to participate in society and the market (2010, 174; 2015, 19, 36, 38ff., 177).

Yet, as Žižek points out, while basic income programs may better help reconcile freedom and equality, we remain very much *"within* capitalism—social production remains predominantly capitalist, and redistribution is imposed from the outside by the state apparatus" (2011, 236, italics added).[22] This means that it is business as usual for the (transnational) corporate sector, which in the southern African context especially results in the continued production of socioeconomic inequalities, unevenness, and environmental destruction (particularly given the heavy presence of, and reliance on, extractive industries there) (see Bond 2006; Mensah 2008). Basic income schemes help tinker with liberal democratic capitalism, adding an extra element of social redistribution but nonetheless posing little threat to the overall framework. Ultimately, such schemes appear to let capitalism off the hook, allowing for its continued smooth functioning.

The problem here is that Ferguson fails to show how neoliberal governmentality is being "repurposed" or in which way so-called "radically *distributive* politics" (2015, 198, italics in original) can help transform capitalism in southern Africa. Toward the end of his book he even admits as much, confessing to the limits of actually existing programs: "it is not clear how the southern African BIG campaign is capable of achieving the sort of political traction that would be necessary to achieve its goals" (2015, 200).[23] He stops short, then, of providing the necessary evidence or arguments to show how basic income can challenge (or help the marginalized mobilize against) liberal political economy. Instead, what he offers is a "capitalism with a human face"—a system made more socially responsible but left fundamentally intact; a program that attends to the worst manifestations of neoliberalism (e.g., the dispossession of the poor) yet thereby ensures its prolongation.

In the end, Ferguson simply gives us more welfarism (or social democracy). The social stigma of such welfarism has perhaps been attenuated,[24] but the overall bureaucratic, bourgeois state-led schema remains. Ironically, his redistributive politics depends on a relatively strong bureaucratic state, the very one of whose politics of survival/expansion he was previously critical. Nowhere does he explain how and why such a top-down setup would acquiesce to anything that deviates from the mainstream or threaten the power (and desires and enjoyments) of bureaucrats. Most importantly, his basic income idea continues to count on the liberal or social democratic compromise with capital that *is* welfarism—give the poor a small piece of the pie, but first ensure capital accumulation; leave the market mostly intact . . . and attend to its socioenvironmental problems only *after* the fact.

But none of this should come as a surprise since, as mentioned earlier, Ferguson touts at the outset how "leftist and rightist regimes alike" have embraced basic income. Rather than a hopeful sign, to my mind this underscores precisely the liberal democratic compromise that his basic income proposal cannot escape (rightist regimes, and in fact many social democratic ones, are unlikely to compromise on anything that overly threatens market capitalism).

## Fetishistic Disavowal: Capitalism Is Bad . . . but It's Here to Stay

Post-Development may well aspire to a radical Left politics, yet what emerges from the above is its avoidance of the traumatic Real, that is, its notable evasion of any direct confrontation with the state or capital. Instead, in the vein of John Holloway's plea to "change the world without taking power" (2010), what Escobar and Esteva resort to is an anxious defense of local resistance and autonomy that outwardly withdraws from the state yet, as emphasized earlier, unconsciously needs and materially depends on it. The two analysts back social movements, yet the latter's localized and moralistic politics tends to be increasingly tolerated if not embraced by the state and capital, thus constructing a relationship of "mutual parasitism" (Žižek 2008, 349).

Ferguson similarly refrains from adequately transforming (let alone threatening) the state by offering up a quasi-welfarist politics that operates within the rules already laid down by liberal democratic capitalism. His reworked governmentality essentially amounts to capitalism with a human face, relying on the bureaucratic bourgeois state to address the worst manifestations of inequality, all the while maintaining the very market economy that creates such inequality. The proof of the pudding is his conception of basic income as a "rightful share" of national wealth: why is he proffering such a mysteriously abstract conception, which obfuscates the nature and quantity of both "share" and "national wealth" (how would one legitimately determine "real" national wealth or the worth of a just share?),[25] as opposed to something more concrete and precise such as corporate or workplace shares, which would give the poor much more substantive control over their jobs and the economy? The answer surely is that such abstractness allows him to avoid the traumatic Real of (liberal democratic) capitalism. He gentrifies his distributive politics so as not to have to address the key social antagonisms that pit the poor against the wealthy or the proletariat against the bourgeoisie. He anesthetizes redistribution against the messy politics of dispossession and inequality by simply extending bureaucratic bourgeois welfarism.[26]

But then why such avoidance on the part of Post-Development? Why the unwillingness to confront the Real? I want to suggest that, psychoanalytically speaking, it is a case of fetishistic disavowal (as defined above). Escobar, Ferguson, and Esteva call for a radical politics of development, but end up relying on liberal political economy; they want to resist neoliberal capitalism, but ultimately tolerate if not require the bourgeois state and market. In other words, despite their critique, they have unconsciously surrendered to global capitalism. They may tinker at the edges of it, but they have silently accepted that neoliberal economy, along with its political arrangement—liberal democracy—are here to stay. Hence their avoidance of the traumatic Real of capitalism.

Now psychoanalysis points to the unconscious libidinal investments we make, so that in spite of knowing better, we act against our best interests. Unconscious desire trumps knowledge, enjoyment overwhelms reason or intention. So it is that the Post-Development analysts appear to have unconsciously bought into (i.e., fetishized) neoliberal capitalism, despite their outward intellectual protestations and condemnations. This is because, as I have been suggesting, they neither attend to the libidinal underpinnings of power nor have the theoretical inclination or resources to do so, given their Foucauldian orientations. The result is a "return of the repressed": Post-Development's disavowal of unconscious desires paves the way for its ultimate acquiescence to global capitalism.

If this is true, then we should not be surprised when the likes of Escobar and Esteva resort to hyperbole and romanticization, as stressed earlier. The latter is an anxious acting out of, an overcompensation for, the weak grounds for resistance to capitalism and the absence of a psychoanalysis to adequately confront the Real (excess, antagonism) of their desires.

But I do not want to suggest that these Post-Development analysts are uniquely fetishistic. I side with Žižek (1989, 18, 32–33) in claiming that fetishistic disavowal is the key ideological phenomenon of our age. Global capitalism seduces us all by producing fantasies or objects that libidinally capture us, despite our best intentions; this is why, not just the subjects of development, but the very critical (Post-Development) analysts who study them can (and do) easily succumb to its charms. In fact, Žižek takes several key Left figures to task (including the likes of Antonio Negri, Simon Critchley, Yannis Stavraka-kis, and Ernesto Laclau) for their seemingly radical yet ultimately reformist politics. According to him, all tend to yield to a polite, unthreatening, and half-hearted politics, and the proof is that the status quo tolerates, acknowledges, and even accedes to many of their so-called radical demands ("third way" so-cial democracy, gay rights, local cooperatives, autonomous collectives, etc.). All deplore and criticize capitalism and its attendant penchant for inequality and unevenness, but ultimately, for Žižek, all manifest a secret desire that noth-ing too much must change (2008, 337ff.).

The great challenge, then, is acknowledging and squarely facing the Real of our age (see chapters 3, 8–10, and 12). Knowledge and critical intellectual distance are not nearly enough, it seems. If we are to conceive of an "alterna-tive to development," to be able to meaningfully look beyond the immensely dominant horizon of global capitalism, psychoanalysis suggests that, as first step at least, we need to recognize and confront our unconscious desires.

## Conclusion

I have claimed that Post-Development ignores at its own peril the role of de-sire in its critique of capitalist development. By not considering unconscious passions, it cannot explain how people enjoy rather than reject development, so that capitalism continues to flourish, not perish, globally. Moreover, by not attending to the Real of its own desires, Post-Development ends up buying into global capitalism. Despite its critique of both state and capital, it not only fears confronting them but also winds up relying on them.

I have suggested that part of the problem is Post-Development's depen-dence on Foucauldian discourse analysis, which provides meager resources for resistance to capitalism, while also refusing any form of transcendence (e.g., the psychoanalytic Real) that would enable stronger forms of agency. Post-Development suffers precisely from this lack of grounding for a radical politics. Yet my proposal that Post-Development engages in fetishistic disavowal points to a more endemic problem—that discourse analysis is itself a surren-der to global capitalism, and that it offers only resistance, not radicalism or agency, precisely to honor this surrender (see chapters 7, 8). This aligns with Fredric Jameson's argument (1991) that postmodernism is but the cultural logic of late capitalism and hence critical but unthreatening. It also adheres to Gillian Hart's claim, specifically concerning Post-Development—that it is part and par-cel of the development of capitalism. Recalling Polanyi's notion of capitalism's "double movement," whereby market forces unleash social havoc that in turn generates demands for social justice, she characterizes Post-Development critiques as "expressions of the opposing forces contained within capitalism" (2001, 650).[27] For her, Post-Development's so-called radicalism is thus integral to the development of development. I agree, except that I would want to supplement her political economy analysis with a psychoanalysis.

## Notes

1. Toward the end of *The Anti-Politics Machine* (1990, 275–276), Ferguson makes fleeting reference to Deleuze and "desire," even mentioning the "unacknowledged" and "non-discursive" structures embedded in development discourse. But he refrains once again from elaborating these ideas or their psychoanalytic implications. In other words, by evading the psychoanalytic route, he appears to implicitly accept the Foucauldian notion of desire as discursively produced, as opposed to seeing desire as an unconscious, nondiscursive remainder à la Lacan. More on the latter below.

2. I will use the terms "global capitalism" and "liberal democratic capitalism" interchangeably here, as in my view global capitalism and liberal democracy go together: Liberal democracy is the political arrangement for much of (global) capitalism (the other main political-economic arrangement being "authoritarian capitalism," as found in Singapore, China, Russia, etc.).

3. It should be noted that, while both Escobar and Ferguson have mostly stuck to their Foucauldianism, their more recent work does diverge, with Escobar embracing a more utopian decoloniality perspective (e.g., Mignolo and Escobar 2010) and Ferguson a more realist welfarism (see below).

4. See, for example, Ziai (2004) and Brigg (2002). For instance, while Foucault advocates a historically contingent and sensitive notion of discourse, Esteva tends to view development discourse as monolithic, seeing power exercised, not biopolitically as Foucault would have it, but by a single "Western" force (Brigg 2002, 424–425; Esteva 1992, 6, 17).

5. Esteva's 1987 piece is perhaps his most Foucauldian, using the term "development discourse" and citing Foucault (Esteva 1987, 137, 146). His later works make more fleeting references to Foucault, although still identifying with "postmodern" ideas more generally (as witnessed, for example, by his coauthored book, Esteva and Prakash 1998, entitled *Grassroots Post-Modernism*).

6. Escobar's statement closely follows Said's famous definition of Orientalism as "the enormously systematic discipline by which European culture was able to manage—and even produce—the Orient politically, sociologically, militarily, ideologically, scientifically, and imaginatively during the post-Enlightenment period" (1979, 3).

7. See Esteva (1987, 146) and Ferguson (1990, 8).

8. In his later work, Foucault is quite critical of psychoanalysis, seeing it (along with medicine generally) as a normalizing technology in the service of our disciplinary societies.

9. See Fraser (1989, 31), Harstock (1990, 168–170), Sawicki (1988). See also chapter 8.

10. Lacan calls the Real "extimate" (une *extimité*), that is, intimately external or internally transcendent (1997, 71; see also Žižek and Daly 2004, 76). See Chapter 3 for Žižek's argument about why this extimacy makes the Real a negative universal.

11. Note, as the rest of this paragraph/section underlines, that I am not trying to replace Ferguson's argument here, but to enrich and complicate it with a psychoanalytic argument. As I shall claim later (see the section "Universal Basic Income"), the fact that there is a not-to-be-missed passionate enjoyment in bureaucratic politics further undermines Ferguson's recent attempt at "repurposing" neoliberal governmentality: it is improbable that bureaucrats passionately invested in the system (and their own bureaucratic power/privilege) would be easily amenable to change, and Ferguson fails to specify otherwise.

12. Chapters 4 and 12 go further into this, but institutional expansion can be explained more precisely by what Lacanians call "drive," which is to be distinguished from desire. Institutional growth happens through the enjoyment of power (i.e., drive). And while such drive may have an impersonal dimension (in chapter 4, I speak, for example, of the quasi-impersonal way in which capitalists are "driven" by the dictates of Capital), the enjoyment of it is still interiorized at the level of the subject, even if the latter remains unconscious.

13. See Esteva (1999, 163, 155ff.; 2001, 126). See also Esteva, Babones, and Babcicky (2013, 124ff.) and Esteva and Prakash (1998, 152ff., 172ff.).

14. See Aronowitz (2006, 1ff., 109ff.), Della Porta (2015), Kirsch (2014), and McMichael (2017, 213ff.).

15. Escobar (1984, 381, italics added). See also a series of similar statements on page 393, including: "a strategy of resistance *must* develop . . ." and "the discourse of development *must* be dismantled" (italics added); and in Escobar (1995, 98, 110, 209, 222). This is an illustrative not exhaustive list, as is the case with the examples from Esteva's work listed in notes 17 and 18 below.

16. See Esteva, Babones, and Babcicky (2013).

17. Esteva, Babones, and Babcicky (2013, 70), and Esteva (2001, 142). Other examples of moral exhortation can be found in Esteva (1999, 169), Esteva, Babones, and Babcicky (2013, x, 117), and Esteva and Prakash (1998, 42ff.).

18. Esteva (1999, 162) and Esteva and Prakash (1998, xiv). Other examples of such generalizations and bravura can be found in Esteva (1999, 162, 174; 2001, 139), and Esteva and Prakash (1998, 8, 204). Esteva rationalizes his "broad brush strokes" by stating that he aims at "breaking the prison of academic disciplinary boundaries" in order to speak to "non-specialists" (Esteva and Prakash 1998, 8). But I am suggesting they are more likely an unconscious cover/compensation for ineffectual arguments and theoretical grounding.

19. Esteva has worked as an advisor to the Zapatista Army for National Liberation (EZLN) in Chiapas, especially in connection with its negotiations with the Mexican government. So perhaps it is no coincidence that the EZLN's moralistic politics has rubbed off on him, or indeed that his own moralistic stance has been, at least to a small degree, reproduced in the EZLN.

20. The North American Free Trade Agreement (NAFTA), which has now been replaced by the United States-Mexico-Canada Agreement (USMCA).

21. Vergara-Camus (2014) makes a compelling case for the Zapatista movement as an example of autonomy and decommodification of rural social life. And while I agree, what appears to be missing is how such a model is or can be generalized: while Vergara-Camus does focus on Zapatista alliance building, the crucial question that remains is how such bridge-building helps transform the largely urban (or indeed even other rural) capitalist economies of Mexico and beyond.

22. It should be noted that, ironically, Ferguson marshals Žižek's statement that universal basic income is "arguably the Left's only original economic idea of the last few decades" (Žižek 2011, 233) to back up his case (Ferguson 2015, 193), but he does so disingenuously since Žižek is in fact highly critical of the idea, despite it seeming attractive.

23. Note that Ferguson's book is scattered with sentences that favor what he calls a certain "empiricism" and "inductivism" so that, according to him, his project can start from what people do "instead of from some theorist's idea of what they ought to do" (2015, 140; on p. 32 he even approvingly quotes Foucault on the need for "a certain empiricism"). Yet by the same token, given his admission of the currently unfavorable record of basic income in southern Africa, his arguments must succumb to these same empiricist predilections.

24. The paternalism Ferguson is worried about may be reduced through basic income programs, but it would by no means be eliminated. Society would still be divided into "basic income" and (let's say) "productive" citizens, so that hierarchical distinctions and social stigma and resentment would still remain. See Žižek (2011, 240–241).

25. Per capita income could be one measure, but as is well known, this is not an unproblematic indicator, given its tendency to hide sometimes wide inequalities (in income, gender, racialized positioning, etc.) and the environmental costs of development (see chapter 6).

26. Japhy Wilson (2014, 1156) accuses Ferguson's variant of Post-Development of being "complicit in the reproduction of relations of domination" by excluding the dimension of desire and the Real.

27. Ray Kiely (1999, 48) makes a similar argument.

## References

Alvarez, Sonia E., Evelina Dagnino, and Arturo Escobar, eds. 1998. *Cultures of Politics/Politics of Cultures: Re-Visioning Latin American Social Movements.* Boulder, CO: Westview.

Aronowitz, Stanley. 2006. *Left Turn: Forging a New Political Future.* New York: Routledge.

Bond, Patrick. 2006. *Looting Africa: The Economics of Exploitation.* London: Zed.

Brigg, Morgan. 2002. "Post-Development, Foucault and the Colonisation Metaphor." *Third World Quarterly* 23 (3): 421–436.

Center for Science in the Public Interest (CSPI). 2016. "Soda Companies Turning to Low- and Middle-Income Countries to Replace Sagging US Soda Sales." Center for Science in the Public Interest. https://cspinet.org/new/201602091.html.

Copjec, Joan. 1994. *Read My Desire: Lacan against the Historicists*. London: Verso.

Della Porta, Donatella. 2015. *Social Movements in Times of Austerity*. Cambridge: Polity.

de Vries, Pieter. 2007. "Don't Compromise Your Desire for Development! A Lacanian/Deleuzian Rethinking of the Anti-Politics Machine." *Third World Quarterly* 28 (1): 25–43.

Escobar, Arturo. 1984. "Discourse and Power in Development: Michel Foucault and the Relevance of His Work to the Third World." *Alternatives* 10: 377–400.

——. 1995. *Encountering Development: The Making and Unmaking of the Third World*. Princeton, NJ: Princeton University Press.

——. 2000. "Beyond the Search for a Paradigm? Post-Development and Beyond." *Development* 43 (4): 11–14.

——. 2008. *Territories of Difference: Place, Movements, Life, Redes*. Durham, NC: Duke University Press.

Escobar, Arturo, and Sonia E. Alvarez, eds. 1992. *The Making of Social Movements in Latin America: Identity, Strategy, and Democracy*. Boulder, CO: Westview.

Esteva, Gustavo. 1987. "Regenerating People's Space." *Alternatives* 12 (1): 125–152.

——. 1992. "Development." In *The Development Dictionary: A Guide to Knowledge as Power*, edited by Wolfgang Sachs, 6–25. London: Zed.

——. 1999. "The Zapatistas and People's Power." *Capital and Class* 23 (2): 153–182.

——. 2001. "The Meaning and Scope of the Struggle for Autonomy." *Latin American Perspectives* 28 (2): 120–148.

Esteva, Gustavo, Salvatore Babones, and Philipp Babcicky. 2013. *The Future of Development: A Radical Manifesto*. Bristol: Policy.

Esteva, Gustavo, and Madhu Suri Prakash. 1998. *Grassroots Post-Modernism: Remaking the Soil of Cultures*. London: Zed.

Ferguson, James. 1990. *The Anti-Politics Machine: "Development," Depoliticization, and Bureaucratic Power in Lesotho*. Minneapolis: University of Minnesota Press.

——. 2010. "The Uses of Neoliberalism." *Antipode* 41 (January): 166–184.

——. 2015. *Give a Man a Fish: Reflections on the New Politics of Distribution*. Durham, NC: Duke University Press.

Foucault, Michel. 1979. *The History of Sexuality*. Vol. 1, *An Introduction*. New York: Allen Lane.

——. 1980. *Power/Knowledge: Selected Interviews and Other Writings, 1972–1977*. Edited by Colin Gordon. New York: Pantheon.

——. 1991. *The Foucault Effect: Studies in Governmentality*. Edited by Graham Burchell, Colin Gordon, and Peter Miller. London: Harvester Wheatsheaf.

——. 2002. *The Archaeology of Knowledge*. Translated by A. M. Sheridan Smith. London: Routledge.

Fraser, Nancy. 1989. *Unruly Practices: Power, Discourse, and Gender in Contemporary Social Theory*. Minneapolis: University of Minnesota Press.

Harstock, Nancy. 1990. "Foucault on Power: A Theory for Women?" In *Feminism/Postmodernism*, edited by Linda J. Nicholson, 157–175. London and New York: Routledge.

Hart, Gillian. 2001. "Development Critiques in the 1990s: Culs de Sac and Promising Paths." *Progress in Human Geography* 25 (4): 649–658.

Holloway, John. 2010. *Change the World without Taking Power*. London: Pluto.

Homer, Sean. 2004. *Jacques Lacan*. London: Routledge.

Jameson, Fredric. 1991. *Postmodernism, or The Cultural Logic of Late Capitalism.* London: Verso.

Kapoor, Ilan. 2008. *The Postcolonial Politics of Development.* London: Routledge.

———. 2013. *Celebrity Humanitarianism: The Ideology of Global Charity.* London: Routledge.

Kiely, Ray. 1999. "The Last Refuge of the Noble Savage? A Critical Assessment of Post-Development Theory." *European Journal of Development Research* 11 (1): 30–55. https://doi.org/10.1080/09578819908426726.

Kirsch, Stuart. 2014. *Mining Capitalism: The Relationship Between Corporations and Their Critics.* Oakland: University of California Press.

Lacan, Jacques. 1977. *Écrits: A Selection.* Translated by Alan Sheridan. New York: Norton.

———. 1997. *The Ethics of Psychoanalysis: The Seminar of Jacques Lacan, Book VII.* Edited by Jacques-Alain Miller. New York: Norton.

———. 2014. *Anxiety: The Seminar of Jacques Lacan, Book X.* Edited by Jacques-Alain Miller. Cambridge: Polity.

McMichael, Philip. 2017. *Development and Social Change: A Global Perspective.* Thousand Oaks, CA: Sage.

Mensah, Joseph, ed. 2008. *Globalization in Africa: Contestations on the Embattled Continent.* New York: Palgrave Macmillan.

Mignolo, Walter D., and Arturo Escobar. 2010. *Globalization and the Decolonial Option.* London: Routledge.

Pieterse, Jan Nederveen. 2000. "After Post-Development." *Third World Quarterly* 21 (2): 175–191.

Rigg, Jonathan. 1997. *Southeast Asia: The Human Landscape of Modernization and Development.* London: Routledge.

Said, Edward W. 1979. *Orientalism.* New York: Vintage.

Sawicki, Jana. 1988. "Feminism and the Power of Discourse." In *After Foucault: Humanistic Knowledge, Postmodern Challenges*, edited by Jonathan Arac, 161–178. New Brunswick, NJ: Rutgers University Press.

Storey, Andy. 2000. "Post-Development Theory: Romanticism and Pontius Pilate Politics." *Development* 43 (4): 40–46.

Vergara-Camus, Leandro. 2014. *Land and Freedom: The MST, the Zapatistas and Peasant Alternatives to Neoliberalism.* London: Zed.

Vighi, Fabio, and Heiko Feldner. 2007. *Žižek: Beyond Foucault.* Basingstoke: Palgrave-Macmillan.

Wilson, Japhy. 2014. "Fantasy Machine: Philanthrocapitalism as an Ideological Formation." *Third World Quarterly* 35 (7): 1144–1161.

———. 2015. "The Joy of Inequality: The Libidinal Economy of Compassionate Consumerism." *International Journal of Žižek Studies* 9 (2). http://zizekstudies.org/index.php/IJZS/article/view/815/820.

Ziai, Aram. 2004. "The Ambivalence of Post-Development: Between Reactionary Populism and Radical Democracy." *Third World Quarterly* 25 (1): 1045–1060.

———. 2015. "Post-Development: Premature Burials and Haunting Ghosts." *Development and Change* 46 (6): 833–854.

Žižek, Slavoj. 1989. *The Sublime Object of Ideology.* London: Verso.

——. 1992. *Enjoy Your Symptom! Jacques Lacan in Hollywood and Out.* New York: Routledge.

——. 1999. *The Ticklish Subject: The Absent Centre of Political Ontology.* London: Verso.

——. 2008. *In Defense of Lost Causes.* London: Verso.

——. 2011. *Living in the End Times.* London: Verso.

——. 2012. *Organs without Bodies: On Deleuze and Consequences.* London: Routledge.

Žižek, Slavoj, and Glyn Daly. 2004. *Conversations with Žižek.* Cambridge: Polity.

# PART TWO

## *Keywords / Essays*

# Chapter 3

# The Universalist Dimensions of Antagonism

Keyword: *Antagonism*

## Introduction

As chapter 1 intimated, for Lacanian psychoanalysis, antagonism is ontological. There is no escape from it: the traumatic Real is constitutive of the human condition. In fact, according to Žižek, the social emerges from human efforts to struggle against or avoid trauma so that reality is constructed and materialized as a response to antagonism (1989, 5–6). Ideologies propagated by the state or market (e.g., multiculturalism, neoliberalism) aim at covering up this fundamental deadlock (e.g., social contradictions such as inequality or class struggle) in order to present reality as unified, complete, or pristine. The goal of Žižekian ideology critique, then, is to uncover these contradictions in order for us to better face our social traumas. Yet such antagonisms are to be identified not just in the Other, but also in our midst. The most difficult task of ideology critique is coming to terms with our own unconscious investments in obscuring and perpetuating social antagonisms; to be meaningful, therefore, such a critique needs to be universalist—in the sense of nondiscriminating—in order to confront the antagonisms of every side, including and especially one's own.

But Žižek relies on the idea of antagonism to expound another key argument: if the traumatic Real is ontological, this means that it can form the basis for a shared politics. Social traumas—oppressive socioeconomic and cultural systems—are what a plurality of people and groups across the globe face in common, thereby providing a platform to work together. Antagonism here becomes a negative horizon enabling a universalist politics.

In this chapter, I focus on two recent controversies in which Žižek has been embroiled—the European refugee crisis and the issue of Eurocentrism—to illustrate these two universalist dimensions of antagonism. The two controversies are, of course, directly pertinent to international development, since the one (the refugee crisis) is closely entwined with North-South relations and the global politics of inequality, while the other (Eurocentrism) is a key cause of concern for those (postcolonial, decolonial) development theorists and practitioners focusing on continuing patterns of Western domination. Žižek's stand on both issues has been the subject of notable disapproval, if not denunciation. Critics reproach him for being Eurocentric and even racist, charges which he has repeatedly countered. I will examine the differing theoretical and political positions in these debates, underlining what Žižek's critics miss or misunderstand about the key notion of antagonism.

## The Refugee Controversy

In 2015, at the height of the European refugee crisis, Žižek wrote three controversial articles on the issue (2015a, 2015b, 2015c) in the *London Review of Books* and *In These Times*. He begins by emphasizing the heavy responsibility of Western powers in creating the crisis—military interventions and political meddling in Iraq, Libya, and Syria, and imperial engagements in such places as the Congo and Central African Republic, all of which have brought about war, "failed states" and untold dispossession and inequality. He is scathing about the racist, anti-immigrant political discourse in Europe, particularly in Eastern European countries such as Hungary and Slovakia, writing that "the principal threat to Europe is not Muslim immigration but its anti-immigrant, populist leaders [such as Hungary's Viktor Orbán]" (2015a). He also singles out the wealthy oil states of the Middle East (Saudi Arabia, Qatar, Emirates, etc.) for being so unwelcoming to refugees and turning a blind eye to indentured labor practices for foreign workers, who are essential to these countries' economies.

Žižek supports admitting many more refugees into Europe but, on the other hand, he is critical of those who advocate "open borders," accusing them of a naïve and unrealistic humanitarianism that "would instantly trigger a populist revolt" across Europe (2015a, 2015b). But his most controversial remarks are apropos the refugees themselves. He asserts that European authorities should not hesitate to "impose clear rules and regulations" that assure refugees of their safety, while at the same time requiring them to "accept the destination allo-cated to them." The latter condition, he says, is a response to reports about refu-gees in Slovenia and Southern Italy preferring to move to Scandinavian countries rather than stay where they are: they "assert their dreams as their unconditional right, and demand from the European authorities not only proper food and medical care but also transportation to the destination of their choice. . . . But the hard truth to be faced by the refugees is that 'there is no Norway,' even in Norway" (2015a). He also insists that European authorities should eschew the pretense of "multicultural tolerance" and require refugees to respect the laws and social norms of states (e.g., individual freedoms, religious tolerance, re-spect for women's and gay rights, etc.) "without fear that such norms will ap-pear 'Eurocentric'. . . . Such rules privilege the Western European way of life, but that is the price to be paid for European hospitality" (Žižek 2015a, 2015c).

Finally, given what he sees as haphazard refugee resettlement policies amidst the rising tide of populist anti-immigrant racism across Europe, Žižek advo-cates for the establishment of resettlement centers near crisis areas (Lebanon, Turkey, the Libyan coast, etc.), with transportation of refugees from there to European destinations. He also suggests relying on the military to help orga-nize these resettlement efforts in a way that "avoids the neocolonial traps of the recent past" (2015a).

Žižek's interventions elicited vociferous rebukes from a number of liberal/Left quarters, with critics accusing him of racism, Eurocentrism, and Islamo-phobia (Alarian 2016; Kriss 2015a; Riemer 2015; Sørensen 2015). Riemer (2015) characterizes Žižek's position as "reactionary," endorsing "an elitist vision of politics—the enlightened political class versus a racist and ignorant popula-tion"; while Alarian (2016) depicts him as an "orientalist . . . a wolf in sheep's clothing—masquerading as a leftist while flaunting the most obscene right-wing sentiments." Kriss's response is more sustained; he and Žižek engaged in a lengthy to-and-fro (Kriss 2015a, 2015b; Žižek 2015c). He sees as xenopho-bic the idea that "migration threatens some posited European way of life," reproaching Žižek for being patronizing and prescriptive for requiring refugees to settle in destinations allocated to them and wanting to impose rules and regulations on people already traumatized by dislocation. In the face of rising anti-immigrant political discourse, he argues that Žižek has it wrong: it is not "Europe experiencing a migrant crisis" but "migrants experiencing a Euro-pean crisis" (2015a). He also criticizes Žižek for wrongly assuming refugees are "backward," or misogynist or racist, pointing out that many Syrian refu-gees are in fact secular, eager to integrate into European life rather than clinging on to their "particularism." For him, Žižek too easily presumes that migrants have no agency and are wholly determined by their culture.

Žižek does soften his stance a little in the face of this barrage of criticism, for example striking a more conciliatory note on the question of refugee settlement by admitting that European authorities would need to balance the "desires of refugees (taking into account their wish to move to countries where they already have relatives, etc.) and the capacities of different countries" (Žižek 2015c). But mostly he sticks to his position, which I suggest has to do with being faithful to ideology critique or what I would call his "hermeneutics of antagonism."[1] As Adam Kotsko (2015) puts it, Žižek is always trying to "highlight a fundamental conflict or deadlock." This is true when he discusses the European side of the refugee crisis, calling out both the European complicity in creating it and the rise of anti-immigrant nationalist-populist discourse across the continent. He thus couldn't be further from the position of defending "Fortress Europe," as his critics are wont to insinuate. He even points the finger at the Left for allowing the Right to dominate Europe's immigration agenda, while not shying away from highlighting anti-immigrant racism within the ranks of the traditional Left: "Yes, unfortunately, a large part of the working class in Europe *is* racist and anti-immigrant, a fact which should in no way be dismissed as the result of the manipulation of an essentially 'progressive' working class" (Žižek 2015c).

But as underlined earlier, Žižek also has a go at the refugees, and in this sense he is more an "equal opportunity antagonist" (so to speak) than an "elitist" (as Riemer alleges). His is an attempt at a universalist or nondiscriminating ideology critique. He excoriates guilt-ridden liberal multiculturalists for not daring to say negative things about immigrants/refugees, seeing it as a reinforcement, not a renunciation, of the white man's burden.[2] For him, not to identify the prejudices (i.e., gaps, antagonisms) of the Other is itself racism, since it "condescendingly treats [others] as morally inferior beings who should not be held to normal human standards" (Žižek 2015c). Far from denying refugees agency, as his critics suggest, his point is that, like all of us, refugees and immigrants are also ideologically interpellated, so that it is romanticizing them or refraining from criticizing them that denies them agency, disregarding their (as is everyone's) proclivity to makes mistakes. It also disavows or underestimates the horrors of poverty, dispossession, and forced migration, which can often destabilize and brutalize refugees (as it would anyone). In this sense, impoverishment for Žižek is not likely to make for noble people (2015c).

It is for this reason that Žižek does not hesitate to speak out against oppressive sociocultural practices—be they those of refugees, Muslims, or indeed Europeans: "Some say I am more right wing, which I am absolutely not. On the refugee crisis, we should drop the patronizing 'They are warm people.'

No, there are murderers among them in the same way there are among us. The liberal left prohibit writing anything bad about refugees" (Žižek 2016c). And he continues with: "[M]ulticulturalist or anti-colonialist's defense of different 'ways of life' is also false. Such defenses cover up the antagonisms within each of these particular ways of life by justifying acts of brutality, sexism and racism as expressions of a particular way of life that we have no right to measure with foreign, i.e. Western values" (Žižek 2015c). Evident here once again is Žižek's determination to prod the limits and deadlocks of any particularism, European or not.

Žižek's concern is that the Left's tendency to be silent, or make strategic compromises, on questions of culture "results in the anti-immigrant right monopolising" the immigration and refugee agenda (Žižek 2016c). For him, politically correct multiculturalism ends up conceding the terrain of culture to the Right, aiding and abetting anti-refugee populism. Perhaps what worries him most is the complicity of the Left in covering up the Real of our age: as Kotsko underlines (2015), the "entire basis of [Žižek's] critique of mainstream liberalism . . . has been that it enables right-wing reaction as a way of deflecting attention from the fundamental contradictions of capitalism." In this sense, the refugee crisis serves as an ideological diversion. The real question is not the refugee/immigrant threat, but what this very question tells us about Europe and the global capitalist order. Accepting more refugees or instituting racist immigration policies helps displace the fundamental antagonisms of capitalism, avoiding having to address them (see Žižek 1993, 210; 2009, 66). The challenge for the Left, according to Žižek, is therefore to envision "radical economic change which would abolish the [very] conditions that create refugees" (2015b). And it is because the Left has given up on the possibility of such change—the prospect of a post-capitalist world—that it ends up compromising on right-wing demands on refugees and immigration: "The real task is to build bridges between 'our' and 'their' working classes. Without this unity (which includes the critique and self-critique of both sides) class critique proper regresses into a clash of civilizations" (Žižek 2015c). The latter point is a reference precisely to the second dimension of antagonism that I would now like to highlight: the possibility of a negative universal politics.

## The Eurocentrism Controversy

In 2012, academic Santiago Zabala wrote a piece for *Al Jazeera* (2012) extolling several contemporary philosophers, and focusing on Žižek in particular as a "thinker of our age." The piece provoked vehement responses (also in

*Al Jazeera*) from Columbia University cultural critic Hamid Dabashi ("Can Non-Europeans Think?," 2013) and decolonial theorist Walter Mignolo ("Yes, We Can," 2013), both of whom reproach Zabala for Eurocentrism and ethnocentrism. Zabala does indeed praise Western thinkers such as Žižek, Derrida, and Butler as important public intellectuals, while referring to non-Western ones only as "others working in Brazil . . . and China," without specifically naming any. Dabashi (2013) counters by mentioning a slew of non-Western thinkers—from Chatterjee and Achebe to Bishara and Karatani—who, according to him, also merit the labels "philosopher" and "public intellectual," and who offer "alternative . . . visions of reality more rooted in the lived experiences of people in Africa, in Asia, in Latin America."

Mignolo argues along the same lines, taking aim at Žižek. To Žižek's tongue-in-cheek claim in "A Leftist Plea for 'Eurocentrism'" (1998, 988) that "When one says Eurocentrism, every self-respecting postmodern leftist intellectual has as violent a reaction as Joseph Goebbels had to culture—to reach for a gun, hurling accusations of proto-fascist Eurocentrist cultural imperialism," Mignolo (2013) responds with: "A self-respecting decolonial intellectual will reach instead to Frantz Fanon." Mignolo then draws on Fanon to argue that decolonial intellectuals "'have better things to do' . . . than being engaged with issues debated by European philosophers." He maintains that, in the non-European world, Žižek's work is less relevant than that of the likes of Lewis Ricardo Gordon, Nawal El Saadawi, or Enrique Dussel, and that Žižek's advocacy of communism is an "abstract universal," only one of many other possible alternatives/solutions to the problem of global capitalism (Mignolo 2013; see also Nigam 2013).

In 2013, Žižek responded in a public lecture at the London School of Economics (LSE), entitled "Reply to My Critics." He begins by asking jokingly if Mignolo is "as stupid in real life as he sounds," and then, in relation to Mignolo's exhortation that decolonial intellectuals should ignore European philosophers, he asks "OK fuck you, who are these much more interesting intellectuals?" (Žižek 2013a at 42:09 and 44:40). In a later written piece, Žižek insists the "fuck you" was "a general exclamation addressed (if at anyone) at my public" (Žižek 2016d; see also Marder and Žižek 2016), but Dabashi counters with an acerbic retort, (mis)quoting Žižek as saying "Fuck you, Walter Mignolo!" (Dabashi 2015, 1). Dabashi's response forms part of his 2015 volume brought out by Zed, *Can Non-Europeans Think?*, with a preface by Mignolo and an introduction that he publishes as an online blog on Zed's website, entitled "Fuck you, Žižek!" Here, Dabashi expands on his 2013 *Al Jazeera* article: he is critical of what he believes are "limited and now exhausted [colonial/European] epistemics," claiming that the likes of Zabala and Žižek are out of touch with the realities of the global South, have no interest in what non-Europeans have to say, and only end up assimilating the world "into what they already know." As a result, for Dabashi, it is important for non-Europeans to overcome the "myth of 'the West' as the measure of truth" (Dabash 2015, 8, 28, 2).

The problem with Dabashi's text is that it is replete with mistakes, causing at least one writer to characterize it as a "post-colonial comedy of errors" (Marder 2013). Like Mignolo, Dabashi champions Fanon as an exemplar of the postcolonial public intellectual, but in the midst of a critique of Eurocentrism, he wrongly attributes a passage by Fanon on European racism to Žižek, proceeding to do a critique of the passage over several pages (2015, 8ff.)—in effect criticizing Fanon, his exemplar, instead of Žižek. To make matters worse, Dabashi appears not to have actually listened to the audio of Žižek's LSE talk (during which he mistakenly claims Žižek uttered "Fuck you, Walter Mignolo!"), relying instead on a *second-hand* online account of it (Wolters 2013). It is from this second-hand account that Dabashi quotes the Fanon passage wrongly attributed to Žižek (Dabashi 2015, 8n5). Worse still, the second-hand account itself correctly attributes the quoted passage to Fanon! It is therefore hard not to see Dabashi's polemic as careless, if not slipshod, at least in the form of it. Needless to say, in a subsequent reflection, Žižek makes hay of this comedy of errors, remarking that "I thought we had reached the lowest point, although in a more recent contribution to Al-Jazeera, Dabashi puts me into the same line with Breivik, the Norwegian racist mass murderer" (Žižek 2016d; see also Marder and Žižek 2016).

Putting aside the (schoolboy?) name calling in both camps of this debate, let me deal specifically with the accusation that Žižek is Eurocentric: as the title of his 1998 piece, "A Leftist Plea for 'Eurocentrism,'" makes clear, he is unapologetic about the fact that he *is*. But his is not a run-of-the-mill kind of Eurocentrism that papers over European colonial history and sees the continent as the flag-bearer of liberal democracy and human rights. Instead, Žižek's is a critical Eurocentrism: he acknowledges his inescapable European background and carries out a critique of many of its legacies (colonialism, liberalism, racism, the Holocaust, exploitation, misogyny, etc.) (Žižek 1998). He is even unafraid of characterizing his native Slovenia as a "shitty country" for this reason (Žižek 2016a at 27:45). But nonetheless, he insists on defending and reinvigorating such *Left* European legacies as radical egalitarianism, universal emancipation, justice, and the welfare state (1998, 1009).

Crucially, Žižek aligns his critical Eurocentrism with his concept of universality. Once again, this is not the neocolonial form of universalism that parades itself as neutral or objective while advancing European interests (e.g., the rights of white men as universal rights), but a universality that centers on negativity and contradiction—and this is where the second important dimension of antagonism enters the picture. Here, the universal is the result of shared antagonisms rather than identities: for example, workers, women, or LGBTI people around the world may respond in unique ways to the traumatic inequalities wrought by global capitalism, but what they have in common is not their particular identities as workers, women, or queers—in fact, these are what often divides them across cultures—but precisely their shared trauma. Žižek explains it this way: "[The Universal is about] an antagonistic struggle which does not take place between particular communities, but splits from within each community, so that the 'trans-cultural' link between communities is that of a shared struggle" (2010b; see also Flemming 2015, 170; Žižek 1998, 1006; 2006, 7ff.). The universal is thus not about finding a common positive element but a shared excluded element so that, under our current global capitalist system, solidarity around the world is to be forged on the basis of shared experiences of exploitation and marginalization. It is for this reason that Žižek wishes to appropriate from the European Left tradition those political values (equality, justice, emancipation, etc.) central to the struggle of the excluded and marginalized.

Žižek's critical Eurocentrism/negative universality therefore avoids the trap of both a narrow or ghettoized particularism and a neocolonial universalism. It neither pretends to transcend the particular nor imposes a positive universalized norm. Rather, it works in and through the particular and the universal negatively to bring out the antagonistic element(s) in both. To repeat the Eisenstein and McGowan (2012, 69) quote from chapter 1: "[t]here are no transcendent principles that every society shares, but there is a constitutive failure that marks every society." In the same vein, Žižek declares: "What all epochs share is not some trans-epochal constant feature; it is, rather, that they are all answers to the same deadlock" (Žižek and Daly 2004, 76).

The problem with Dabashi's and Mignolo's critiques is that they fail to meaningfully engage with Žižek's argument and end up advocating a narrow particularism. Dabashi appears to be unaware of the idea of a critical Eurocentrism when he accuses Žižek of assimilating the world into "what [he] already knows," claiming that there is "a direct and unmitigated structural link between an empire, or an imperial frame of reference, and the presumed universality of a thinker thinking in the bosom of that empire" (Dabashi 2013). As outlined above and elaborated further below, Žižek is highly critical of European empire, while nonetheless being able to retrieve from it a Left antagonistic universal dimension (emancipation, justice, equality) that speaks to struggles against empire, marginalization, and exploitation in other parts of the world.

Mignolo, like Dabashi, seems to equate non-European particularity with a certain authenticity, as though a distinct or pristine non-European identity can be retrieved in the wake of colonialism and the globalization of capital. As noted above, he appeals to Fanon to justify ignoring European philosophy and relying instead on intellectuals rooted in the global South. Yet as Žižek points out (2013a at 48:30), much of Fanon's work draws precisely on the likes of Hegel, Sartre, Freud, and Lacan. Moreover, Fanon is himself highly critical of a politics of identity and authenticity: he sees the *négritude* movement, for example, as a "blind alley"—a narrow "racism of defense" that is nothing but the "logical antithesis" of White European prejudice against Blacks (1963, 163–164, 214, 212). Žižek concurs, arguing that in "his primitive anti-Eurocentrism" Mignolo "is way too Eurocentric" (2016a at 59:00).

The idea here is not just that anti-Eurocentrism is a knee-jerk reaction to Eurocentrism, but also that "the 'postcolonial' critique of Eurocentrism is, in its intellectual background and the tools it mobilizes, a 'Eurocentric' endeavor par excellence" (Žižek 2002b, 580). The Western legacy, for Žižek, may well be (and is indeed) imperialist domination and plunder, but it is also "that of the self-critical examination of the violence and exploitation the West itself brought to the Third World . . . the West supplied the very standards by which it (and its critics) measures its own criminal past" (2009, 115). To posit authentic "non-European" intellectual space(s), discrete and untainted, as Dabashi and Mignolo tend to do, is therefore to deny both the violence of (post)colonialism and the subversive intellectual tools that enable Dabashi and Mignolo's Eurocentric critique in the first place.

Rather than mourning loss/fall (from some mythical precolonial roots), engaging in *ressentiment* (against European philosophers), or searching for (impossible) non-European authenticity, Žižek suggests facing the antagonism of the fall head-on (2013a): the loss of roots provides the (post)colonial subject with the opportunity to become more emancipated (and hence more universal) than the European subject. By fully immersing oneself in the fall, by mastering the Master's language better (or more creatively) than her/him, one may be able to exploit the liberatory potential of the fall and outsmart Europeans on their own terrain. Such an argument is reminiscent of Gayatri Spivak's about colonialism's "enabling violation" and the persistent transformation of "conditions of impossibility into possibility" (Spivak 1987, 198–201; 1996, 19); but Žižek turns instead to Malcolm X, who, according to him, views racism and slavery as traumatic, depriving Black people of their roots but nonetheless opening up a creative space—the "X" in Malcolm X—by inventing a new universal (Islamic) identity (Žižek 2013a at 65:30).

Implicit in Žižek's argument is that, in the wake of European imperial dom-ination, the European symbolic order is the de facto global symbolic order (see chapter 1 and Kapoor 2018a), so that the postcolonial subject in the global North as much as the South has no choice but to work with it. This is why, like it or not, an anti-Eurocentric viewpoint cannot escape a Eurocentric back-ground. It is also why the non-European's search for roots can never recover a pure or authentic local tradition: the search is always a retroactive one, made possible only in *the* terms of the dominant European Symbolic, so that a search for roots is always a tainted one. There are, of course, innumerably important "non-European" philosophical texts, past and present, but these are inescapably written, read, and interpreted in the light of the postcolonial present. No won-der that for Žižek, a (postcolonial) emancipatory project lies in retrieving from both the European Symbolic and (retroactive) "tradition" their respective an-tagonistic dimension, from which to invent a new universal identity.

But perhaps the more important problem with upholding an authentic par-ticularism for Žižek is that, despite outward protestations against imperial power, it aids and abets that most dominant form of imperial power—global capitalism. Particularism suits imperial economic interests well—you do your own thing, celebrate your language, identity, and festivals, as long as you don't interfere with the free mobility of capital. Such postmodern multicultural pol-itics is the politicocultural arrangement of global capitalism, according to Žižek. Particular identities and minority demands (e.g., gender, LGBTI, eth-nic, indigenous rights) are unthreatening to the smooth functioning of the System and can be (and are) quite readily accommodated (i.e., assigned a "proper" place) and commodified (e.g., the corporate niche-marketing of prod-ucts to women, minorities, environmentalists, etc.) (Žižek 1997, 1998, 2010b). So by opting for particularism, Dabashi and Mignolo are enabling the unfet-tered globalization of capital.

Dabashi and Mignolo also appear to be giving up entirely on the notion of a universal, seeing it as necessarily complicit with Eurocentrism. Yet once again, what they miss is Žižek's important point that not all universals are bad, and in fact that a negative, antagonistic version of it is oriented towards sub-altern emancipation. For Žižek, the globalization of capital cannot be meted out through fragmentation and localized particularisms (which are all too eas-ily blunted, colonized, or co-opted, as mentioned above; see also chapters 2 and 8); it can be challenged only through a universalized political project. And such a project would not ignore the local or particular, but retrieve from it an antagonistic dimension (e.g., the experience of being marginalized under global capitalism) that then forms the basis for a shared and universalized strug-gle, most especially for the Excluded/subaltern.

It is in this sense that Žižek proposes the idea of communism, viewing it not as an "abstract universal" or a positive or definitive solution to the problem of global capitalism, as Mignolo seems to think (see above), but as a determination of the problem (of the antagonism) of capitalist self-reproduction (Žižek 2013a at 56:30; see also Douzinas and Žižek 2010). Žižek is highly critical of twentieth-century communism (in Russia, China, and his own country Yugoslavia / Slovenia), but insists on not throwing out the baby with the bath water. It is because neoliberal capitalism dispossesses so many around the globe that the possibility of a "new" open and broadly conceived communist project—a commons of nature, biogenetics, intellectual property, etc.—emerges. For Žižek, the project may well not happen at all, or if it goes ahead, it may fail or take on different local forms, but in any case, it would have to be the product not of an externally imposed program, but the politicization by the dispossessed themselves of a commonly perceived and experienced deadlock within capitalism (see chapter 12).

Let me note, to conclude this section, that some years ago, Žižek engaged in not dissimilar debates with William Hart (in 2002–2003) and Gayatri Menon (in 2010), both of them accusing him of being Eurocentric for treating Western Christianity as the height of religious evolution (see Basu Thakur 2013; Hart 2002, 2003; Menon 2010; Žižek 2002b). Indeed, Žižek has written extensively on Christianity (Žižek 2001a, 2001b, 2003; Žižek and Gunjević 2012), but he takes a radical atheistic view of it, arguing that the history of Christianity centers on covering up its radicalism. He once again readily admits to his (critical) Eurocentric view of Christianity, but true to his antagonistic-political hermeneutics, retrieves from within it not religious faith or belief but notions of universal justice, egalitarianism, and the absence of any guarantee of meaning.

But Hart and Menon are suspicious, asking whether Žižek thinks his universality "is legitimate for any other religions" (Menon 2010) and if he can "imagine the agonistic universalization of non-European difference?" (Hart 2002, 559). It seems to me that the answer is "yes" in both cases, since Žižek has consistently viewed the rise of global Islam, for example, with much hope, seeing an "emancipatory underground tendency" in it (Žižek 2016c), characterizing Malcolm X's inflection of it with enthusiasm (as underlined earlier), and stating that "instead of celebrating the greatness of true Islam against its misuse by fundamentalist terrorists, or of bemoaning the fact that, of all great religions, Islam is the one most resistant to modernization, one should rather conceive this resistance as an open chance: it does not necessarily lead to 'Islamo-Fascism,' it can also be articulated into a Socialist project. Precisely because Islam harbors the 'worst' potentials of the Fascist answer to our present predicament, it can also turn out to be the site for the 'best'" (Žižek 2004, 48–49).[3]

But Žižek also responds to Hart by saying that the onus is on Hart and others, not him, to either demonstrate that he is wrong in retrieving emancipatory features in the Judeo-Christian tradition or to "find [emancipatory] features that I attribute to Christianity in Buddhism or Hinduism?" (Žižek 2002b, 579). Once again, like Dabashi and Mignolo, what Hart and Menon miss is the antagonistic dimension of Žižek's Eurocentrism, which sees universality emerge not from outside, transcendent principles but from the deadlocks/traumas that are constitutive of every particular.[4]

## Conclusion

I have emphasized two key dimensions of antagonism, relying on Žižek's recent interventions on refugee politics and Eurocentrism. The dimension of ideology critique (or "hermeneutics of antagonism") comes through in his intervention on the European refugee crisis, highlighting the fundamental deadlocks on each side—the European Left (for disavowing the problems of global capitalism, thus enabling the rise of right-wing populism and anti-immigrant racism) and refugees (for failing to adequately face up to the limits of their "dreams"). Antagonism also underpins Žižek's conception of critical Eurocentrism, enabling him to readily admit to his European partisanship, while retrieving a negative universal dimension, which opens up to articulation with other (equally partisan) non-European positions in shared struggle.

It is important to note again that Žižek has been a frequent critic of postcolonialism (e.g., Žižek 2002a, 545–546; 2008, 147–148), and while several analysts (including me) have taken him to task for overreaching (e.g., Almond 2012; Basu Thakur 2013, 70; Gilbert 2007, 66; Kapoor 2018, 20–21; Stam and Shohat 2012, 118–121), I think he raises a crucial claim: that postcolonialism/decoloniality of the type professed by Dabashi and Mignolo has lost its way by focusing on questions of identity, which often leads to cultural relativism, declarations of authenticity, and, as raised in chapters 2 and 8, a lack of grounding for a transversal politics (e.g., the non-Western is always better, you can speak about the global South only if you are from there, the local and the subaltern is necessarily good, etc.). Žižek's hermeneutics/politics of antagonism moves away from these essentialist traps by dwelling instead on the traumatic Real, which authorizes both a thoroughgoing ideological critique and a critical horizon for common struggle (between and across socioeconomic and North-South divides). The positivity of identity politics may well valorize the particular and the local, but it is also what disunites and disables a broad-based politics in the face of the dominant global capitalist order. In contrast, as we have seen, the criticality of antagonistic politics may well dwell on the negative, but it thereby enables the joining of the particular to a broader transversal, subaltern, and anticapitalist politics (see chapters 8, 9, 12).

## Notes

1. I mean hermeneutics here in the broad, phenomenological sense of not just interpretation of texts, but interpretation that is always already bound up with an engagement in the world. This is especially the case with Žižek's work, where antagonism is a negative ontological condition and hence integral to life and politics. A "hermeneutics of antagonism" is then at the same time a politics of antagonism.

2. Žižek has said that he is not in the least bit interested in hosting a refugee in his home—he wouldn't even want to do that with family members. But on the other hand, he would be willing to have the state deduct half his salary to support refugees (see Khader 2015). His position is underpinned philosophically by a view, not of the goodness of the refugee qua neighbor, but of the "monstrosity of the neighbour" (Žižek 2016b). In stark contrast to a liberal multicultural position of tolerance and celebration of alterity, he sees the Other as inaccessible, unknowable, incommensurable. My neighbor is a traumatic intrusion and makes me anxious (which has to do with anxiety about the stranger in myself). S/he is not "exotic" or "interesting," someone I want to eagerly engage with, but rather someone I must maintain at a certain distance, suspending the desire to "understand" or empathize because this invariably translates into trying to incorporate or control her/him (Žižek 2005). The post-capitalist, postmulticultural society for Žižek, then, is one in which there is social diversity but people politely ignore each other. They live alongside one another, despite the existential gap between them and in a way that recognizes and faces such a gap. In this sense, true communication with the Other has nothing to do with reciprocal identification. Meaningful social encounters happen in unexpected or rare moments of solidarity and shared battle.

3. Žižek has also engaged with Buddhism (2010a, 335–336, 2013b, 127–135), seeing parallels between it and some aspects of Lacanian thought (e.g., the void as not unlike the Real, *nirvana* as mirroring the idea of "traversing the fantasy," etc.). But in contrast, he has been very critical of *Western* Buddhism (e.g., 2003, 26), characterizing it as a paradigmatic ideology of late capitalism.

4. While I think Menon and Basu Thakur (who is sympathetic to Menon over and against Žižek) make many valuable criticisms of Žižek, I tend not to agree with them. Once again, I think both misinterpret (or ignore) Žižek's conception of the universal, wrongly attributing to it positive features while missing its negative or antagonistic dimensions (see the main text below regarding Menon). Basu Thakur mistakenly suggests, for example, that Žižekian universality is about an "invitation" being offered "to the particular to join the universal," which would of course result in the subaltern's subordination to the hegemon (2013, 767, 764; see also Flemming 2015, 170). But as Flemming puts it, "for Žižek, to be universal is not to be a positive element within a symbolic system that asserts itself and is accepted as equal, but an excluded element

that enters the frame and thereby negates the frame" (2015, 115). Žižekian politics, after all, is never about being accepted or tolerated by the dominant but engaging agonistically in a struggle to defeat the dominant, and thereby fashion a new politics.

## References

Alarian, Riad. 2016. "Self-Proclaimed Leftist Slavoj Žižek Makes Right-Wing Remarks About the Syrian Refugee Crisis." Muftah. https://muftah.org/self -proclaimed-leftist-slavoj-zizek-makes-right-wing-remarks-about-the-syrian -refugee-crisis/.

Almond, Ian. 2012. "Anti-Capitalist Objections to the Postcolonial: Some Conciliatory Remarks on Žižek and Context." Ariel: A Review of International English Literature 43 (1): 1–21.

Basu Thakur, Gautam. 2013. "The Menon-Žižek Debate: 'The Tale of the (Never-Marked) (But Secretly Coded) Universal and the (Always Marked) Particular . . .'." Slavic Review 72 (4): 750–770.

Dabashi, Hamid. 2013. "Can Non-Europeans Think?" Al Jazeera, January 15. https://www.aljazeera.com/indepth/opinion/2013/01/201311414263 8797542.html.

Dabashi, Hamid. 2015. Can Non-Europeans Think? London: Zed.

Douzinas, Costas, and Slavoj Žižek. 2010. The Idea of Communism. London: Verso.

Eisenstein, Paul, and Todd McGowan. 2012. Rupture: On the Emergence of the Political. Evanston, IL: Northwestern University Press.

Fanon, Frantz. 1963. The Wretched of the Earth. Translated by Richard Philcox. New York: Grove.

Flemming, Gregory C. 2015. "By Mutual Opposition to Nothing." Angelaki 20 (4): 157–177.

Gilbert, Jeremy. 2007. "All the Right Questions, All the Wrong Answers." In The Truth of Žižek, edited by Paul Bowman and Richard Stamp, 61–81. London: Continuum.

Hart, William David. 2002. "Slavoj Žižek and the Imperial/Colonial Model of Religion." Nepantla: Views from South 3 (3): 553–578.

———. 2003. "Can a Judgment Be Read? A Response to Slavoj Žižek." Nepantla: Views from South 4 (1): 191–194.

Kapoor, Ilan, ed. 2018a. Psychoanalysis and the GlObal. Lincoln: University of Nebraska Press.

———. 2018b. "Žižek, Antagonism and Politics Now: Three Recent Controversies." International Journal of Žižek Studies 12 (1). https://zizekstudies.org/index.php /IJZS/article/view/1041/1071.

Khader, Jamil. 2015. "Why Zizek's Critics Are Wrong—and Where They Could Have Gotten it Right." In These Times, December 11. http://inthesetimes .com/article/18683/why-zizeks-critics-are-wrong-and-where-they-could-have -gotten-it-right.

Kotsko, Adam. 2015. "How to Read Žižek on the Refugee Crisis." An und für sich, November 25. https://itself.blog/2015/11/25/how-to-read-zizek-on-the -refugee-crisis/.

Kriss, Sam. 2015a. "Building Norway: A Critique of Slavoj Žižek." Idiot Joy Show-
    land, September 11. https://samkriss.com/2015/09/11/building-norway-a
    -critique-of-slavoj-zizek/.
——. 2015b. "Why Slavoj Zizek Is Wrong About the Syrian Refugee Crisis—And
    Psychoanalysis." In These Times, November 17. http://inthesetimes.com
    /article/18615/in-defense-of-fantasy-a-response-to-slavoj-zizek.
Marder, Michael. 2013. "A Post-Colonial Comedy of Errors." Al Jazeera, 13 April.
    http://www.aljazeera.com/indepth/opinion/2013/03/201331411225576
    1369.html.
Marder, Michael, and Slavoj Žižek. 2016. "The Breakdown of Rational Argumenta-
    tion." The Philosophical Salon, October 3. http://thephilosophicalsalon.com
    /the-breakdown-of-rational-argumentation/.
Menon, Nivedita. 2010. "The Two Zizeks." Kafila, January 7. https://kafila.online
    /2010/01/07/the-two-zizeks/.
Mignolo, Walter D. 2013. "Yes, We Can: Non-European Thinkers and Philosophers."
    Al Jazeera, February 19. http://www.aljazeera.com/indepth/opinion/2013
    /02/20132672747320891.html.
Nigam, Aditya. 2013. "End of Postcolonialism and the Challenge for 'Non-European'
    Thought." Critical Encounters, May 19. https://criticalencounters.net/2013/05
    /19/end-of-postcolonialism-and-the-challenge-for-non-european-thought/.
Riemer, Nick. 2015. "How to Justify a Crisis." Jacobin, October 5. http://jacobinmag
    .com/2015/10/refugee-crisis-europe-zizek-habermas-singer-greece-syria
    -academia/.
Sørensen, Esben Bøgh. 2015. "Slavoj Žižek: Fortress Europe's Staunch Defender on
    the Left." ROAR, November 29. https://roarmag.org/essays/zizek-refugee
    -crisis-critique/.
Spivak, Gayatri Chakravorty. 1987. In Other Worlds: Essays in Cultural Politics. New
    York: Methuen.
——. 1996. The Spivak Reader: Selected Works of Gayatri Chakravorty Spivak. Edited by
    Donna Landry and Gerald MacLean. New York and London: Routledge.
Stam, Robert, and Ella Shohat. 2012. Race in Translation: Culture Wars around the
    Postcolonial Atlantic. New York: New York University Press.
Wolters, Eugene. 2013. "The Critical-Theory Guide to that Time Zizek Pissed
    Everyone Off (Again)." Critical-Theory, May 22. http://www.critical-theory
    .com/the-critical-theory-guide-to-that-time-zizek-pissed-everyone-off-again/.
Zabala, Santiago. 2012. "Slavoj Zizek and the Role of the Philosopher." Al Jazeera,
    December 25. http://www.aljazeera.com/indepth/opinion/2012/12
    /20121224122215406939.html.
Žižek, Slavoj. 1989. The Sublime Object of Ideology. London: Verso.
——. 1993. Tarrying with the Negative: Kant, Hegel, and the Critique of Ideology.
    Durham, NC: Duke University Press.
——. 1997. "Multiculturalism, or, the Cultural Logic of Multinational Capitalism."
    New Left Review 225 (1): 28–51.
——. 1998. "A Leftist Plea for 'Eurocentrism.'" Critical Inquiry 24 (4): 988–1009.
——. 2001a. On Belief. London: Routledge.
——. 2001b. The Fragile Absolute or, Why is the Christian Legacy Worth Fighting for?
    London: Verso.

———. 2002a. "A Plea for Leninist Intolerance." *Critical Inquiry* 28 (2): 542–566.

———. 2002b. "I Plead Guilty—But Where Is the Judgment?" *Nepantla: Views from South* 3 (3): 579–583.

———. 2003. *The Puppet and the Dwarf: the Perverse Core of Christianity*. Cambridge, MA: MIT Press.

———. 2004. *Iraq: The Borrowed Kettle*. London: Verso.

———. 2005. "Neighbors and Other Monsters: A Plea for Ethical Violence." In *The Neighbor: Three Inquiries in Political Theology*, edited by Slavoj Žižek, Eric L. Santner, and Kenneth Reinhard, 134–190. Chicago: University of Chicago Press.

———. 2006. *The Parallax View*. Cambridge, MA: MIT Press.

———. 2008. *Violence: Six Sideways Reflections*. New York: Picador.

———. 2009. *First as Tragedy, Then as Farce*. London: Verso.

———. 2010a. *Interrogating the Real*. Edited by Rex Butler and Scott Stephens. London: Continuum.

———. 2010b. "Appendix: Multiculturalism, the Reality of an Illusion." Lacan.com, September 1. http://www.lacan.com/essays/?page_id=454.

———. 2013a. "A Reply to My Critics." London: Birkbeck Institute for the Humanities, University of London. Podcast, Backdoor Broadcasting Company, February 28. https://backdoorbroadcasting.net/2013/02/slavoj-zizek-a-reply-to-my-critics/.

———. 2013b. *Less than Nothing: Hegel and the Shadow of Dialectical Materialism*. London: Verso.

———. 2015a. "In the Wake of Paris Attacks the Left Must Embrace Its Radical Western Roots." In These Times, November 16. http://inthesetimes.com/article/18605/breaking-the-taboos-in-the-wake-of-paris-attacks-the-left-must-embrace-its.

———. 2015b. "The Non-Existence of Norway." *London Review of Books* 37 (17), September 10. https://www.lrb.co.uk/2015/09/09/slavoj-zizek/the-non-existence-of-norway.

———. 2015c. "We Can't Address the EU Refugee Crisis without Confronting Global Capitalism." In These Times, September 9. http://inthesetimes.com/article/18385/slavoj-zizek-european-refugee-crisis-and-global-capitalism.

———. 2016a. "Against the Double Blackmail." https://www.youtube.com/watch?v=T4QsgUIbBoM.

———. 2016b. *Against the Double Blackmail: Refugees, Terror and Other Troubles with the Neighbours*. London: Allen Lane.

———. 2016c. "Slavoj Žižek: 'We Are all Basically Evil, Egotistical, Disgusting.'" *The Guardian*, December 10. https://www.theguardian.com/lifeandstyle/2016/dec/10/slavoj-zizek-we-are-all-basically-evil-egotistical-disgusting.

Žižek, Slavoj, and Boris Gunjević. 2012. *God in Pain: Inversions of Apocalypse*. New York: Seven Stories.

# CHAPTER 4

# What "Drives" Capitalist Development?

KEYWORD: *Drive*

## Introduction

As mentioned in chapter 1 (see also Kapoor 2014), there is a tendency in international development to be suspicious of human passions. The mind-body dualism, so pervasive in social science, has pitted the coolness and calm of reason against the unpredictability and uncontrollability of the passions, the former most often being charged with the need to tame the latter. The realm of emotions, moreover, frequently represented as immaterial and feminine, tends to be relegated to the private sphere, excluded from what are seen as the more significant and palpable spheres of the public and the political.

Lacanian psychoanalysis, as we have been insisting, averts any such dualism; it claims that human passions play, not a supplementary or trivial, but a *constitutive* role in the construction of social reality. For Lacan, our emergence from nature into culture is accompanied by a deep sense of loss and alienation, which we inevitably bring to all our pursuits, be they private or public, material or symbolic, economic or political. Thus, not only can reason not be divorced from passion, but as we have seen and shall develop further below, it is always tainted with, and often overwhelmed by, the irrationality of *jouissance* (enjoyment); and not only is the market unavoidably imbued with human desire, but it is invariably overdetermined, if not overtaken, by drive.

I would like, in this chapter, to underline the importance of (unconscious) social passions in the socioeconomic system so central to development—capitalism. I will focus on the Lacanian notion of "drive," a compulsion that stems from our ontological loss as linguistic beings, to suggest that capitalist development is propelled by an accumulation drive. Unlike desire, which capitalism manipulates at the level of consumption (e.g., the enjoyment of shopping), drive involves the more fundamental compulsion to repeat endlessly, which manifests as the circular drive to accumulate for the sake of accumulation. In late capitalism, such a drive has resulted in a crisis of overaccumulation, which as Harvey (2005) has pointed out, results in imperialism and "accumulation by dispossession," especially in the global South. The capitalist development drive thus turns crisis into triumph, generating enjoyment, not from success, but from repeated failure. It is this libidinal kick (*jouissance*) which accompanies drive that helps explain capitalism's continued obstinacy and endurance. I conclude the chapter by reflecting on the possibilities of disrupting capitalist development through drive.

But before proceeding, a note on the term "capitalist development." I use it to counter the term "economic growth" (or "economic development"), which is the expression most widely employed in international development, but which I see as an ideological mystification. It tends to characterize the typical "Third World" economy as an independent entity to be "managed,"[1] rather than inextricably linked to a historically constructed, global capitalist system that produces wealth alongside inequality and unevenness. I therefore subscribe to the Marxist/neo-Marxist view (e.g., Frank 1967; Sweezy 1970) that "economic development" is de facto "capitalist development." Much of my discussion about the libidinal underpinnings of development is, as a result, about the capitalist system, applicable as much to the global South as to the North. Nonetheless, my analysis will focus on the implications of the capitalist logics of "drive" for the global South.

## Drive

The notion of drive, famously attributed to Freud,[2] is usually equated with sexual libido, a primordial biological stimulus. But Lacan desubstantializes the notion, seeing it as arising not from bodily need but the subject's entrapment in the symbolic order (Homer 2005, 75–77; Johnston 2005, 211; Kingsbury and Pile 2014, 19–26; Lacan 1997, 92; 2014, 66–67).[3] For him, as we have observed, the emergence of human animals from nature into culture is accompanied by traumatic loss. Such loss is irrepressible: we are never able to forget or let go of it. Our initiation into language thus introduces a fundamental absence (of a mythical sense of plenitude) that forever haunts us. And drive takes its stimulus from this lack. It is an unconscious and relentless remainder or excess inscribed in the Symbolic, a constant compulsion to reenact our loss.[4]

Lacan (1998, 179) distinguishes the aim of the drive (its route or way) from its goal (its final destination). While the goal of the drive is the object around which it circulates, its true aim, according to him, is continuous circulation. It aspires not to obtain the object or reach a destination, but to encircle it. Its insistent reenactment of the subject's imaginary primordial loss yields to a self-propelling circuit, an unending looping and repetition (see Johnston 2005, xxxiii; Žižek 1991, 5; 2010, 73).

Lacan closely associates drive with *jouissance* (1998, 183–184). *Jouissance* as we know is much more than "enjoyment": it reaches beyond pleasure toward the excessive and ecstatic, causing the subject to do irrational, if not dangerous, things. Accordingly, given that the aim of drive is not to get the object but to encircle it, it is the process of constantly missing the object that is satisfying. The source of drive's *jouissance* lies in endless repetition and circulation. Thus, paradoxically, drive derives pleasure from repeated failure—from never reaching its goal despite obstinately trying. Failure is inherent to its structure, and the subject revels in it. Eisenstein and McGowan put it this way: "The inhumanity of the human manifests itself in the human capacity for finding satisfaction in—and repeating—failure. Subjects repeat their acts not in order to one day succeed but in order to continue to fail" (2012, 195).

Not only do we get satisfaction from constant failure, but we do so to the point of our own peril. There is a sadomasochistic dimension to drive, which sees the subject unconsciously delighting when attempts at moderation and rationality are undermined and (self-)sabotaged. Think of how we imbibe those extra few drinks despite the impending hangover, goad our enemy despite his violent tendencies, or spend wildly despite being on a budget: we most often do these things, not "despite" their recklessness, but *because* of it. We perversely enjoy, and so frequently repeat, such painful, traumatic, and self-destructive behavior:

> The ultimate lesson of psychoanalysis is that human life is never "just life": humans are not simply alive, they are possessed by the strange drive to enjoy life in excess, passionately attached to a surplus which sticks out and derails the ordinary run of things. (Žižek 2006, 62)

Lacan describes human drives as the expression of the "death drive" (1997, 211). By this, he does *not* mean the human predilection toward self-annihilation and death, which is the usual (Freudian) meaning attributed to the term. In fact, for him, the death drive is quite the opposite of death. As Žižek explains, it is more like an eternal undeadness, the "horrible fate of being caught in the endless repetitive cycle of wandering around in guilt and pain" (2006, 62; see also Homer 2005, 76; Žižek 1996, 106; 1999, 294). Such a cruel and torturous sort of immortality[5] is the consequence of the inescapability of drive and *jouissance*: never able to free ourselves from their constant needling and excess, we are condemned to circuitousness and immoderate gratification. Like it or not, the (death) drive compels us both to suffer enjoyment and to enjoy suffering.

Finally, the contrast between "drive" and "desire" is worth pondering. In the Lacanian scheme of things, both terms are closely related but not synonymous. Like drive, desire stems from our ontological loss as linguistic beings.[6] But desire targets a lost object to cover up our lack—an object that is never found; whereas drive, as we have seen, targets the experience of loss itself as the object. In shifting from object to object, desire moves directly towards each but fixates on none; while in encircling objects, drive misses them all and fixates instead on the libidinal circuit (see Johnston 2005, 211; Kingsbury 2010; Žižek 2006, 62).

Such contrasting behavior is perhaps nowhere more evident than in relation to *jouissance*. Desire's quest for enjoyment can never be attained (no object satisfies), whereas drive's search is always satisfied (in reenacting loss). Desire is egged on by trying, yet failing, to fill the ontological lack; while such recurring failure is the very source of drive's enjoyment. But of course, drive's "success" is hardly that, since, as per the death drive, *jouissance* is experienced without one ever being able to free oneself of it. Žižek summarizes it this way:

> desire desperately strives to achieve *jouissance*, its ultimate object which forever eludes it; while drive, on the contrary, involves the opposite impossibility—not the impossibility of attaining *jouissance*, but the impossibility of getting *rid of it*. (1999, 293, italics in original)

## Capitalist Development: The Drive to Overaccumulate

How, then, to connect drive, and its interplay with desire, to the workings of capitalist development? In a crucial passage in *The Parallax View*, Žižek does just that, arguing for the constitutive position that both desire and drive play in capitalism's expansive movement:

At the immediate level of addressing individuals, capitalism . . . interpellates [us] as consumers, as subjects of desire, soliciting in [us] ever new perverse and excessive desires (for which it offers products to satisfy them). . . . Drive inheres to capitalism at a more fundamental, *systemic* level: drive is that which propels the whole capitalist machinery, it is the impersonal compulsion to engage in the endless circular movement of expanded self-reproduction. (2006, 61, italics in original)

Let me tease out, first, how desire operates at the level of the interpellated subject of consumption. What Žižek has in mind is the way in which, under capitalism, subjects are primarily *desiring* subjects, in the Lacanian sense of that term: they engage in endless shopping, moving from one commodity to the next, forever searching for that "real thing," which always proves elusive (see chapter 5). Capitalism thus successfully exploits the fundamental (unconscious) lack that lies at the heart of our desires. To ensure the endless expansion of its productive engine, it provides a panoply of commodities and services that promise to satisfy us (and fill our lack). It also deploys a massive advertising machine to stimulate desire by constructing a social fantasy around the products to be sold (see Kapoor 2013, 76ff.; Stavrakakis 2006).

But the fantasy we are promised is fleeting. The object consumed turns out *not* to be the sublime object advertised (the "it" in Coke's "This is it!" or Nike's "Just do it!"), never quite delivering. And capitalism manipulates this frustration to ensure the system's material reproduction. Advertising's social fantasy must remain an unfulfilled promise both to enable commodity fetishism and to subjectivize us as desiring-machines. It is this unending cycle of enjoyment-disappointment that explains why companies must continuously offer new brands, personalized choices, and differentiated products, to keep us coming back for better and more.

But as Žižek avers, if desire operates at the subjective level of consumer society, drive plays a more fundamental,[7] structural role at the level of capital. That is, in capitalism, drive becomes an accumulation drive, which is what enables capital's compulsive movement and underlies the reproduction of the capitalist system itself (Boyle 2008, 17; Özselçuk and Madra, 2007, 96). In this regard, Marxist political economy has long maintained that accumulation is the law of motion of capitalism. Echoing Marx's credo in *Capital*, "Accumulate, accumulate! That is Moses and the prophets!," Paul Sweezy writes, for example, that "the form of the profit-making process itself produces the pressure to accumulate, and accumulation generates innovation as a means of preserving the profit-making mechanism and the class structure on which it rests" (1953, 282; see also Sweezy 1970). What Lacanian Marxists such as Žižek are adding here is the unconscious libidinal content—in this case, drive—of such a law of motion.

Žižek's (above-stated) view that drive is an "impersonal" and quasi-objective law of motion should come as no surprise, given that drive arises not from some inherent individual libido, but from our common ensnarement in the Symbolic, which operates above and beyond individual subjects (this is why, in Lacanianese, the Symbolic is often referred to as the "big Other"). Hence capitalism may well be sustained by the selfish greed and competitive spirit of the bourgeoisie, but such passions are themselves "subordinated to the impersonal striving of capital to reproduce and expand" (Žižek 2010, 132). And so, just as capitalism interpellates us as consumers at the level of desire, so capitalists (bankers, stock brokers, corporate managers, self-made entrepreneurs, etc.) do the tasks, and enact the social passions, that are necessary to keep capitalism going (Boyle 2008, 14): they are moved and subjectivized by capital's accumulation drive.

Not only does the accumulation drive propel the capitalist system, it also prevents it from ever standing still. Marx writes, in this regard, that the "law of capitalist production" is the "tendency to accumulate, the *drive* to expand capital and produce surplus value on an extended scale" (1967, 244, italics added). The continuous striving and circulation of capital, the production and expansion of surplus value, are therefore required if the system is to reproduce itself. Jodi Dean holds, in fact, that "[t]he fundamental structure of capitalism is a circuit. . . . [Capital] circulates, ceasing to be capital if this circulation stops" (2012, 3).

Such circulation—capital's accumulation drive—manifests at many levels of the economy. At the level of the firm, it is in the way surplus (primarily in the form of profits, but also surplus cash, commodities, stocks, derivatives, credit, etc.)[8] is repeatedly reinvested to produce more capital, and technology is perpetually revolutionized to reduce production costs and increase profits. At the level of consumer society, as we saw earlier, it is in the striving to always offer more and differentiated or niche-marketed products and services to keep the economy going. And in the context of the new information economy ("communicative capitalism"), it is in the endless circuit of information creation, dissemination, remixing, repetition, sampling, and so on, that help expand corporate media and the news and information industry (see Dean 2010a, 2010b). Capital's circulation may therefore be said to hinge, so to speak, on the "GOD imperative" (Grow or Die).

From a structural-historical viewpoint, the accumulation drive's circular and repetitive movement is nowhere better visible than in global capitalism's recurring cycle of booms and busts. Perhaps counterintuitively, drive's insistent and unyielding movement continually threatens the stability of the capitalist order, ruling out any steady-state or equilibrium. Accumulation, to be sure, inevitably runs into blockages—bankruptcy, insufficient or excessive liquidity, immoderate financial speculation, overextended credit, rising labor costs, diminishing markets—that result in periodic crises around the globe, and have done so since global capitalism's inception. The Third World debt crisis (1980s to the 1990s), the Asian financial crisis (1997), and the global financial crisis (2007–2008) are just some of the more obvious, recent examples that come to mind. But while failure is written into the very DNA of capitalism, so is capital's drive to overcome them ("expansion through contradiction"). Crises prepare the ground for a new round of accumulation. As a result, every obstacle or limit (e.g., the environmental crisis) makes for new opportunities (e.g., "green capitalism"), allowing capital to expand beyond measure.

Capital's endless circuit and limitless expansion, in spite (or *because*) of obstructions and crises, yields to what several Marxist political economists have called "accumulation for accumulation's sake" (Harvey 1982, 24; see also Sweezy 1970). That is, in late capitalist societies, accumulation overtakes and overdetermines the logic of the system, leading to excess and, as we shall see below, overaccumulation. Yet, such overtaking, such excess, is precisely a key feature of drive. Its unconscious reenactment of loss has no limits, to the point of excess. From the perspective of *jouissance*, this means that enjoyment is derived not simply from accumulation but from extravagant wealth and luxury. No wonder that late capitalist societies (in both the global South and North) are characterized by the normalization of excess—the desire for the grandest, tallest, biggest, and the best, whether we are talking buildings, dams, or space programs (see chapter 5 for details; and Dean 2006, 37–38).

But let us turn specifically to the issue of overaccumulation. Focusing mainly on the chronic problems of overaccumulation in the global economy from the 1970s onward, Harvey (1982, 2005) argues that overaccumulation is integral to capital's search for surplus value: capital is liable to accumulate over and above what can be reinvested profitably. But the risk is that substantial capital devaluation can occur when the market is flooded in this way. Capitalism faces a crisis, then, when surpluses of capital "lie idle with no profitable outlets in sight" (2005, 149). A solution to this predicament is the "spatio-temporal fix," that is, temporal deferral and geographic expansion (2004, 63–64; 2005, 139). In the first case, the crisis is deferred through investments in long-term infrastructure projects—both social (e.g., education, research) and physical (e.g., dams, subways, suburbanization, large commercial/residential real-estate projects)—that will yield future profits. In the second case, the crisis is moved geographically. This involves spatial expansion and reorganization by opening up new markets as profitable sites for trade and investment, while also enabling access to lower-cost inputs (raw materials, labor). Here, Harvey specifically has in mind the rapid acceleration of multinational corporate investment after the mid-1980s that flowed primarily from advanced capitalist countries toward the global South. This acceleration was facilitated by the Bretton Woods institutions, which helped pry open Third World markets through the imposition of neoliberal conditionalities (structural adjustment).

If we are to follow Harvey's lead, then, the logic of the accumulation drive is overaccumulation, which in turn can (and does) bring about geographic expansion—that is, imperialism:[9] "The general thrust [drive?] . . . is not that territories should be held back from capitalist development, but they should be continuously opened up" (Harvey 2005, 139). Imperialism allows surplus capital to be absorbed, creating further opportunities for accumulation, while at the same time (temporarily) helping to stabilize the capitalist system.

## The (Thrilling) Drive to Accumulate by Dispossession

But not only can the drive to (over)accumulate bring about imperialism through geographic expansion, it can also result in the appropriation of new wealth through what Marx calls "primitive accumulation" and Harvey renames as "accumulation by dispossession" (Harvey 2004; 2005, 137ff.). Indeed, Marx contends that the prelude to capitalism involves capital accumulation by means of robbery, trickery, and fraud; Harvey extends this claim by arguing that accumulation by dispossession plays not merely a "primitive" or originary role in capitalism, but a key and recurring one. According to him, while postwar and Cold War economic growth in the West entailed mainly reconstruction and infrastructural development with little resort to accumulation by dispossession, the 1970s witnessed a crisis of overaccumulation (including in the oil-rich Third World). During the neoliberal era that followed, accumulation by dispossession moved from the background to the dominant form of capital accumulation (Harvey 2005, 172). It has essentially meant bringing public goods (land, water, public utilities, etc.) into the private sphere to create further surplus value: "What accumulation by dispossession does is to release a set of assets . . . at very low (and in some instances zero) cost. Overaccumulated capital can seize hold of such assets and immediately turn them to profitable use" (149).

The state (in both the global South and North) has played a vital role in facilitating accumulation by dispossession. It has canceled or diluted regulatory frameworks seen as hindering accumulation (e.g., labor or environment laws), while strengthening others touted as "private-sector friendly" (e.g., taxation, private property laws). As a result, writes Harvey, accumulation by dispossession has led to:

> the commodification and privatization of land and the forceful expulsion of peasant populations; the conversion of various forms of property rights (common, collective, state, etc.) into exclusive private property rights . . . the commodification of labour power and the suppression of alternative (and indigenous) forms of production and consumption; colonial, neo-colonial and imperial processes of appropriation of assets [including the biopiracy of Third World genetic materials and seed plasma] . . . [and] the monetization of exchange and taxation, particularly of land. (2005, 145)

To be sure, accumulation by dispossession has been a feature of capitalist economies around the globe since the 1980s. In post-Soviet Eastern Europe, it has manifested in the form of the rapid liberalization of markets (through "shock therapy") and the massive privatization and distribution of state assets in favor of political and economic elites (often resulting in "crony capitalism," especially in Russia). In the West, it has taken the predominant form of privatization of education, social services (health care, social housing, public utilities), and state enterprises, frequently jeopardizing universal access to public services, particularly for the most marginalized (see Braedley and Luxton 2010). And such erosion of the public sphere has been exacerbated by the neo-liberalization of legal and regulatory frameworks. McCarthy (2004) shows, for example, how recent free trade agreements, especially in North America, have helped impose an expansion of private property rights, thereby shrinking public/state rights.

But I would like to dwell a little on the drive to accumulate by dispossession in the global South, which has seen particularly widespread and virulent forms of it. Austerity programs in Third World countries, in many cases imposed by the IMF and World Bank as a condition for debt relief, have inaugurated a wave of privatization of social services and nationalized industries—in areas ranging from water, sewerage, and transportation to health, energy, and telecommunications—with negative social impacts. In South Africa, for example, the privatization of municipal water has meant that people now have to pay for a basic service they used to receive from their local government. Not only are thousands unable to afford such paid access, but as a consequence they face fines and evictions, and health problems from restricted access (McDonald and Ruiters 2005). In China, the closure and privatization of state enterprises has created a huge pool of unemployed workers, now deprived of welfare and pensions (Harvey 2005, 155–156).

The enclosure of the natural commons (especially land and forests), as a result of privatization, commoditization, or deregulation, is of particular relevance here. In many countries (e.g., Mexico, India, Brazil), it has entailed the eviction and displacement of millions of peasants and indigenous communities from communal or ancestral lands, creating a sizable class of pauperized and landless people, as well as notable rebellion (e.g., the Zapatistas in Chiapas, the Naxalites in Eastern India, the Kayapo in the Brazilian Amazon). In India, state-led hydroelectric dam construction has displaced some thirty million people since the country's independence, submerging vast arable lands and destroying precious biodiversity (see Whitehead 2010). For the mostly indigenous communities displaced, such dam construction has also meant the devastation of their sociocultural livelihoods and institutions.

"Land grabs" are one of the most recent incarnations of the commoditization of the commons. They involve the (foreign) purchase of public forests and lands previously used for subsistence food production, which are converted for cash-crop exports and biofuel production. They are a way for liquidity to be channeled to the global South in the form of land and agricultural investment, helping to hedge against recent financial instability as well as sustain growing global demand for food and energy. Although figures vary, it is estimated that between fifteen and twenty million hectares changed hands for this purpose in the global South between 2006 and 2009 (International Food Policy Research Institute, quoted in Bush, Bujra, and Littlejohn 2011, 187; see also Borras and Franco 2012, 37). In all cases, land grabs are facilitated by the state, with peasant communities sometimes being forcibly evicted. There are, in fact, several examples (e.g., in Colombia and Cambodia) of paramilitary or military forces being used to remove people from their land (Borras and Franco 2012, 42; Grajales 2011). The overall result, once again, is the dispossession of rural and indigenous people (see Borras and Franco 2012; Bush, Bujra, and Littlejohn 2011; Hall 2011;), the creation of new landless classes (as a result of labor-saving technologies used in large-scale cultivation), and, especially in sub-Saharan Africa, food insecurity (from favoring cash crops rather than food crops).

A noteworthy feature of land grabs is that, while they are often driven by Western multinational corporations and financial speculators (Borras and Franco 2012, 37), several are planned and directed by Third World states (usually on behalf of Third World food and energy MNCs/businesses) to ensure greater food security. Thus, South Africa has facilitated the purchase of vast land tracts in the Republic of Congo for dairy, poultry, maize, and soya production by powerful South African agro-industrial concerns, and is negotiating other purchases in Tanzania, Malawi, Uganda, and Mozambique. Egypt has been doing much of the same in Northern Sudan, while China, South Korea, and the Gulf states have targeted forests and farm lands across sub-Saharan Africa (see Borras and Franco 2012, 38; Bush, Bujra, and Littlejohn 2011, 188; Hall 2011).

Finally, it is important to mention the significant role played by MNCs in the drive to accumulate by dispossession. They have been some of the main beneficiaries of the post-1980s liberalization and deregulation of Third World economies, profiting from new markets, lax environmental laws, cheap labor, and global protection of their intellectual property rights (under the WTO TRIPS agreement).[10] Most often, it is MNCs that have gained from the above-mentioned privatization of nationalized industries and enclosure of the natural commons (including through land grabs).

Of particular concern here have been the global operations of extractive industries (oil and minerals), which have repeatedly led to the forceful uprooting of local communities (see Petras and Veltmeyer 2014; Zalik 2009). The Canadian mining industry's operations in Latin America since the 1990s are a case in point. Gordon and Webber (2008) analyze how these have been facilitated by the Canadian state (through trade agreements and foreign aid) and welcomed by several Latin American governments (e.g., allowing foreign MNCs increased royalties and profit repatriation). As a result, the companies have established about 1200 sites across the subcontinent (especially in Chile, Colombia, Argentina, Bolivia, and Peru), extracting such minerals as selenium, iodine, lithium, iron, copper, coal, gold, and silver (2008, 70). Their activities have been met with significant local resistance, particularly from farming and indigenous communities, who have been dispossessed of their land with little compensation, often suffering health problems caused by mining's notorious environmental havoc. In Colombia, the Canadian companies played a major role in perpetuating the civil war, and have been accused of significant human rights violations in the eviction and displacement of indigenous and Afro-Colombian peasant communities (77–78).

What emerges from the above is that accumulation by dispossession in the global South is the outcome not only of Western imperialism and Euro-North American-based MNC operations, but equally of intra–Third World imperialism and global South–based business activity. It is, therefore, part of the *global* logic—or drive—of late capitalism. It may well involve a diverse range of players and take on different local manifestations, but it invariably translates into the fraudulent or forcible appropriation of the commons.

But what about the libidinal investments of this drive to accumulate by dispossession? If *jouissance* is integral to the drive to accumulate, how are we to understand it in terms of the drive to accumulate *by dispossession*? To begin, there is the satisfaction that comes from accumulating wealth, all the more so when that, in turn, enables further wealth creation. But drive, let us recall, is ultimately not about the goal (surplus value) but the aim (the continuous circulation of capital). From the point of view of *jouissance*, this means that enjoyment is not derived simply from accumulation but from the processes, rituals, and challenges (e.g., industrial organization, planning, investment, marketing, lobbying government, labor unrest, technological obsolescence, etc.) involved in such accumulation. The capitalist may well enjoy her/his profits, but s/he also takes comfort from the routines, repetition, and dictates of doing business.

In particular, it is finding ways of resolving capitalism's limits and contradictions—in this case, discovering new terrains for profitability to stave off the problem of overaccumulation—that is enjoyable. Opening up new markets in the Third World, privatizing the commons, negotiating land grabs—all these become creatively satisfying ways of (temporarily) resolving the antagonisms of late capitalism—and not just resolving them, but transforming them into opportunities for further accumulation. Drive, in this sense, "turns failure into triumph"; it derives pleasure, not from accumulation per se, but from the challenges of finding new paths to accumulation. And to the extent that capitalism is crisis-prone, each of its new ambitions ultimately being thwarted, then drive finds satisfaction in the repetition of failure. The more capitalism misses its mark, the more drive enjoys:

> a drive does not bring satisfaction because its object is a stand-in for the Thing, but because a drive, as it were, turns failure into triumph—in it, the very failure to reach its goal, the repetition of this failure, the endless circulation around the object, generates a satisfaction of its own. (Žižek 2006, 63)

It is important to underline once again the quasi-impersonal (and lest we forget, *unconscious*) dimension of the drive to accumulate, as a result of which, as pointed out earlier, capitalists carry out the rituals and procedures necessary to keep capital circulating. The logic of capital plays out *through* the actions of the capitalist; s/he may well find unique and creative ways around obstacles, but such creativity still obeys the chief dictate of capital—"accumulate!" There is, then, an intransitive and quasi-mechanical dimension to ensuring the reproduction of capital, captured well by the notion of "accumulation for accumulation's sake." And from the perspective of *jouissance*, the drive to accumulate for accumulation's sake effectively translates into the compulsion to enjoy for capital's sake. Here, the bourgeois enjoys but only in the name of Capital-as-master-signifier (more on this below).[11]

Things take an unmistakable sadomasochistic turn when it comes to the drive to accumulate by dispossession, since the necessary effect is enjoyment of, not only the privatization of the commons, but also the negative impacts on communities and natural environment (eviction, displacement, human right abuses, pollution, ecological damage, etc.). But, in keeping with drive's structural characteristics, this is an impersonal type of sadomasochism: although some capitalists (and/or collaborating politicians and state officials) may well get a thrill out of dispossession, on the whole they are primarily enjoying and following capital's drive to accumulate, no matter (or despite) its socioenvironmental impacts. Once again, Capital serves as master signifier, a sacred object or rallying term—like God, Nation, Democracy—that people identify with and enjoy without really knowing what it implies (see Žižek 1993, 78). Capitalists and state managers go about their business or bureaucratic plans and rituals, unaware, inattentive, or callously unconcerned about the consequences. Hence it is as if it is Capital (as the big Other) that is perversely delighting in its creative destruction, getting off, not despite dispossession's implied robbery, fraudulence, and recklessness, but *because* of them.

Accumulation by dispossession highlights, consequently, the multiple nuggets of enjoyment inherent in the accumulation drive. For, perverse satisfaction is to be obtained not only from continuous accumulation, but also from the rituals and challenges involved in accumulation, the "robbery" of the commons, and the resulting displacement of people. No wonder that Lacan equates drive with the "death drive": in capitalist development, one can never *not* enjoy, even in the face of people's suffering or misfortune. Yet, it is precisely the inescapability and multiplicity of *jouissance* in capitalist development—its death drive—that help explain its obduracy and longevity. People are easily seduced by it, captured by it, stuck in its seemingly limitless and thrilling circuits, repetitions, and challenges. In fact, no credible or enticing horizons appear to exist outside neoliberal development these days, so libidinally captivating are its charms.

Accumulation by dispossession in the global South also brings home how drive (and enjoyment) can overtake and overwhelm, to the point of fraudulence, callousness, and irresponsibility. In the same way that nationalist fervor can get so caught up in collective *jouissance* that "rational" people end up doing irrational things (e.g., targeting "outsiders"), so the relentlessness of the drive to accumulate can (and does) overdetermine capitalist development, leading to imperialism and reckless dispossession. So overwhelming can the accumulation drive be, in fact, that it can undermine capitalist development itself, to the extent of threatening the latter's existence. Here, the current global environmental crisis is the most obvious case in point, illustrating the long-term self-destructiveness of the capitalist system. While such a system may well thrive on crises, *this* crisis more than any other until now appears to have the better of us, confronting us with how we can continue to invest in activities that so exceed human and ecological life and the good of the very planet.

## Conclusion

I have stressed the important contributions that psychoanalysis can make to the political economy of development by focusing on the "drive." It is a concept that helps explain the excess underlying capitalist development: it sheds light on the relentlessness with which capital circulates, despite (and because) of blockages, leading to such late capitalist phenomena as overaccumulation, imperialism, and dispossession in the Third World; and it elucidates the unavoidable libidinal investments people make in global capitalism, helping to better understand the latter's continued persistence.

But in the face of the capitalist drive's relentlessness and apparent unstoppability, what are the possibilities for change? To what extent can the accumulation drive be resisted? As evidence of such resistance, Harvey cites multiple global struggles, old and new, against dispossession and enclosure of the commons (a few were alluded to earlier). He emphasizes the "traditional" Left trade-unionist politics centered on class struggle and anticapitalism, as well as the more novel politics of social movements that responds to injustice, globalization, and dispossession from the perspective of environment, health, indigeneity, gender, class, and so forth (2005, 176–178). While he endorses both types of politics as necessary to challenge the power of capital and the state, he also points out their weaknesses, including that they tend to be too localized and parochial (especially social movement politics). What is most lacking for the effective confrontation of global capitalist power, according to him, is "connectivity between struggles" (179).

I agree with Harvey, but in keeping with my attempt to complement political economy with libidinal economy, I would like to add three main qualifications to his argument that stem from the consideration of drive. Firstly, seriously challenging capitalist development would require a drive at least as relentless and obdurate as the accumulation drive. This would mean fully inhabiting (the death) drive, since it is its excess that enables breaking boundaries and limits (see chapter 10).[12] In fact, for Žižek, because the death drive allows us to defy constraints, it is the very source of human freedom and autonomy (Žižek 1999, 248; Žižek and Daly 2004, 135). Following Lacan, he often cites Antigone as an illustration—she insists on burying her brother despite the law and everyone around her stipulating otherwise, to the point of self-endangerment (Žižek 1989, 117). The implication is that an anticapitalist politics, to be effective, would need to insist on its enjoyment (of the disruption of accumulation or a post-capitalist alternative) to the very end; and do everything to achieve it, including braving risk and peril. In other words, an anticapitalist drive would need to be nothing less than uncompromising in the face of the capitalist drive's dogged persistence (see chapter 10).

This is all the more the case given that both labor and new social movements have a recent history of compromise. The development of a privileged worker-management class (a "labor aristocracy") has meant that some, although certainly not all, trade unions in both the global South and North have cozied up to corporate capital and the state, with several of their members even voting for conservative and right-wing nationalist parties (du Toit 2010; Kautsky 2002). Similarly, neoliberal capitalism has been able to co-opt many social movements, taming them by culturalizing and commodifying their demands—for example, by logoizing "multiculturalism" and niche-marketing products for the likes of gays and lesbians, young women, "ethnic" and racialized communities, organic food lovers, and so on. A global anticapitalist movement would need to learn from these mistakes by daring not to compromise its desires.

Secondly, and relatedly, it is an anticapitalist fervor (i.e., drive) that would help lay the basis of global connectivity and networking between and among labor / social movements. Without an obdurate spirit, without inhabiting drive's derailed excess, it is hard to see how a broad global coalition could persist energetically or indeed could adequately oppose the power of capital.

And finally, challenging the accumulation drive would require recognizing capital as a common adversary. As chapters 2, 3, and 8 argue, social movement politics has been plagued by fragmentation and parochialism as a result of the absence precisely of such commonality. While accumulation may not be the only source of inequality and dispossession, it certainly is one of the primary ones (if not *the* primary one), invariably intersecting with gender, racialization, indigeneity, queerness, environment, health, etc. Constructing capital as the common adversary would likely drive disparate radical groups to coalesce, solidify their collective resolve, and persist in their struggles. Let me quote Žižek at length on this final point:

[The undermining of a radical politics today] is directly due to the depoliticization of economics, to the common acceptance of Capital and market mechanisms as neutral tools/procedures to be exploited . . . all the talk about new forms of politics bursting out all over, focused on particular issues (gay rights, ecology, ethnic minorities . . .) . . . has something inauthentic about it, and ultimately resembles the obsessional neurotic who talks all the time . . . to ensure that something—what *really matters*—will *not* be disturbed . . . So, instead of celebrating the new freedoms and responsibilities . . . it is much more crucial to focus on what *remains the same* in this global fluidity . . . : the inexorable logic of Capital. (1999, 353–354, italics in original)

## Notes

1. This is due, in my view, to the continuing hegemony of Modernization theory in international development: steeped in Cold War ideology, it initially sought to contain Soviet power in the Third World through the spread of capitalism and liberal democracy, thereby making international development an experiment in social engineering. The "traditional" developing country needed, accordingly, to imitate the "modernized" West by adopting the "right" values and institutions (capitalist liberal democratic ones) and liberalizing markets. International development continues to bear this ideological inheritance, as witnessed by the strong influence to date of the Bretton Woods institutions in Third World debt, trade, and development programming and policy.

2. In fact, Freud has a more complex reading of drive than a purely biological one, seeing it as a "psychic" or "mythical" representation of biological processes: "Drives are mythical entities, magnificent in their indefiniteness" (1989, 95).

3. The Lacanian concept of drive, then, is animal instinct mediated by the signifier. Libido becomes excess or remainder when filtered through language. See Eisenstein and McGowan (2012, 194).

4. The Lacanian literature I am drawing upon in this chapter (especially Žižek and Dean) tends to refer to the drive in the singular, and I will mostly follow suit. But we should bear in mind that drives are partial and plural: the Lacanian subject is never unified, with the result that there can never be a single, integrated, or harmonious resolution of the drives. Lacan speaks of four bodily drives (oral, anal, scopic, invocatory), and as Johnston explains, such bodily/erotic energy is "always-already channeled through non-natural mediums, namely vicissitudes organized by images and ideas" (2005, 261). In what follows, I argue that under capitalist development, the drive becomes an "accumulation drive"; and in the Conclusion, I argue for an uncompromising "anticapitalist drive" to counter the relentlessness of the accumulation drive.

5. Lacan is not, of course, suggesting humans are immortal, but that as long as we remain alive, we cannot escape drive or *jouissance*; they are unendingly inscribed in human life.

6. As chapter 1 explained, desire and drive are two ways in which human animals deal with the primordial loss, desire operating on the premise that enjoyment can be regained through a lost object, drive operating on the premise that enjoyment lies in the repetition of loss.

7. I read Žižek as saying that desire is always restricted to consumption and its interpellated subjects and thus secondary to the drives. This is because desire, by definition, is an impossible longing for fullness that gets fixated onto partial objects (of consumption). Whereas drive is not an infinite longing for an object, but fixation itself: a universal thrust and stuckness (i.e., accumulation) that, while never transcending particular objects, is condemned to always circulate around them.

8. Most of these (credit, stocks, derivatives) are themselves the embodiment of the accumulation drive, aimed at producing further surplus value. Jodi Dean writes, for example, that "derivatives should be understood as commodified forms of drive" (2012, 6).

9. Harvey (2005, 26–29) distinguishes between an imperialism with a "territorial logic of power" (state-led empire building aimed at commanding territory) and an imperialism with a "capitalist logic of power" (a more diffuse, business-led spatial expansion growing out of capital accumulation). It is the second that relates to the "spatio-temporal fix."

10. In 1994, the World Trade Organization (WTO) reached an agreement on Trade-Related Aspects of Intellectual Property Rights (TRIPS) that protects trademarks, copyrights, and patents, the vast majority of which are held by MNCs globally.

11. One could say that while the drive is impersonal, it is interiorized—mediated subjectively—through (personal) enjoyment.

12. It is true that desire, too, could be mobilized in favor of a post-capitalist alternative (by constructing a post-capitalist Left fantasy, for example, that would help reorient people's desires). However, in the Lacanian scheme of things, desire is mainly associated with the Symbolic, which tends to be the realm of the conventional, safe, and banal (since it comes to us from the Other). In contrast, the drive is associated with the Real, and hence is comparatively more subversive, unpredictable, and relentless. This is why it is drive more than desire that Žižek takes up as a pathway to a radical politics. As Jodi Dean suggests, "while some theorists focus on the subject of desire, . . . Žižek has opened up the category of drive, confronting what it is that impels us, that invests us in activities or patterns or objects exceeding interest, life, even our own good" (2012, 2).

# References

Borras, Saturnino M., Jr., and Jennifer C. Franco. 2012. "Global Land Grabbing and Trajectories of Agrarian Change: A Preliminary Analysis." *Journal of Agrarian Change* 12 (1): 34–59.

Boyle, Kirk. 2008. "The Four Fundamental Concepts of Slavoj Žižek's Psychoanalytic Marxism." *International Journal of Žižek Studies* 2 (1): 1–19. https://zizek studies.org/index.php/IJZS/article/view/59/56.

Braedley, Susan, and Meg Luxton, eds. 2010. *Neoliberalism and Everyday Life.* Montreal: McGill-Queen's University Press.

Bush, Ray, Janet Bujra, and Gary Littlejohn. 2011. "Editorial: The Accumulation of Dispossession." *Review of African Political Economy* 38 (128): 187–192.

Dean, Jodi. 2006. *Žižek's Politics*. New York: Routledge.

——. 2010a. "The Real Internet." *International Journal of Žižek Studies* 4 (1): 1–22. https://zizekstudies.org/index.php/IJZS/article/view/280/280.

——. 2010b. *Blog Theory: Feedback and Capture in the Circuits of Drive*. Cambridge: Polity.

——. 2012. "Still Dancing: Drive as a Category of Political Economy." *International Journal of Žižek Studies* 6 (1): 1–19. https://zizekstudies.org/index.php/IJZS/article/view/598/603.

du Toit, Damien. 2010. *Capital and Labour in South Africa: Class Struggle in the 1970s*. London: Routledge.

Eisenstein, Paul, and Todd McGowan. 2012. *Rupture: On the Emergence of the Political*. Evanston, IL: Northwestern University Press.

Frank, Andre Gunder. 1967. *Capitalism and Underdevelopment in Latin America*. New York: Monthly Review.

Freud, Sigmund. 1989. *New Introductory Lectures on Psycho-Analysis*. Translated and edited by James Strachey. New York: Norton.

Gordon, Todd, and Jeffery R. Webber. 2008. "Imperialism and Resistance: Canadian Mining Companies in Latin America." *Third World Quarterly* 29 (1): 63–87.

Grajales, Jacobo. 2011. "The Rifle and the Title: Paramilitary Violence and Land Control in Colombia." *Journal of Peasant Studies* 38 (4): 771–792.

Hall, Ruth. 2011. "Land Grabbing in Southern Africa: the Many Faces of the Investor Rush." *Review of African Political Economy* 38 (128): 193–214.

Harvey, David. 1982. *The Limits to Capital*. Chicago: University of Chicago Press.

——. 2004. "The 'New' Imperialism: Accumulation by Dispossession." *Socialist Register* 40: 63–87.

——. 2005. *The New Imperialism*. Oxford: Oxford University Press.

Homer, Sean. 2005. *Jacques Lacan*. London: Routledge.

Johnston, Adrian. 2005. *Time Driven: Metapsychology and the Splitting of the Drive*. Evanston, IL: Northwestern University Press.

Kapoor, Ilan. 2013. *Celebrity Humanitarianism: The Ideology of Global Charity*. London: Routledge.

——. 2014. "Psychoanalysis and Development: Contributions, Examples, Limits." *Third World Quarterly* 35 (7): 1120–1143.

Kautsky, John H. 2002. *Social Democracy and the Aristocracy: Why Socialist Labor Movements Developed in Some Industrial Countries and Not in Others*. New Brunswick, NJ: Transaction.

Kingsbury, Paul. 2010. "Locating the Melody of the Drives." *Professional Geographer* 62 (4): 519–533.

Kingsbury, Paul, and Steve Pile. 2014. "Introduction: Transference, Drives, Repetition and other Things Tied to Geography." In *Psychoanalytic Geographies*, edited by Paul Kingsbury and Steve Pile, 1–38. Farnham: Ashgate.

Lacan, Jacques. 1997. *The Ethics of Psychoanalysis: The Seminar of Jacques Lacan, Book VII*. Edited by Jacques-Alain Miller. New York: Norton.

———. 1998. *The Four Fundamental Concepts of Psychoanalysis: The Seminar of Jacques Lacan, Book XI*. Edited by Jacques-Alain Miller. New York: Norton.

———. 2014. *Anxiety: The Seminar of Jacques Lacan, Book X*. Edited by Jacques-Alain Miller. Cambridge: Polity.

Marx, Karl. 1967. *Capital*. Vol. 3, *The Process of Capitalist Production as a Whole*. Edited by Friedrich Engels. New York: International Publishers.

McCarthy, James. 2004. "Privatizing Conditions of Production: Trade Agreements as Neoliberal Environmental Governance." *Geoforum* 35: 327–341

McDonald, David A., and Greg Ruiters, eds. 2005. *The Age of Commodity: Water Privatization in Southern Africa*. London: Earthscan.

McGowan, Todd. 2004. *The End of Dissatisfaction? Jacques Lacan and the Emerging Society of Enjoyment*. Albany: SUNY Press.

Özselçuk, Ceren, and Yahya M. Madra. 2007. "Economy, Surplus, Politics: Some Questions on Žižek's Political Economy Critique of Capitalism." In *Did Somebody Say Ideology? On Slavoj Žižek and Consequences*, edited by Fabio Vighi and Heiko Feldner, 78–107. Newcastle: Cambridge Scholars Publishing.

Petras, James, and Henry Veltmeyer. 2014. *Extractive Imperialism in the Americas: Capitalism's New Frontier*. Leiden: Brill.

Stavrakakis, Yannis. 2006. "Objects of Consumption, Causes of Desire: Consumerism and Advertising in Societies of Commanded Enjoyment." *Gramma* 14: 83–105.

Sweezy, Paul M. 1953. *The Present as History*. New York: Monthly Review.

———. 1970. *The Theory of Capitalist Development*. New York: Monthly Review.

Whitehead, Judith. 2010. *Development and Dispossession in the Narmada Valley*. New Delhi: Dorling Kindersley.

Zalik, Anna. 2009. "Zones of Exclusion: Offshore Extraction, the Contestation of Space and Physical Displacement in the Nigerian Delta and the Mexican Gulf." *Antipode* 41 (3): 557–582.

Žižek, Slavoj. 1989. *The Sublime Object of Ideology*. London: Verso.

———. 1991. *Looking Awry: An Introduction to Jacques Lacan through Popular Culture*. Cambridge: MIT Press.

———. 1993. *Tarrying with the Negative: Kant, Hegel, and the Critique of Ideology*. Durham, NC: Duke University Press.

———. 1996. *The Indivisible Remainder*. London: Verso.

———. 1999. *The Ticklish Subject: The Absent Centre of Political Ontology*. London: Verso

———. 2006. *The Parallax View*. Cambridge, MA: MIT Press.

———. 2010. *Living in the End Times*. London: Verso.

Žižek, Slavoj, and Glyn Daly. 2004. *Conversations with Žižek*. Cambridge: Polity.

# CHAPTER 5

# Capitalism as Envy-Machine

KEYWORD: *Envy*

## Introduction

Jassi's beautiful house in Lodhi Colony is the envy of his neighbors, especially his immediate neighbor, Manish, whose abode is comparatively small and modest. So when Manish holds his annual neighborhood party, Jassi makes it a point to go up to him and say: "A lovely party. Thank you for your hostility!"

A genie appears to a farming family. It offers to bestow upon them anything they wish, but with the caveat that their neighbors will receive twice as much. The family huddle together, and having quickly reached their decision, shout out in unison: "blind us in one eye"!

Envy is often an unspeakable social passion. That's because it involves not just coveting others' good fortune, but harboring an ill-will toward them that dare not be publicly admitted or acknowledged. In fact, in precapitalist societies, there were prohibitions on it in order to maintain a modicum of congenial family and community relations (Wrenn 2015, 503). Christian communities counted it as one of the "seven deadly sins." Some cultures encouraged outward displays of modesty (e.g., refraining from wearing fine clothes or jewelry) to avoid the envious gaze of strangers, while others engaged in public ceremonial "expenditures" (e.g., gift-giving, potlatch) as a way of dissipating socioeconomic surplus and minimizing envy. Many societies invested objects, idols, or charms with the power to ward off curses or the evil eye, aiming thereby to protect property, children, or valuables (see Foster 1972; Gell 1986; Kaster 2005; Wrenn 2015, 503–504). There is, moreover, the repeated caution of mythology and folklore from across the globe against sibling or social rivalry—think of Cain murdering Abel, Set usurping his brother Osiris's throne, Vali breaking his fraternal bonds with Sugriv (in the *Ramayana*), Zubaydah punishing her two half-sisters (in the *Arabian Nights*), Iago bringing down Othello, or Cinderella being needled by her cruel stepsisters. Curiously, even the current practice of restaurant tipping is said to take its origins in envy-avoidance: sharing a small portion of your good fortune with your server so s/he doesn't envy you your wealth.[1]

But if precapitalist societies tended to curb envy, capitalist ones increasingly encourage it, indeed depend on it. To be sure, this chapter claims that the dominant affect of late global capitalism is not egoism, as is commonly held, but envy: the social inequality inherent in capitalist accumulation in the global South (and North) breeds a mix of coveting and malice, so that it is not just that those on top of the social hierarchy must win but equally that those on the bottom must lose, generating enjoyment (*jouissance*) on both sides. The chapter focuses on two contemporary manifestations of such an envy-machine: consumption, which exploits the urge to "keep up with the Joneses"; and corruption, born of socioeconomic resentment and aspiration. Each case involves enjoyment—both in envying and being envied—thus helping to reproduce capitalist development and social inequality.

# The Psychoanalytic Underpinnings of Envy

Envy is closely associated with the gaze; it derives, in fact, from the Latin *invidere* ("to look askance at somebody"), taking on, as just mentioned, the malicious signification of evil eye or begrudging scrutiny (Kaster 2005, 85–86; Vidaillet 2008, 282). Indeed, this is how Lacan conceptualizes the notion (1998b, 116; see also 1998a): when referring to it, he often recalls the scene from Augustine's *Confessions* (1980, 28), in which a young infant enviously gazes at his stepbrother suckling at his mother's breast.[2] This is evidently a portrayal of sibling rivalry in which the infant sees his stepbrother usurping his close relationship to his parent; what Lacan emphasizes though is that it is because the infant is unconsciously reminded of the originary unbearable loss (of enjoyment) that he is envious. That is, the infant's envious gaze harkens back to a primal fantasy of plenitude and is therefore an attempt at compensating for it, at filling up the void.

The crucial implication is that the infant envies not the Other's object but the Other's *enjoyment*. The goal of envy, in other words, is not to possess or steal some prized object, but rather, to put it starkly, to "destroy the Other's ability/capacity to enjoy the object" (Žižek 2008b, 90). This point is brought home, for example, when comparing envy to jealousy (see Copjec 2002, 159): jealousy is about losing an object one already "possesses" (e.g., one's lover to a rival), while envy is about hungering to possess what one lacks (e.g., full enjoyment, plenitude); jealousy involves love (i.e., fear of losing the loved object), while envy involves hostility or hatred toward the obstacle preventing one from enjoying; and jealousy centers on a prized object, whereas envy centers on (a fantasy about) the Other's enjoyment.[3]

To be sure, fantasy works hand-in-hand with envy because the envious places intrinsic value, not on the object per se, or even on the Other per se, but rather on the *fictionalized* Other, specifically the fantasy of the Other enjoying ("look at how much s/he is enjoying that object"!). And the danger and cruelty of the evil eye of envy lies in its *construction* of the Other's enjoyment; so strong and desperate is its yearning for a return to full *jouissance* that it may seek not only to steal the Other's enjoyment but also to eliminate any interceding obstruction. As Dupuy (2013, 165–167) and Žižek (2008b, 91) remind us, it is likely this feature that Rousseau (2011, 63–65, 106) was troubled by when he distinguished egotism (*amour-de-soi*), which he saw as benignly "natural," from self-love (*amour-propre*), which he saw as so perverse as to destroy anything standing in its way.

Implicit here is that it is the impasse of enjoyment that leads to the pathology of envy. We are unable, it seems, to enjoy by ourselves; we can only enjoy through the Other's enjoyment. The search for enjoyment, then, is never ending, since satisfaction always lies elsewhere and is forever imbricated with an Other's. As Žižek puts it, the "problem with human desire is that . . . it is always a 'desire for the Other' in all the senses of the term: desire for the Other, desire to be desired by the Other, and especially desire for what the Other desires. This last makes envy . . . [a] constitutive component of human desire" (2005; 2006, 36; 2008b, 87).

## Capitalism, Inequality, and Envy

To say that envy is constitutive of human desire (i.e., it results from the fundamental loss we suffer as we emerge as sociolinguistic beings) is to say that it is operative in all societies. But different societies elicit, amplify, or constrain this unconscious impulse differently. Many precapitalist ones, as underlined earlier, tried to contain it to keep a lid on social animosity. Capitalist societies, on the other hand, have encouraged it. In fact, Žižek, echoing several other analysts (see Deleuze and Guattari 1977, 247; Sloterdijk 2010, 64, 202–203), argues that "today's capitalism functions as the 'institutionalization of envy'" (2011a, xiii).

This is because capitalism thrives on instability (and inequality). Precapitalist social systems saw volatility as a threat, but capitalism sees it as an opportunity (see chapter 4). Crises—economic, environmental, social—open up possibilities for increasing profit, market share, and commoditization (e.g., the financialization of debt in response to the global debt crisis; the greening of the economy in response to the environmental crisis; or the aggressive marketing of tobacco and alcohol in the global South in response to the growing crisis of youth unemployment).[4] Most often, these crises are generated by the inequality integral to capitalism. The recent financialization of global markets, for example, is the consequence of rapidly rising income inequalities, which have allowed global financial elites ("the 1 percent") to use their liquidity to make drastically more "money from money," leaving the liquidity-strapped "99 percent" of the world significantly worse off (Storm 2018). In this sense, not only does capitalism engender social and spatial inequalities, but the latter themselves become its driving forces. Inequality breeds competition, rivalry, struggle, deadlock: it may well end up pitting rich against poor and "developed" against "underdeveloped," but it also functions as putative motivator for innovation and creativity. "Inequality and—by extension—envy are thus heralded as the prime catalysts of economic activity" (Wrenn 2015, 503).

To be sure, the history of global capitalism is written in unevenness and inequality (see chapters 1, 4, and 12). As dependency theory and world-systems analysis have now well established (Amin 1976; Cardoso and Faletto 1979; Frank 1967; Wallerstein 2004; see also Harvey 2006; Smith 1991), starting around the sixteenth century, the deepening international division of labor produced a world economic system in which "core" (mostly Western) countries have dominated "peripheral" ones (mostly in the Third World). Over time, this system has become more geographically differentiated, with the emergence of "semiperipheral" countries (e.g., the decline of Portugal and Spain at the turn of the twentieth century, the rise of South Korea, China, Brazil, South Africa, or Saudi Arabia today). And such spatial differentiation has manifested not only at the national or regional level, but also at the local level (Sassen 2006; Taylor 2004), creating an uneven and hierarchical network of cities (e.g., such current "global" cities as London, Cape Town, or São Paulo in contrast to such "hinterland" cities as Salford, Butembo, or Wuhan).

Of late, this geographic inequality has been increasing. The world's poorest countries' GDP per capita in 2010 (averaging about $252) was less than half of what it was in 1900 (around $545). Between 1960 and 2010, the GDP per capita gap between the richest and poorest countries increased by 252 percent (i.e., inequality almost tripled during this period). The same trend emerges regionally: between 1960 and 2010, inequality between the United States and Latin America grew by 206 percent (again, as measured by GDP per capita), with the corresponding figures comparing the United States to the Middle East/North Africa region, sub-Saharan Africa, and South Asia standing at 155 percent, 207 percent, and 196 percent, respectively (Hickel 2017, 2214, 2217; see also Piketty 2014). Breaking down such spatial inequality along current production/investment lines, one finds that about four-fifths of global manufacturing and services production, and almost two-thirds of world agricultural production, are centered in just fifteen countries. Over half of inward foreign direct investment (FDI) in the global South, likewise, is concentrated in just five host countries, with almost one-third going to China (Dicken 2009).

Finally, while extreme poverty worldwide has fallen and millions have joined the ranks of the middle class during the last fifty years (especially in China and India), this has not prevented income inequalities from growing sharply (see chapter 12). The 2010–2015 Palma ratio (measuring the difference between the top and bottom income brackets) reveals a growing divide between the richest and poorest in almost all countries of the global South, with South Africa, Haiti, and Central African Republic leading the pack (Barr 2017).

Relatedly, of note since the 1990s has been spectacular wealth accumulation in the hands of the few. The emergence of billionaires, multimillionaires, and a highly remunerated corporate bourgeoisie (earning fat-cat salaries, bonuses, and stock options) stands alongside growing underclass made up of sweatshop labor (mostly composed of women, children, and migrants), unemployed youth, rural subalterns, the precariat (insecure and part-time labor), and urban and suburban slum-dwellers. The world's richest 1 percent today holds as much wealth as the rest of the world combined, with the richest sixty-two people owning as much wealth as the poorest half of the globe (BBC 2016). In South Africa, the top 1 percent owns 70.9 percent of the country's wealth, while the bottom 60 percent holds just 7 percent (Greenwood 2018). China fares not much better—the top 1 percent currently owns a third of the country's wealth (Leng 2017); nor does Brazil, where the six richest men own the same wealth as the poorest 50 percent (i.e., 100 million people) (Oxfam International 2018).[5]

My point in outlining this growing inequality and unevenness is to suggest not only how they depend on envy, when this unevenness motivates a competitive ethic as just discussed, but also how they breed (further) envy.[6] Social and spatial difference, after all, forms the basis for comparison, thereby generating envy. This is a fortiori the case in today's mediatic age, when the starkness of wealth versus poverty, glamour versus depravity, is made even more visible, providing an augmented basis for (envious) social comparison. Witness for example the promotion and popularity of media programs in the global South devoted to the lives of the rich and famous, game shows that promise instant wealth (e.g., local variations of *Who Wants to Be a Millionaire?*), or reality TV productions valorizing self-responsible, entrepreneurial subjectivity (e.g., variations of *Apprentice*, *Survivor*, or *Amazing Race*).[7]

Neoliberalism (and neoliberal communicative capitalism) stimulates envy by propagating market mechanisms, hyperindividualism, and performance measurements. We find this at work not only in media spectacles of individual striving and class conflict, but also in interstate rivalries (e.g., clashes over land and water) and regional power struggles (e.g., tensions over federal transfers from wealthier to poorer provinces, or between resource-rich and resource-deprived regions). The latter antagonisms, it should be said, are most often intensified by the creation of scarcity (e.g., the production of oil scarcity by multinationals and OPEC to drive up prices, or the privatization of the commons in favor of corporate farmers at the expense of the landless). Scarcity construction ups the competitive stakes, creating the myth there is not enough to go around and naturalizing the idea that there are winners and losers (Wrenn 2015, 508).

Envy is, in this sense, integral to late capitalist culture. Our global symbolic order elicits and amplifies people's envy in order to reproduce capitalist accumulation. On the one hand, it encourages socially desirable (i.e., envy-laden, capitalistic) values and practices—competition, entrepreneurialism, hyperindividualism, high performance, wealth, profit, greed, fame, success, winning. And on the other hand, it rationalizes the social and spatial inequalities that keep capitalism (and envy) going. Central here is the way in which it naturalizes hierarchy—for example, by propounding beliefs in "equal opportunity" and "the work ethic." For, if anyone can "make it," if getting rich and famous is about working hard, then inequality becomes acceptable, even desirable (for spurring competition, innovation, wealth accumulation, etc.). Frequently, such capitalistic beliefs are reinforced by "traditional" or religious ones (e.g., one's social position is the result of "good/bad fortune" or "the will of God") thus further rationalizing inequalities. All of this is why various forms of social apartheid—shanty towns besides gated communities, sweatshops alongside wealthy corporate headquarters—are tolerated if not normalized. In the Third World, one comes to believe in social mobility, while at the same time accepting that, as Eduardo Galeano puts it, the underclass should "sell newspapers they cannot read, sew clothes they cannot wear, polish cars they will never own and construct buildings where they will never live" (1990).

Capitalist culture, then, is the (Lacanian) "big Other," the symbolic order that (putatively) provides a guarantee of the subject's identity. It encourages capitalist accumulation and inequality, while propagating the myth of social mobility. It frames and unconsciously elicits the values, goals, and objects coveted by the subject (profit, competition, success, iPhones, etc.) as a way of soothing the subject's ontological lack or loss of enjoyment. The implication is that envy involves not just two subjects—the envious and the envied—but three: it is the big Other that provides the cultural background enabling each of the two subjects' identification process (Vidaillet 2007, 1693; 2008, 281). It is this big Other that helps validate each subject's perception of itself as whole and good. So the envious (are encouraged to) covet the Other's enjoyment in the belief that capturing it will satisfy their hunger, while the envied (are encouraged to) covet the prospect of even more enjoyment to satiate their (insatiable) appetite. And this triadic interrelationship is what helps keep capitalism going.

Implicit here though is that the capitalist big Other never quite delivers on its promises (of stability, plenitude, enjoyment); it always falls short, and is in fact premised on never reaching the mark since that is what keeps the machine churning. Despite ideological attempts at naturalizing social and spatial hierarchy, envy acts as the antagonistic element disrupting the status quo. For the envious, it means having to admit one's inferiority, resulting in bruised self-esteem and feelings of frustration and impotence. Indicative in this regard is the keen recent interest in "happiness" studies and measurements, which ironically speak to the relative *unhappiness* of the aspiring classes—they enjoy material comforts yet by all accounts appear to be experiencing an existential crisis. In recent happiness rankings, for example, "the happiest nations . . . [are also the ones that] tend to have the highest levels of suicide [revealing that happiness is not the same thing as satisfaction with one's life. This only points up] the key role of envy—what counts is not what you have so much as what others have (the middle classes are far less satisfied than the poor, for they take as their reference point the very wealthy, whose income and status they will be hard pushed to match; the poor, meanwhile, take as their reference point the middle earners, who are more within their reach)" (Žižek 2008a, 45). Ultimately then, through the mechanism of envy, the inequality of late capitalist development guarantees only every subject's *unhappiness*.

But of course envy's negativity manifests not simply in unhappiness; in our late capitalist times, it can also take on (and has taken on) hostile and destructive forms. This stems from the envious subject's profound, if not irrational, preoccupation with the Other's *jouissance*. Perhaps the most obvious example here is the rise of religious fundamentalist violence in the global South (and North), which not coincidentally parallels the rise of global inequality. Speaking in relation to both the 1995 Oklahoma bombing and the 9/11 attack on the Twin Towers, Žižek claims that "we are dealing with hatred pure and simple: destroying the obstacle, the Oklahoma City Federal Building, the World Trade Center, was what really mattered, not achieving the noble goal of a truly Christian or Muslim society" (2008b, 92). This is to say that it is not anger so much as envy that motivates such violence: far from being concerned about preserving (Muslim, Hindu, Buddhist, Jewish, Christian) culture or opposing "Westernization," the religious fundamentalist can be understood as having secretly internalized Western capitalist standards so that, despite his outward protestations, he is actually measuring himself *by* them, in the end coveting what he hates (Žižek 2005). Hence the pathological preoccupation by the likes of extremist religious groups (e.g., Boko Haram, the 969 Movement, Rashtriya Swayamsevak Sangh) with the Other's enjoyment (sexual mores, gender equality, consumerism, etc.); and hence the resulting need not simply to win through acts of "terror," but for the Other to lose. For, one's victory, it seems, is made all the more enjoyable by one's enemy's loss.

A similar proclivity can be discerned in what Mbembe calls "the emergence of the urban mob with its culture of rioting and racketeering" (2001, 56, 93, 111). The "youth bulge," in particular, sees 60 percent of such global South countries as Nigeria, Pakistan, and Afghanistan composed of young people (see Prashad 2012, 15ff.; Yousef 2003), contributing to not infrequent urban youth riots, looting, vandalism, and car torching. While unemployment and disaffection certainly have a lot to do with it, so does envy: the outbursts are generally not political, in that they make no outward demands; they are instead meaningless and destructive acts, with looting in particular motivated by consumerist *ressentiment* (since it takes the form of violent shoplifting of consumer goods) (Žižek 2007, 51; 2011c). These eruptions thus reveal how the capitalist big Other pervades the ranks of not just the "unhappy" rich and powerful, but also the disaffected poor and unemployed. Looting and vandalization of property allow the latter to enjoy what they have stolen or destroyed, but also to revel in what others have been deprived of. And while the capitalist powers that be may condemn and clamp down on such "irrational" and violent flare-ups, they can sleep comfortably in the knowledge that such isolated eruptions ultimately remain unthreatening to the System. The envy/enjoyment of such outbursts is perhaps taken too far, but lacking any political goal, the latter express well the capitalist superego command to "enjoy!" (more on that below).

That this negative and destructive dimension of envy is a crucial feature of human desire (and late capitalism) appears to elude the likes of John Rawls, whose idea of (liberal) justice is one which specifically brackets envy, or at least only admits a "benign" form of it (Rawls 1999, 124, 473). His idea of the just society is one where people are egoists, not envy seekers, and social inequality is accepted to the extent that those on the bottom of the social ladder are taken care of by those on top (through a modicum of socioeconomic distribution, which is to say, a welfare state). By bracketing envy, though, what Rawls misses is that people begrudge not objects or wealth per se, but others' enjoyment. If it were just a matter of those at the bottom needing to possess goods, they could resort, for example, to theft and that would satisfy; but envy's irrationality, as we have seen, involves much worse—destroying the Other's ability to enjoy (Copjec 2002, 165–166).

What Rawls ignores, in other words, is how a "just" society such as his would "create conditions for an uncontrolled explosion of *ressentiment*: in it, I would know that my lower status is fully 'justified' and would thus be deprived of the ploy of using my failure as the result of social injustice" (Žižek 2006, 36; 2008b, 88). Rawls thus overlooks that it would be unbearable for the (envious) subject to think it *deserves* its lower social position. For, accepting my unequal status knowing it is the result of an impersonal social force, rather than my "natural" (in)capacity, is much easier. This is Jean-Pierre Dupuy's argument in *The Mark of the Sacred* (2013, 157–164), where he claims that social inequalities can be made ideologically acceptable (and nonhumiliating) in four different ways: an externally imposed hierarchy (my lower status is predetermined, and hence unrelated to my social worth or personal abilities); demystification (my social status is based not on merit but on objective or hidden power struggles); contingency (my status depends on chance or social lottery); and complexity (my status is the result of uncontrollable social forces such as the "invisible hand" of the market).

It is ideological justifications such as these which, as underlined earlier, capitalist development deploys to make envy operational and inequality palatable. The knowledge that my social position is contingent (on outside, impersonal, or market forces) and can be changed (based on the myths of "hard work" and "equal opportunity") renders it bearable. This means that, on the one hand, the biggest threat to capitalism is the denial of such contingency (as suggested in Rawls), since it would result in bitterly hurt pride for all those in lower social positions; and on the other, that capitalist development is socially acceptable not because it is just but *unjust*. It is precisely inequality that enables me to tolerate that my failure is due to luck or accident, not my inferior abilities (Žižek 2007, 54; 2008b, 89).

# Consumption

One of the most obvious places where envy is at work is consumption. This is because consumption exploits not only the human desire for what is missing (I consume the object to fulfill my constitutive lack), but also human coveting (I desire the object only insofar as it is desired by the Other). Social comparison, "keeping up with the Joneses," is the linchpin of consumption in our late capitalist times; and the goal, as underlined earlier, is not so much to possess the Other's object as to enjoy the way the Other is enjoying.

The chief means by which such mimetic enjoyment is activated and maintained is advertising (see chapter 4). The latter induces one to enjoy (Coke's "Enjoy!" says as much), binding one to continuous shopping. As Stavrakakis argues (2006; see also Böhm and Batta 2010), advertising does not so much dupe subjects, as many like to claim, as *seduce* them, appealing to their passions (i.e., they get hooked despite knowing they are being duped). Product promotion stimulates desire by constructing a fantasy—usually in the form of a beautiful model or famous celebrity enjoying the good life—pledging to fill one's lack: it thus promises me enjoyment by staging an Other's. What I buy when I consume a product is not so much the physical object, but the mystique surrounding it, the fantasy of others'—and by association, my own—Edenic enjoyment.

But as argued in chapter 4, the fantasy promised is fleeting and temporary. The object consumed turns out to be less than fully satisfying, never quite delivering on what was staged and expected (this is what Lacan calls *objet petit a*). Needless to say, capitalism exploits this frustrated enjoyment, since that is what keeps shopper's coming back, thereby ensuring the reproduction of the System. Advertising's fantasy must forever remain an unfulfilled promise so that we can continue to be subjectivized as envy-machines. And so, before too long, a "new and improved" product is packaged and promoted, pledging more and better thrill. This is the deliberate strategy of "product differentiation"; and it works because it exploits people's enjoyment of small differences—the hope and yearning, however faint, that maybe this time full enjoyment will be procured.

Note the importance here of the gaze, since, as stressed earlier, consumption/advertising involves not simply the gaze of the (envious) consumer on the (envied) Other, but most importantly the gaze of the big Other (see chapter 7): it is the latter that constitutes the background—the consumer culture—that helps produce (envious) shoppers, promising to deliver them from their lack. As Todd McGowan explains (2004), late capitalist culture doesn't merely encourage us to enjoy, it (unconsciously) commands us to enjoy; the System's productive engine depends on it. This is evidenced, in the global South as in the global North, by the naturalization of enjoyment-as-excess (see chapter 1): the desire for the tallest, biggest, wealthiest, flashiest, most original or outrageous (think of the gratuitous displays of wealth by rich kids across the Third World, the legendary shopping sprees by Saudi royal families or Grace Mugabe, or billionaire Ambani's twenty-seven-story, 400,000 square foot skyscraper home in Mumbai); the ubiquity of the colossal, from beverages to architecture (e.g., "venti" drinks, the Burj Khalifa, the Shanghai or Petronas Towers, or the recently built African Renaissance Monument in Dakar or Chimalli Warrior in Mexico State); and the surfeit of choice from jeans and fast food to films and dating partners. In this regard, the excess of the powerful and wealthy itself serves as advertisement, spurring mimetic consumption by those at the middle and bottom of the social ladder. This certainly explains the massive success of luxury products—from high-end brands such as Graff, Van Cleef, and Rolex to the more "affordable" ones such as Coach, Swatch, and Veuve Clicquot—or indeed the plethora of knock-offs and faux luxury items, meant to provide those at the bottom a taste of (and *for*) the high life. It also explains the excessive commercialization of festive holidays around the world (birthdays, Christmas, Eid, Diwali, Dia de las Reyes, Kwanzaa, Purim, Chinese New Year, Tet, Festa Junina): here people feel the pressure not simply to buy gifts but to ensure they are offering the "right" or "worthy" gifts (in relation to what they expect to receive and what others will be giving). Holiday shopping capitalizes on both "keeping up with the Joneses" and the pleasure/pain/stress (*jouissance*) of gift giving, thus helping to produce the excess we have now become inured to.

Lest we think that envy-driven consumption is limited only to rich and middle-class people, research shows just the opposite. Not only are brand corporations now targeting poorer sections of the population, but marketing that focuses on the elite and middle classes is "democratically" heard and watched by those at the bottom through radio, television, social media, and billboards. Advertising now infiltrates the slums of Calcutta, Nairobi, and Mexico, where homes with TVs and Wi-Fi outnumber those with running water and sanitation (Mueller 1996, 250; see also Raynolds 2017; Trentmann 2016). What is more, recent consumer studies (see Hill 2011; Iqani 2016) show that social comparisons appear to be even more powerful determinants of life satisfaction and consumption for the poor compared to the wealthy (and for poorer countries in contrast to richer ones). That is, while the poor take their shopping cues from those better off than them (the "demonstration effect"), they also appear to be most satisfied when they are able to make "downward" comparisons (when they are successfully able to compare themselves to those who have even less). Nothing illustrates envy better than that.

Social media come close though, since in many ways, they are the embodiment of upward and downward comparisons (see Appel, Gerlach, and Crusius 2016; Krasnova et al. 2013). While ostensibly a tool for social communication, they hinge on advertising and promotion. I am referring here not simply to the targeted ads based on tracked user online behavior, but more importantly to user posts (on Facebook, Instagram, Snapchat, etc.). For, under the guise of personal "news," these posts often serve as self-promotion and advertising: text/images/selfies depicting films, clothes, homes, holidays, books, cars, jobs, concerts, weddings, birthdays, and the like, are a form of (1) braggadocio, aimed at recognition and social status, and/or (2) consumption, helping elicit others' desires. Followers and "friends" act as tribes, whose views and tastes you share and shape, and over whom you sometimes lord it with your accomplishments and purchases. In this sense, social media institutionalize envy-driven consumption and consumption-driven envy, with users jockeying to establish their social status and rank.

Now there are those who condone this type of envy, claiming that consumption under our global capitalist order encourages "benign" forms of it. Russell Belk, for example, argues that current-day consumption is "driven far more by benign envy involving a desire to 'level up' through consumption emulation rather than 'level down' by harming others. . . . Compared to the impotent rage and hatred provoked by malicious envy, the emulative urges prompted by benign envy, into which malicious envy has been sublimated, seem relatively innocent" (2011, 117, 128). For him, benign envy today has been "democratized" in that it successfully elicits people to consume: "We have far more possessions now [than before] and they have branded and model names. . . . We have greater discretionary income and more access to consumer credit" (2011, 122–123, 130).

But I couldn't agree less. For one, there are plenty of contemporary manifestations of consumption-related malicious envy: theft, looting, vandalism (by urban rioters, as discussed earlier), or "money burning" (the purposeful destruction of money to reduce one's own wealth, but equally to prevent it from enriching others). Each is precisely an attempt at leveling down, robbing, or destroying goods or property in order to prevent the Other from enjoying. The broader point though is that benign envy is the intimate other side of malicious envy, no more so than under capitalism, which breeds inequality and feeds off competition, hostility, and rivalry. Every act of (so to speak) "happy shopping"—which Belk appears to be extolling—is thus based on a series of acts of hostile competition that help produce the consumable product in the first place, while also generating the unequal conditions that foster acts of theft, looting, vandalism, and so on. Belk's "we" is therefore elite-centered, not democratic: in the global schema, only very few benignly envious consumers *do* have "discretionary income" and "access to consumer credit," and it is they who lord it over those very many who don't, thereby (further) enabling malicious envy. How, in such an unequal structural relationship, is Belk able to determine where the benign ends and the malicious begins?

In other words, Belk is an apologist for neoliberal capitalism.[8] His is an attempt to sanitize consumption's dirty underside. He not only neglects the malicious dimensions of shopping but also conveniently delinks consumption from production. In the latter regard, he sidelines Marx's warning about commodity fetishism (1990, 164–165), as a result of which we are seduced into shopping without regard to the exploitative socioecological relations involved in production (e.g., sweatshop labor, environmental degradation) (see chapter 6). Malicious envy is, as a result, not "sublimated" when "we" shop but covered over to ensure a worry-free shopping experience.

## Corruption

Corruption has become a catch-all explanation for "underdevelopment" in the Third World, often blamed on moral decay, "dishonest" behavior, and the lack of boundaries between the public and private. Usually defined as the misuse of public resources for private gain, it has served as pretext for Western browbeating of Third World governments, particularly in Africa and the Middle East, where the state is frequently portrayed as authoritarian and beholden to family and "tribal" loyalties (Sile 2017; World Bank 1997b, 162). Spearheaded by the World Bank and the international NGO Transparency International, anticorruption activities have gained increasing prominence, particularly since the 1990s (see World Bank 1997a; 2018). For these agencies, corruption damages incentive structures and negatively affects investment and growth (Pope 2000, 3); it is seen as so threatening to development, in fact, that the World Bank has not hesitated to make anticorruption activity an aid conditionality, even withholding loans (for such countries as Chad, Kenya, Congo, India, Bangladesh, Uzbekistan, Yemen, and Argentina) because of the perceived lack of recipient government action against graft (Bretton Woods Project 2006).

But I want to suggest that corruption is the symptom, not the cause, of "underdevelopment"; and moreover that its bedfellow is envy / enjoyment, of corrupt Third World officials, of course, but equally of anticorruption Western advocates.

To say corruption is symptomatic is to say that it is a consequence of the inequality inherent in (capitalist) development. Indeed, the reason corruption is relatively widespread in several countries of the global South is not because of moral but of socioeconomic lack and a comparatively high degree of inequality. Corruption is, in this sense, a coping mechanism, a safety net for people to make ends meet in the absence of an adequate welfare state. For civil servants, for example, it helps complement their often meager wages, sometimes allowing for patronage (diverting government funds or jobs) to similarly struggling family members and friends. Many analysts point out, in fact, that the World Bank's structural adjustment programs have themselves caused or worsened corruption: Mbembe suggests, for example, that, given the severity of adjustment in sub-Saharan Africa, bribery has likely acted as a safety valve, preventing a "slide into completely arbitrary rule and raw violence" (2001, 75; see also Bukovansky 2006, 196); while Diawara makes a case for black-market corruption and smuggling, which provide more choice and lower prices, thereby helping people cope with the hardships of cuts to social programs (2009, 123).

Corruption can and has thus become a common practice as a direct response to inequality. The fact that it is systemic and institutionalized is evidence not of some cultural defect, but of the continuing need for people to survive in the face of continuing inequality. And the fact that it is a widespread response to the pervasiveness and depth of inequality means that, in many countries, it has become the object not of social opprobrium but approval and acceptance. Yet, this corruption-as-coping-mechanism ("low-level corruption") must be distinguished from its more nefarious form, perpetrated by the powerful and wealthy ("high-level corruption"). They are of course related, stemming as they both do from capitalist inequality. But whereas the former tends to see low-level officials and ordinary citizens trying to negotiate their relative socioeconomic deprivation, the latter tends to see elites (domestic and international) further rewarding and enriching themselves by pilfering public resources. And it is here that the evil eye of envy rears its head.

High-level corruption comprises a variety of activities—pillaging state resources, instituting government tolls and taxes for private gain, trafficking and extortion, tax avoidance (through the use of offshore tax havens),[9] cybercrime and hacking, buying the influence of the courts or political leaders, patronage (in the form of favors, jobs, and contracts) to family members and party/ community allies, and so on. Often these practices involve a vast network of international and local actors and intermediaries, all aiming to acquire favor, power, and wealth. Mbembe summarizes it well:

> [Corruption entails] an economy based on concessions, made up of lucrative monopolies, secret contracts, private deals, and privileges in the tobacco, timber, transport, transit, and agro-industry sectors, in

large-scale projects, in oil, uranium, lithium, manganese, and arms pur-
chasing, in the training and officering of armies and tribal militias, and
in the recruitment of mercenaries. . . . [It is] a process in which international networks of foreign traffickers, middlemen, and businessmen
are linking with, and becoming entwined with, local businessmen, "tech-
nocrats," and warlords, causing whole areas of Africa's international
economic relations to be swept underground, making it possible to consolidate methods of government that rest on indiscriminate violence
and high-level corruption. (2001, 85–86; see also Gupta 2012, 74ff.)

In many ways, such high-level corruption is a form of "accumulation by dispossession" (Harvey 2004) (see also chapter 4), since it entails elite acquisition
of wealth and power by looting public assets. Onoge (1983) claims, in fact, that
such corruption is merely a continuation of the corruption already endemic
to capitalism—the misappropriation of social surplus by the bourgeoisie (and
other social elites), although in this case not through market mechanisms but
through neopatrimonialism, fraud, and theft.[10]

It is not hard to see the link between such fraudulent misappropriation and
envy. High-level corruption is about desiring objects (wealth, power) only in
so far as they are desired by those better socially positioned than me in the
global capitalist hierarchy. I attribute to the Other some mysterious access to
full enjoyment, which is what gives rise to envy: the (imagined) Other's access to enjoyment excludes me, haunts me; hence my proclivity to engage in
bribery and fraud. Such a propensity centers not simply on making do and
surviving (low-level corruption) but on a deeper yearning for the good life,
for acquiring and consuming wealth; so much so, in fact, that I resort to non-
market practices—bribery, fraud, patronage, and so on—to achieve a market
goal (wealth accumulation). High-level corruption is thus not just generated
by capitalist inequality; it is driven by envy to the point of short-circuiting "normal" practices (market-based competition, innovation) to win capitalism's
ultimate prize—greater wealth (and higher status). Such envy-based corruption is, to an extent, a quick and dirty (albeit risky) way of subverting the myths
of equal opportunity, merit, and the "invisible hand of the market" to improve
social status. It is also a way of bending the system (and bending to the system) in order to maintain patron-client relationships and obligations (the latter rooted, it must be mentioned, not in "traditional" cultural institutions but
in colonial practices of rent seeking and resource extraction) (see Clapham
1982). Neopatrimonialism thus articulates with the neoliberal market economy through envy-driven corruption.

The maliciousness of envy can be seen here in the perverse pleasure fraudsters take in pilfering the state (and the public) to improve their social position. No doubt such pleasure is mixed with guilt and anxiety, but again, that is precisely what *jouissance* entails. To be sure, there is a whole economy of enjoyment to be had in "creatively" devising a corrupt scheme (perhaps especially in cahoots with others), bucking the smooth or "normal" operation of the system, depriving others of resources, profits, or jobs (the state, the public, taxpayers, other job-seekers, corporate competitors, etc.), and of course enjoying the fruits of one's chicanery (wealth, power) (see Awa 1964, 156; Brehm and Gates 2010; Caiden 2009; Gilbert 2016; Ibekwe 2014; Mitchell 2011, 144ff.; Olupohunda 2016; Poon 2018). The last of these (relishing the prize) is undeniably important, but it is the middle two pleasures (sabotaging the system, depriving others) that are revealing of the sadomasochism of envy ("if I can't enjoy, then neither should others," and "if others are enjoying, so must I").

But envy and enjoyment are to be detected not just on the part of the fraudsters but also on the part of the very Western anticorruption advocates who sit in judgment (World Bank, Transparency International, aid agencies, etc.). This is all the more the case given that the moralizing and hectoring of the latter are often disingenuous and hypocritical. When (former) World Bank president Kim declares, for example, that corruption is "public enemy number one in developing countries" (World Bank 2013), he is conveniently sidelining the spate of recent (and not so recent) corruption scandals in the "developed" West (bribery, nepotism, tax avoidance, and clientelism involving the likes of former NATO secretary-general Willy Claes, President Jacque Chirac, German chancellor Helmut Kohl, Italian prime minister Silvio Berlusconi, "friends" and associates of Presidents Mitterrand and Trump, Elf Aquitaine, Enron, WorldCom, Hollinger, Savings and Loans, SNC-Lavalin, FIFA, etc.) (see Szeftel 2000, 296–297). Such scandals are further evidence that corruption is not a Third World problem but a global one, that is to say, endemic to global capitalism/inequality.

Anticorruption discourse is based on a series of ideological myths:

1. That capitalism is a well-functioning system, corrupted by rogue individuals and decaying culture, which if eliminated would allow a return to wholesomeness, purity, transparency, integrity. What such a fantasy cannot admit, and aims at masking, is what we have been suggesting all along—that global capitalism is a system rotten from the start (because inequality and unevenness are always already written into it).

2. That corruption is a function of "underdevelopment," that is, that there is an "inverse correlation" between corruption and economic development/democracy. The bribery scandals that have plagued the West from the beginning of the industrial revolution to the present, as well as the fact that countries with high levels of growth can have and have had high levels of corruption (e.g., Japan, China, the Asian Tigers), suggest just the contrary—that corruption is part and parcel of economic development and not necessarily tied to the presence or absence of democracy (see Della Porta and Vannucci 1999, 5). Some research even submits that in cases where there is rigid and centralized decision making, "corruption may actually improve efficiency and help growth," for example by speeding up approvals processes (Bardhan 1997, 1322–1323; Rose-Ackerman 1978).[11]

3. That structural adjustment, coupled with anticorruption measures, can help alleviate the problems of bribery, fraud, and so on. The problem here, as was pointed out earlier, is that adjustment has itself induced new forms of corruption: opening markets to foreign investment has spawned new opportunities for (mostly Western) corporate graft; new regulatory frameworks have brought about novel "gatekeeping" opportunities for civil servants and local intermediaries (e.g., the need for new trade licenses, contract requirements, etc.); and state retrenchment and privatization have created a new class of fraudsters from the ranks of those displaced and dispossessed (Szeftel 2000, 295, 302).

4. That the private and the public can be easily separated, by specifying clear civil service rules and procedures. Such a view relies on idealized Weberian notions of a "rational" and "objective" bureaucracy, denying that all decision making involves at least a degree of subjective assessment and interpretation, individual discretion, personalism, and flexibility in applying rules (see chapters 2, 7, and 12). This Weberian bureaucratic ideal, moreover, comes out of a particular Euro–North American history, which cannot be arbitrarily or indiscriminately imposed on the diversity of Third World states. Many African and Middle Eastern governments, for example, do have clientelist practices; but these have complex colonial and sociopolitical origins, as underlined earlier. Attempts at eliminating such practices or establishing "clear" lines between the public and private to create a professional civil service—lines which, importantly, do not pass muster even in the West—are therefore doomed to failure.

Not only are the above anticorruption myths aimed at diverting attention away from the relationship between corruption and capitalism—that is what makes them ideological—but like all ideologies, their foundation rests on the unconscious. Which is to say that, at the heart of anticorruption discourse is enjoyment and envy. Our first clue here is the self-righteous and moralizing tone and intent of such a discourse. There is no mistaking the perverse (superegoic) pleasure taken when anticorruption advocates such as the World Bank or Transparency International torment a Third World government, rank it (e.g., by publishing the annual "Corruptions Perception Index"), threaten it (through adjustment or aid conditionalities), audit it, accuse it, embarrass it, make it comply, require that it institute "integrity" measures, and so forth. In addition to neocolonialism, is there not a certain pornographic voyeurism, if not a sadomasochism, that pervades much of this? Moreover, like the proponents of all depoliticized, moral discourses (especially across the North-South divide), are not anticorruption advocates only too quick to blame the problem on "greedy" individuals and faulty culture rather than broader socioeconomic and corporate structures? Along with local allies,[12] they gleefully push for "whodunnit" investigations, demanding their pound of flesh, and helping to criminalize and shame perpetrators, boast victories, and whip up public support for further investigations. The irony, of course, is that there is a never-ending supply of new cases and investigations, despite the institution of "integrity" measures.

Yet that is precisely the point: targeting the symptom (corruption) rather than the cause (inequality) is what ensures an unlimited logjam of cases (and enjoyment).[13] It is this interminable cycle that not only makes anticorruption discourse a self-fulfilling prophecy, but guarantees the maintenance and multiplication of the anticorruption institutional machinery. Witness the plethora of activities now undertaken in this sector: constructing an integrity "culture" through seminars, conferences, training workshops, and so on; carrying out institutional reform by creating anticorruption commissions, drug enforcement agencies, new tax regimes, public sector financial management, and so on; strengthening judicial and policing capabilities; and encouraging civil society and media to better hold states to account (Szeftel 2000, 290). This is what I have been calling "institutional enjoyment" (see chapters 2, 7, and 12), that is, institutional development as an enjoyment-responding and -producing machine that secures the reproduction and aggrandizement of the system.

As to the envy of these anticorruption advocates (or "warriors"?), it is to be gleaned in the way in which they appear to be haunted by (their construction of) the prohibited pleasures of fraudsters. Psychoanalytically, such a preoccupation is revealing of both an attraction to and a repulsion by the Other's enjoyment. Indeed, despite (or because) of their outward protestations, it is hard not to see these advocates as secretly envying the latter's flaunting and subversion of the Law (see chapters 9 and 11)—the fraudsters' gumption in engaging in devious forms of accumulation, diverting resources for personal gain, using quick and dirty methods to succeed, refusing to follow the commands of the market ("work hard!" and "compete!" are replaced by "be cunning!" and "commandeer!"), and so forth. At the same time, the advocates' envy is enlivened by fantasies of "theft of enjoyment," in which the Other prevents one from properly or adequately enjoying (hence the moral mission to stamp out corruption, find the culprits, institute integrity measures, etc.). Not unlike the fraudsters themselves, then, the advocates secretly believe the Other has some exclusive path to happiness, some secret to life. Their envy is grounded in the (mis)perception of the object causing their lack: "this illusion sustains the longing to regain the lost object, as if this object has a positive substantial identity independently of its being lost" (Žižek 2001, 68). The anticorruption advocates, in this sense, *need* the fraudsters (i.e., they have a libidinal interest in them), in order to sustain their enjoyment and indeed to keep the anticorruption business in business.

Consequently, envy and enjoyment are what enable the effectivity of the ideology of corruption. It is because people get libidinally invested in the practices of (anti)corruption that they end up believing in the ideology. They get so caught up in everyday survival (low-level corruption) or in the thrills of envy and enjoyment (high-level corruption, anticorruption advocacy) that the relationship between corruption and capitalism/inequality is in effect masked. They may get mad and frustrated at having to pay bribes, they may demand that perpetrators be caught and publicly shamed, but ultimately all this becomes an (enjoyable) "ritual practice" to purge and sublimate public anger, "thus allowing normal practice to continue" (Girling 1997, viii). Corruption at low and high levels, as much as efforts to fight it, become mutually reinforcing endeavors sustained by envy and enjoyment, all of which ensures that capitalism and inequality continue unabated.

## Conclusion

I have attempted to show how capitalist development uses and abuses envy to ensure its survival. Indeed, the spatial and socioeconomic inequality inherent in the capitalist system depends on and encourages upward and downward social comparisons to drive competition and entrepreneurialism, while also

naturalizing social hierarchy through the propagation of beliefs in equal opportunity, hard work, fate, and so forth. But the problem with envy is its excessive
preoccupation with the Other's enjoyment, as evidenced today by the rise of
such phenomena as religious fundamentalist violence or mob vandalism and
looting. I have dwelled, in particular, on two areas where such malicious envy
manifests to varying degrees: consumption, premised on the subject coveting
the Other's *jouissance*, while sidelining the socioeconomic strife and exploitation
required to keep worry-free consumerism going; and high-level corruption and
its corollary—anticorruption advocacy—which mutually reinforce one another
in enjoyably sadomasochistic ways. Both examples demonstrate how envy is
integral to capitalist development, helping to sustain growth and inequality.

But the question that now arises is: can envy be oriented toward social justice? Freud suggests that it can, because it is in fact the very condition of social justice. He writes that social collectivities derive from "envy. No one must
want to put himself forward, every one must be the same and have the same.
Social justice means that we deny ourselves many things so that others may
have to do without them as well, or, what is the same thing, may not be able
to ask for them. This demand for equality is the root of social conscience and
the sense of duty" (1949, 88). Envy is thus not a barrier to justice (as Rawls
suggests) but its prerequisite, since the demand for justice implies that the Other's enjoyment be limited in order that everyone have equal access to enjoyment (Copjec 2002, 165; Žižek 2006, 37; 2008b, 89).

The problem is that, within the current capitalist socioeconomic coordi-
nates, envy in the service of social justice risks resulting in the revenge of the
"weak" over the elites (i.e., eliminating the Other in order to access enjoyment). This is what Sloterdijk (2010, 213ff.) suggests has been the fate of such
"revolutionary" movements as communism and political Islam, often culmi-
nating in the mere replacement of one elite by another (i.e., apparatchiks and
mullahs instead of capitalists). But Žižek takes him to task, accusing him of
too easily "denouncing every global emancipatory project as a case of envy
and resentment. Wherefrom his obsessive-compulsive urge to find beneath
solidarity the envy of the weak and their thirst for revenge?" (2008b, 194).[14]
While readily acknowledging that envy can take the form of vindictiveness
of the oppressed, Žižek gestures toward an "authentic resentment" (2008b,
190; see also Copjec 2002, 165; Zalloua 2012, 56–57) that is oriented toward a
demand for equality, as a result of which, and in keeping with Freud's above
proposition, people agree to submit themselves to the same limitations on
enjoyment as they submit to the Other.

This implies a thoroughgoing politicization of envy. It means fiercely resisting the status quo by refusing to accede to the enjoyment of elites (celebrities,

the rich, the powerful), since that would result in merely replacing one privilege with another, thus perpetuating inequality. Envy in the service of social justice involves a movement away from neoliberal hyperindividualism, which readily aspires to the entitlements of elites, in favor of a collective ethicopolitical stance that involves an agreement to *curb* entitlements for all. The challenge here is not merely refusing to be seduced by the goodies offered by the System, or fighting uncompromisingly against inequality—no small tasks themselves—but also facing up to the stupidity of envy. As Todd McGowan puts it,

> The antagonism between the society and the individual develops out of the envy that subjects experience when they believe other members of the society have greater access to the privileged object than they do. For the subject who grasps that this object only exists—and can only be enjoyed—through its loss, envy is no longer inevitable. The composition of nothing is such that no one can have more of it than anyone else; there can be no hierarchy of loss, because everyone alike loses nothing. The authentic society of subjects connected through the embrace of trauma would be a society that could recognize that nothing is something after all. (2013, 165–166)

Indeed, the significant psychoanalytic and political test of social justice is learning to embrace common loss (of enjoyment): collectively understanding that this loss is everyone's to bear, so that no one really loses more than anyone else because there is nothing actually lost in the first place. So it is not just about appreciating that wealth does not necessarily lead to the (capitalist) "good life" (or "happiness"), especially when such wealth is achieved at the expense of others; but also about coming to terms with the fact that the good life or happiness is itself an ideological fantasy covering up the antagonism and loss that lies at the heart of sociohuman existence.

Implied in such a politicization of envy is its universalization. That is, solidarity among and between groups struggling against global development is to be forged on the basis not of shared identity (as workers, urban youth, queers, women, environmentalists, etc.), which often disunites people across class/gender/spatial divides, but common loss—the shared experience of being marginalized by the neoliberal capitalist order (see chapters 3, 8, and 12). Envy here is transformed into a desire for egalitarian justice for all (i.e., enjoyment of common loss and social justice), rather than a demand for socioeconomic privilege or recognition of particular identities and rights. Drawing on Žižek, Zahi Zalloua perspicaciously calls this the "'public use of *ressentiment*' for the (potentially) Excluded . . . staged as the uncompromising feeling for social justice . . . [so that it transforms into] a collective moral feeling, based on a shared but unacceptable condition of exclusion" (2012, 62). This collective and solidary form of envy is one in which people join together by refusing to allow such social traumas as inequality and dispossession to be normalized, domesticated, or reproduced.

Finally, a crucial ingredient for the politicization of envy is a vision of social justice. Part of the weakness of recent urban youth protests in the global South, as pointed out earlier, has been their lack of such a vision, causing them not only to have little significant or lasting political impact but ultimately to be tolerated by those in power. In this regard, Žižek expresses doubt about similar recent movements such as the 2005 Paris youth uprising, the 2011 London riots, or the 2018–2019 "Yellow Vest" populist demonstrations across France (Žižek 2005; 2011c; 2018): while certainly symptomatic of growing socioeconomic marginalization and inequality, each has tended to show opposition to the System but without a realistic or meaningful utopic project: "this is the fatal weakness of recent protests: they express an authentic rage which is not able to transform itself into a positive programme of sociopolitical change" (Žižek 2011c). These movements might well be spontaneous and leaderless outbursts directed at the System, yet that is precisely their Achilles's heel—what they lack is "a leader who would not only listen to the people but translate their protest into a new, coherent vision of society" (Žižek 2018).

Which is to say that the politicization of envy, while possible and (arguably) politically desirable, is certainly never given or guaranteed. It is contingent on so very much, including political and psychoanalytic resolve, leadership, organization, vision, timing, and so on (hence the relative "success" of the Tunisian, in contrast to the Egyptian, revolution; see chapter 9). In any case, were envy to be miraculously[15] deployed to destabilize rather than maintain the System, there would be no getting rid of it: even in a society of relative egalitarian justice, the pathology of the envy of the Other would continue to function as antagonism, decidedly preventing any (lasting) social harmony, collectivity, or solidarity.

# Notes

1. In fact, the French word for tip is *pourboire* ("for drinking"), that is, "drink-money" for your (less fortunate) server, with the English term "tip" similarly deriving from the old English "tipple," meaning drink (Foster 1972, 181). Today, the practice of tipping is often couched as rewarding the server for her/his service, but it can (also or mainly) be seen as an individual act of charity that attempts to lessen the gap (the socioeconomic inequality) separating the patron from the server, thereby trying to ward off

the latter's envy. Only in a handful of countries is tipping a rarity these days—in Denmark, for example, where waiters/waitresses tend to be paid well enough that no tip is generally required or expected.

2. The gaze is key to Freud's understanding of envy (1949; 1977), too, since his argument about "penis envy" is rooted in a girl's desirous gaze on the male organ (a biologism for which he has been roundly criticized). For her part, Melanie Klein (1957) makes envy central to her understanding of child development, with the child *perceiving* the mother's breast as both a "good" object (providing a sense of safety and security) and a "bad" one (causing intense frustration when the infant realizes it cannot possess the coveted object).

3. Of course jealousy also involves fantasy, but jealousy's fantasy revolves around the object, while envy's revolves around enjoyment (one's own, but mediated through the Other's).

4. These responses themselves generate further crises, such as when "derivatives" contribute to market crashes, as they did in 2008.

5. Göran Therborn (2013) argues that such inequality can be measured not just in terms of the widening gaps in income or wealth but also in terms of health and lifespan, which in turn affect people's dignity and freedom.

6. This is why envy, more than egoism, is the appropriate social passion of our times: egoism is self-enclosing, more preoccupied with the self, whereas envy is *relational and comparative*, more preoccupied with others. Egoism describes, for example, rich people consumed by their wealth, while envy describes rich people deriving pleasure from their superiority over, and undermining of, others in the social hierarchy. The insidiousness of envy is that one can obsess about the Other's enjoyment to the point of hostility and violence, sometimes even being compelled to act against one's own interest as long as it means sabotaging the Other's (e.g., the suicide bomber, risking his life to inflict suffering on others). Thus, Žižek claims, the "true opposite of egoistic self-love is not altruism, a concern for the common Good, but envy, *ressentiment*, which makes me act *against* my own interests" (2008a, 346; 2008b, 87; see also Zalloua 2012, 55).

7. Rebroadcasts, variations, and spin-offs of *Who Wants to be a Millionaire?* have appeared in such countries as in the Philippines, Mauritius, Sri Lanka, Venezuela, and Chile; of *The Apprentice* in Nigeria, Ghana, Tanzania, Lebanon, Colombia, and Vietnam; of *Survivor* in Botswana, Ethiopia, Namibia, Argentina, Brazil, Ecuador, Pakistan, and Turkey; and of *Amazing Race* in Brunei, Cambodia, Malaysia, Mongolia, Papua New Guinea, Costa Rica, Curaçao, Guyana, Jamaica, and Trinidad and Tobago. See the Wikipedia entries for these shows for a full list of countries.

8. Belk is Kraft Foods Canada Chair in Marketing at the Schulich School of Business, York University (the university where I work, too). His ideological position thus appears to reflect his professional title and position, bearing witness to the increasing corporatization of the university in which we academics function.

9. The recent leaks of the Panama and Paradise papers have exposed the pervasive use of shady (although not always "illegal") offshore tax regimes by global elites and corporations, involving world leaders and/or their families (e.g., Nawaz Sharif, Xi Jinping, Najib Razak, Jacob Zuma, Kojo Annan, Luis Caputo, Blairo Borges Maggi, Jayant Sinha, Alaa Mubarak, Ahmed al-Mirghani, Hamad bin Khalifa Al Thani, Mounir Majidi, Sam Nujoma, Vladimir Putin, David Cameron, Marine Le Pen, Queen Noor, the Spanish and Qatari Royal families, etc.), celebrities (Jackie Chan, Amitabh Bach-

chan, Edith Gonzalez, Willian, Sarah Ferguson, Mark Thatcher, etc.), and corporate brands (Apple, Facebook, Twitter, Glencore, Grupo Salinas, UBS Bank, Hinduja Group, Jindal Steel, etc.) (see Harding 2016; Pegg 2017).

10. High-level corruption frequently involves extensive networks of foreign (often corporate) and local actors, including low-level government officials and intermediaries. And while the latter may be in it simply to cope / survive, they are nonetheless part of a network aimed at accumulating wealth and power for the benefit of high-level actors and elites. Low-level corruption (corruption as coping mechanism) is thus linked to, and in the service of, high-level corruption (corruption as wealth accumulation). The two types of corruption are related and often mutually reinforcing (although the latter is dominant / more powerful, while the former is more widespread / common).

11. But the same research suggests the opposite may also be true: delaying approval processes can be a way for civil servants to extract more and higher bribes (Bardhan 1997, 1322–1323); which is to say, once again, that the correlation between democratic development and corruption is weak at best, and that this line of thinking diverts from the actual correlation—between capitalist-induced inequality and corruption.

12. Several Third World government agencies, political parties, and members of the judiciary are fervent supporters of anticorruption measures (e.g., Afghanistan's National Procurement Authority, India's Aam Aadmi Party, Brazil's anticorruption judge and Minister of Justice Sergio Moro, etc.).

13. My implication is that there is nothing necessarily wrong with anticorruption measures per se, only with those that fail to target its causes. It is the latter that end up being depoliticized, neocolonial, and moral, blaming individuals and culture rather than socioeconomic structures, and Third World states (which are of course not blameless) rather than global inequality.

14. Žižek appears to be implying that Sloterdijk's generalized suspicion of social justice movements may itself be rooted in envy!

15. There are of course always excuses for people *not* to act and so many reasons for which protest movements don't happen or fail—repression or co-optation by the System, lack of resources and organization, or political will and determination, and so on. Nonetheless, radical movements can and *do* materialize. Žižek often muses that sometimes "miracles happen" (see for example Žižek 2011b; Žižek and Daly 2004, 139ff.), which is to say that sometimes people can and do act *despite* all the excuses and reasons not to: they act because it must be done, uncoupling from the big Other (which dictates why and what we should and shouldn't do), falling into the void, so to speak. This for Žižek is the expression of the true political Act (see also chapter 12).

# References

Amin, Samir. 1976. *Unequal Development: An Essay on the Social Formations of Peripheral Capitalism*. New York: Monthly Review.

Appel, Helmut, Alexander L. Gerlach, and Jan Crusius. 2016. "The Interplay between Facebook Use, Social Comparison, Envy, and Depression." *Current Opinion in Psychology* 9 (June): 44–49. https://doi.org/10.1016/j.copsyc.2015.10.006.

Augustine. 1980. *Confessions*. Translated by R. S. Pine-Coffin. Harmondsworth: Penguin.

Awa, Eme O. 1964. *Federal Government in Nigeria*. Berkeley: University of California Press.

Bardhan, Pranab. 1997. "Corruption and Development: A Review of Issues." *Journal of Economic Literature* 35 (3): 1320–1346.

Barr, Caelainn. 2017. "Inequality Index: Where Are the World's Most Unequal Countries?" *The Guardian*, April 26. https://www.theguardian.com/inequality /datablog/2017/apr/26/inequality-index-where-are-the-worlds-most-unequal -countries.

BBC. 2016. "Wealth of Top 1% 'Equal to Other 99%.'" BBC Business, January 18. https://www.bbc.com/news/business-35339475.

Belk, Russell. 2011. "Benign Envy." *AMS Review* 1 (December): 117–134.

Böhm, Steffen, and Aanka Batta. 2010. "Just Doing It: Enjoying Commodity Fetishism with Lacan." *Organization* 17 (3): 345–361.

Brehm, John, and Scott Gates. 2010. *Working, Shirking, and Sabotage: Bureaucratic Response to a Democratic Public*. Ann Arbor: University of Michigan Press.

Bretton Woods Project. 2006. "The World Bank Weeds out Corruption: Will It Touch the Roots?" Bretton Woods Project, April 8. https://www .brettonwoodsproject.org/2006/04/art-531789/.

Bukovansky, Mlada. 2006. "The Hollowness of Anti-Corruption Discourse." *Review of International Political Economy* 13 (2): 181–209.

Caiden, Gerald E. 2009. "A Parabolic Theory of Bureaucracy or Max Weber through the Looking Glass." In *Bureaucracy and Administration*, edited by Ali Farazmand, 111–124. Boca Raton, FL: CRC.

Cardoso, Fernando Henrique, and Enzo Faletto. 1979. *Dependency and Development in Latin America*. Berkeley: University of California Press.

Clapham, Christopher, ed. 1982. *Private Patronage and Public Power: Political Clientelism in the Modern State*. London: Frances Pinter.

Copjec, Joan. 2002. *Imagine There's No Woman: Ethics and Sublimation*. Cambridge, MA: MIT Press.

Deleuze, Gilles, and Félix Guattari. 1977. *Anti-Oedipus: Capitalism and Schizophrenia*. Translated by Robert Hurley, Mark Seem, and Helen R. Lane. New York: Viking.

Della Porta, Donatella, and Alberto Vannucci. 1999. *Corrupt Exchanges: Actors, Resources, and Mechanisms of Political Corruption*. New York: Aldine de Gruyter.

Diawara, Manthia. 2009. *In Search of Africa*. Cambridge, MA: Harvard University Press.

Dicken, Peter. 2009. "The World Is 'Not' Flat: The Intense Geographical Unevenness of Globalization." In *The Multiple Faces of Globalization*, edited by Francisco González. BBVA Group. https://www.bbvaopenmind.com/en/articles/the -world-is-not-flat-the-intense-geographical-unevenness-of-globalization/.

Dupuy, Jean-Pierre. 2013. *The Mark of the Sacred*. Stanford, CA: Stanford University Press.

Foster, George M. 1972. "The Anatomy of Envy: A Study in Symbolic Behavior." *Current Anthropology* 13 (2): 165–202.

Frank, Andre Gunder. 1967. *Capitalism and Underdevelopment in Latin America*. New York: Monthly Review.

Freud, Sigmund. 1949. *Group Psychology and the Analysis of the Ego*. Translated by James Strachey. London: Hogarth.

——. 1977. *On Sexuality: Three Essays on the Theory of Sexuality and Other Works*. Edited by James Strachey. Harmondsworth: Penguin.

Galeano, Eduardo. 1990. "The Other Wall." *New Internationalist* 213 (November). https://newint.org/features/1990/11/05/other.

Gell, Alfred. 1986. "Newcomers to the World of Goods: Consumption among the Muria Gonds." In *The Social Life of Things*, edited by Arjun Appadurai, 110–138. Cambridge: Cambridge University Press.

Gilbert, Zanna. 2016. "Bureaucratic Sabotage: Knocking at the Door of the 'Big Monster.'" In *Sabotage Art: Politics and Iconoclasm in Contemporary Latin America*, edited by Sophie Halart and Mara Polgovsky Ezcurra, 84–104. London: I. B. Tauris.

Girling, John. 1997. *Corruption, Capitalism and Democracy*. London: Routledge.

Greenwood, Xavier. 2018. "South Africa Is the Most Unequal Country in the World, Says World Bank." *Independent*, April 4. https://www.independent.co.uk /news/world/africa/south-africa-unequal-country-poverty-legacy-apartheid -world-bank-a8288986.html.

Gupta, Akhil. 2012. *Red Tape: Bureaucracy, Structural Violence and Poverty in India*. Durham, NC: Duke University Press.

Harding, Luke. 2016. "What Are the Panama Papers? A Guide to History's Biggest Data Leak." *The Guardian*, April 5. https://www.theguardian.com/news /2016/apr/03/what-you-need-to-know-about-the-panama-papers.

Harvey, David. 2004. "The 'New' Imperialism: Accumulation by Dispossession." *Socialist Register* 40: 63–87.

——. 2006. *Spaces of Global Capitalism*. London: Verso.

Hickel, Jason. 2017. "Is Global Inequality Getting Better or Worse? A Critique of the World Bank's Convergence Narrative." *Third World Quarterly* 38 (10): 2208–2222.

Hill, Ronald. 2011. "Why Consumers In Poor Countries Try Harder To 'Keep Up With The Joneses.'" *Forbes*, November 16. https://www.forbes.com/sites /onmarketing/2011/11/16/why-consumers-in-poor-countries-try-harder-to -keep-up-with-the-joneses/.

Ibekwe, Chux. 2014. "Corruption in Oil Revenue Distribution and Conflict in Bayelsa State, Nigeria." PhD diss., International Conflict Management, Kennesaw State University, Georgia. https://digitalcommons.kennesaw.edu /cgi/viewcontent.cgi?article=1001&context=incmdoc_etd.

Iqani, Mehita. 2016. *Consumption, Media and the Global South: Aspiration Contested*. Basingstoke: Palgrave Macmillan.

Kaster, Robert A. 2005. *Emotion, Restraint, and Community in Ancient Rome*. Oxford: Oxford University Press.

Klein, Melanie. 1957. *Envy and Gratitude: A Study of Unconscious Sources*. London: Tavistock.

Krasnova, Hanna, Helena Wenninger, Thomas Widjaja, and Peter Buxmann. 2013. "Envy on Facebook: A Hidden Threat to Users' Life Satisfaction?" In *Proceedings*

*of the 11th International Conference on Wirtschaftsinformatik (WI2013)*, 2:1477–
    1491. Universität Leipzig, Germany. https://boris.unibe.ch/47080/.

Lacan, Jacques. 1998a. *Encore. On Feminine Sexuality, the Limits of Love and Knowledge:*
    *The Seminar of Jacques Lacan, Book XX.* Edited by Jacques-Alain Miller.
    Translated by Bruce Fink. New York: Norton.

——. 1998b. *The Four Fundamental Concepts of Psychoanalysis: The Seminar of Jacques*
    *Lacan, Book XI.* Edited by Jacques-Alain Miller. New York: W.W. Norton.

Leng, Sidney. 2017. "China's Dirty Little Secret: Its Growing Wealth Gap." *South*
    *China Morning Post,* July 7. https://www.scmp.com/news/china/economy
    /article/2101775/chinas-rich-grabbing-bigger-slice-pie-ever.

Marx, Karl. 1990. *Capital.* Vol. 1. Translated by Ben Fowkes. Harmondsworth:
    Penguin.

Mbembe, Achille. 2001. *On the Postcolony.* Berkeley: University of California Press.

McGowan, Todd. 2004. *The End of Dissatisfaction? Jacques Lacan and the Emerging*
    *Society of Enjoyment.* Albany: SUNY Press.

——. 2013. *Enjoying What We Don't Have: The Political Project of Psychoanalysis.*
    Lincoln: University of Nebraska Press.

Mitchell, Timothy. 2011. *Carbon Democracy: Political Power in the Age of Oil.* London:
    Verso.

Mueller, Barbara. 1996. *International Advertising: Communicating Across Cultures.*
    Belmont: Wadsworth.

Olupohunda, Bayo. 2016. "The Cost of Vandalising Public Properties." Punch,
    April 12. https://punchng.com/the-cost-of-vandalising-public-properties/.

Onoge, Femi O. 1983. "Corruption and the Nigerian Social System: Notes for a
    Materialist Ethnography." In *Nigeria: Corruption in Development,* edited by Femi
    Odekunle. 1982 Proceedings of the Nigerian Anthropological and Sociologi-
    cal Association. Ibadan: Ibadan University Press.

Oxfam International. 2018. "Brazil: Extreme Inequality in Numbers." Oxfam
    International, November 13. https://www.oxfam.org/en/even-it-brazil
    /brazil-extreme-inequality-numbers.

Pegg, David. 2017. "Paradise Papers: Who's Who in the Leak of Offshore Secrets."
    *The Guardian,* November 11. https://www.theguardian.com/news/ng
    -interactive/2017/nov/11/paradise-papers-whos-who-leak-offshore-secrets.

Piketty, Thomas. 2014. *Capital in the Twenty-First Century.* Translated by Arthur
    Goldhammer. Cambridge, MA: Belknap Press of Harvard University Press.

Poon, Patrick. 2018. "Judge Attacks Civil Servant's Excuse for Web Site Attack."
    *South China Morning Post,* December 23. https://www.scmp.com/article
    /388340/judge-attacks-civil-servants-excuse-web-site-attack.

Pope, Jeremy. 2000. *TI Source Book: Confronting Corruption. The Elements of a National*
    *Integrity System.* Berlin: Transparency International.

Prashad, Vijay. 2012. *The Poorer Nations: A Possible History of the Global South.* London:
    Verso.

Rawls, John. 1999. *A Theory of Justice.* Cambridge, MA: Belknap Press of Harvard
    University Press.

Raynolds, Laura T. 2017. "Bridging North/South Divides through Consumer-Driven
    Networks." In *Routledge Handbook on Consumption,* edited by Margit Keller,

Bente Halkier, Terhi-Anna Wilska, and Monica Truninger, 167–178. London and New York: Routledge.

Rose-Ackerman, Susan. 1978. *Corruption: A Study in Political Economy*. New York: Academic.

Rousseau, Jean-Jacques. 2011. *The Basic Political Writings*. Translated by Donald A. Cress. 2nd ed. Indianapolis, IN: Hackett.

Sassen, Saskia. 2006. *Cities in a World Economy*. 3rd ed. Thousand Oaks, CA: Pine Forge.

Sile, Aza Wee. 2017. "These Are the World's Most Corrupt Countries." CNBC, January 24. https://www.cnbc.com/2017/01/24/these-are-the-worlds-most-corrupt-countries.html.

Sloterdijk, Peter. 2010. *Rage and Time: A Psychopolitical Investigation*. New York: Columbia University Press.

Smith, Neil. 1991. *Uneven Development: Nature, Capital, and the Production of Space*. Oxford: Blackwell.

Stavrakakis, Yannis. 2006. "Objects of Consumption, Causes of Desire: Consumerism and Advertising in Societies of Commanded Enjoyment." *Gramma* 14: 83–105.

Storm, Servaas. 2018. "Financial Markets Have Taken Over the Economy: To Prevent Another Crisis, They Must Be Brought to Heel." Institute for New Economic Thinking, February 13. https://www.ineteconomics.org/perspectives/blog/financial-markets-have-taken-over-the-economy-to-stop-the-next-crisis-they-must-be-brought-to-heel.

Szeftel, Morris. 2000. "Between Governance & Under-development: Accumulation & Africa's 'Catastrophic Corruption.'" *Review of African Political Economy* 27 (84): 287–306.

Taylor, Peter J. 2004. *World City Network: A Global Urban Analysis*. London: Routledge.

Therborn, Göran. 2013. *The Killing Fields of Inequality*. Cambridge: Polity.

Trentmann, Frank. 2016. *Empire of Things: How We Became a World of Consumers, from the Fifteenth Century to the Twenty-First*. New York: HarperCollins.

Vidaillet, Benedicte. 2007. "Lacanian Theory's Contribution to the Study of Workplace Envy." *Human Relations* 60 (11): 1669–1700.

——. 2008. "Psychoanalytic Contributions to Understanding Envy: Classic and Contemporary Perspectives." In *Envy: Theory and Research*, edited by Richard H. Smith, 267–289. Oxford: Oxford University Press.

Wallerstein, Immanuel Maurice. 2004. *World-Systems Analysis: An Introduction*. Durham, NC: Duke University Press.

World Bank. 1997a. *Helping Countries Combat Corruption: The Role of the World Bank*. Washington, DC: World Bank.

——. 1997b. *World Development Report 1997: The State in a Changing World*. Washington DC: World Bank.

——. 2013. "Corruption Is 'Public Enemy Number One' in Developing Countries, Says World Bank Group President Kim." World Bank, December 29. http://www.worldbank.org/en/news/press-release/2013/12/19/corruption-developing-countries-world-bank-group-president-kim.

———. 2018. "Combating Corruption." World Bank, October 4. http://www
.worldbank.org/en/topic/governance/brief/anti-corruption.

Wrenn, Mary V. 2015. "Envy in Neoliberalism: Revisiting Veblen's Emulation and
Invidious Distinction." *Journal of Economic Issues* 49 (2): 503–510.

Yousef, Tarik. 2003. "Youth in the Middle East and North Africa: Demography,
Employment, and Conflict." In *Youth Explosion in Developing World Cities:
Approaches to Reducing Poverty and Conflict in an Urban Age*, edited by Blair A.
Ruble, Joseph S. Tulchin, Diana H. Varat, and Lisa M. Hanley, 9–24. Washington, DC: Woodrow Wilson International Center for Scholars.

Zalloua, Zahi. 2012. "Betting on Ressentiment: Žižek with Nietzsche." *Symploke*
20 (1–2): 53–63.

Žižek, Slavoj. 2001. *On Belief*. London: Routledge.

———. 2005. "Some Politically Incorrect Reflections on Violence in France and
Related Matters." Lacan.Com. http://www.lacan.com/zizfrance.htm.

———. 2006. *How to Read Lacan*. London: Granta.

———. 2007. "Multitude, Surplus, and Envy." *Rethinking Marxism* 19 (1): 46–58.

———. 2008a. *In Defense of Lost Causes*. London: Verso.

———. 2008b. *Violence: Six Sideways Reflections*. New York: Picador.

———. 2011a. *Living in the End Times*. London: Verso.

———. 2011b. "For Egypt, This Is the Miracle of Tahrir Square." *The Guardian*,
February 10. https://www.theguardian.com/global/2011/feb/10/egypt
-miracle-tahrir-square.

———. 2011c. "Shoplifters of the World Unite." *London Review of Books*. 33 (16),
August 19. http://www.lrb.co.uk/2011/08/19/slavoj-zizek/shoplifters-of-the
-world-unite.

———. 2018. "How Mao Would Have Evaluated the Yellow Vests." RT, December 21.
https://www.rt.com/op-ed/447155-zizek-yellow-vests-france/.

Žižek, Slavoj, and Glyn Daly. 2004. *Conversations with Žižek*. Cambridge: Polity.

# CHAPTER 6

# Fetishism in International Development

## Domination, Disavowal, and Foreclosure

KEYWORD: *Fetishism*

## Introduction

The term "fetish" comes to us from the Latin *factīcius*, meaning artificial or manufactured, and the late medieval Portuguese word *feitiço*, meaning charm or allurement. It was reportedly used by Portuguese explorers and traders to describe the worshipping practices of fifteenth-century West Coast Africans, wherein objects were revered for their mysterious and magical powers (Böhm and Batta 2010, 348; Pietz 1985). Later, during the height of European imperialism (seventeenth to nineteenth centuries), the term was popularized as a way of distinguishing Europe from its colonized Others: the European saw himself as master of his own destiny—rational and enlightened—in contrast to the colonized, constructed as men of nature, primitive, fetishistic, superstitious.

Psychoanalytic thought from Freud onward draws on this etymology but adds an unconscious dimension to it: the fetish is not just a pleasurable and magical object, it is also one that enables the subject to (unconsciously) deny the harshness of reality. As a substitute for fundamental trauma, the fetish is a site of disavowal, allowing the subject to better master her world by ridding it of lack and difference. Additionally, by behaving single-mindedly toward the fetish object as if it possesses a sublime quality, the fetishist forecloses other possible worthy objects or sociopolitical goals. Mastery, disavowal, and foreclosure thus become the hallmarks of fetishism.

In this chapter, I apply these psychoanalytic insights to international development—particularly its dominant Modernization variant—by focusing on two of the latter's top fetishes: growth and technology. I examine how to each fetish is ascribed extraordinary powers (e.g., prosperity, progress, super-intelligence), with several important socioenvironmental implications: the domination of the Other (i.e., the Third World, the subaltern, nature); the dis-avowal of social inequalities and environmental degradation; and the fore-closure of politics.

## Psychoanalysis and Fetishism

According to Freud, fetishism relates to the "phallic phase" of childhood de-velopment, during which the child experiences castration anxiety: the boy's first sight of his mother's genitals causes a deep fear that his own penis will be cut off. His unconscious recourse is to adopt a fetish to ward off this anxiety, with fur and velvet as the most likely fetish objects as they recall the sight of pubic hair (in addition to feet, shoes, and underclothing, imagery that crystal-lizes the moment of his mother's undressing). As Freud puts it, "the fetish is a substitute for the woman's (the mother's) penis that the little boy once be-lieved in and . . . does not want to give up" (1977, 351–352).

What are significant are the unconscious processes at play here. While the horror of female castration leads to unmistakable disavowal, Freud suggests a dual attitude of sustaining a belief that the child simultaneously denies (1977, 352). That is, the child knows very well that the woman does not have a penis but all the same believes she does (this is what Žižek famously calls "fetishistic disavowal"; see Žižek 1989, 18; see also chapter 1). The result none-theless is the boy's disavowal of sexual difference. His is an attempt to control his environment by resorting to a fetish, thereby denying, covering up, his trauma. The fetishist, in this sense, attempts to master his world through a fantasy of sameness.

Lacan extends the Freudian notion of fetishism to the wider symbolic realm, shedding both its androcentrism and biologism. For him, the "phallus" is not a sexual organ but a signifier of our inherent lack as linguistic beings (Lacan 1977, 312; see also Tomšič 2015, 179). The result is that disavowal and castration anxiety are symptoms for everyone—and for people of any gender (not just men, as in Freud)—with the fetish helping to fill out the void of our fundamen-tal lack (see chapter 8). Of course, the Lacanian notion of the fetish retains the

Freudian meaning of a substitute for that which must remain repressed, a prosthetic organ of lack aimed at soothing and controlling one's world.

In addition to seeing the fetish as a site of mastery or control and the disavowal of difference, Lacan and Lacanians underline other related mechanisms (see, for example, Cowie 1997, 261–281; Dean 2008, 112–115; Evans 2006, 64–66; Lacan 1977, 157, 160; 1988, 43–59), including:

- *displacement*: the fetish is not simply a substitute for castration and loss, it is also an object onto which the fetishist displaces her fantasies of authority and mastery by assigning her fetish magical powers; she overinvests it in order to give the banal a sense of the extraordinary;
- *jouissance* (enjoyment): the phallus for Lacan is a signifier of both lack *and* enjoyment, with the result that the fetish acts not just as cover for loss but also as pleasurable object. The fetishist becomes greatly attached to his chosen object for comforting and reassuring him (against trauma), as well as for enchanting him (with its spellbinding powers);
- *condensation*: this is about the "superimposition of signifiers" so that one signifier becomes a substitute for a chain of signifiers. Lacan associates condensation with the metaphor, which abbreviates, erases, or mystifies meaning (e.g., "big is better"). The fetish thus becomes a symptom of a repressed or disavowed content; and
- *foreclosure*: by narrowly fixating on an object, by reducing and simplifying the world in order to better master it, the fetishist excludes difference, foreclosing anything that cannot be assimilated into it.

There are, therefore, multiple operations at work under the rubric of fetishism, and although I will refer to all of them, in what follows I will emphasize those relating to mastery, disavowal, and foreclosure (counting "condensation" as a form of disavowal). Our next task, then, is to examine how these intersect with the field of international development, particularly its fetishization of growth and technology.[1]

# Growth Fetish

## The Fetishization of Growth

Economic growth has undoubtedly been the main fixation of modernity, whether in the West or the global South. Governments of the Right as much as the Left have made achieving it *the* top priority, to such an extent that growth has become a question of national pride, holding out the promise of happiness and bliss (Hamilton 2004, 4). Today, the question of growth grips China like never before, so much so that annual GNP growth rates of less than 5 percent are seen as less than adequate; but of course economic modernization has been the key preoccupation of all post-colonial states since at least the Second World War. In India, for example, large-scale industrialization was the hallmark of Nehru's 1950s "socialist" economic planning, a priority that endures even today, albeit under Modi's right-wing, neoliberal leadership. Similarly, in Turkey, modernization has been the longstanding goal of the state since the advent of the modern republic, with the idea of catching up with the West a matter of national urgency. The stated commitment of successive Turkish governments has been rapid economic growth, supported by modern science and technology and the need to overcome "backward and traditional institutions and values" (Akbulut and Adaman 2014; Bozdoğan and Kasaba 1997). Like in many other post-colonial states, Turkey's economic policies have focused on large-scale public works (dams, highways, power plants, bridges, canals) to sustain a modern capitalist economy, and increasingly, the privatization of public services and lands, ostensibly to stimulate economic and urban "renewal."

At least part of the impetus to prioritize growth in the global South has come from Modernization theory, whose ideological grip on international development since the 1950s cannot be overstated. True, during the Cold War years, (neo-)Marxist development theory, which also advocated a growth-oriented worldview despite being critical of global capitalism, *did* present an ideological challenge to Modernization (see Kapoor 2008, 19ff.). But it is Modernization's procapitalist bandwagon that appears to have won the day, especially in the wake of the fall of the Berlin Wall and the onset of neoliberal globalization.

As Peet and Hartwick put it (2009, 104), "Modernization theory basically says: if you want to develop, be like us (the West)"—a dictum that most "developing" countries appear to have followed by and large. Indeed, Modernization constructs development as an evolutionary process moving from "tradition" to modernity, with the ideal end-state exemplified by Western capitalist liberal democracies. The expansion of capitalist markets is spotlighted, with the modernization of "backward" economies requiring specialization of economic activities, bolstered by science, technology, and communications (see Eisenstadt 1973; Peet and Hartwick 2009, 122). Even the "psycho-cultural" version of Modernization (Lerner 1958; McClelland 1967) is strongly growth-centered advocating the need for not local or indigenous cultural values but only those "modern" (read: Western) ones that will ensure capitalist accumulation—individual achievement, ambition, entrepreneurialism, scientific reasoning, urbanity.

Much of such thinking is encapsulated by Walt Rostow's notorious book *The Stages of Economic Growth: A Non-Communist Manifesto* (1960). As is well known, he prescribes five stages that all societies must go through to become modern: traditional societies, preconditions for take-off, take-off, the drive toward maturity, and high mass consumption. And as chapter 1 emphasized, lest we think that such blatantly ethnocentric and ideological argumentation is tired or passé, we only have to look at Jeffrey Sachs's popular and influential *The End of Poverty* (2005) to be disabused of the idea. Sachs mostly reproduces Rostow's universalist and evolutionary history, defending a capitalist model of growth and even prescribing "ladders of economic development."

The neoclassical economics that grounds Modernization theory, and mainstream economic thinking generally, is decidedly positivist, putting a heavy onus on the need to measure and quantify growth. Not surprisingly, this tendency to mathematize economics has its origins in the development of capitalism itself: Frank Swetz (2012) shows, for example, that the elaboration of algorithms and abstract calculation coincides with the early rise of mercantilism, facilitating the increasingly complex activities of bankers, money changers, and traders. Since then, much economic theorizing—from equilibrium theory and Keynesian economics to contemporary computerized economic modeling and forecasting—hinges on such mathematization, to the point of mathematics itself becoming the economist's fetish (Benson 2008, 11–12; Zein-Elabdin 2004, 105–6).

The most significant measure of growth has become gross national product (GNP), which is the total annual money value of all domestic goods and services produced in a country.[2] Despite the availability of many less narrowly economic indicators (e.g., Human Development Index, Index for Social Progress, Genuine Progress Indicator), it is GNP that dominates global development discourse, and has done so since the Second World War. As Clive Hamilton suggests, "GNP appears to provide a measure of prosperity that is immune to argument" (2004, 2). It is a key indicator of economic performance for governments, donors, and global economic organizations alike (World Bank, International Monetary Fund, World Trade Organization), guiding them in socioeconomic policy making or foreign aid and debt computations. Perhaps most importantly, it has become the principle global measure of economic success and failure—a comparative tool that ranks national economies along a developed/developing/least-developed scale. GNP has thus enabled a global economic hierarchy, constructing the top Western countries as models, especially when it comes to the need to structurally adjust "failing" developing economies.

## A Psychoanalysis of the Growth Fetish

Since resorting to a fetish is, as we saw earlier, about the disavowal of trauma that results in the denial of (sexual) difference, I would like in this section to examine how the fetishization of growth is an attempt to preserve privilege by dominating the Other (the Third World, the subaltern) through the fantasy of sameness. The discourse of growth is, in this line of thinking, a way for the West and Third World elites to manage their sociopolitical position in the global hierarchy.

Let us not forget that Modernization arises as a consequence of the Cold War, when Western powers, in their drive to "contain" the threat of communism, construct the West as a model of capitalist growth and democracy (this is why Rostow subtitles his book "a non-communist manifesto"). The main ideological task of Modernization—in relation to both the Soviet Bloc *and* the postcolonial world—is therefore to produce a strong and idealized West, free of wounds or blemishes (see chapter 1). In this sense, growth becomes the magical fetish which masks through substitution the West's trauma (i.e., the perceived Soviet menace, the appearance of weakness or deficiency). The growth fetish is, as Freud puts it, an emblem of triumph over the threat of castration: "the horror of castration . . . set[s] up a memorial to itself" (1977, 353). The mythologization of (Western) capitalist growth offers the fantasy of a castration-free society—wealthy, democratic, rational—while at the same time warding off anxieties about disunity, instability, or vulnerability.

Here GNP emerges as a Western "memorial" of particular note. It is no mere coincidence that it has become *the* measure of economic growth: GNP is deployed and valorized in international development because it centers the West globally in precisely the realm in which the latter dominates—capitalism. Narcissistic desire is thus transferred onto GNP as a numerical proxy, the latter serving as fetish object to help stabilize the West's self-worth (see Benson 2008, 5). The GNP-as-fetish becomes, in fact, an object of narcissistic pleasure (*jouissance*), allowing the West to revel in pride, while lording it over its "inferior" Third World Other. So in fetishizing growth, Western economists such as Rostow and Sachs are preserving—and enjoy preserving—the "purity" and immortality of Western capitalist modernity, helping assert its superiority. And in mimicking their Western counterparts by revering GNP and growth-related statistics, Third World/development policy makers are helping reproduce both capitalist social relations and the fantasy that the "West is the best."

At the heart of castration, as we have also pointed out, is the denial or denigration of difference. Fetishism is the devaluation of the Other in order to soothe one's trauma/lack and maintain one's central position. The discourse of Modernization goes about this in two ways. First, it deploys a "temporal freezing" that both includes and excludes the (Third World) Other (see Tomšič 2015, 160):[3] the primitive Other is frozen in time, relegated to an ahistorical past in order to impose the West's economic history on her/him by presenting it as universal. In this way, the Other is recognized (inclusion), but only in some distant past that culminates in the West's own present (exclusion). Modernization's growth fetish thus enables the West to assume a transcendental fantasmatic position in which, as Said argues, a unilinear history "uniting humanity either culminated in or was observed from the vantage point of Europe, or the West" (1985, 22). In this way, it is not just capitalism, but the way capitalism develops in Europe and North America that is "made to stand for History" (Prakash 1992, 15). Third World countries thereby become specimens of "tradition," with capitalist economic growth as the unquestioned goal to emulate.

Such Western suprematism engages in several crucial occlusions. It conveniently glosses over that it has not been able to live up to its own ideal of a "rational" modernity, with such horrors/excesses/deadlocks as the Nazi concentration camps, global warming, periodic crises of capitalist accumulation (e.g., in 1929, 1973, 2008), and the nuclear obliteration of Hiroshima as prescient reminders of the limits of Western rationality. Similarly, it disavows its own complicity in the "underdevelopment" of the Third World—its imperial plunder, central to both enabling Europe's modernity and impoverishing the very (post)colonies that it now characterizes as "traditional" (Frank 1967; see also chapter 1). It fails to recognize, in particular, the multiple histories of the precolonial societies disrupted by their forced integration into a Western-dominated global capitalist system. Finally, what this fantasy of a pure and uncastrated West sidelines is its ethnocentrism and hybridity: how Afro-Asian ideas and institutions influenced the very Greco-Roman culture that founds "Western civilization" (Bernal 1987; Braudel 1982); how subaltern and indigenous practices have shaped North America socioculturally (Anzaldúa 1987; Mignolo 2012); and how Europe and North America have not always been the historical centers of global commerce, science, and industry (Blaut 1989; Frank 1998).

A second way in which difference is devalued is through stereotyping. The stereotype alleviates the fetishist's anxiety (about lack) by fixing the Other, thereby denying the "play of difference" (Bhabha 1994, 75). Modernization proceeds, accordingly, by stereotyping the Third World Other as static and uncomplicated, ascribing it characteristics mostly associated with femininity (or homosexuality?)—the Other as traditional, irrational, underdeveloped, passive, libidinous, wild (see chapter 10; and Kapoor 2015). The Third World is thus castrated in the properly Freudian sense, enabling the development-policy-maker-as-fetishist to secure his own manhood, while at the same time prescribing how this feminized Other can now be masculinized/phallicized. This recalls Louise Kaplan's notion of "Pygmalions" (1991; see also Fernbach 2002, 23–24), men involved in the fashion industry who transform women into "beguiling images of femininity." They identify some shabby, underachieving creature and deploy their Pygmalion fantasy of the need for her to be rehabilitated. To twist Kaplan's words for our purposes: "Our modern-day Pygmalion enjoys nothing so much as taking an unformed girl and transforming her into a highly valued, sexually exciting [man]—the ideal phallic [man] he wishes he could be" (1991, 263). What Kaplan helps underline for us, once again, is how the fetishist's deployment of the gender stereotype (or of temporal freezing), although outwardly about masking the Other's lack, is really about masking the fetishist's own lack. It is about the mistaken belief in the nonuniversality of castration, a desperate attempt to memorialize and immortalize oneself.

Of course, as I have suggested above, the fetishization of growth in development happens not just along West–Third World lines, but also *within* the Third World. In particular, it is Third World economic and political elites who are enamored of modernization, mostly although not exclusively because they are the main benefactors of capitalist growth. Drawing on Fanon and Bhabha, Benson sees such fetishism as the product of a "narcissism of mastery," which for her is a "widespread symptom of postcolonial trauma" (2008, 4–5; see also Bhabha 1994, 110–116; Fanon 1963, 98). The narcissism of the postcolonial elite is a condition of both humiliation and superiority: humiliation from having to mimic the master's ideal without ever living up to it—graduating from "developing" to "emerging" power perhaps, but never quite arriving (one wonders when the BRICS[4] will be deemed fully "developed"); and superiority from embracing the modernization ideal, thereby gaining from capitalist wealth creation. The goal of capital, as Tomšič underlines, is to value itself, so that wealth is prized by, and remains the property of, the wealthy: "No other system in history [is] more successful [than capitalism] in turning social inequalities and structural contradictions into the privileged source of value" (2015, 163). By mimicking the master's wealth creation, the postcolonial fetishist believes s/he will share in some *je ne sais quoi* essence of wealth. The master's riches are thought to be transmissible and contagious; so maintaining ties with him allows one to gain access to his secret of accumulation. One can then confidently engage in the public display of one's *own* wealth to establish and maintain one's *own* superior knowledge and social standing. There is, in this sense, not just a materialist but also a fetishistic foundation to the neocolonialism and conspicuous consumption of postcolonial elites in the global South.

Frequently, the postcolonial fetishist not only conflates economic value and self-worth like his erstwhile master but also overcompensates for his inferiority in the global hierarchy. This is often where growth fetish meets hypermasculinity: in order to cover over the deep wounds of (neo)colonialism—continuing patterns of economic humiliation, patriarchal imperialism, racialized dehumanization—postcolonial states have sometimes opted for a hypermasculinized modernity: cases in point are high spending on military equipment and technology or substantial public investments in huge or spectacular projects (megadams, supersized monuments and buildings, space programs, state-of-the-art hospitals, etc.). They are symptomatic of the fetishist's ardent desire to assert his phallic identity and authority, although such exaggerated virility can at times turn into its opposite: like Hamlet's Player Queen protesting "too much," or the hypermasculine gay leatherman, or indeed the gigantic North Korean military parade, it ends up exhibiting rather than concealing its deep anxiety, trauma, or lack, mutating into a form of camp (see Fernbach 2002, 147ff.)

Let me turn to a key aspect of the growth fetish that I have until now only implied under the rubric of disavowal: condensation. This refers, it will be recalled, to the way in which the fetishist fixates on an object, thereby wresting it from its symbolic or social relationships. Growth and GNP are of particular relevance here since, for the fetishist, their "magical" aura conceals their sociohistorical determinations, effectively screening their process of value making. On the issue of growth, there are multiple layers of condensation worth uncovering. There is, first, the seemingly obvious but notably ideological sleight of hand in the very use of the term "growth," which neoclassical economics, and development economists more generally, accept as given, obscuring that it is a particular type of growth—*capitalist* growth—that they favor (a point stressed in chapter 4). For them, capitalist markets are what regulate and solve social problems. But even in so doing they are positing a "nonrelation." As Alenka Zupančič suggests, the fundamental discovery of capitalism is that "non-relation is profitable. . . . Adam Smith's 'capital' idea starts out by positing a social non-relation as a fundamental state . . . as elements of social order individuals are driven by egoistic drives and pursuit of self-interest. But out of these purely egoistic pursuits grows a society of an optimal general welfare and justice" (2016, 97). It is precisely such nonrelation that Marx is most preoccupied with, since for him, it curtains over the social inequality, dispossession, and unevenness integral to market-driven capitalist development. According to him, "commodity fetishism" is the most immediate form of capitalist nonrelation: "The mysterious character of the commodity-form consists . . . in the fact that the commodity reflects the social characteristics of men's labour as objective characteristics of the products of labour themselves, as the socio-natural properties of these things" (Marx 1990, 164–165). Such mystification means that the social relations between producers are transformed into a relation between things. So by fetishizing capitalist growth, one is de facto fetishizing commodities, thereby masking oppressive and exploitative social relations.

As a quick but important aside, it is worth pointing out the irony of history here: at the very time that European colonizers (and later, Modernization theorists) were labelling the "primitive" Other as irrational, superstitious fetishists, they were themselves engaging in commodity fetishism. Baudrillard is quick to emphasize, in this regard, how the fetish can "turn against those who use it" and that "the knowledge [the colonizers] produced of the 'primitive Other' reflected their *own* relation to commodities, money and capital" (1981, 90, emphasis added).

But like growth, GNP is also an ideologically mystifying object. Much ink has been spilled on the problem, so I will only summarize the key points (see for example Haque 2004; Szirmai 2005). The main issue is that GNP measures only the quantity of economic growth, not the broader quality of development. That is, GNP may grow but result in, or be supported by, "maldevelopment"—for example, high military spending, overreliance on foreign aid, inadequate social investments, or authoritarian government. This problem is perhaps best illustrated by pre–civil war Sri Lanka and postindependence Kerala, where impressive state investments in health and education were made despite only moderate growth in GNP; versus Brazil in the late 1960s and 1970s, where there was quite rapid GNP growth but little change in poverty levels or state social spending (Szirmai 2005, 7). Part of the difficulty here is GNP's fixation on the economic, which ends up reflecting only market-valued production and excluding the many social activities that happen outside the market (e.g., self-produced food, housing, and clothing; informal/subsistence-sector activities; eldercare; or the unpaid household and reproductive labor of women). Also discounted are the many hidden costs of economic growth, including the depletion of biodiversity, the degradation of land and water, environmental health hazards, or crime and mental illness resulting from "maldevelopment." The absurdity of GNP, in fact, is that it counts many of these hidden costs (e.g., deforestation, pollution, crime) as gains.

Finally, of course, there is the all-important issue that GNP obscures inequality. Per capita GNP is not really an alternative, since it is simply an arithmetic division of annual growth by population size, telling us nothing about *actual* wealth distribution. The catch is that while Third World countries have grown in fits and starts since the Second World War and relative poverty levels have declined, absolute numbers of "poor" people have increased (Szirmai 2005, 30). Latin American countries (especially Brazil and Chile) remain some of the most unequal worldwide despite overall increases in wealth accumulation (Institute for Policy Studies 2016). Meanwhile, globally, the gap between rich and poor has risen dramatically over time, in spite of a massive expansion of overall global wealth (see chapters 5 and 12). The broader problem, to be sure, is not just that GNP is an ahistorical and insensitive measure—it dispenses with socioeconomic inequality as much as gender and racial inequalities—but that it is integral to a discourse of growth which, as mentioned earlier, is focused on wealth creation and has little concern for the question of social relations and distribution. Fetishizing GNP therefore masks the social antagonisms of capitalist development and effectively endorses the politics of "trickle down" growth that has overwhelmingly benefitted a small group (economic and political elites).

This condensation and mystification/disavowal of social relations, it must be noted, happens not really at the level of illusion or distorted knowledge, but is built into the fabric of social reality itself. The neglect of inequality becomes *the very condition* of social activity under the regime of growth, so that the fetishist's misrepresentation is a constitutive element of capitalist political economy. This is why the fetishization of GNP, as underlined above, does not just operate as an idea but translates into actual policies and planning that affect resource allocation, division of wealth, and relations between people. This points up once again how the unconscious mechanisms of the fetish are not an "inside" condition of the mind but are radically external, inscribed into our social practices (see Žižek 1989, 28–30).

To conclude this section, let me tease out the political implications of the fetishization of growth. For fetishism here is not only about control (e.g., over capitalist accumulation), but across the North-South divide it is also a technology of domination. As we have noted, it helps symbolically castrate the

Third World in order to prop up the West's self-worth (and preserve the [fraudulent] Western "phallus" from extinction). But more than that, it enables Western powers to assess and judge the economic performance of Third World countries, and to hold them to account, for example through loan, aid, and debt restructuring conditionalities. Structural adjustment programs are, after all, one of the key neocolonial tools for reproducing capitalism, ensuring the West's central position in the global capitalist hierarchy. Restructuring Third World economies has largely meant their opening up to Western capital and MNCs. In this sense, the phallic ideal of (Western-centered) economic development doesn't simply confirm Western cultural dominance but also helps maintain a degree of Third World global economic subjugation and dependence.

In Third World countries themselves, the fantasy of modernization appears to have taken firm root, allowing elites to maintain and advance their socioeconomic superiority. Modernization, in this sense, is a politically conservative discourse tending toward the foreclosure of politics. Because it privileges elite-driven capitalist accumulation, it tends toward social control (Peet and Hartwick 2009, 119), the protection of private property, and the need to keep dissidence under wraps to assure the smooth functioning of the economy. State priority to GNP growth at all costs often legitimizes authoritarian rule, visible in the last three decades in the political repression accompanying the wave of economic deregulation and privatization across the global South. In countries as varied as Turkey, Egypt, Argentina, Nigeria, Mozambique, and Indonesia, class inequalities have been put aside in favor of what is constructed as the "collective" interest in neoliberal modernization (see Akbulut and Adaman 2014; Gibbon, Bangura, and Ofstad 1992; Gwynne and Kay 2004; Pepinsky 2009). High growth rates, and growth statistics themselves, have become "pedagogical and disciplinary" tools aimed at taming the population (Appadurai 1996, 120, 123). And with political dissent increasingly foreclosed, people are positioned less as citizens and more as taxpayers and consumers.

The growth fetish, consequently, concedes enormous power to Third World economic and political elites, legitimizing political violence against antigovernment protesters, while narrowing avenues for debate and contestation. In a sense, fetishizing capitalist growth forecloses politics *in advance*: for elites to enjoy their magical fantasy of modernization, the stain of difference and opposition must be eliminated. So the fixation on growth rests on the prior exclusion of political messiness or disturbance.

# Technofetishism
## Fetishizing Technology

Technofetishism often goes hand in hand with growth fetishism. The belief in technological progress, the notion that technology can solve (all) social problems, is what underpins the fetishist's growth discourse: science and technology are viewed as the very motors of economic modernization. This is reflected in President Harry Truman's 1949 speech—the one that many see as inaugurating not only his full term as president but also the discourse of development—when he declares that "the key to greater production is a wider and more vigorous application of modern scientific and technical knowledge" (quoted in Ullrich 1992, 275). This is also reflected in the thinking of influential postwar development economists such as Robert Heilbroner, who argues that the main bottleneck for developing countries is low productivity, requiring improved technologies (Heilbroner 1968; Ivory 1998, 326, 337). The idea here is that capitalism *depends* on technological innovation: superior technology is a source of higher profits because it helps increase productivity. As David Harvey points out, "Capitalist entrepreneurs and corporations innovate not because they want to but because they have to in order to either acquire . . . or retain . . . their status as capitalists" (2003, 7). Obsolete technology is thus believed to lead to low productivity. And like Heilbroner, Rostow and his fellow Modernization theorists see the Third World as having limited productive capacity because of "traditional" cultural barriers and "pre-Newtonian science and technology" (Rostow 1960, 4, xxiv). They therefore prescribe significant cultural change in "traditional societies" to ensure the spread of science and facilitate the transfer of technologies and capital.

Their call has been duly taken up by post-colonial states and international development policy makers alike. Despite the occasional critical voices (e.g., M. K. Gandhi, E. F. Schumacher, Vandana Shiva), there has in fact been near religious faith in science and technology, as witnessed for example by Nehru's famous characterization of hydroelectric dams as the "temples of modern India" or Nkrumah's statement about the need to "mobilize our total manpower for the industrial, economic, technological and scientific reconstruction of Ghana" (quoted in Coleman and Rosberg 1964, 260). Development's postwar technofetishism is witnessed, for example, by large state investments in nuclear and hydroelectric power for electricity generation to support urban and industrial growth; military aid and spending to help guarantee military and geopolitical superiority; and more recently, the development of an information and communications technologies (ICTs) infrastructure to increase market productivity, efficiency, and service delivery (see OECD 2010).

The aggressive promotion of the "green revolution" is another notable case, highlighting the extent of the global mobilization of resources in favor of technology. Over the last fifty years, backed by the World Bank, USAID, and the Rockefeller, Ford, and Gates foundations, many post-colonial states have jumped on board the campaign to persuade farmers to adopt high-yielding and weather-resistant varieties of rice, maize, and wheat seeds (and subsequently, a range of other cash-crop seeds) to increase agricultural production. True to the spirit of Modernization, the idea has been to replace "traditional" agricultural practices and institutions (i.e., animal power, rain-fed water systems, natural fertilizers, communal or family farming) with modern scientific ones (i.e., mechanically powered tractors and pumps, irrigation, pesticides, biotechnology, large-scale private agriculture). In countries such as Turkey, Tanzania, and India, the state has ensured the "success" of the green revolution through massive investments in dams and irrigation, the supply of subsidized agricultural inputs, and the adoption of favorable pricing mechanisms (see Prabhakar 2011; Shiva 2016).

Technofetishism has thus become a key feature of capitalist development. More than just an ingredient of development, technology has gripped post-colonial decision makers and business interests, who see it as a way of unlocking the secret of prosperity and progress. There may well be problems associated with technology (e.g., pollution, environmental destruction), but for the technofetishist, the solution is not less but more and better technology. It is this kind of technological fix that provides the reassurance and comfort that unlimited growth is possible.

## A Psychoanalysis of Technofetishism

As with growth fetishism, technofetishism is about the construction of a fantasy of development, which holds out the promise of abundance, wealth, unity, social stability. The technofetishist displaces her hopes and dreams onto the technological object (nuclear energy, dams, computers, bioengineering), so that all she needs is a technological fix and modernization will be achieved, nature will be mastered, and society will progress and be bettered. Such overinvestment produces a magical object, so much so that, as just underlined, any technological flaw or problem is addressed not through critical questioning but by the prescription of more, newer, and higher technology: for instance, terror threats are met with drone surveillance; an increase in cancers or diabetes is addressed with new high-tech treatments; and pest infestation from new seed varieties is fought with more newly engineered seeds and pesticides. The magical technological object, in turn, becomes the source of tremendous glee and gratification (*jouissance*)—and the higher the tech, the greater the glee, it seems. This is witnessed, for instance, by the remarkable display of national pride and pageantry across the global South relating to space and satellite programs, military and nuclear hardware, computerization (of business, education, health programs), food exports from the green revolution, and so on.

But by the same token, technofetishism is a site of disavowal. Like growth fetishism, it functions as a stand-in for castration. The technofetishist constructs her fantasy—a techno-developmental heaven—in order to cover over her fundamental lack. It is because she knows that nature cannot be dominated (climate change, pollution, nuclear waste, environmental health hazards are just a few of the many symptoms) that the fetish must be invented as substitute savior. It is because science cannot explain or guarantee everything, despite its pretensions, that triumphant science fiction is required. It is because social order and unlimited growth are elusive that a technological fix needs to be conjured. And it is because one's body—the body in flesh, but also the body of the nation or the military-industrial complex—is deficient that a technological prosthetic must be found (iPhones, rockets, robots). The technofetish, in this sense, is not just a screen onto which dreams are displaced, but also an object to *screen out* fundamental antagonism, danger, and lack. And such lack, it must be emphasized, is not so much repressed as disavowed: the technofetishist is well aware of the dangers of using technology indiscriminately, but proceeds nonetheless. This is the "fetishistic disavowal" that we referred to earlier, wherein one's social practice (using technology indiscriminately) outweighs one's knowledge (being aware of the socioenvironmental consequences).

Importantly, what the technofetishist disavows is technology's broader social context ("condensation"). It is as though the technological object emerges magically on its own—through immaculate conception or self-generated production—independent of the market, labor process, or social and environmental resources and relationships. The technofetishist misrecognizes the relationship between a social network and one of its elements: the effect of social relations appears as the immediate property of only one of the elements (Žižek 1989, 24). Hence the technofetishist's attribution of supernatural properties to his fetish and its placement outside of its social determinations.

Such condensation is evident in the above-mentioned Modernization belief that superior technology leads to greater profits and growth. What is disavowed is that profit and growth always happen relative to the social relations between capital and labor, and technology is almost always biased in favor of the former. New technology often implies labor costs in the form of either lower wages or lay-offs; it is these, not technology per se, that help increase productivity. The overall effect is the weakening of the power of labor and unions. "In the hands of the capitalist, the purpose of machinery is to extract more profits from laborers and not to lighten their load." For the capitalist, robots don't answer back, complain, strike, or demand higher wages; his technofetishist fantasy thus rests on "total control over the laborer via technology" (Harvey 2003, 13).

Technological change can frequently lead to new divisions of labor, driving out small businesses that cannot afford new technology, and facilitating the concentration of capital (one thinks here of the recent dramatic rise of global monopoly capital in the high-tech, banking, and communications industries as represented by likes of Microsoft, Visa, or Murdoch) (see Harvey 2003, 9–10). It can also often result in a gender division of labor, for instance when men replace women in the move from subsistence to agro-industrial farming (see Modersitzki 2009). The broader result of technological change may thus well be growth and modernization, but it can equally be a rise in unemployment, inequality, and feminization of poverty.

Not to be overlooked is technofetishism's condensation of socioenvironmental linkages. The trouble is that technology's so-called magic is myopic, so that the ardent desire for modernization leads to a call for quick results and short-term calculations. Issues about technology's impacts on flora and fauna, future generations, or indeed people living in remote or marginalized areas, end up becoming abstract, not immediately visible or palpable (Ullrich 1992, 283).

On the one hand, the consequence of such myopia has been historically unprecedented environmental degradation on a global scale. Energy- and technology-biased development has meant that "[j]uxtaposed to the 10,000 year duration of the agrarian system, the industrial system appears as a brief, one-time paroxysm of intoxication in which the resources gathered over many millions of years are used up in a couple of hundred" (Rolf Peter Sieferle quoted in Ullrich 1992, 280). Not only is such global degradation a transfer of costs to future generations, it also makes the fantasy of unlimited capitalist accumulation impossible. The Western model of modernity is consequently generalizable for perhaps only a few more generations, if that.

And on the other hand, such myopia has had specifically socioenvironmental impacts. Businesses, rich farmers, and urban areas have certainly benefitted from technologically driven development (e.g., dams, nuclear plants, the green revolution). But the costs of such development—air and water pollution, desertification, toxic waste dumping, deforestation, biodiversity reduction— have been disproportionately borne by subalterns (indigenous peoples, racialized minorities, migrant workers, poor farmers, subaltern women) (see Byrne, Glover, and Martinez 2002). The green revolution, for example, while certainly leading to increases in food production and cash crop exports, has also been accompanied by a host of problems: increasing privatization of communal and public lands ("accumulation by dispossession"), resulting in the displacement of the landless, poor farming communities, and indigenous people; the concentration of wealth in the hands of rich farmers and global agro-industrial corporations; and the loss of biodiversity and salinization/silting of land due to agricultural intensification, which in turn brings about loss of livelihood and human displacement (see Akbulut and Adaman 2014; Prabhakar 2011; Shiva 2016).

Finally, let me mention the global context, so often disavowed by development technofetishists. The fantasy of embracing technology in favor of modernization is belied by the significant global inequalities in ownership of, and access to, such technology: the overwhelming proportion of scientific R&D takes place in the global North. The vast majority of patents are registered there and fifty of the largest multinationals currently own the bulk of them (especially in electronics, software, pharmaceuticals, and biotechnology) (Cimoli et al. 2014; Szirmai 2005, 129ff.). Many global South countries, therefore, either cannot afford technology or may have access to it only if they honor intellectual property rights agreements (e.g., TRIPS) and open up their markets to multinational investment. Technology has thus become another instrument for the North, and for large multinationals, to dominate the global South (Ivory 1998, 339). It allows for the imposition of foreign technological practices that may disrupt local life-worlds ("cultural imperialism," for example in the form labor-saving technologies or a productivist work ethic) and limit the choice of moving toward more "appropriate technologies."[5]

Now an important word about the political dimensions of technofetishism: given technofetishism's strong attachment to, and fascination with, technology, given its tendency to mask the fetish object's social determinations, it is by definition averse to democratic governance. The decision to opt for a particular technological solution forecloses politics, relying on an a priori dismissal of social antagonism, debate, or contestation. As Jodi Dean puts it, the technofetishist's fantasy is one in which "there is no politics; there is already agreement" (2008, 117).

This is especially evident in a technology such as nuclear power: it requires substantial investments (by the state and/or private sector) that, once made, are difficult to withdraw; and it is high risk, particularly in this post-Chernobyl and post-Fukushima era. It therefore necessitates strong, centralized, and hierarchical forms of decision making (by politicians and "expert" scientists), which tend to exclude in advance any meaningful participation by citizens, especially those concerned about cost, safety, or radioactive waste (Harvey 2003, 5–6). The same is true of other complex and high-investment technologies such as those in the chlorine, synthesizing chemistry, chemicalized agriculture, and extractive industries. All are notoriously averse to public scrutiny, intent on erasing their socioenvironmental determinations and impacts. All point to how technological hardware—what the technofetishist fixates on—matters most, to the exclusion of technological software and design—its sociopolitical organizational forms.

Even the internet, often extolled for enabling citizen participation and democratic governance ("electronic democracy"; see Browning 2002), is not as "empowering" as it first seems. Emailing, blogging, chatting give the impression of public interaction and virtual communities, but as Todd McGowan notes, it is a public world "that seems to have everything save actual physical interaction. . . . [It] merely increases the range of the subject's private world" (2004, 156–157). True, the Internet can be (and has been) used to important effect in the organization of social movements and popular protest (e.g., most recently during the "Arab Spring"; see chapter 9); but while the technology is a useful tool for political campaigning and organizing, it tends to foreclose the space for the *political* proper—struggle, conflict, disagreement, debate (in the Arab Spring, these happened not virtually but in actual physical-social spaces such as Tahrir Square). Dean goes so far as to argue that "communicative capitalism" is really about the circulation of messages, which don't so much have a sender or receiver as become part of an endless stream of information that people click on, "like," copy, paste, forward. Some messages may well be received and make a difference (as in the case of the Arab Spring), but in the overall communicative network, the "exchange value of messages overtakes their use value. . . . The only thing that is relevant is circulation" (2008, 107; see also 2010). Consequently, people on the Internet think they are interacting with others, but they do so from the security of their home or office without actually getting too involved with other people. Messages *are* sent, and exchange *does* happen, but these tend to be stripped of struggles, problems, unpredictability. So one experiences the Other without actually encountering the (antagonism of the) Other. This is the point at which, as Ullrich underlines, "scientistic technology" becomes a "dream of happiness without sacrifice" (1992, 278). Seen in this light, the Internet is a technology invented for virtual interaction to save us from the trauma of political (and physical) interaction.

We thus see how a technofetish such as the Internet becomes a substitute that screens the antagonisms of the political. It is a magical object on which people (or indeed the state) rely, in this case relieving them of the need to act. This is a phenomenon that Žižek calls "interpassivity" (1997, 144–147): in contrast to interactivity, where people enjoy through participation, interpassivity is when people enjoy through an Other—here, the Internet-as-fetish-object. They lead busy lives but try and make a difference—by clicking on a button, forwarding a message, or adding their name to a petition. They believe they are acting, linking with others, but actually it is the Internet-as-fetish that is acting in their stead so that they themselves are passive. Frenetic activity happens, messages circulate and recirculate, but the fetish prevents any meaningful transformation. The sweat and tears of political organizing and struggle are elided through displacement, and "this displacement, in turn, secures and protects the space of 'official' politics" (Dean 2008, 10). Technology acts instead of us so we can continue our busy daily lives; it covers over our relative impotence while making us feel we are making a difference. But the overall effect is unthreatening and acquiescent to the prevailing technocapitalist order.

## Conclusion

Focusing on the growth and technological fetishes, I have argued that fetishism is deeply ingrained in international development. This is because it is much more than just a psychoanalytic idea; it is an unconscious process manifested externally and materially in social and institutional practices. Thus, as rational, progressive, and scientific as the discourses of growth and technology might purport to be, they are tainted by, on the one hand, magical thinking—ironically underlining a continuity (not a break) between so-called tradition and modernity—and on the other, unconscious tendencies to disavow, dominate, and foreclose. Indeed, as we have noted, the fetishization of growth and technology is at the same time a disavowal of their own fundamental lack and deficiency, which implies the masking of their socioenvironmental determinations (e.g., inequality, gender division of labor, environmental degradation). Such masking happens through the construction of a seductive technocapitalist fantasy that props up the self-worth of the West and Third World economic and political elites. In turn, this implies the denigration of difference and the domination of the Other—the symbolic castration of the Third World, mastery over nature, and social and economic control over "poor" countries and subalterns. Finally, as emphasized, the fetishization of growth and technology forecloses politics: its elite-driven fixation on capitalist accumulation gives way to hierarchical and undemocratic decision making aimed at maintaining the status quo. It manages to seduce people with its magical and

communicative possibilities, but its a priori exclusion of political antagonism ensures that nothing fundamental will change.

So what is to be done? Of course, there is no question of getting rid of fetishism; for Lacanians, it is constitutive of the subject, and of all societies: the
fetish allows us to cope with our fundamental lack, so that many of the (material and symbolic) objects that surround us—from money, cell phones, and
images to religious and political icons and ideas—become props onto which
we displace our hopes and dreams. The problem is when the fetish is articulated in the form of broader ideologies such as technocapitalist modernization, with, as we have seen, serious socioenvironmental consequences. The
challenge then is to engage in ideology critique, which as we have noted (in
chapter 1) happens *not* just at the level of knowledge. Deconstructing an ideological fetish on the basis of information and knowledge can assist as a first
step, since it helps politicize the fetish, putting it in a sociopolitical context and
making it stand for something beyond itself. In the case of technofetishism,
for instance, this would allow one to grasp that what matters is not just better
control of technology but better accountability of the epistemic *and* material
systems (i.e., modernization discourse, state and corporate structures) that
control or regulate technology.

But as important as such demystification might be, it is not nearly enough.
This is because, as pointed out earlier, knowledge / awareness can simply take
the form of "fetishistic disavowal": I am aware that money is not magical, but
I still invest it with great importance in my life; I know very well that GNP
does violence to the social, but nonetheless I continue to use it; I understand
that nuclear energy has safety implications, but I still wish to opt for it . . . No,
the more crucial step for Lacanians is to identify, and come to terms with, the
unconscious processes at play in ideological fetishism—the kernel of enjoyment that makes us choose the fetish despite knowing better (see Kapoor 2014,
1133–1135; Žižek 2008, 329ff.). It is by facing up to our unconscious desires,
to the deep seduction of the fetish, that we can "traverse the fantasy" of the
fetish: only then can we start to meaningfully demystify it.

## Notes

1. Although implied, let me specify the *subjects* of the fetishism that I discuss in this
chapter: while we are admittedly all fetishists, my critique is directed primarily at the
development establishment elites (national and transnational economic and political
elites, policy makers, Modernization theorists), who help propagate and benefit from
the dominant fantasy of technocapitalism. The political task for all of us, including
the subalterns who pay the highest price of such fetishism, is to demystify and "tra-

verse" this ideological fantasy (see the concluding section of this chapter). I thank Mustapha Pasha for prompting me to address this question.

2. GNP is to be distinguished from gross domestic product (GDP), a measure which also includes foreign loans, repatriated profits, and the like (see Szirmai 2005, 13).

3. See also Bhabha (1994, 274–275, 353), who refers to this as a "time-lag."

4. BRICS refers to the group of increasingly powerful "emerging" countries (Brazil, Russia, India, China, and South Africa).

5. It should be clear that my argument is not a Luddite one here: I am not arguing against technology (nor are critics of technofetishism such as Gandhi or Schumacher), but against its indiscriminate and unaccountable use, its deployment outside of its socioenvironmental, political, and psychoanalytic contexts.

# References

Akbulut, Bengi, and Fikret Adaman. 2014. "The Unbearable Appeal of Modernization: The Fetish of Growth." Heinrich Böll Stiftung Derneği, Istanbul. https://tr.boell.org/de/2014/06/16/unbearable-appeal-modernization-fetish-growth-publikationen.

Anzaldúa, Gloria. 1987. *Borderlands / La Frontera: The New Mestiza*. San Francisco: Spinsters/Aunt Lute.

Appadurai, Arjun. 1996. *Modernity at Large: Cultural Dimensions of Globalization*. Minneapolis: University of Minnesota Press.

Baudrillard, Jean. 1981. *For a Critique of the Political Economy of the Sign*. Translated by Charles Levin. St. Louis, MO: Telos.

Benson, Melanie R. 2008. *Disturbing Calculations: The Economics of Identity in Postcolonial Southern Literature, 1912–2002*. Athens: University of Georgia Press.

Bernal, Martin. 1987. *Black Athena: The Afroasiatic Roots of Classical Civilization*. New Brunswick, NJ: Rutgers University Press.

Bhabha, Homi K. 1994. *The Location of Culture*. London: Routledge.

Blaut, James M. 1989. "Colonialism and the Rise of Capitalism." *Antipode* 8 (2): 1–11.

Böhm, Steffen, and Aanka Batta. 2010. "Just Doing It: Enjoying Commodity Fetishism with Lacan." *Organization* 17 (3): 345–361.

Bozdoğan, Sibel, and Reşat Kasaba. 1997. *Rethinking Modernity and National Identity in Turkey*. Seattle: University of Washington Press.

Braudel, Fernand. 1982. *Civilization and Capitalism, 15th–18th Century*. Vol. 2: *The Wheels of Commerce*. Translated by Siân Reynolds. New York: Harper and Row.

Browning, Graeme. 2002. *Electronic Democracy: Using the Internet to Transform American Politics*. Medford, NJ: CyberAge.

Byrne, John, Leigh Glover, and Cecilia Martinez, eds. 2002. *Environmental Justice: Discourses in International Political Economy*. New Brunswick, NJ: Transaction.

Cimoli, Mario, Giovanni Dosi, Keith E. Maskus, Ruth L. Okediji, Jerome H. Reichman, and Joseph E. Stiglitz, eds. 2014. *Intellectual Property Rights: Legal and Economic Challenges for Development*. Oxford: Oxford University Press.

Coleman, James Smoot, and Carl Gustav Rosberg. 1964. *Political Parties and National Integration in Tropical Africa*. Berkeley: University of California Press.

Cowie, Elizabeth. 1997. *Representing the Woman: Cinema and Psychoanalysis*. London: Macmillan.

Dean, Jodi. 2008. "Communicative Capitalism: Circulation and the Foreclosure of Politics." In *Digital Media and Democracy: Tactics in Hard Times*, edited by Megan Boler, 101–121. Cambridge, MA: MIT Press.

———. 2010. *Blog Theory: Feedback and Capture in the Circuits of Drive*. Cambridge: Polity.

Eisenstadt, Shmuel Noah. 1973. *Tradition, Change and Modernity*. New York: Wiley.

Evans, Dylan. 2006. *An Introductory Dictionary of Lacanian Psychoanalysis*. London: Routledge.

Fanon, Frantz. 1963. *The Wretched of the Earth*. Translated by Richard Philcox. New York: Grove.

Fernbach, Amanda. 2002. *Fantasies of Fetishism: From Decadence to the Post-Human*. Edinburgh: Edinburgh University Press.

Frank, Andre Gunder. 1967. *Capitalism and Underdevelopment in Latin America*. New York: Monthly Review.

———. 1998. *ReOrient: Global Economy in the Asian Age*. Berkeley: University of California Press.

Freud, Sigmund. 1977. *On Sexuality: Three Essays on the Theory of Sexuality and Other Works*. Edited by James Strachey. Harmondsworth: Penguin.

Gibbon, Peter, Yusuf Bangura, and Arve Ofstad, eds. 1992. *Authoritarianism, Democracy, and Adjustment: The Politics of Economic Reform in Africa*. Uppsala: Nordiska Afrikainstitutet.

Gwynne, Robert N., and Cristóbal Kay, eds. 2004. *Latin America Transformed: Globalization and Modernity*. London: Arnold.

Hamilton, Clive. 2004. *Growth Fetish*. London and Sterling, VA: Pluto.

Haque, M. Shamsul. 2004. "The Myths of Economic Growth (GNP): Implications for Human Development." In *Handbook of Development Policy Studies*, edited by Gordon M. Mudacumura and M. Shamsul Haque, 1–24. New York: Marcel Dekker.

Harvey, David. 2003. "The Fetish of Technology: Causes and Consequences." *Macalester International* 13 (1): 3–30.

Heilbroner, Robert L. 1968. *The Great Ascent: The Struggle for Economic Development in Our Time*. New York: Harper and Row.

Institute for Policy Studies. 2016. "Global Inequality." Inequality.Org. http://inequality .org/global-inequality/.

Ivory, Ming. 1998. "Doctrines of Science, Technology, and Development Assistance." *Alternatives: Global, Local, Political* 23 (3): 321–374.

Kaplan, Louise. 1991. *Female Perversions: The Temptations of Emma Bovary*. New York: Anchor.

Kapoor, Ilan. 2008. *The Postcolonial Politics of Development*. London: Routledge.

———. 2014. "Psychoanalysis and Development: Contributions, Examples, Limits." *Third World Quarterly* 35 (7): 1120–1143.

———. 2015. "The Queer Third World." *Third World Quarterly* 36 (9): 1611–1628.

Lacan, Jacques. 1977. *Écrits: A Selection*. Translated by Alan Sheridan. New York: Norton.

——. 1988. *Freud's Papers on Technique, 1953–1954: The Seminar of Jacques Lacan, Book I.* Edited by Jacques-Alain Miller. New York: Norton.

Lerner, David. 1958. *The Passing of Traditional Society: Modernizing the Middle East.* New York: Free Press.

Marx, Karl. 1990. *Capital.* Vol. 1. Translated by Ben Fowkes. Harmondsworth: Penguin.

McClelland, David. 1967. *The Achieving Society.* New York: Free Press.

McGowan, Todd. 2004. *The End of Dissatisfaction? Jacques Lacan and the Emerging Society of Enjoyment.* Albany: SUNY Press.

Mignolo, Walter D. 2012. *Local Histories/Global Designs: Coloniality, Subaltern Knowledges, and Border Thinking.* Princeton, NJ: Princeton University Press.

Modersitzki, Anna Falth. 2009. "The Dynamics of Technology and Gender Roles." In *Globalization of Technology*, edited by Prasada Reddy, 253–278. Oxford: Eolss.

Organisation for Economic Co-operation and Development (OECD). 2010. *ICTs for Development: Improving Policy Coherence.* Paris: Organisation for Economic Co-operation and Development. https://read.oecd-ilibrary.org/development/icts-for-development_9789264077409-en#.

Peet, Richard, and Elaine Hartwick. 2009. *Theories of Development: Contentions, Arguments, Alternatives.* New York: Guilford.

Pepinsky, Thomas B. 2009. *Economic Crises and the Breakdown of Authoritarian Regimes: Indonesia and Malaysia in Comparative Perspective.* Cambridge: Cambridge University Press.

Pietz, William. 1985. "The Problem of the Fetish, I." *Res* 9: 5–17.

Prabhakar, Akhilesh Chandra. 2011. *Green Revolution: A Comparative Study of Africa and Asia.* Saarbrucken: Lambert Academic.

Prakash, Gyan. 1992. "Postcolonial Criticism and Indian Historiography." *Social Text* 31/32: 8–19. https://doi.org/10.2307/466216.

Rostow, Walt W. 1960. *The Stages of Economic Growth: A Non-Communist Manifesto.* Cambridge: Cambridge University Press.

Sachs, Jeffrey D. 2005. *The End of Poverty: Economic Possibilities for Our Time.* New York: Penguin.

Said, Edward W. 1985. "Orientalism Reconsidered." In *Europe and Its Others: Proceedings of the Essex Conference on the Sociology of Literature, July 1984*, edited by Francis Barker, 1:201–226. Colchester: University of Essex.

Shiva, Vandana. 2016. *The Violence of the Green Revolution: Third World Agriculture, Ecology, and Politics.* Lexington: University Press of Kentucky.

Swetz, Frank J. 2012. *Mathematical Expeditions: Exploring Word Problems across the Ages.* Baltimore, MD: Johns Hopkins University Press.

Szirmai, Adam. 2005. *The Dynamics of Socio-Economic Development: An Introduction.* Cambridge: Cambridge University Press.

Tomšič, Samo. 2015. *The Capitalist Unconscious: Marx and Lacan.* London: Verso.

Ullrich, Otto. 1992. "Technology." In *The Development Dictionary: A Guide to Knowledge as Power*, edited by Wolfgang Sachs, 308–322. London: Zed.

Zein-Elabdin, Eiman O. 2004. "Articulating the Postcolonial (with Economics in Mind)." In *Postcolonialism Meets Economics*, edited by Eiman O. Zein-Elabdin and S. Charusheela, 21–39. London: Routledge.

Žižek, Slavoj. 1989. *The Sublime Object of Ideology*. London: Verso.

——. 1997. *The Plague of Fantasies*. London: Verso.

——. 2008. *In Defense of Lost Causes*. London: Verso.

Zupančič, Alenka. 2016. "Sexual Is Political?" In *Jacques Lacan: Between Psychoanalysis and Politics*, edited by Samo Tomšič and Andreja Zevnik, 86–100. London: Routledge.

CHAPTER 7

# The "Gaze" in Participatory Development
Panoptic or Traumatic?

KEYWORD: *Gaze*

## Introduction

Over the past three decades, participatory development—development programming that promotes local community "empowerment"—has become notably mainstream, with most NGOs and foreign and multilateral aid agencies now integrating it into their projects (Chambers 1994a, 1994b, 1997; World Bank 1995). But such mainstreaming has also brought with it a backlash: several analysts warn against its proclivities for gender bias (Mayoux 1995; Parpart 2000), localism (Mohan and Stokke 2000), and neocolonialism (Kapoor 2005, 2008). In particular, recent critics have tended to deploy a Foucauldian notion of the gaze, emphasizing participation's panoptic dimensions (e.g., Cooke and Kothari 2001; Kapoor 2002, 2004a, 2005; Mosse 1994, 1997, 2001): for example, how people's participation can be a technology of surveillance, allowing donors to better supervise project participants while enabling village leaders to better keep a watch on their constituencies (particularly women).

In this chapter, I contrast this Foucauldian view with a Lacanian take on the gaze, stressing its affective dimensions. Here, the desire is less to master the Other than to perpetuate oneself, for example by masochistically manipulating the gaze of the Other in a way that is nonthreatening and pleasurable. Participatory development projects, in this sense, are a way of shoring up the donor's self-image (of benevolence) and enjoyment. Yet the gaze, for Lacan, is a point of distortion or trauma, wherein the subject not only enjoys but also secretly envies the Other's enjoyment (which remains unattainable). This opens up possibilities for exploiting the master's insecurities and need for recognition, disrupting his gaze by looking back threateningly (Bhabha 2004, 86), thus enabling participants in development projects to hijack participation for their own purposes.

## Participation and the Foucauldian Gaze: Mastering the Other

In *Discipline and Punish*, Foucault develops a notion of the gaze that involves mastering and dominating the Other (1977, 239).[1] As is well known, he illustrates this by way of Bentham's "panopticon," an eighteenth-century architectural model for a prison, consisting of an annular building surrounding a central tower that allows for the constant surveillance of inmates (204). For Foucault, the panoptic or "inspecting" gaze is about watching and disciplining without being watched—"eyes that must see without being seen," he writes (1984, 189)—the ultimate form of domination. Not only does such an architectural arrangement allow for continuous supervision, but after a time, inmates end up internalizing their surveillance.

For Foucault, the panopticon is a metaphor for the governance of modern societies, in which "everyone is watched, according to his position within the system, by all or by certain of the others" (1996, 235). The notion of the panoptic gaze becomes central to his arguments about "biopower" and "governmentality" (aptly referred to as the "conduct of conduct"), whereby populations are controlled through disciplining technologies of power, producing subjectivities that self-correct, -police, and -govern (Foucault 1991, 2, 87ff.).

It is easy to see why Foucault's notion of the gaze lends itself to a critical analysis of participatory development. The inherently public character of participation makes panopticism a distinct possibility. For example, one of the key tools of participatory development is Participatory Rural Appraisal (PRA), which aims at ensuring inclusive and "bottom-up" planning and decision making for a range of development projects, from forestry management and health to irrigation and urban slum improvement (Chambers 1994a, 1994b, 1997). PRAs are made up of public events (meetings, social/community gatherings) involving face-to-face discussions and interactions, typically between community members and leaders, local authorities, and NGO and donor agency representatives. PRAs are thus a type of spectacle, in which people perform roles under the watchful eyes of all those gathered. The community gaze is omnipresent in discussions and social interactions, so that to participate is to play to an audience, live up to an expectation, or act out a socially sanctioned duty.

Drawing on Foucault, the critics of participatory development home in on four of the latter's main panoptic (and performative) dimensions, which I would now like to outline.

## Panoptic Consensus Making

A key objective of participatory development is to arrive at a consensus. Once the main stakeholders are brought together, relevant information has been sifted through, and people have aired their opinions, a collective decision is reached (Chambers 1994a). The consensus that ensues is thus taken by not being imposed from the top or "outside," but as reflective of the community's own interests and needs. But as both Cooke (2001, 102ff.) and Kothari (2001, 145–146) point out, there is a "tyranny" at work in group decision making as a result of which participants' views can be influenced by (the gaze of) others, resulting for example in intimidation and self-censorship. The use of rhetoric—polemical or sensationalist arguments, technical or esoteric language, misrepresentation or overrepresentation of evidence, loud or aggressive speech, spectacular or melodramatic images, monopolization of air time by a participant—can unduly influence opinion or silence participants (Kapoor 2004a; 2008, 66). Such rhetoric can sometimes be overt, but sometimes it can be subtle, too, as when government or NGO officials bring in scientific "experts" to address (read: persuade) community members about, say, the necessity and viability of a hydroelectric dam (Kapoor 2004a).

The presence of facilitating organizations may further reinforce this type of conduct. As Mosse underscores repeatedly (1994, 520; 1997, 255; 2001, 20; 2005, 85), in the case of an outside-funded program especially, people will tend to say and do what they believe is expected of them. Rather than dissent, they may feel obliged, under the scrutiny of the donor and government officials, to give only the "official story." In the presence of the funder, they may feel encouraged to work harder and deliver better results, or hide their disappointment when something promised by the funder or local government is undelivered.

The panoptic gaze can thus constrain or coerce consensus making. This is particularly true, as I have noted elsewhere (Kapoor 2004a; 2005, 1209–1210), because of the tendency to seek a single consensus or policy decision, which risks stifling social plurality. Panopticism, coupled with the demand for a single outcome, sets up an all-or-nothing situation in which some community members win (usually powerful elites, who feel entitled to speak up) and others lose (usually minorities or the disadvantaged, who feel constrained and intimidated to participate). Consensus making assumes a monolithic community, prescribing one formula for all women, classes, disabled people, or racialized groups, irrespective of differences, inequalities, and tensions between them.

But in addition to constricting people's participation, the panoptic gaze also constricts discussion topics, agendas, and outcomes. It emboldens the powerful to raise, defend, and advance their interests (e.g., private property, leadership, religious privileges, law and order), while constraining or silencing subaltern voices. Frequently, this means ignoring precisely those issues that are most difficult to address—class and caste inequality, patriarchy, racism (Kapoor 2004b, 637; Mohan and Stokke 2000; Mosse 2001, 22). Thus, Kelsall and Mercer (2003) write about a World Vision participatory community development project in Northern Tanzania, which ends up concentrating power in the hands of established elites (church elders and employees, village council members, rich farmers) to the exclusion of poorer farmers and women. Not only is decision making monopolized by these elites, but so are project resources (access to funds and training, allocation of free cattle), thereby "reproducing existing inequalities" (Kelsall and Mercer 2003, 302; see also Mosse 1994, 508).

In all the above instances of panoptic and power-induced consensus making, the political result may well be that elites win. It is precisely the latter's socioeconomic, cultural and patriarchal power that allows for biased decisions or a coerced single consensus, so that subalterns end up effectively being disenfranchised or asked to put aside their aspirations for the sake of the "community good" (Kapoor 2004b, 637–638). Thus, despite the trappings of empowerment for the "poor," participatory processes can end up reproducing or even advancing elite domination.

## Imposed "Local Knowledge"

Participatory development prides itself on valuing local, and especially subaltern, knowledge. Much pain is taken to ensure that the "catalytic" or facilitating organizations—NGOs, local government organizations, and/or international development agencies—help coordinate and support, not extract or impose, local knowledge through inclusive participatory mechanisms (Chambers 1994a, 1997). Yet, critics point out that panopticism can cause participatory development to do just what it sets out not to do: rather than reflecting the diversity of knowledge of the local community, it can bias knowledge production in favor of outsiders and elites.

Mosse's research on PRA highlights this problem. He finds that what is taken to be "local" knowledge can be a reflection of the preferences and biases, not of the community, but of outside authorities (e.g., donor and NGO representatives, local government officials). Thus, *adivasi* (indigenous) villagers in Western India are found to prefer using eucalyptus as timber for housing. Yet they do so, not because they are drawing on "traditional knowledge" or have had prior experience with this tree species, but because the local Forest Department favors it—it is a faster-growing tree, compared to, say, oak (Mosse 2001, 20–21, 17; see also 1997, 255; 2005, 94). In a similar vein, Mosse maintains that often local "needs" identified in PRAs are not necessarily what local community members believe in, but what they think the outside donor can realistically deliver: they "increasingly [anticipate] and [comply] with outsiders' points of view" (2005, 93; see also 2001, 19–20; Kothari 2001, 146–147). In this sense, for him, PRAs are "disciplinary exercises in right thinking; techniques through which outsiders [control] the knowledge that others [possess]" (Mosse 2005, 96).

Not just outsiders influence local knowledge; so do local elites. As was the case with consensus making, knowledge making can be prejudiced for the benefit of local leaders and power brokers. Mosse avers (2005, 82) that "[t]hrough PRAs, men of influence [can] mobilise participation in such a way that [wins] public support for private interests"—for example, preferred crop choices and tree species or agronomic and pest control methods. As time passes, NGO staff and local authorities begin to treat these same elites as "knowledgeable, open, innovative, organised, cooperative, clear sighted and able to speak for others" (Mosse 2005, 84). And before long, what were once elite concerns are taken for granted: they become naturalized, passing off as "consensus," "community will," or "traditional knowledge" (Kapoor 2005, 1212–1213).

So participation's panoptic gaze may well help redefine knowledge, but knowledge cannot be divorced from power, as Foucault is quick to remind us. Indeed, far from reconfiguring knowledge in favor of the community at large (let alone the subaltern), participatory development ends up reflecting, and being shaped by, power inequalities. Thus, outsiders and elites can each deploy panopticism to their advantage, so that external agendas become local concerns and dominant "regimes of truth" are normalized as "traditional knowledge."

## Gender Constrictions

The panoptic gaze plays a notable role in shaping gender relations. Women, for example, whom participatory development takes great pains to include in decision-making, can both feel and be intimidated when speaking publicly. This is particularly the case when they are expected to openly raise such sensitive issues as sex, rape, or violence (Mayoux 1995; Mosse 1994, 509–510; 2005, 85; Parpart 2000). As a consequence, rather than speaking frankly or expressing direct dissent, they either resort to letting men articulate their concerns or, as Mosse notes, they "have to clothe their ideas and encode their desires in particular ways to make them heard and accepted as legitimate in the public domain of the PRA. But often, their particular concerns do not find a place in the consensus which a PRA generates" (1994, 515).

It is, of course, the panoptic operations of a patriarchal society that are at play here. The public character of participatory development means that patriarchs—both symbolic and real—monitor and normalize women's (and community members') behaviors (Kapoor 2002, 113–114; 2005, 1212). So women have to "encode" their communicative interactions in the presence of the larger community, particularly men. And it is not just that the (heteropatriarchal) male gaze takes possession of the female-as-object to ogle at it or gain power over it; it is also, to follow Foucault, that women end up monitoring *themselves* with a patriarchal eye. The patriarchic gaze is internalized by women, and for that matter, by all community members, female as much as male, heterosexual as much as queer, constricting their participation.

## Securitization

The increasing securitization of societies, especially over the last decade and a half, has meant a greater pervasiveness of surveillance—CCTV, collection of social security or tax data, populationwide security assessments, cybersurveillance, and so on. Not surprisingly, such securitization has also crept into development, with the rising presence of security firms and the military, in the humanitarian sector for example. And not surprisingly, critics warn of the securitization of participatory development, particularly in light of its panoptic dimensions (Kapoor 2013, 110–111; Nelson and Wright 1995, 8–9).

The idea here is that, to the extent that panopticism is a technology of surveillance, it provides the opportunity to monitor the Other for various purposes, including for security reasons. In this sense, securitization—constructing and managing the Other as a threat—may not be integral to the panoptic gaze, but it is likely facilitated by it. While more field research is required here, the claim is that, with regard to participatory development, donors, NGOs and government officials may all find participation helps monitor the community: it may allow them, for example, to keep tabs on community members seen as threatening, or to co-opt those seen as potential allies, organizers, or leaders. Gradually, as I have pointed out (Kapoor 2004a; 2005, 1212–1213), everyone may develop an interest in such surveillance: husbands/fathers may use it to watch over their wives/children; elites may see in it an opportunity for keeping dissent in check; and subalterns may find it useful for monitoring both their peers and foes. Once again, this amounts to what Foucault calls "governmentality," although here subjects self-govern through the lens of security.

To conclude this section, the main argument by the critics of participatory development is that participation's panoptic gaze disciplines subjects, affecting the way people interact, decisions are made, and knowledge is produced. Most often, panopticism molds itself to the prevailing power structures, so that far from mounting a challenge to dominant power/knowledge, it "can lead to the reification of social norms through self-surveillance and consensus-building" (Kothari 2001, 142). Participatory development yields, in this sense, to the privileging of some voices (elites, donors, NGOs, government), and the suppression and exclusion of others (women, subalterns).

# Participation and the Lacanian Gaze: The Traumatic Loss of Mastery

If the Foucauldian concept of the gaze is linked to power, the Lacanian concept is linked to desire and libidinal attachment. Turning our attention to the latter will allow us to examine how participatory development is libidinally invested.

In his early writings, Lacan develops a notion of the gaze that parallels Foucault's. For Lacan, in the "mirror stage," the child deludes itself into thinking that it has mastery over its body (because it perceives its body-image as whole and unified), in spite of the fact that what it experiences is a lack of bodily control (poor verbal ability, coordination, etc.) (Lacan 1977, 2). The Lacanian gaze here is an illusory sense of mastery, an act of imaginative deception. But in later work (1998, 67ff.), Lacan revises this view, removing any sense of complete mastery while maintaining the notion of self-delusion. In fact, the gaze for him becomes the point at which mastery fails (Copjec 1994, 30ff.).

The later Lacan distinguishes between the "eye" and the "gaze": the eye belongs to the subject looking at the object, whereas the gaze belongs to the object looking back (1998, 67). The gaze for him, then, is not about the inspecting subject (à la Foucault), but the point at which the object is scrutinizing the subject. And the crucial claim is that, while I may be looking at the object, it is always already looking back at me, although from a perspective of which I am unaware (Lacan 1998, 109; Žižek 1997, 109, 125–126). As Žižek explains, the gaze is a "kind of formal 'condition of possibility' of our seeing anything at all" (1996, 90). It preexists the subject, in the sense that we are all born into a historically constructed visual world. But importantly, our perception depends on exclusion, with the result that for us to see, something must be left out. The gaze, to be sure, is the expression of the "remainder" of "symbolic identification," the rupture in any functioning ideology (Žižek 1992, 4, 1996, 113). What Lacan is getting at, therefore, is the inherent "lack" in the visual/symbolic field, the unavoidable gap within the subject's seemingly omnipotent look (Lacan 1998, 73; McGowan 2007, 6).

Following Lacan (1998, 74, 104), I would like to differentiate between two different forms of the gaze—as "stain" (or "spot") and as "lure"—with a view to examining how they play out in participatory development. The stain is that which is absent or mislaid in the symbolic order, whereas the lure is that inexpressible characteristic of the Other which makes me desire her/him.

## The "Stain" of Participatory Development

In his Seminar XI, Lacan (1998, 88–89) illustrates his notion of the gaze with the help of Hans Holbein's famous work *The Ambassadors*. At first glance, the painting depicts two well-dressed, rich travelers; but looking at it carefully, one discovers an oval, distorted figure at the bottom of the work that turns out to be a skull—the figure of death that, unbeknownst to the travelers, haunts them. The skull, in this light, is the stain or blind spot that marks the disruption of the visual/symbolic field, a point of indeterminacy that the subject fails to see. Others might be able to glimpse it, but if the subject were able to see the stain, there would be no gaze: "I see only from one point," writes Lacan, "but in my existence I am looked at from all sides" (1998, 72; see also Copjec 1994, 34–35).

The gaze-as-stain is thus the point at which something is left unrevealed, remaining invisible to the subject. In particular, what Lacan has in mind here are the subject's unconscious desires, which distort the field of vision. We invest our desires in everything we do, yet we are often barely cognizant of them and rarely attuned to how they frame and limit our perspective. As McGowan puts it, "the gaze is nothing but the way that the subject's desire deforms what it sees" (2013, 11). Our desires, in this sense, disrupt our ability to remain detached, neutral, or all-perceiving.

So what, then, are participatory development's desires? Where are we to locate its skulls and skeletons? Its ostensible goal is the Other's "empowerment." Yet, as I have noted above and underline further below, participation projects center not so much on the Other as the Self (e.g., the donor, the out-side convener, the NGO-as-facilitator). Here the gaze-as-stain is to be found in the way the convener's perspective is distorted, indicating her/his critical involvement in the scene from which s/he is supposedly excluded. The dis-course of empowerment thus conceals the external actor's (fervent?) desire to be the central agent.

What is surprising is that participatory development programs go to great lengths to cover over the most obvious: it is not the program "beneficiaries" but the donor/convener who is in control. It is the latter who provides the nec-essary financial and institutional resources, and who directs and manages the project, in most cases from start to finish. Moreover, at community meetings, the facilitator may well portray herself as neutral and fair, but the fact is that she manages the proceedings almost every step of the way—deciding on the need for, and objectives of, the meeting; choosing who to include or exclude on the invitation list; composing the agenda; selecting which participants speak, on what topic and for how long; and/or shaping the form and use of the meet-ing outputs (Kapoor 2005, 1207; Mosse 2005, 91). Power is tilted decidedly in favor of the convener, and as we have seen, while it may well be used account-ably, it can just as easily be abused (by donors, elites, local authorities).

The convener's desire to be at the center of the scene is evidenced, addi-tionally, by the remarkable absence of politics in participatory development. Community empowerment is meant to politicize development, making it more responsive and accountable, particularly to the subaltern. But the prob-lem is that the participatory space is purposefully artificial and anesthetized: projects take place in geographically bounded places (villages, neighborhoods) that are easier to isolate from the "outside" world precisely in order to avoid political complications—the inconveniences and messiness of such things as capitalist globalization, regional disparities, or broader racial tensions and so-cial protest (Kapoor 2008, 74; see also Mohan and Hickey 2004). By cleansing the space of the political (disagreement, debate, disorderliness), the convener can thus more easily stage-manage and control it: community consensus is eas-ier to construct (or coerce), elites are more easily co-opted, and subalterns more easily assuaged.

We looked into some instances of stage management earlier, but the ten-dency toward constructing a nonthreatening, depoliticized, and hence more manageable participatory space is also evinced by two other inclinations. First, while donors/conveners appear all too ready to take up participatory devel-opment in the global South, very rarely if ever are their *own* (First World) decision-making structures participatory—in fact, most are hierarchical and bureaucratic. This means, ironically, that the approval of "open" and "inclusive" participation programs is the result of mainly closed and top-down bureaucratic decision making (Kapoor 2005, 1217). No wonder, as we have seen, that such openness and inclusion are frequently compromised in project implementation, reflective of the convener's desire to set aside meaningful politics in favor of a manageable project that centers on her/him.

And second, as I have argued elsewhere (Kapoor 2005, 1217), while the proponents of participation seem eager to initiate projects in such areas as health, education, or forestry, almost never do they take them up in more politically difficult areas such as, say, manufacturing. Social economy—making the economic sector more socially accountable—remains a taboo in participatory development, most likely because it would entail grappling with fraught and fractious worker-management relationships, trade union politics, and private property laws and protections. This speaks once again to participatory development's tendencies toward the relatively safe and controllable.

The blind spot of participatory development is thus the failure to see that the convener is far from fair, neutral, or objective in the empowerment process: his/her desires are in fact central, principally in wanting to create a manageable participatory space, cleansed of the untidiness and unpredictability of the political. The gaze-as-stain thereby exposes the constructedness and tendentiousness of participatory development. But it also foregrounds the fantasy that the convener must create in order to maintain the illusion of "doing good," of "helping" the Other. This fantasy is vital to domesticating the trauma of the gaze; it is a way of concealing the fundamental agency of the external actor in the Other's empowerment process. To put it in Lacanian terms: participatory development is structured around a fantasy (the Other's empowerment), which aims at avoiding the Real (trauma) of the gaze, that is, at sustaining the fiction that the convener's desires have little to do with it.

## The "Lure" of Participatory Development: Enjoyment and Submission to the Other

In addition to the stain is the lure. Lacan maintains that "the relation between the gaze and what one wishes to see involves a lure" (1998, 104). What he has in mind here is the *objet petit a* (or *objet a*, for short)—the illusive object that, according to him, we, as human animals, must abandon when we emerge from nature into culture as desiring subjects. It is a fictional and unobtainable object, yet without it we feel incomplete and insecure (Lacan 1977, ii, 73, 76–77, 164). It is less a positive entity than a lacuna, and for Lacan this "*objet a* in the field of the visible is the gaze" (1998, 105; see also McGowan 2007, 6). The reason the *"gaze as objet a"* is a lure is because it acts to trigger our desire—Lacan calls it "the object-cause of desire" (1998, 17, 62). Our look is compelled and mesmerized by some unseen mystery or secret, a *je ne sais quoi*, to which the gaze appears to offer access. And we derive a certain enjoyment (*jouissance*)[2] in our search for this mysterious object, so much so that we seek it out relentlessly and insatiably, even though it may well be fleeting and fictional.

I want to suggest that participatory development holds out the promise of enjoyment in the way that it deploys the *"gaze as objet a."* The primary way it does this is by seeking out the Other's gaze as a guarantee for the donor's/convener's being. That is, participatory development enables the donor to attract the gaze of the Other—project participants, other donors, the media, the wider public—as an assurance of social recognition (see chapter 5). As Žižek states, "I exist only in so far as I am looked at all the time . . . today, anxiety seems to arise from the prospect of NOT being exposed to the Other's gaze all the time, so that the subject needs the [Other's] gaze as a kind of ontological guarantee of his/her being" (2002, 225).

There are several ways in which seeking the Other's gaze manifests itself in participatory development. Keeping in mind that the fantasmatic *objet a* points not to what you see but how you'd like to be seen, then it could be said that what enthralls the Western donor promoting participation is not so much Third World "empowerment" but the Third World's gaze on the West. Even though public participation and democracy in the West have several limitations (corruption, low voter turnout, social inequalities, etc.), donors fantasize that the Third World admires and wishes to imitate Western democratic/participatory practices. As several analysts have underlined (e.g., Escobar 1995; Sachs 1992), the very notion of international development is premised on this Third World–First World or tradition-modernity hierarchy. In this sense, the Third World gaze becomes the *objet a*, with donors *desiring to be desired*, that is, fantasizing about being liked and admired. The gaze elicited by participatory development is thus meant to shore up the Western donor's identity. Žižek affirms, in this regard, that "[t]he most elementary fantasmatic scene . . . [is] the notion of 'someone out there looking at us'; it is [not so much a dream as] the notion that 'we are the objects in someone [else's] dream'" (2002, 225).

In this post-Fordist age, seeking the Other's recognition often happens through branding. And in the context of international development, participatory development has indeed become a kind of brand (Kapoor 2008, 67–68; Mosse 2001, 23–24; see also chapter 3). For donors, it provides a certain cachet, a mark of respectability, which brings instant approbation and value, while enabling development agencies to build long-term trust and loyalty with their "clients" (governments, communities, NGOs). As a brand, participation is therefore a means of inviting the Other's gaze, thereby contributing to the donor's self-image as caring, benevolent, and generous.

Within the participatory space itself, moreover, there are several ways that "desiring the Other's desire" is expressed and realized. As I have written elsewhere,

> [Participatory development] creates a "feel good" community experi-
> ence, but elides the behind-the-scenes stage management. It promotes
> the sharing of power, but manages to centralise power by personalising
> and mythologising the role of the facilitator. The latter feature is per-
> haps what makes [participatory development] so desirable to the devel-
> opment establishment—its narcissistic pleasurability: not only does one
> get to stage the empowerment process, but one also gets to be the cen-
> tre of attention, deriving enjoyment and praise for it. (Kapoor 2005,
> 1208)

Here, the depoliticization of the participatory space, as discussed earlier, is central to ensuring the Other's recognition and approbation. By creating an anesthetized and tame environment, relatively free of internal dissent or out-side complications, the convener confirms the likelihood of a friendly, docile, and admiring audience. The Other's gaze is constructed, if not manipulated, so that the convener sees itself reflected in community members' eyes in a way that makes it feel good. Depoliticization thus helps avert trauma and anxiety in favor of a palatable, sympathetic, and pleasurable gaze. The "community gaze as *objet a*" becomes the bearer once again of a certain *jouissance*.

Three implications follow. First, participatory development, it seems, is a kind of pleasurable "reality show," almost like *Big Brother*. The participatory project is not only an artificially created space, but also a stage where people appear to play themselves "for real." The conveners/donors play the benevo-lent and generous overseers; NGO and local government staff play the expert managers who care; and community members act out their "real" lives and struggles, albeit in a participatory way. All of them know the space is an arti-ficial one—it is donor funded and managed, and participatory only in a limited and provisional sense; yet they act as if that were not so, playing "for real" to an audience (themselves, the wider public, etc.), that is, for the benefit of a gaze. To twist what Žižek has to say about *Big Brother*, "[t]he standard dis-claimer of a novel ('characters in this text are fictional, any resemblance with real life characters is purely coincidental') also holds for [participatory development]: what we see there are fictional characters, even if they play themselves for real" (2002, 227).

It is when one examines the libidinal economy which supports this fantasy space that things get more troubling. There is surely an exhibitionist and voyeuristic dimension to the gaze (Lacan 1998, 181–183). In participatory development, this manifests in the way people can get a kick from role playing and acting (out) for others, or enjoy gossiping about the day's revelations about their neighbors (Kapoor 2008, 69; see also Wilson 2014, 2015). Talking, dialoguing, rumor-mongering, performing—all can and do become a source of pleasure, which, it must be noted, puts paid to any Habermasian notion of "undistorted" communication (Habermas 1985): it is not necessarily clarity or transparency but the enjoyment of talking/performing that can become the goal of communicative action; people can get invested in it (see chapter 4).

Yet this kind of *jouissance* is derived by *all* project participants, whether community members or donor, government, and NGO staff. More disturbing is that, since it is the donors/conveners who are in the driving seat, their enjoyment is more accurately described as both narcissistic and sadomasochistic: they get off on the secret fantasies (of benevolence) they invest in participatory development, their powerful role as stage director (or puppeteer?), the manipulated adulation of community members, or the mesmerizing gaze of the Other to be seduced and impressed. There is also a class and racial dimension to this sadomasochism, with mainly privileged white donors lording it over mostly nonwhite subalterns (see chapter 11). The undergirding (supremacist) fantasy here, once again, is that "these poor nonwhite people really want to become more like us." Hence the need to direct (and bend) them.

The second implication is that, from the point of view of the donor, participatory development is an enjoyment-producing machine. As we have noted, participation helps shore up the donor's identity, bringing approbation and respectability; it elicits a nonthreatening, manageable, and admiring community gaze; and it is the source of sadomasochistic pleasures that confirm the donor's dominant role. No wonder that development agencies have become deeply invested in participation. Its libidinal returns help explain, in fact, why participation programs proliferate among the development community (as pointed out above). This in spite of the fact that the logic of participation dictates the contrary: conveners are supposed to work themselves out of a job by handing over to self-determining communities. That institutional expansion ensues shows instead that desire and *jouissance* are central factors in the operations of these organizations (this is what I have been calling "institutional enjoyment"; see chapters 2 and 12). It should not be forgotten, in this regard, that ultimately desire is never about finding its object but about perpetuating itself, continually moving on to new objects and producing new pleasures (see Fletcher 2013, 2015; Kapoor 2015, 1129; McGowan 2007, 9; and chapter 4). So it is hardly surprising that participatory development is less about empowering the Other than gratifying and aggrandizing the donor.

Finally, we come to a crucial yet perhaps counterintuitive psychoanalytic idea: despite donors' powerful, neocolonial position in participatory development, they are notably vulnerable to the Other. This is because, psychoanalytically speaking, we seek our lack in the field of the Other, which is ultimately unknowable. That is, desire emerges in response to an *objet a* that constantly eludes our grasp, not because it is a transcendent or powerful object, but simply because it cannot be apprehended: its secret is that there is no secret, yet we nonetheless continue our search for it (McGowan 2003, 35). The donors' desire arises therefore in response to the indecipherable gaze of the Other—they never really know who this Other is, what s/he is really thinking, or whether his/her admiration is authentic or feigned. Yet, donors need and want to believe in the Other's gaze (the fictional *objet a* as lure), seeking *jouissance* in it.

In a sense, then, donors are *submitting* to the Other: the gaze triggers their desire because it seems to hold the secret, not to their completeness, but as McGowan puts it, "the disappearance of self in the experience of enjoyment" (2007, 11). In fact, it could be said that donors *enjoy* submitting to the Other, since by never being able to fully apprehend the Other, by always failing to get the object, the experience of enjoyment is constantly renewed (and institutional aggrandizement assured). There is, as a consequence, remarkable instability to the donors' sense of self and need for recognition: the Other's gaze may well help shore up their identity but, by the same token, such a gaze is never guaranteed or predictable—which unmistakably opens up avenues for the Other's agency.

## Mimicry and (Subaltern) Agency

It is because the subject is always lacking and never fully interpellated that, for Lacan, any mastery of the Other must ultimately fail (McGowan 2007, 35; Žižek 1999, 262). The notion of the gaze is meant precisely to bring such failure to the fore, since it constitutes the blind spot in the donor's/convener's look, which the Other can potentially exploit as I want to suggest below. So donor-initiated participatory development may well manipulate the Other sadomasochistically, but in the end it succeeds only in giving an illusory sense of control.

In this regard, let us turn briefly to Bhabha's work, as it gives the Lacanian notion of the gaze a notable political inflection.[3] In the context of colonialism, Bhabha disturbs the idea of any totalizing colonial authority, seeing it instead as always split and hybrid. This is because the colonizer can never produce a stable discourse of legitimation, trying to assert both the master's difference from, yet commonality with, the colonized. For Bhabha, such a contradictory and ambivalent discourse can empower the colonized to resist and interrupt it: "The ambivalence at the source of traditional discourses on authority enables a form of subversion, founded on the undecidability that turns the discursive conditions of dominance into the grounds of intervention" (1994, 112).

Bhabha illustrates his argument with several instances of subaltern agency, most notably in his essay "Of Mimicry and Man." There, he writes about the colonizer's attempt at promoting a colonial civilizing mission by creating "mimic men," that is, recognizable Others who are *almost the same, but not quite*" (1994, 86, italics in original). But this ambivalence ("same"/"not quite") is exploitable: mimicry easily serves as camouflage for menace or mockery, with the native denying, or threatening to deny, her master's desire for recognition or imitation. Mimicry, then, is a mixture of deference and destabilization, bowing to the master but refusing to become his replica. As a result, the master can recognize himself only in an image which is alluring but also "alienating and hence potentially confrontational . . . always threatened by lack . . . [and the] return of the look [i.e., the gaze]" (77, 81).

In participatory development, the donor's authority is replete with the ambivalences and contradictions that Bhabha is alluding to: wanting to be recognized and admired but unable to decipher the Other's gaze; empowering the Other while remaining at the center of the process; aspiring to appear benevolent and other-regarding, but nonetheless directing and stage-managing meetings; seeking consensus, yet ensuring it is single, smooth, and relatively uncontested; and so on. These slippages, in turn, open up multiple possible spaces for political action by community members. To name just a few: demanding more transparent rules for community deliberation and project management; praising and obliging donors/elites inside meetings, but badmouthing them outside; highlighting community differences and inequalities rather than commonalities and consensus; organizing for participation to be extended to other spheres of community life; manipulating donors' need to appear benevolent by cajoling them into providing more funding or, say, better minority/subaltern political representation; and diverting project resources for other, nonproject purposes. All are attempts at denying the master full recognition, refusing to be his docile or palatable subject. The idea instead is for community members to manipulate the manipulator—to mimic the master while mocking him, to listen intently to him while reinterpreting his rules or appropriating his resources for other uses.

Such a "politics of estrangement," so to speak, is not just theoretical or speculative; there is already some evidence of it:

- Waddington and Mohan (2004) examine the ways in which a Village AiD project in Ghana has inspired women to strengthen their bargaining position outside the project vis-à-vis local elites/patriarchs.
- Hildyard et al. (2001, 60) show how women participants in a participatory project, rather than using project loans to buy dairy cattle, have diverted the funds for their own purposes (e.g., to recover family heirlooms used as loan equity).
- Nagar and Swarr (2004) write about a community school program in India, whose unintended consequence has been to allow lesbians to organize against homophobia and social prejudice.
- Jenkins and Goetz (1999) document how a participation project has inspired a right-to-information campaign challenging government corruption and accountability in Rajasthan (India).
- Mitlin (2004) indicates that participation programs can inspire people to mobilize against elites during local elections.
- McKinnon (2006) studies how NGO-initiated participatory practices have been put to a range of successful regional political uses by marginalized groups in northern Thailand.
- Finally, in India's Western Ghats, villagers are reported to have used the knowledge and organizational skills gained from a participatory forestry project to help close down a nearby hazardous mine, as well as secure the construction of a long-promised road from the local government (Prem Kare, cited in Hildyard et al. 2001, 68).

All of these are instances of a kind of hijacking of participatory development—its twisting, reinterpretation, or reappropriation by community members. But we should bear in mind that such events are neither pervasive nor necessarily overwhelming; they tend, in fact, to be relatively uncommon, involving not so much a reversal of power as its diversion and estrangement. The power of donors (or elites) still tends to remain hegemonic, although certainly not stable or totalizing. There is always the possibility of a more coordinated and persistent creative resistance campaign (see Kapoor 2003; 2008, 132ff.), but as far as I am aware, there is no evidence of this to date in regard specifically to participatory development (which speaks perhaps to a broader limitation of what in chapter 8 I call "performative" politics).[4] We should also bear in mind that such a politics of estrangement is not necessarily the preserve of the subaltern. While several of the instances cited above involve the subaltern divergence of power, there is no necessary reason that local elites could not also creatively bend power for their own interests. Indeed, more often than not they do bend (and have bent) power in this way: recall earlier-mentioned cases of elites coercing consensus and diverting project resources.

Nonetheless, from the point of view of the donor/convener, these moments of deflection disturb any sense of mastery or omnipotence. They are precisely instances of the gaze, in the Lacanian sense of that term—blind spots that the master is unaware of, uncanny moments that makes him aware of his smugness,[5] disruptive and traumatic events that bring to the fore his instabilities and insecurities. Try as donors may for their participatory projects to turn out one way, such instances demonstrate that projects can be turned in so many unexpected ways. If, as pointed out earlier, the donor's main preoccupation is not so much the Other's empowerment but the need for recognition/admiration, then these moments of disruption show that the Other's main preoccupation is not so much admiration but using the project for other purposes. If Western donors dream about being in the Third World's dreams, then the above instances reveal that the Third World dreams of places where the donor plays a peripheral—not central—role.

## Conclusion: Foucault or Lacan?

It must be noted that, whether drawing on Foucault or Lacan, the critics of participatory development (myself included) are not against participation per se. I have previously stated, echoing Foucault, that it is not that participation is bad, it is that it is dangerous (2008, 72–73). That is, its practice is neither straightforward nor necessarily benign, particularly in the context of international development, where ironically, it can often take on neocolonial and exclusionary dimensions.

In this chapter, I have focused on the gaze as a way of drawing attention precisely to several of these dangers. Foucault's conception of the gaze helps bring out participation's panopticism—its tendencies toward mastering the Other by coercing consensus, producing docile subjects (particularly subalterns and women), and biasing knowledge production in favor of donors and local elites. In contrast, Lacan's notion of the gaze helps focus on participation's desires—the convener's desire to be center stage, depoliticize the empowerment process, and be admired by the Other to the point of submission.

Both Foucault and Lacan are important in helping alert us to different political facets of participatory development, the one elucidating its power/ knowledge characteristics, the other its libidinal investments. In a sense, Foucault's critical analysis places us inside the participatory scene, where we experience the restrictions and prescriptions of the panoptic gaze, while Lacan's places us backstage, where we decipher what fails to appear on stage, thus making the scene suspect. As Copjec suggests, Foucault's gaze is a caring and knowing one—it takes you seriously to the point of keeping tabs on you— whereas Lacan's is a blind eye: it is "not a seen gaze, but a gaze imagined by me in the field of the Other" that is illusory and delusive (Copjec 1994, 32, 84; see also Krips 2010).

But importantly, I do want to argue that Lacan's analysis adds two crucial elements missing in Foucault's. First, as underlined in chapter 2, while Foucault is helpful in studying panoptic regimes, his work has little to say about how such regimes come about, and crucially, why they persist. Indeed, as previously discussed, he has been taken to task over these issues (e.g., Copjec 1994; McNay 1994, chap. 3; Vighi and Feldner 2007), with critics finding little in his writing explaining why people are drawn to or seduced by power. Lacan's emphasis on questions of desire and *jouissance* is much more amenable here, providing a libidinal explanation of how and why the gaze comes about and endures. Thus, as we have seen, it is because participatory development is an "enjoyment-producing machine" that we can understand why donors are eager to promote it, so much so that participation programs currently proliferate in the international development community. In this regard, the link between enjoyment and institutional politics/expansion (what I have termed "institutional enjoyment") is an important one worthy of much more study and research, I believe.

And second, while Foucault's strength lies in his analysis of the microtechnics of power, he has relatively little to say about agency (in contradistinction to "resistance"). Once again, as stressed in chapter 2 and developed further in chapter 8, he has been taken to task on this question also, with several critics arguing that he so reduces subjectivity to relations of power that it leaves not much room for agency (Brown 1995; Copjec 1994; Fraser 1989; Harstock 1990).[6] Once again, Lacan comes to the rescue, showing how the subject's mastery of the Other turns into its opposite—submission—enabling the Other to pry open the interstices of power in favor of (creative forms of) agency.[7] This is because no matter how much power the master has, there is always something missing (*objet a*)—an allure of the Other that he needs and secretly envies, yet an allure that the Other need not, and indeed cannot, divulge.

## Notes

1. Note that Foucault first develops the notion of the gaze in his earlier *Birth of the Clinic* (2003).

2. The excess of enjoyment is to be seen, as I am about to show, in how much conveners enjoy participatory development, to the point of manipulating the gaze of the Other in order to appear benevolent.

3. Ashis Nandy's work (1983), which is also psychoanalytically inflected (and which Bhabha draws on), makes a similar argument by underlining the cultural and psychological resources (e.g., Gandhian nonviolence) that can be deployed by the colonized to resist colonialism.

4. My implication here is that subaltern mimicry, to be politically efficacious and more broadly impactful, needs to accompanied by a negative universalist politics, which I discuss in chapters 3, 8, and 12. Without the latter, mimicry likely ends up as just another form of "performative" politics of the type advocated by Butler and Mahmood (see chapter 8).

5. Lacan's notion of the gaze here is akin to a *parabasis*, when the Chorus in ancient Greek dramas suddenly (and uncannily) faces and addresses the audience, breaking the dramatic fantasy and making the audience more aware of the artificiality of the staging.

6. As these critics point out, Foucault does have a notion of resistance (for him, wherever there is power, there is resistance), but it is a weak and undeveloped one, which leaves one wondering for what ethical-political reason the subject would resist and what room is left for a politics beyond mere resistance (see Brown 1995; Fraser 1989; Harstock 1990). See chapter 8.

7. Lacan does stress issues of power/mastery, as we have alluded to, but for him, ultimately the desire for power is not central to the subject. Rather, as McGowan explains (2007, 11), mastery is an avoidance of unconscious desires, a short-circuit to derive enjoyment without the experience of trauma, a way of regulating enjoyment so it does not allow one to be overcome by it. This underlines once again Foucault's overemphasis on power/mastery and failure to adequately consider unconscious desire, which in the Lacanian scheme of things is an opening for the Other's agency despite mastery.

## References

Bhabha, Homi K. 1994. *The Location of Culture*. London: Routledge.

Brown, Wendy. 1995. *States of Injury: Power and Freedom in Late Modernity*. Princeton, NJ: Princeton University Press.

Chambers, Robert. 1994a. "The Origins and Practice of Participatory Rural Appraisal." *World Development* 22 (7): 953–969.

———. 1994b. "Participatory Rural Appraisal (PRA): Analysis of Experience." *World Development* 22 (9): 1253–1268.

———. 1997. *Whose Reality Counts? Putting the First Last.* London: Intermediate Technology Publications.

Cooke Bill. 2001. "The Social Psychological Limits of Participation?" In *Participation: The New Tyranny?*, edited by Bill Cooke and Uma Kothari, 102–138. London: Zed.

Cooke, Bill, and Uma Kothari, eds. 2001. *Participation: The New Tyranny?* London: Zed.

Copjec, Joan. 1994. *Read My Desire: Lacan against the Historicists.* London: Verso.

Escobar, Arturo. 1995. *Encountering Development: The Making and Unmaking of the Third World.* Princeton, NJ: Princeton University Press.

Fletcher, Robert. 2013. "How I Learned to Stop Worrying and Love the Market: Virtualism, Disavowal, and Public Secrecy in Neoliberal Environmental Conservation." *Environment and Planning D: Society and Space* 31: 796–812.

———. 2015. "Blinded by the Stars? Celebrity, Fantasy, and Sesire in Neoliberal Environmental Governance." *Celebrity Studies* 6 (4): 457–470.

Foucault, Michel. 1977. *Discipline and Punish: The Birth of the Prison.* Translated by Alan Sheridan. New York: Pantheon.

———. 1984. *The Foucault Reader.* Edited by Paul Rabinow. New York: Pantheon.

———. 1991. *The Foucault Effect: Studies in Governmentality.* Edited by Graham Burchell, Colin Gordon, and Peter Miller. London: Harvester Wheatsheaf.

———. 1996. *Foucault Live: Interviews, 1961–1984.* Edited by Sylvère Lotringer. New York: Semiotext(e).

———. 2003. *The Birth of the Clinic: An Archaeology of Medical Perception.* Translated by Alan Sheridan. London: Routledge.

Fraser, Nancy. 1989. *Unruly Practices: Power, Discourse and Gender in Contemporary Social Theory.* Minneapolis: University of Minnesota Press.

Habermas, Jürgen. 1985. *The Theory of Communicative Action.* Vol. 1. New York: Beacon.

Harstock, Nancy. 1990. "Foucault on Power: A Theory for Women?" In *Feminism/Postmodernism*, edited by Linda J. Nicholson, 157–175. London and New York: Routledge.

Henkel, Heiko, and Roderick Stirrat. 2001. "Participation as Spiritual Duty; Empowerment as Secular Subjection." In *Participation: The New Tyranny?*, edited by Bill Cooke and Uma Kothari, 168–184. London: Zed.

Hildyard, Nicholas, Pandurang Hegde, Paul Wolvenkamp, and Somsekhare Reddy. 2001. "Pluralism, Participation and Power: Joint Forest Management in India." In *Participation: The New Tyranny?*, edited by Bill Cooke and Uma Kothari, 56–71. London: Zed.

Jenkins, Rob, and Anne Marie Goetz. 1999. "Accounts and Accountability: Theoretical Implications of the Right-to-Information Movement in India." *Third World Quarterly* 20 (3): 603–622.

Kapoor, Ilan. 2002. "The Devil's in the Theory: A Critical Assessment of Robert Chambers' Work on Participatory Development." *Third World Quarterly* 23(1): 101–17.

——. 2003. "Acting in a Tight Spot: Homi Bhabha's Postcolonial Politics." *New Political Science* 25 (4): 561–577.

——. 2004a. "Concluding Remarks: The Power of Participation." *Current Issues in Comparative Education* 6 (2): 125–129. https://www.tc.columbia.edu/cice/pdf/25731_6_2_Kapoor.pdf.

——. 2004b. "Hyper-Self-Reflexive Development? Spivak on Representing the Third World 'Other.'" *Third World Quarterly* 25 (4): 627–647.

——. 2005. "Participatory Development, Complicity and Desire." *Third World Quarterly* 26 (8): 1203–1220.

——. 2008. *The Postcolonial Politics of Development*. London: Routledge.

——. 2013. *Celebrity Humanitarianism: The Ideology of Global Charity*. London: Routledge.

——. 2015. "Psychoanalysis and Development: Contributions, Examples, Limits." *Third World Quarterly* 35 (7): 1120–1143.

Kelsall, Tim, and Claire Mercer. 2003. "Empowering People? World Vision and the 'Transformatory Development' in Tanzania." *Review of African Political Economy* 96: 293–304.

Kothari, Uma. 2001. "Power, Knowledge and Social Control in Participatory Development." In *Participation: The New Tyranny?*, edited by Bill Cooke and Uma Kothari, 139–152. London: Zed.

Krips, Henry. 2010. "The Politics of the Gaze: Foucault, Lacan and Žižek." *Culture Unbound* 2: 91–102.

Lacan, Jacques. 1977. *Écrits: A Selection*. Translated by Alan Sheridan. New York: Norton.

——. 1998. *The Four Fundamental Concepts of Psychoanalysis: The Seminar of Jacques Lacan, Book XI*. Edited by Jacques-Alain Miller. New York: Norton.

Mayoux, Linda. 1995. "Beyond Naivety: Women, Gender Inequality and Participatory Development." *Development and Change* 26 (2): 235–258.

McGowan, Todd. 2003. "Looking for the Gaze: Lacanian Film Theory and Its Vicissitudes." *Cinema Journal* 42 (3): 27–47.

——. 2007. *The Real Gaze: Film Theory after Lacan*. Albany: SUNY Press.

——. 2013. "The Capitalist Gaze." *Discourse* 35 (1): 3–23.

McKinnon, Katharine Islay. 2006. "An Orthodoxy of 'The Local': Post-Colonialism, Participation and Professionalism in Northern Thailand." *The Geographical Journal* 172 (1): 22–34.

McNay, Lois. 1994. *Foucault: A Critical Introduction*. Cambridge: Polity.

Mitlin, Diana. 2004. "Securing Voice and Transforming Practice in Local Government: The Role of Federating in Grassroots Development." In *Participation: From Tyranny to Transformation? Exploring New Approaches to Participation in Development*, edited by Samuel Hickey and Giles Mohan, 175–189. London: Zed.

Mohan, Giles, and Samuel Hickey. 2004. "Relocating Participation within a Radical Politics of Development: Critical Modernism and Citizenship." In *Participation: From Tyranny to Transformation? Exploring New Approaches to Participation in Development*, edited by Samuel Hickey and Giles Mohan, 59–74. London: Zed.

Mohan, Giles, and Kristian Stokke. 2000. "Participatory Development and Empowerment: The Dangers of Localism." *Third World Quarterly* 21 (2): 247–268.

Mosse, David. 1994. "Authority, Gender and Knowledge: Theoretical Reflections on the Practice of Participatory Rural Appraisal." *Development and Change* 25 (4): 497–526.

——. 1997. "The Ideology and Politics of Community Participation: Tank Irrigation Development in Colonial and Contemporary Tamil Nadu." In *Discourses of Development: Anthropological Perspectives*, edited by R. D. Grillo and R. L. Stirrat, 255–291. Oxford: Berg.

——. 2001. "'People's Knowledge', Participation and Patronage: Operations and Representations in Rural Development." In *Participation: The New Tyranny?*, edited by Bill Cooke and Uma Kothari, 16–35. London: Zed.

——. 2005. *Cultivating Development: An Ethnography of Aid Policy and Practice.* London: Pluto.

Nagar, Richa, and Amanda L. Swarr. 2004. "Organising from the Margins: Grappling with 'Empowerment' in India and South Africa." In *A Companion to Feminist Geography*, edited by Lise Nelson and Joni Seager, 291–304. Oxford: Blackwell.

Nandy, Ashis. 1983. *The Intimate Enemy: Loss and Recovery of Self under Colonialism.* Delhi: Oxford University Press.

Nelson, Nici, and Susan Wright. 1995. "Participation and Power." In *Power and Participatory Development*, edited by Nici Nelson and Susan Wright, 1–8. London: Intermediate Technology.

Parpart, Jane. 2000. "Rethinking Participation, Empowerment, and Development from a Gender Perspective." In *Transforming Development: Foreign Aid for a Changing World*, edited by Jim Freedman, 222–234. Toronto: University of Toronto Press.

Sachs, Wolfgang, ed. 1992. *The Development Dictionary: A Guide to Knowledge as Power.* London: Zed.

Vighi, Fabio, and Heiko Feldner. 2007. *Žižek: Beyond Foucault.* Basingstoke: Palgrave Macmillan.

Waddington, Mark, and Giles Mohan. 2004. "Failing Forward: Going beyond PRA and Imposed Forms of Participation." In *Participation: From Tyranny to Transformation? Exploring New Approaches to Participation in Development*, edited by Samuel Hickey and Giles Mohan, 219–234. London: Zed.

Wilson, Japhy. 2014. "Fantasy Machine: Philanthrocapitalism as an Ideological Formation." *Third World Quarterly* 35 (7): 1144–1161.

——. 2015. "The Joy of Inequality: The Libidinal Economy of Compassionate Consumerism." *International Journal of Žižek Studies* 9 (2). http://zizekstudies.org/index.php/IJZS/article/view/815/820.

World Bank. 1995. *World Bank Participation Sourcebook.* Washington, DC: World Bank, Social Policy and Resettlement Division.

Žižek, Slavoj. 1991. *Looking Awry: An Introduction to Jacques Lacan Through Popular Culture.* Cambridge, MA: MIT Press.

——. 1992. *Enjoy Your Symptom! Jacques Lacan in Hollywood and Out.* New York: Routledge.

——. 1996. "'I Hear You with My Eyes'; or, the Invisible Master." In *Gaze and Voice as Love Objects*, edited by Renata Salecl and Slavoj Žižek, 90–126. Durham, NC: Duke University Press.

——. 1999. *The Žižek Reader*. Edited by Elizabeth Wright and Edmond Leo Wright. Oxford: Blackwell.

——. 2002. "Big Brother, or, the Triumph of the Gaze over the Eye." In *Ctrl [Space]: Rhetorics of Surveillance from Bentham to Big Brother*, edited by Thomas Y. Levin, Ursula Frohne, and Peter Weibel, 224–227. Cambridge, MA: MIT Press.

# CHAPTER 8

# When Sex = (Socially Constructed) Gender, What Is Lost, Politically?

## Psychoanalytic Reflections on Gender and Development

KEYWORDS: *Gender/Sex*

## Introduction

This chapter takes the Lacanian view that sexual difference is neither a biological position nor a discursive construct but a negative ontological category:
it is the name of the deadlock (the Real) inherent in the symbolic order
(Copjec 2012; Lacan 1998a; Zupančič 2017). Sex thus refers to the condition
of being split—out of joint and never whole. This contrasts sharply with recent feminist theory's tendency to ignore sexual difference in favor of gender
as social construction, which has caused it to overlook the negativity and
"trouble" inherent in sex, thereby missing an important way of radicalizing
feminist politics. The chapter focuses on two recent variants of the gender and
development literature—postmodern feminism and Butlerian performativity—
arguing that each prescribes a politics founded on discursivity (resistance,
transgressive repetition) that yields to a timid and fragmented politics that is
ultimately unthreatening to the neoliberal and patriarchal capitalist order. The
chapter seeks to valorize instead a feminist politics of development centered
on sex as the domain of the "too much" (i.e., excess, drive) and the "not enough"
(i.e., lack), amenable to both a more radical politics and universal collective
action.

## Social Construction: Postmodern and Performative Perspectives on Gender and Development

### Postmodern Critique/Politics

The rise of the feminist movement is closely associated with deconstructing the long-held notion that "anatomy is destiny"—sex is reducible to sexual organs, femininity is a fixed and universal essence, women are passive and unpredictable (in contrast to men, who are active and rational), and so on. Simone de Beauvoir ([1949] 1989) was one of the first to question such an ontologization of sexual difference, famously claiming that one is not born but becomes a woman. Her view was taken up by several subsequent feminist scholars (e.g., Chodorow 1978; Haslanger 1995; MacKinnon 1989; Millett 1970), who argue that gender differences and power relationships are socially determined, so that femininity and masculinity are not inherent but the result of family rearing and social learning and conditioning. Implicit if not explicit here is a movement away from sex, seen as too strongly associated with biologism, toward gender, seen as socially constructed.

The work of Chandra Mohanty and Aihwa Ong encapsulates such thinking, and I would like to briefly focus on two of their influential articles (Mohanty 1984; Ong 1988), with particular reference to implications for the politics of international development. Indeed, what both writers bring to the discussion is an important postmodern "Third World" feminist lens.

Drawing on Foucauldian discourse analysis, Mohanty's groundbreaking piece, "Under Western Eyes" (1984), seizes on three texts in Zed's "Women in the Third World" book series to carry out a critique of Western feminist scholarship about women of the global South. She claims that such scholarship tends to replicate orientalist images of the Third World woman—the veiled woman, the chaste virgin, the obedient wife—thus producing the latter as a "singular monolithic subject" (333, 352). Accordingly, Third World women are homogenized as a coherent and undifferentiated group, with identical interests and desires, irrespective of class, ethnicity, or race. They are represented as universally "traditional," "illiterate," and oppressed, victims of a cross-culturally "monolithic notion of patriarchy" (335). What is significant for Mohanty is the neocolonial thinking that pervades such discourse: for, the binary opposites upon which such categorization rests (tradition-modernity, illiterate-educated, subordinate-liberated) is predicated on the construction of a modern, secular, and emancipated Western woman. It is the latter who stands as primary reference point, making possible the production and evaluation of the Third World woman.

Overcoming such essentialist knowledge/politics requires, according to Mohanty, better addressing the diversity and difference of Third World women, that is, their "specification in local cultural and historical contexts" (1984, 347, 344–346).[1] And although she does not develop the point, she aligns the need for such a discursive approach with a typically postmodern feminist politics: a localized identity politics that eschews universalism in favor of "strategic coalitions which construct oppositional political identities for themselves" (349).

Ong's famed piece, "Colonialism and Modernity" (1988), in many ways mirrors Mohanty's, arguing against the ahistorical and decontextualized use of the category "woman." For Ong, Western feminist scholarship deploys such Western standards as rationality and individualism to evaluate Third World women, thus "unconsciously echo[ing] . . . [a] masculinist will to power in its relation to non-Western societies" (80). Such a will to power is discernible in Modernization discourse, as much as Marxist political economy, both of which according to Ong frame the Third World in essentialist and neocolonial terms, positing Western modernity as the universal benchmark; and it is equally discernible in neoliberal corporate discourse, which employs an "instrumental-biological representation of women" (e.g., "oriental" female, "nimble" fingers) to justify its sweatshop assembly operations (89, 82). Like Mohanty, Ong underlines the need for feminist/development scholars to "recognize other forms of gender- and culture-based subjectivities" and, drawing on Foucault, she ends her piece by advocating for an "understanding of gender as constructed by . . . the play of power relations in a cultural context" (90, 88).[2]

The undeniable strength of the postmodern view of gender as social construction, encapsulated by the work of Mohanty and Ong, is its dismantling of representations of "woman" as the undifferentiated Other. It helps us better understand the multiplicity of women's subject positions in the global South (and North)—how, for example, addressing gender inequalities requires paying close attention to the discursive, historical, spatial, and sociocultural contexts in which women live. By claiming that gender difference cannot be isolated from such questions as class, race, sexual orientation, ethnicity, indigeneity, ability, or nationality, it also responds to the voices of those who have been historically marginalized (women, LGBTI people, racialized minorities, indigenous communities, the disabled, the socioeconomically oppressed of the Third World, etc.) (see Anthias, Yuval-Davis, and Cain 1993; Anzaldúa 1990; hooks 1984). Here, deconstructing essentialist representations of women and opening up to the multiple axes that shape their lives is at the same time a means of clearing the space for marginalized identities to be expressed and recognized.

Yet the strength of such antiessentialism is also its weakness. As several feminist scholars have pointed out (e.g., Glynos 2000, 90; Narayan 1998; Scott 1996, 3–4), the risk of challenging one set of essentialisms is that you can end up creating others. This is the perennial limitation of postmodern identity politics, as chapters 2 and 3 have argued: championing or fixing an identity can result in a politics of parochialism ("everything from the global South is good," "any criticism from the West is suspect") and authenticity ("women are closer to nature than men"), which is often exclusionary. There is always a person or group that deviates or does not quite belong (e.g., indigenous communities in environmental movements or LGBTI people in women's movements in the global South [and North]). Thus, while uncovering and criticizing the nature / culture binary that underpins gender inequalities, postmodern social construction is not only unable to escape such a binary, but can also ends up reproducing it in inverted form (i.e., essentializing culture-as-identity).

Moreover, a fundamental political problem with antiessentialism is that, by celebrating the fluidity of identities, it often yields to a fragmented and localized politics, thereby preventing collective feminist action (see Bordo 1990; Di Stefano 1990; Nicholson 1990). As Linda Alcoff puts it, "If gender is simply a social construct, the need and even the possibility of a feminist politics becomes immediately problematic. What can we demand in the name of women if 'women' do not exist and demands in their name simply reinforce the myth that they do?" (1988, 420). Mridula Udayagiri takes Mohanty and Ong, in particular, to task on this question: "If there is no connectedness between the two realms, 'us' and 'other,' then how is it possible to form strategic coalitions across class, race, and national boundaries?" (Udayagiri 1995, 166; see also Nzomo 1995, 134; Parpart 1993; 1995b, 263–264; Parpart and Marchand 1995, 18). Thus, social construction may well reject universalism, but it fails to specify alternative ways of creating solidarity and political alliances, especially, as Udayagiri underlines, across the sociocultural and spatial (race, class, ethnicity, nation, region, etc.), axes that so often *divide* groups and communities.

The related issue is that Mohanty and Ong's credence of Foucault implies a weak conception of women's agency. Indeed, as we have rehearsed before (chapters 2 and 7), Foucault so reduces subjectivity to relations of power that he leaves not much room for politics, often wavering between determinism and voluntarism. The best he offers is a notion of resistance ("Where there is power, there is resistance"; 1979, 95), leaving many feminist critics incredulous (Brown 1995; Fraser 1989; Harstock 1990, 167). At worst, then, his discursive politics pushes women back into docility, and at best it makes them resilient;

but what it fails to provide is the possibility of a broad and transformatory feminist project.

Such a proclivity certainly appears to be reflected in postmodern studies of women's agency. Raissiguier, for example, examines how Algerian-French school girls are able to construct their identities at the intersection of a dominant French discourse of assimilation, on the one hand, and a marginal, patriarchal discourse of a French Algerian community, on the other. She concludes from her enquiry that "What we have here is neither pure resistance nor pure accommodation to already available scripts" (1995, 87). Similarly, Bald explores ways in which migrant South Asian women in Britain are able to "empower" themselves through community antiracism coalition building. For Bald, this allows the women to become more self-reliant, making their life in the margins of British society more bearable and livable (1995, 112). While such coping strategies and daily acts of resistance are certainly not to be devalued, it remains unclear how they add up to broader structural change. Indeed, they could be seen as wholly consistent with liberal multiculturalism—struggles that are tolerated, if not encouraged, by liberalism because they both confirm that multicultural democracy works and remain unthreatening to the System. In this regard, Nzomo (1995, 138) decries the overemphasis in postmodern feminist politics on representational/identity struggles to the detriment of political economy struggles (over property, work, equal pay, etc.). I would add that this has much to do, once again, with the culturalization of politics under liberal capitalist regimes—you can celebrate your identities and customs, you can even protest to have your rights recognized, as long as you don't interfere with capital accumulation and mobility. In this sense, postmodern feminist "resistance" suits (capitalist) multicultural liberal democracies just fine.

## Performative Politics

Now Judith Butler's influential concept of performativity is also a species of "gender as social construction," although it overcomes an important postmodern limitation—the rigidity of identity politics. Butler well understands that the mistake of postmodern feminism is its attempt to define "woman" as a bearer of certain culturally produced attributes, which ends up on the slippery slope of a politics of authenticity and exclusion (1990, 9). So rather than seeing gender as expressing a fixed or predetermined essence or identity, she views it as a performative act: it is instituted "through a *stylized repetition of* [habitual] *acts*" (179; see also McNay 2000, 33ff.). It relates, in this sense, not to what one is but to how one acts. Moreover, it is the result not of a priori social norms, but their recurring enactment: gender roles are routinized and institutionalized, and it is because of such continuous reinscription and reinforcement that they solidify. What we take as a given or prescribed gender identity is really the consequence of repeated performance and congealment. And for Butler, it is power structures that largely dictate the extent of such incrustation. Gender norms—patriarchal practices, heteronormativity, sexual "perversion"—are not only constructed but also propagated/imposed by a society's prevalent sociocultural institutions (1990, 42). What is portrayed as "normal" and "natural," then, is a reflection of such a society's dominant sociocultural groups and structures.

We should note here that Butler suggests doing away with the concept of sex in favor of gender. She writes, in this regard, that the "construct called 'sex' is as culturally constructed as gender . . . with the consequence that the distinction between sex and gender turns out to be no distinction at all" (1990, 10–11). This is due to the fact that, for her, physical/sexed bodies, just like gendered ones, are discursively performed and produced: they never exist outside the social, so that we can perceive or understand them only as a result of socially instituted systems of classification.

It is because gender is a construction that it can be undone, according to Butler, and this is where her politics enters the picture: gender is a "performatively enacted signification . . . that, released from its naturalized interiority and surface, can occasion the parodic proliferation and subversive play of gendered meaning" (1990, 33). Accordingly, she spends a good deal of time deconstructing and denaturalizing the binaries of gender and sexual difference (nature/culture, feminine/masculine, normal/perverse, heterosexuality/homosexuality, etc.). But her key contribution to feminist theory is the notion of performative politics implied in the above quotation: since gender roles and identities always involve repetition, the possibility for subversion and difference creeps in. The performative reinscription of social norms contains a margin of freedom. Gendered agents can defiantly resignify, creatively rearticulate, mis-cite, or fail to repeat. Thus, societies may well set limits on the woman-as-subject, but through a performative politics, she can subversively destabilize and dislocate them.

This is precisely the import of (the late) Saba Mahmood's well-known book *Politics of Piety* (2011), which draws on Butler's notion of performativity to make an argument about the agency of Muslim women in Egypt. Based on ethnographic work in Cairo, the book examines the women's mosque movement, which formed part of the broader "piety movement" in the country during the 1990s. Mahmood focuses on how women alter the male character of the mosques by, among other things, organizing public meetings to teach one another Islamic doctrine. Her intent is not only to valorize Muslim

women's agency but more importantly to recognize that it differs from secular liberal/progressive feminist views of agency. Following Butler, she rejects
the conception of politics in terms of a transcendental, autonomous subject,
arguing instead for it to be understood as a performative act of resignifica-
tion: "the meaning and sense of agency cannot be fixed in advance, but
must emerge through an analysis of the particular concepts that enable specific
modes of being, responsibility and effectivity" (Mahmood 2011, 14–15). Accordingly, the women she studies seek not so much to overturn the system of
inequality and patriarchy of the mosque as to "flourish despite its constraints,"
to use the "resources and capacities . . . [that] a pious lifestyle make[s]
available"—ranging from demanding better access to religious instruction and
changes in women's dress to learning about financial and household management and the provision of services to the poor (168, 104–105). In this sense, the
mosque movement for Mahmood is a "non-liberal movement," desirous not of
liberal rights and freedoms but religious virtues, hopes, and welfare.

Mahmood repeatedly anticipates the key criticism of her project (a performative act in itself), stating that "what may appear to be a case of deplorable
passivity and docility from a progressive point of view, may actually be a form
of agency" (2011, 14–15; see also 34, 154, 175, 179–180). Yet while predictive,
duplicating one's claim and anticipating counterclaims is revealing precisely
of an anxiety about one's argument. The problem, it seems to me, is not con-
ceptualizing the Muslim women as performative agents—Mahmood makes a
good case, perhaps too good a case, on that score—but what such agency
amounts to politically. The author appears so intent on demonstrating how
the women-as-agents gain a modicum of influence at the mosques that there
is nary any criticism of the conservative religious regime they are perforce buying into or propping up. When advancing one's status in the mosque happens
despite continuing overall submission to male authority, then the space for politics is meager indeed.

Mahmood's project appears, then, as a rationalization of conservative religious politics. This is all the more the case considering Asef Bayat's contention (2007, 155–161; see also Bangstad 2010, 217) that the mosque movement
in the 1990s was made up of mainly upper-class Egyptian women, an important detail that Mahmood elides. Bayat argues, in fact, that the movement "em-
powered" well-off Egyptian women by enhancing their personal autonomy
(religious education, salvation), "yet also reproduced patriarchal constraints . . .
[thereby shutting down] possibilities for other women" (2007, 156). In this light,
Sindre Bangstad is adamant that the "alternative which Mahmood offers is one
in which women's rights in the Muslim world are subordinated to the over-
riding aim of so-called 'preservation of life forms' . . . which regretfully does

not provide any sustainable ground for a much required critical feminist engagement with the lives of contemporary Muslim women" (2010, 218; see also Jamal 2008, 128).

Mahmood's study thus illustrates well the political limitations of Butler's performative politics. While Butler and Mahmood no doubt escape the essentialist trap of postmodern identity politics, the problems of a timid and localized or fragmented politics remain. This is because, as several critics have underlined (e.g., McNay 2000, 131), performativity tends to be straightjacketed by the discursive system from which it emerges. As Butler herself admits, "it is only *within* the practices of repetitive signifying that a subversion of identity becomes possible" (1990, 145). Agency, in this sense, is hamstrung by the terms of a given discourse, enabling only a minor deviation, or as Joan Copjec puts it, "a banal difference: mere variation" (2014, 6; see also 1994, 210; 2012, 35). Like postmodern feminism, moreover, such agency is localized and fragmented: it is confined to a specific discursive construction, sensitive to difference no doubt (gender, class, race, etc.) but lacking a common, crosscutting political vision or project. Indeed, Butlerian performativity pointedly rejects a notion of the universal in favor of historically and culturally specific categories (Butler and Scott 1992).

No wonder that, in the case of Mahmood's study, (upper-class) women's performativity is limited by, and cannot meaningfully displace, religious conservatism; it can only repeat with slim differences an inherited patriarchal (and class-interested) discourse. Constrained by its sociocultural inheritance, it lacks political ambition or reach, opting for a localized politics of personal self-improvement that remains unthreatening to, and in fact sustains, the broader System (Egypt's authoritarian rule during the 1990s and beyond, the country's continued integration into global capitalism, etc.).[3]

The issue of sustaining the global capitalist order is particularly germane since the fluidity and mobility of identities that a performative politics so valorizes (be they gender or sexual), fits well into late capitalism, which thrives on the production and commodification of new identities and desires. Jodi Dean suggests that this "fit" is even more prevalent in our internet and social media age: "the key attribute of global capitalist technoculture with its flows of capital information, images, and DNA, is the collapse of symbolic efficiency. . . . It means that there are all sorts of ways to perform, stylize, and signify gender that will circulate and recombine and mean all sorts of different, difficult to determine, things" (2006, 82–83). The endless repetition and circulation of sound bites, memes, words, stories, or (fake) news is precisely about the rearticulation and restylization inherent to performativity. What this means, then, is that a performative feminist politics, which dwells so much on the need for historical specificity, must itself be historicized, emerging as it does in the specific historical formation that is late capitalism (see Žižek 2017, 56; and chapter 2).

# The Psychoanalytic Recuperation of Sex: Toward a Radical and Universal Politics

Let me now contrast the above arguments about gender as social construction with the psychoanalytic take on sex. In so doing, I wish *not* to discard social construction but to try and move beyond its two main political limitations—placidity and fragmentation—which lead to an inability, if not reluctance, to embrace a radical and broad feminist politics. I want to argue that the psychoanalytic perspective on sex helps address both limitations: it is consistent with social construction, seeing language (i.e., the sociosymbolic order) as constitutive of reality, yet it varies significantly by adding a negative and destabilizing dimension. It is such negativity that enables a disruptive and universal feminist project, while escaping the latter's homogenizing tendencies.

## The Psychoanalysis of Sex

As implied above, in Lacanian psychoanalysis, sex (or sexual difference, or "sexuation") is a negative ontological category. It does not refer to a substantive reality or essence; in fact, it designates the very limit of substance, and in this sense is the "inherent twist, or stumbling block" in (symbolically mediated) reality (Zupančič 2017, 3; see also Glynos 2000, 94; Lacan 1998a, 83ff.). The subject is the point of inherent failure of symbolization, which is to say, first, that the subject is not constructed by language but results from the inherent gap in language, and second, that the subject which emerges from this gap is, by definition, always already sexed. Sex, in this sense, denotes the antagonism involved in the structuring of reality itself and indeed in our own very being. As sexed subjects, we are always uncomfortably ensnared in the Symbolic, mismatched and out of joint.

What is noteworthy about the postmodern and performative views of gender is, as I underlined earlier, that they either ignore sex as a category or sex becomes secondary, subsumed under the more significant notion of gender. Partly, such a devaluation has to do with the association of sex with fixed biology/anatomy, but partly it has to do, as Copjec claims, with the removal of sex from sex: "The elimination of sexual difference in favor of a study of the social technologies of gender construction left biology behind altogether and produced subjects without any vitality, subjects without bodies or, more precisely, *subjects without sexual organs*" (Copjec 2012, 38, 31–32). Copjec is not, of course, advocating a return to sex as biology but rather seeing in this "neutering" of gender a disavowal of the trouble and "naughtiness" implied in sex.

But why such disavowal? Alenka Zupančič (2016, 88; 2017, 5ff.) suggests that it is the result of the dimension of "negativity" in sex: either sex is discomforting for us (it is considered "dirty" and "risqué") or, in this age of sexual permissiveness, there is never enough of it (e.g., despite the fact that porn literally shows us everything, it still lacks something, never quite satisfying, the upshot being that there is always a need for something else, often resulting in the need to watch even more porn). But in both cases, it is the impasse of sex itself that is being played out, according to Zupančič: "The cause of embarrassment in sexuality [or of its insatiability] is not simply something which is there, on display in it, but on the contrary, something which is not there . . . the lack at stake is not a possible lack of sex, but a lack at the very heart of sex" (2017, 23, 141). The implication is that it is because we cannot face the incompleteness at the center of our being that we (unconsciously) find ways of avoiding or disavowing it: we try to cover it up (e.g., with ideological mystifications, essentialist/racist/sexist stereotypes), fill it up (e.g., with fetish objects, consumer products, porn), and/or gentrify it (e.g., with a neutered conception of gender, as social construction does).

Now to say that the sexed subject embodies a fundamental antagonism is to insist that sexual difference is the *key* difference, rather than one sociosymbolic difference among many, as social construction contends. The point is not that the instability in the Symbolic (stemming from the endless play of signifiers) is reflected in sexuality but that sexuality is itself this instability: whereas "differences are inscribed in the symbolic, sexual difference is not. . . . [Sexual difference] is a real and not a symbolic difference" (Copjec 1994, 207).

Moreover, it is the antagonism that sexual difference embodies which enables sociosymbolic difference in the first place. Antagonism (the Real) is, in this sense, the originary cut that brings forth the very field in which social difference appears. Or to put it differently, sexual difference is not a differential difference: the antagonism it denotes "never simply exists between conflicting parties [e.g., sociocultural groups, identities]; it is the very structuring principle of this conflict, and of the elements involved in it" (Zupančič 2012). Society/culture, in this sense, follows on from antagonism. This is precisely what Freud had in mind in *Civilization and Its Discontents* (1962) when he claimed that culture is driven by the trauma that is sex. We construct social norms and cultural identities to respond—through processes of repression, disavowal, displacement, compensation, and so on—to the fundamental deadlock that is sex. (Hence the disavowal referred to above in relation to social construction's "neutering" of gender.)

The important further implication is that social difference, and indeed social construction itself, follows from sexual difference. Sexuality is the split/division across which sociocultural difference is joined: "It is always a sexed subject who assumes each racial, class, or ethnic identity" (Copjec 1994, 208). Acknowledging diverse sociocultural identities is important, as social construction is right to underline, but equally important is acknowledging the fundamental void or impossibility that lies in each identity's midst. So for example, gender identity may well be fluid, since it is one that the (sexed) subject continuously performs, yet the split (in the) subject always abides. Or, subject positions may well change, intersect, or overlap, but every position is nonetheless responding to the same deadlock.

The psychoanalysis of sex is thus consistent with social construction, but cannot be equated with it. It is antiessentialist in emphasizing the division that besets every positivity. And it is culturally inclined in its endorsement of the symbolic order as constitutive of reality. But it strays appreciably in seeing the sexed subject as the failure of language rather than constructed by it. The difference that matters most to psychoanalysis is the negative ontological one of the split: it is to this vital difference that other (relational) differences—championed by social construction—respond.

## THE PHALLUS AND THE FEMININE/MASCULINE POSITIONS

As we have seen, for Lacan (1977, 324) castration is a symbolic process, as a result of which we get cut off from some imagined state of bliss (a false sense of oneness with the (m)Other). Subjects assume their castration by renouncing the possibility of possessing what Lacan calls the "phallus," which for him is an imaginary object (as distinct from the biological "penis"): "The phallus is the ultimate object of desire that we have lost and always search for but never had in the first place" (Homer 2004, 57; see also Evans 2006, 144; Lacan 1977, 285). As an empty and fraudulent object, the phallus is not, then, a symbol of potency or virility but of lack and failure (see chapter 1).

While everybody is castrated, Lacan distinguishes a feminine from a masculine position as two different ways of responding to fundamental trauma or antagonism, both symbolizing the breakdown of meaning (1998a, 56–57). Each subject position deals differently with the loss of the imagined object that is the phallus. The masculine position (referred to as the "all") is invested in the promise of fullness: it seeks to *have* the phallus, viewing itself as whole and closed. The feminine position ("not all"), in contrast, is invested in evading the structural lack: it seeks to *be* the phallus, seeing itself as able to resist symbolic integration. Both positions are of course untenable for Lacan, with the male pretending to have the (empty) object and the female masquerading as being it. Moreover, for Lacan, both positions can be occupied by people of any sex: the relation of the subject to the phallus is "established without regard to the anatomical difference between the sexes" (1977, 282). The Lacanian viewpoint thus averts what are often seen as Freud's misogynist proclivities on the issue of sexual difference.

It should be noted that the male and female positions are different modalities of desire/enjoyment in relation to the phallus, not to each other. Woman is not the negation of man or vice versa; the relationship between the two is thus incommensurable and nonsymmetrical. Indeed, it is for this reason that Lacan can famously claim both that "woman does not exist" (1998a, 7, 131) and that "there is no sexual relationship" (57): his point is to underline the failure of meaning (of the signifier "woman," or indeed "man") and hence the impossibility of any relationship between or among the sexes. He means by this, not that all relations are doomed to failure due to a lack of relation, but rather the opposite: it is because there is no (sexual) relationship that the opportunity of a tie opens up: "the absence of the relation does of course not prevent the tie (*la liaison*), far from it—it dictates its conditions" (Lacan 2011, 19; see also Copjec 2012, 41; Zupančič 2017, 24). The nonrelation between the sexes makes relationships difficult but still possible. All of which is a way of saying once again that sexual difference is not a differential difference: "there is no contradiction (antagonism) that exists *between* the male and female positions. On the contrary, contradiction, or antagonism, is what the two positions have in common. It is what they share, the very thing that binds them" (Zupančič 2012; see also Salecl 2000, 8).

Now Lacan may well avoid Freud's misogynistic tendencies, but he has nonetheless been taken to task by feminists for his heteronormativity. For Butler (1993, 58ff.), his contention that the subject enters the Symbolic via sexual differentiation ends up condoning compulsory heterosexuality. That is, sexual difference is made into an unchangeable, phallogocentric "'law' prior to all ideological formations" (Butler 1993, 196; see also Butler, Laclau, and Žižek 2000, 145). Thus, the Lacanian viewpoint on sexual difference, according to her, privileges binary sexual difference. Chris Coffman (2013) concurs, although she focuses specifically on the work of Žižek, seeing it as reproducing the same

Lacanian heterosexist account. For her, Žižek's insistence that sexual difference is the fundamental antagonism "fallaciously assumes that (hetero)sexual difference is the motivating fantasy for all people across time," thus creating "problems for theorizing same-sex desire as anything other than a permutation of (hetero)sexual difference." In her view, there is no reason to posit the binary as masculine and feminine, since sexual difference can be (and is) lived and expressed in multiple ways. In this sense, sexuation can be reconstituted in the symbolic order to register "the many possible configurations of desiring subjectivities" (2013).

But Žižek refutes this line of argumentation. What it misses, according to him, is that there is an inescapable "parallax gap" between the masculine and feminine: "there is no third way" because "the one position excludes the other" (2016b; 2017, 58). Indeed, as just underlined, for Lacan, all subjects are positioned differently with respect to the phallus, so that, as Shanna Carlson points out, "every subject is either 'all' or 'not all' under the phallic function." The two positions are not limited by the gender binary as such: for Lacan, there are "two different modes of ex-sistence in the symbolic, two different stances with respect to desire, and (at least) two different types of jouissance. Nothing here indicates 'gender' as we might conventionally conceive of it" (2010, 64).

Sexual difference is thus an impossible difference that precedes what it differentiates: the positive identity (man, woman, trans, etc.) is the result of an attempt to resolve the impossible difference. There is no neutral difference, since sexuation is about resolving the deadlock of difference by taking either one side or the other. As Žižek puts it, sexual difference is not "a secondary imposed frame" and is hence incapable of capturing "the wealth of the unconsciously bisexual subject. There is nothing outside this failure, for subject and language are themselves the outcomes of this primordial failure" (2016b). This is why, for Žižek, "[g]ays are male, lesbians female; transsexuals enforce a passage from one to another; cross-dressing combines the two; bigender floats between the two. . . . Whichever way we turn, the two lurks beneath . . . [so that one can never escape the] normative straightjacket of the binary opposition of masculine and feminine" (Žižek 2016a). Socially constructed gender identity, in this sense, happens only *after* the (unconscious) process of sexuation has taken place and the (never resolved) trauma of having to take a position has played out.

But while I side with Lacan and Žižek in this debate, I do nevertheless wonder why, for each of them, the two mutually exclusive positions vis-à-vis the phallus are labeled "masculine" and "feminine" rather than simply "all" and "not all" (see Kapoor 2018c). Even though all gendered subjects—female, male, trans, bigender, bisexual, and so on—must sexuate either one way or the other, so that females or trans people can be "masculine" and males or bisexuals "feminine," the problem is that the heteronormativity of such labeling remains. It is surely this unease that is expressed in the critiques of Butler and Coffman, even if they may misinterpret the Lacanian notion of sexuation. In other words, it is the heteronormative markers of the two mutually exclusive positions under the phallic function that elicit confusion between gender and sex: people tend to equate the binary ontological deadlock (the unconscious traumatic "choice" of either the "male" or "female" position) with a socially coded compulsory heterosexuality. So the two positions are not limited by the gender binary, as Žižek and Carlson are right to underline, yet they are nonetheless metaphorically tainted by it, a problem which might be averted if they were labelled differently.

The Lacanian point nonetheless is that there are two incommensurable ways in which the subject can deal with its fundamental split. These two ways are not "two species of the same genus, [but] should be read as positions on a Moebius strip" (Copjec 1994, 217, 234). While there is a difference between the two, it is a nonontologizable difference, yet one that always points up the contradiction in both. Perhaps Arun Saldanha summarizes it best: "the question of sexual difference is precisely that, a *question*, not a fact, not a given, a question forever demanding to be answered. No body is ever 'properly' [female or male], but every body from childhood onward must assume such a position to be human at all, regardless of their sex organs, sexual preference, and racial and class identification" (Nast et al. 2016, 264).

## Drive / *Jouissance*

The subject's entry into the Symbolic is associated with castration, which as we saw earlier means surrendering access to unrestrained *jouissance* (i.e., letting go of a mythical sense of wholeness). Thereafter, life consists of a futile and never-ending search for enjoyment, which Lacan denotes by "drive" (1998b, 168, 178). Drive, as we saw in chapter 4, is what remains when the subject enters the Symbolic; it is a surplus or excess closely affiliated with *jouissance*. It is drive / enjoyment that sexualizes the subject, and although it may well be linked to sexual organs and intercourse (libido), its chief characteristic is precisely that it lacks a domain and has no specific object: it involves the impasse of being and the impossibility of attaining full enjoyment (which is why *jouissance* is never just pleasurable, but always involves pain and excess).

Sexual difference is thus to be understood not on the terrain of culture but of drives. And since drives emerge through culture but are not produced by it—they issue from the deadlock of culture—then sexuality is Real, that is, an antagonism internally transcendent to culture: it exists not outside or beyond the symbolic but "'solely as the *curving of the symbolic space that takes place because of the additional something produced with the signifying gesture.* This, and nothing else, is how sexuality is the Real" (Zupančič 2012, emphasis in original). Thus, there is a drive to sex that makes it exceptional, standing at the limit of the sociocultural without being externally imposed or generated. And it is this this extra, this immoderation, that makes for a radical feminist politics.

## Radical Politics: The "Trouble" with Sex

> [Sexuality] is a nothing that walks around and makes trouble.
>
> (Zupančič 2012)

We can now articulate more clearly why psychoanalysis differs markedly from social construction on the question of sex: it is because of the above-mentioned disruptive psychoanalytic "+" that gets added to the social space without being produced by it. The Real of sex is collateral to discourse, an inherent disturbance within the symbolic field. It has an abiding, troublesome presence in the sociodiscursive, while being neither an essence nor an external intrusion. And it is this extra that is sorely missing is postmodern and performative writings on gender and development. For the latter, as we have seen, the gendered subject is sociohistorically produced, a kind of blank slate onto which cultural forces get grafted. Here sex is relegated to the background, with, as Mahmood writes, "all forms of desire . . . discursively organized" (2011, 15, 17). For psychoanalysis, in contrast, desire/drive is precisely not organized by discourse; instead, it is what stands apart, providing the sexed subject with a critical distance from the discursively produced social space.

It is worth briefly noting in this regard that feminist analysts such as Lois McNay (2000, 20, 126–129) and Judith Butler (1993, 202, 207; Butler, Laclau, and Žižek 2000, 12–13, 29–30) have accused Lacanians of elevating the Real (embodied by sex) to an ahistorical category. According to McNay and Butler, the Real lacks social and historical specificity and can thus only be understood as outside the symbolic. But what they miss, as we emphasized in chapters 1 and 3, is the distinction between the Real as transcendent (standing outside history), which Lacanians oppose, and the Real as internally transcendent (standing at the limit of a given historical formation), which Lacanians endorse. This is to say that the Lacanian Real is specific to every discursive formation, marking its impossibility in distinctive ways. The Real is therefore a contextualized antagonism: it is not some unchanging substance, but is immanent to every sociohistorical order, reflecting any such order's inability to fully constitute itself.

But it is not just that the Real of sex is an extra, it is that it is a *troublesome* extra, which is the crucial ingredient missing in social construction's move away from sex in favor of gender. The (relative) disappearance of the category sex has meant, as underlined earlier, the evacuation and gentrification of social antagonism. Thus, postmodern feminism offers a mild Foucauldian resistance, while Butlerian performativity yields to a politics of "mere variation" (which is to say that Butlerian "gender trouble" is not really that much trouble after all!). The politics of both is straightjacketed by the inherited terms of the sociohistorical discourse, thereby lacking any notion of a surmountable limit (Copjec 1994, 210). This is why, as underlined above, the social construction advocated by Mohanty, Ong, and Mahmood gives way to a certain timidity, restricting itself to a localized and tame cultural- or identity-based politics, at the expense of broader and more intransigent (anticapitalist) struggles (see chapter 7, note 3). In contrast, the politics that flow from the Real/drive is more parasitic and riotous,[4] founded as it is on antagonism.

But what does that imply? The paradox of sex is that, as Zupančič articulates in the epigraph to this section, it is a void that nonetheless has political consequences. The negativity at its core orients the sexed subject toward division and disruption. Sex is, in this sense, inherently political, to the extent that both *it* and politics arise from, and respond to, (social) antagonism. The expression "the sexual is political" is to be understood, then, as saying not simply that the domain of sex is where politics plays out, but more broadly that sex is itself the marker of the rupture and disorientation that are the stuff of politics (Zupančič 2017, 24).

I want to suggest that the negativity or gap in sexuality opens up a space for intervention, in particular bringing forth a politics of lack (i.e., of the not enough) and a politics of the Real (i.e., of the too much/excess/drive). A politics of lack involves a critique of those development discourses that lay claim to wholeness, purity, or unity, thereby trying to cover up the void and division at their core. Not unlike social construction's antiessentialism, this entails the unrelenting exposure of fixed notions/norms (e.g., the undifferentiated Third World woman, heteronormativity, patriarchal codes) or claims to authenticity and purity (e.g., "true" identity, "real" women/men, national or racial myths). It is such a critique that helps create spaces for the marginalized to speak, enabling international development to better come to terms with the social pluralism in its midst.

But exposing the inconsistencies of a discourse is not enough: what is crucial to psychoanalysis (and missing in social construction), as I have underlined before, is attending to the unconscious underpinnings of ideological structures (Žižek 1989). For, the main objective of ideology is to cover over its traumatic imperfections, directing subjects to attach themselves passionately to (i.e., to enjoy) fixed social norms and notions of the pure (see chapters 1, 6, and 11). This is why Western feminists can be antiessentialist but still hold on to the idea of the authentic (Third World) woman; people can mock Erdoğan or Modi but be roused by Turkish or Hindu nationalism; and gay male activists can be gay positive but misogynist and transphobic. The danger of identification is that, despite a certain critical or ironic distance, one can nonetheless get libidinally hooked so that one ends up enjoying one's identity as a feminist or gay activist to the point of being confined by it. A politics of lack thus entails not just pointing out the deficiencies and blind spots of development discourse but coming to terms with how it regulates the libidinal investments of its subjects. It means attending to the lack in the other as much as the self, and doing so intellectually as much as psychically (see chapter 3).

But much more troublesome is the politics of the Real implied by sexual difference, which taps into the disruptive excess of the drive. Here, the idea is not resistance but rupture—refusing to accept, work with, or timidly push against the status quo, instead reactivating social antagonisms to break through what is on offer by the powers that be. The problem with the domain of culture, which social construction so valorizes, is that it tends toward the polite and consensual. Yet as Copjec argues in a Freudian vein, "Sexuality has nothing to do with harmony or with this notion of culture, which can be defined precisely as an attempt to resolve or deny the conflicts sexuality introduces. I often speak about sex as an 'exotic force,' since it acts to split the subject, to push the subject away from itself; it is the enemy of harmony" (2014, 6).

Recall that sex/drive is the irreducible other side of culture, which is what enables this politics of (sexual) *disorientation* and division. The drive pushes unrelentingly against given or inherited limits, and while it is accident-prone and unpredictable, it is precisely its excess that is a guarantee against compromise and mere resistance. It allows for a radical and obstinate politics that is not susceptible to co-optation and manipulation. It enables the sexed subject to be uncompromising if not truculent in the face of social injustice, racism, sexism, or homophobia (see chapter 10). Most importantly, it makes for a much needed anticapitalist politics, especially in these present times when the overwhelming global consensus is tilted in favor of a neoliberal capitalist order and, as just underlined, when social construction shies away from confronting political economy in favor of safer and often less fractious cultural or identity politics. The radical and antagonistic politics of sexual difference persists "in the face of gender restylization and in the networks of technoculture. Sexual difference exceeds gender performances; we might even say that *it is* that persistent, inexpressible, and 'unsymbolizable excess'" (Dean 2006, 83). Because it lacks a domain, forever remaining self-divided and undefinable, it cannot easily be pinned down, assimilated, or commodified by capital. Thus, haunted by a fundamental gap, it is oriented toward a politics of the impossible, always dissatisfied, ready to break out of any (liberal capitalist) consensus.

We get glimpses of this politics of the Real in the innumerable (feminist) movements and popular uprisings across the global South in the post-colonial age—from women's participation in the Arab Spring (see chapter 9) and rural women's struggles in India, Mexico, or South Africa to indigenous revolts in Bolivia, Brazil, and Ecuador (see for example Baksh-Soodeen and Harcourt 2015; Vanden, Funke, and Prevost 2017; Waitzkin 2017): in their "drive" for change, their rage, their determination. But the problem with so many of these movements is often compromise and cooptation (by the political mainstream, corporate power), fragmentation and internal divisions (along identity and North-South lines), and lack of broad or transnational linkages (see Kapoor 2018b; Baksh-Soodeen and Harcourt 2015, 23ff.). The enormous challenge for feminist politics is, and remains, holding on uncompromisingly to a radicalism in the face of the many ideological forces (neoliberal, patriarchal) that seek to cover over the traumatic Real, to seduce or force us into settling for gradual reform or indeed the status quo (see chapter 9). This is the challenge that social construction has repeatedly faced, as I have underlined above, and it is one that equally haunts a feminist psychoanalytic politics of the type I am advocating. The big difference though is that the latter has the psychic and philosophical resources to overcome such challenges (i.e., the Real of sex) whereas the former does not (it has already compromised in forgoing the "trouble" of sex in favor of gender).

Moreover, the troublesome politics enabled by the Real of sex is not necessarily oriented towards *Left* radicalism. It is a resource that can be (and has been) employed by right- as much as left-wing movements (the rise of current right-wing populism can be explained precisely by the latter's leveraging of unconscious social passions such as fear and racism; see Kapoor 2018a). But this is no different from the identity politics or the performative transgression of social construction, which is (and has been) pliable equally to the Right as to the Left (and can end up upholding conservative regimes, as I have claimed in relation to Mahmood's performative politics). Yet once again, whereas a politics of the Real is intent on breaking through the status quo, the politics of social construction isn't, despite pleading otherwise.

## A (Negative) Universal Politics

Now sexual difference makes for not just a radical politics but also a universal one. This is because, as intimated earlier, the Real of sex is integral to every discourse, which is to say that the trauma of sex constitutes a negative universal dimension upon which a common political project can be constructed. Thus, as I argue in chapter 3, while each political struggle may be unique and particular, all struggles are responding to a shared trauma. The Real of sex becomes a concrete universal (or a contextualized antagonism as discussed earlier) that forms the basis for a broad and transversal feminist politics. Here, what is cross-cultural is not a positive identity but a shared antagonism (Žižek 2006, 7ff.; 2010). Postmodern and performative feminist politics get bogged down precisely by performative or authentic identity, as we have seen. While coming to terms with sociocultural diversity is important, the problem is that it tends toward a proliferation of identities (gender, sex, class, "race," ability, nationality, etc.), which divides and fragments because it ultimately rests on positive (even if temporary) essences. Yet, as Copjec asks rhetorically, the proliferation of identities "multiplies rather than thinks. Why multiple rather than divided; why not multiple because divided?" (2016, 2; see also 2012, 33).

Indeed, the psychoanalysis of sex allows us to think collective (feminist) action without identity. The idea is that a diverse range of people and groups can unite based not on positive identity but on shared antagonism—marginalization by global capital and patriarchy, inequities from racialization, alienation from work, and so on. The rebellious subject sees itself not as fetishist (relishing its identity), but as part of a global struggle against the destruction of lives/livelihoods. Solidarity is thus a radical relationality, grounded not in a shared substance, history, or humanity, but in the acknowledgment of inhumanity (the Real) as the condition of universality; it is forged partly on the basis of common enemies (capital, political and patriarchal elites), but more importantly on common patterns of social exclusion and antagonism. Each political group takes a side based on its (always) partial perspective and experience, yet expresses a schism that is universal, shared by others. The Real-as-universal is thus to be gleaned only through fractional and engaged political struggle, yet it lays the foundation for global solidarity.

Such a negative conception of universal politics, as noted in chapter 3, avoids the traps of neocolonial forms of universalism, which parade as neutral/objective while imposing external norms (e.g., Western notions of women's/human rights as universal rights). The universality of a feminist politics of the Real is not about importing from outside but having to work through each particular to arrive at a shared traumatic Real; the latter is always, in this sense, a contextualized antagonism. And it is the construction of such a contextualized antagonism that can enable a diversity of groups across the North-South divide to engage in an (always fraught) transversal politics.

The Real of sex thus implies a negative universal politics that averts key problems besetting both performative/identity politics and neoimperial universalism. Through a politics of common traumatic loss, it lays the foundation for a global solidarity of the marginalized and exploited. There are of course never any guarantees of either success or effectiveness, but such a universal politics stands as an important alternative to the fragmented and localized politics of social construction, especially confronted with today's globalizing systems of sexism, racism, homophobia, and above all capital.

## Conclusion

I have argued that social construction has "unsexed" gender to its peril, ending up with coy and fragmented forms of resistance/performativity that barely challenge, and in fact play into the hands of, capitalist development. I have advocated instead for a psychoanalytic feminist perspective, which focuses on the antagonism that is sex and provides the groundwork for a radical and broad-based politics to better confront the power of contemporary global development. What is distinct about the psychoanalysis of sexual difference is that it relies on neither social construction nor foundationalism, yet is able to be antiessentialist; it is culturally and historically sensitive without falling into the trap of determinism; and it upholds the negative core of the sexed subject as resource for a dissident and expansive politics, while averting problems of Eurocentrism and homogenization. Indeed, the curious but troubling paradox of sex is that it is a nothing that has significant political consequences: it foregrounds the void at the center of the subject, yet proffers support for eruptive and far-flung agency.

### Notes

1. Several other feminist scholars (e.g., Parpart 1995a; Rathgeber 1995; Sylvester 1995) have argued along similar lines about the lack of historical and cultural specificity of gender analyses in development, and the tendency of Northern "experts" to represent an undifferentiated "Third World woman."

2. Ong sees both gender and sex as socially constructed, for example referring to the "social meanings of gender and sexuality" (1988, 88–89).

3. Let me make two points in this regard: (1) Mahmood may well characterize the women's mosque movement as "non-liberal," but it appears as merely the other side of the same coin (i.e., it is correlative to, driven by, liberalism): by emerging from within

the confines of a global liberal order, by posing no threat to it, indeed by helping sustain it, it is proof of the very success of liberalism. And (2) while there is not a large literature on performative politics as it relates to international development, the few studies I have found are equally revealing of the political tendencies detected in Mahmood's performative politics: Jackson (2003), for example, draws on Foucault and Butler to examine the emergence of sexual identity / culture in Thailand, while Nayel (2017) focuses on the performative identity of recent Sudanese Muslim women immigrants to Britain. Although I do not wish to take away from the ethnographic importance of these studies, they are once again revealing of both the limits of performativity and the hegemonic political orientation of our late capitalist times: a preference for cultural/identity politics and a concomitant reluctance to espouse a broader project or confront the political-economic.

4. Note that one of the distinguishing features of the drive is also repetition (see chapter 4), but unlike performativity's repetition, which amounts to variation on an *inherited* theme, drive's repetition is lawless and disorderly, founded precisely on escaping meaning and breaking through inheritance (see Copjec 1994, 211).

## References

Alcoff, Linda. 1988. "Cultural Feminism versus Post-Structuralism: The Identity Crisis in Feminist Theory." *Signs* 13 (3): 405–436.

Anthias, Floya, Nira Yuval-Davis, and Harriet Cain. 1993. *Racialized Boundaries: Race, Nation, Gender, Colour and Class and the Anti-Racist Struggle*. London: Routledge.

Anzaldúa, Gloria, ed. 1990. *Making Face, Making Soul / Haciendo Caras: Creative and Critical Perspectives by Feminists of Color*. San Francisco, CA: Aunt Lute.

Baksh-Soodeen, Rawwida, and Wendy Harcourt, eds. 2015. *The Oxford Handbook of Transnational Feminist Movements*. Oxford: Oxford University Press.

Bald, Suresht R. 1995. "Coping with Marginality: South Asian Women Migrants in Britain." In *Feminism/Postmodernism/Development*, edited by Marianne H. Marchand and Jane L. Parpart, 110–126. London: Routledge.

Bangstad, Sindre. 2010. "Book Review: Saba Mahmood, Politics of Piety: The Islamic Revival and the Feminist Subject." *Feminist Theory* 11 (2): 216–218.

Bayat, Asef. 2007. *Making Islam Democratic: Social Movements and the Post-Islamist Turn*. Stanford, CA: Stanford University Press.

Beauvoir, Simone de. (1949) 1989. *The Second Sex*. Translated by H. M. Parshley. New York: Vintage.

Bordo, Susan. 1990. "Feminism, Postmodernism, and Gender-Scepticism." In *Feminism/Postmodernism*, edited by Linda J. Nicholson, 133–156. London and New York: Routledge.

Brown, Wendy. 1995. *States of Injury: Power and Freedom in Late Modernity*. Princeton, NJ: Princeton University Press.

Butler, Judith. 1990. *Gender Trouble: Feminism and the Subversion of Identity*. New York: Routledge.

——. 1993. *Bodies That Matter: On the Discursive Limits of "Sex."* New York: Routledge.

Butler, Judith, Ernesto Laclau, and Slavoj Žižek. 2000. *Contingency, Hegemony, Universality: Contemporary Dialogues on the Left*. London: Verso.

Butler, Judith, and Joan W. Scott, eds. 1992. *Feminists Theorize the Political*. New York: Routledge.

Carlson, Shanna T. 2010. "Transgender Subjectivity and the Logic of Sexual Difference." *Differences* 21 (2): 46–72.

Chodorow, Nancy. 1978. *The Reproduction of Mothering: Psychoanalysis and the Sociology of Gender*. Berkeley: University of California Press.

Coffman, Chris. 2013. "Queering Žižek." *Postmodern Culture* 23 (1): 56–73.

Copjec, Joan. 1994. *Read My Desire: Lacan against the Historicists*. London: Verso.

——. 2012. "The Sexual Compact." *Angelaki* 17 (2): 31–48.

——. 2014. "The Inheritance of Potentiality: An Interview with Joan Copjec." *E-Rea* 12 (1): 1–11.

——. 2016. "Sexual Difference." *Political Concepts* 3 (5): 1–8.

Dean, Jodi. 2006. "Secrets and Drive." In *Sex, Breath, and Force: Sexual Difference in a Post-Feminist Era*, edited by Ellen Mortensen, 81–96. Oxford: Lexington.

Di Stefano, Christine. 1990. "Dilemmas of Difference: Feminism, Modernity, and Postmodernism." In *Feminism/Postmodernism*, edited by Linda J. Nicholson, 63–82. London and New York: Routledge.

Evans, Dylan. 2006. *An Introductory Dictionary of Lacanian Psychoanalysis*. London: Routledge.

Foucault, Michel. 1979. *The History of Sexuality*, Vol. 1, *An Introduction*. New York: Allen Lane.

Fraser, Nancy. 1989. *Unruly Practices: Power, Discourse, and Gender in Contemporary Social Theory*. Minneapolis: University of Minnesota Press.

Freud, Sigmund. 1962. *Civilization and Its Discontents*. 1st American ed. New York: Norton.

Glynos, Jason. 2000. "Sexual Identity, Identification and Difference: A Psychoanalytic Contribution to Discourse Theory." *Philosophy and Social Criticism* 26 (6): 85–108.

Harstock, Nancy. 1990. "Foucault on Power: A Theory for Women?" In *Feminism/Postmodernism*, edited by Linda J. Nicholson, 157–175. London and New York: Routledge.

Haslanger, Sally. 1995. "Ontology and Social Construction." *Philosophical Topics* 23 (2): 95–125.

Homer, Sean. 2004. *Jacques Lacan*. London: Routledge.

hooks, bell. 1984. *Feminist Theory: From Margin to Center*. Boston, MA: South End.

Jackson, Peter. 2003. "Performative Genders, Perverse Desires: A Bio-History of Thailand's Same-Sex and Transgender Cultures." *Intersections: Gender and Sexuality in Asia and the Pacific* 9 (August). http://intersections.anu.edu.au/issue9/jackson.html.

Jamal, Amina. 2008. "Book Review: *Politics of Piety: The Islamic Revival*." *Journal of Middle East Women's Studies* 4 (3): 121–128.

Kapoor, Ilan. 2018a. "Epilogue: Affect and the Global Rise of Populism." In *Psychoanalysis and the GlObal*, edited by Ilan Kapoor, 283–291. Lincoln: University of Nebraska Press.

——. 2018b. "The Pervert versus the Hysteric: Politics at Tahrir Square." In *Psychoanalysis and the GlObal*, edited by Ilan Kapoor, 257–282. Lincoln: University of Nebraska Press.

——. 2018c. "Žižek, Antagonism and Politics Now: Three Recent Controversies." *International Journal of Žižek Studies* 1 (12). https://zizekstudies.org/index.php /IJZS/article/view/1041/1071.

Lacan, Jacques. 1977. *Écrits: A Selection*. Translated by Alan Sheridan. New York: Norton.

——. 1998a. *Encore. On Feminine Sexuality, the Limits of Love and Knowledge: The Seminar of Jacques Lacan, Book XX*. Edited by Jacques-Alain Miller. Translated by Bruce Fink. New York: Norton.

——. 1998b. *The Four Fundamental Concepts of Psychoanalysis: The Seminar of Jacques Lacan, Book XI*. Edited by Jacques-Alain Miller. New York: Norton.

——. 2011. *Le Séminaire, Livre XIX . . . Ou Pire*. Paris: Seuil.

MacKinnon, Catharine A. 1989. *Toward a Feminist Theory of the State*. Cambridge, MA: Harvard University Press.

Mahmood, Saba. 2011. *Politics of Piety: The Islamic Revival and the Feminist Subject*. Princeton, NJ: Princeton University Press.

McNay, Lois. 2000. *Gender and Agency: Reconfiguring the Subject in Feminist and Social Theory*. Cambridge: Polity.

Millett, Kate. 1970. *Sexual Politics*. New York: Avon.

Mohanty, Chandra Talpade. 1984. "Under Western Eyes: Feminist Scholarship and Colonial Discourses." *Boundary 2* 12/13 (3/1): 333–358.

Narayan, Uma. 1998. "Essence of Culture and a Sense of History: A Feminist Critique of Cultural Essentialism." *Hypatia* 13 (2): 86–106.

Nast, Heidi J., Anna Secor, Paul Kingsbury, Richard Hoffman Reinhardt, and Arun Saldanha. 2016. "Sexual Difference between Psychoanalysis and Vitalism." *AAG Review of Books* 4 (4): 255–267.

Nayel, Amina Alrasheed. 2017. *Alternative Performativity of Muslimness: The Intersection of Race, Gender, Religion, and Migration*. Cham, Switzerland: Palgrave Macmillan.

Nicholson, Linda J. 1990. *Feminism/Postmodernism*. London and New York: Routledge.

Nzomo, Maria. 1995. "Women and Democratization Struggles in Africa: What Relevance to Postmodernist Discourse?" In *Feminism/Postmodernism/ Development*, edited by Marianne H. Marchand and Jane L. Parpart, 131–141. London: Routledge.

Ong, Aihwa. 1988. "Colonialism and Modernity: Feminist Re-Presentations of Women in Non-Western Societies." *Inscriptions* 3–4: 79–93.

Parpart, Jane L. 1993. "Who Is the 'Other'?: A Postmodern Feminist Critique of Women and Development Theory and Practice." *Development and Change* 24 (3): 439–464.

——. 1995a. "Deconstructing the Development 'Expert': Gender, Development and the 'Vulnerable Groups.'" In *Feminism/Postmodernism/Development*, edited by Marianne H. Marchand and Jane L. Parpart, 221–243. London: Routledge.

——. 1995b. "Post-Modernism, Gender and Development." In *Power of Development*, edited by Jonathan Crush, 253–265. London and New York: Routledge.

Parpart, Jane L., and Marianne H. Marchand. 1995. "Exploding the Canon: An Introduction/Conclusion." In *Feminism/Postmodernism/Development*, edited by Marianne H. Marchand and Jane L. Parpart, 1–22. London: Routledge.

Raissiguier, Catherine. 1995. "The Construction of Marginal Identities: Working-Class Girls of Algerian Descent in a French School." In *Feminism/Postmodernism/Development*, edited by Marianne H. Marchand and Jane L. Parpart, 79–93. London: Routledge.

Rathgeber, Eva M. 1995. "Gender and Development in Action." In *Feminism/Postmodernism/Development*, edited by Marianne H. Marchand and Jane L. Parpart, 204–220. London: Routledge.

Salecl, Renata. 2000. "Introduction." In *Sexuation*, edited by Renata Salecl, 1–9. Durham, NC: Duke University Press.

Scott, Joan Wallach. 1996. *Only Paradoxes to Offer: French Feminists and the Rights of Man*. Cambridge, MA: Harvard University Press.

Sylvester, Christine. 1995. "'Women' in Rural Producer Groups and the Diverse Politics of Truth in Zimbabwe." In *Feminism/Postmodernism/Development*, edited by Marianne H. Marchand and Jane L. Parpart, 182–203. London: Routledge.

Udayagiri, Mridula. 1995. "Challenging Modernization: Gender and Development, Postmodern Feminism and Activism." In *Feminism/Postmodernism/Development*, edited by Marianne H. Marchand and Jane L. Parpart, 159–177. London: Routledge.

Vanden, Harry E., Peter N. Funke, and Gary Prevost, eds. 2017. *The New Global Politics: Global Social Movements in the Twenty-First Century*. New York: Routledge.

Waitzkin, Howard. 2017. "Revolution Now." *Monthly Review* 69 (6). https://monthlyreview.org/2017/11/01/revolution-now/.

Žižek, Slavoj. 1989. *The Sublime Object of Ideology*. London: Verso.

——. 2006. *The Parallax View*. Cambridge, MA: MIT Press.

——. 2010. "Appendix: Multiculturalism, the Reality of an Illusion." Lacan.Com, September 1. http://www.lacan.com/essays/?page_id=454.

——. 2016a. "The Sexual Is Political." The Philosophical Salon, August 1. http://thephilosophicalsalon.com/the-sexual-is-political/.

——. 2016b. "Reply to My Critics, Part Two." The Philosophical Salon, August 14. http://thephilosophicalsalon.com/reply-to-my-critics-part-two/.

——. 2017. *Incontinence of the Void: Economico-Philosophical Spandrels*. Cambridge, MA: MIT Press.

Zupančič, Alenka. 2012. "Sexual Difference and Ontology." *E-Flux* 32 (February). http://www.e-flux.com/journal/32/68246/sexual-difference-and-ontology/.

——. 2016. "Sexual Is Political?" In *Jacques Lacan: Between Psychoanalysis and Politics*, edited by Samo Tomšič and Andreja Zevnik, 86–100. London: Routledge.

——. 2017. *What Is Sex?* Cambridge, MA: MIT Press.

CHAPTER 9

# The Politics of Perversion and Hysteria in the Tunisian Revolution and Its Aftermath

KEYWORDS: *Perversion/Hysteria*

## Introduction

The 2011 "Arab Spring" was a world-changing event, not simply for those of us on the Left concerned about radical political change, but foremost for those who participated in it: they toppled repressive regimes in the hope of new political beginnings and socioeconomic change. The Tunisian Revolution in particular stands out, partly because it had a democratic domino effect across the region (notably in Egypt), but also because, in hindsight, it has arguably been the most politically successful.

I propose to approach the Tunisian case psychoanalytically. Rather than studying the revolution in a more conventional way, by examining only its socioeconomic and political ingredients, causes, and impacts, I would like to also probe its underlying politics of desire—how subjects can follow the master's Law, despite misgivings about it (a politics of perversion), or choose instead to resist and transgress it, refusing to compromise on their desire for change (a politics of hysteria). The main psychoanalytic question I am asking is: to what extent are subjects *interpellated* by the Law and under what circumstances are they willing to breach it? Framing the issue this way allows me, I hope, to better determine what it takes libidinally for subjects to revolt, particularly in the Tunisian case.

Indeed, the "Jasmine Revolution" saw the overthrow of Ben Ali's despotic rule by broad-based social protest. But while the country subsequently witnessed the establishment of liberal democracy, the two main political forces (the liberal Nidaa Tounes and the Islamic Ennahda) have ended up pursuing many of the same socioeconomic policies of Ben Ali, which have in turn been met with popular opposition. I will examine these events by contrasting (1) the politics of perversion of the ruling Tunisian elites (represented by Nidaa Tounes and Ennahda), which while sometimes appearing to challenge the status quo, ends up confirming it; and (2) the politics of hysteria of the public protesters, which has been expressly more deviant and out of joint, thereby posing a threat to the status quo. I will conclude by briefly comparing the Tunisian to the Egyptian revolution, while also reflecting on the broader psychoanalytic possibilities and perils of popular uprisings, including the risk that a politics of hysteria may transform into a politics of perversion.

## The Lead-up to the Revolution

After the end of French colonial rule in 1956, Tunisia was governed by two repressive regimes—that of Bourguiba and Ben Ali. The Bourguibist regime helped build a modern and secular nation, which grew steadily over two decades, mainly benefitting a small clique of elites. But the global recession of the early 1980s saw the country experience economic failure and social unrest, opening the door to a coup d'état by Ben Ali in 1987.

Despite committing to social and political reforms, Ben Ali proceeded to follow in the footsteps of his predecessor, ruling with an iron hand, while further liberalizing the economy (notably the tourism, mining, and oil and gas sectors). Starting in the mid-1990s, the Tunisian economy grew by an average of 5 percent annually for a decade, with benefits once again accruing mainly to the upper and middle classes (El-Khawas 2012, 1). But the 2008 global economic downturn, especially in Europe, led to economic decline, resulting in slowing exports and tourism, rising poverty, and unpopular food price increases. The recession meant not just that growth stalled, but also that less employment was being generated, especially for the country's youth. In fact, a key factor in the lead-up to the revolution was rising youth unemployment and youth graduate unemployment, which at the end of 2010 stood at 23 percent and 37 percent, respectively (El-Khawas 2012, 7; Honwana 2011, 5; Saidin 2018, 71).

This socioeconomic inequality was accompanied by geographic inequality. For years, the state had systematically marginalized some regions of the country, privileging the industrialized coast and the north with socioeconomic investments, to the detriment of the mainly rural southern, central, and western regions. Such regional disparity was evident, for example, in Ben Ali's last national budget, which allocated 18 percent of funds to the inner regions, in contrast to 82 percent to the coastal towns (Allahoum 2019). These inner regions are the ones that had experienced the highest rates of poverty and unemployment in the country by the time of the revolution (Ayeb 2011; Honwana 2011, 5).

A final factor in the impending social upheaval was Ben Ali's authoritarian and nepotistic governance. His regime's secular and modernist veneer was complemented by increasingly centralized decision making and the elimination of political dissent. While elections were held regularly and a handful of political parties were tolerated, Ben Ali stood unopposed for president, winning some 98 percent of the popular vote each time (in 1989, 1994, and 1998) and even changing the constitution to extend his rule after the three-term limit (El-Khawas 2012, 5). Political opponents and protests were repressed, with the regime often muzzling media and civil society organizations and carrying out anti-Islamist purges under the guise of antiterror measures. A vast state security apparatus was built up over two decades, earning a reputation for widespread human rights abuses, including kidnappings, blackmail, torture, and disappearances.

Ben Ali and his extended family (notably his wife, Leila Trabelsi, and her relatives) also became notorious for their corrupt and clientelist practices. The Ben Ali–Trabelsi clan is estimated to have controlled close to one-third of the Tunisian economy, with major shares in a vast array of sectors, from banking and insurance to real estate and tourism (Honwana 2011, 6; Mahmoud 2018). The clan had a hand, critically, in the development of the most advanced telecommunications and digital networks in the North African region, including the establishment of Internet cafés across the country (Breuer, Landman, and Farquhar 2015, 771; Saidin 2018, 73). Although state censorship of the Internet was common—the frequency of the web error message "404 Not Found" led users to invent a fictional character named Ammar 404—it is ironic that the development of this digital network played a key role in the regime's own undoing: protestors used it to organize the revolution.

## The "Jasmine Revolution" and Its Aftermath

As is well known, the event that triggered the popular uprising was the self-immolation of a street vendor, Mohamed Bouazizi, on December 17, 2010, in protest against the brutality and injustice of police and government officials in Sidi Bouzid. Tellingly, this is one of the country's most marginalized southern cities, which had experienced high rates of recession and unemployment. Within days, antigovernment protests began to spread, starting in the most depressed areas of the country (the southern, central, and western regions) and moving on to the rest of country, notably the capital, Tunis.[1] The majority of those who took to the streets were un- or underemployed youth, joined gradually by a broad-based collection of teachers, students, lawyers, human rights activists, trade unionists, secular intellectuals, journalists, opposition party members/leaders, among others (Honwana 2011, 12). While youth activists played important organizing roles, it was the Tunisian General Labor Union (UGTT) that served as critical coordinator for the popular resistance, holding together the broad coalition against the Ben Ali regime (Honwana 2011, 13; Yousfi 2018).[2] Representing Tunisia's working and middle classes, particularly public sector workers, the UGTT became (and, to some extent, continues to be) the de facto voice for social protest and justice, often acting as power broker and mediator between the radical youth and student groups and the more established and Left-liberal human rights and civil society organizations.

As alluded to above, cyberactivism and social media featured prominently in the organization of the revolution. Often, it was the young tech-savvy bloggers and cyberactivists, some of whom operated from exile outside the country, who helped spread the latest news about the growing political uprising, exposing regime abuses and corruption, and distributing information about protest strategy and organization (Breuer, Landman, and Farquhar 2015, 774; Saidin 2018, 73–74). To get around state censorship of the Internet, these activists created a national intranet, while also receiving help from external cyberhacking groups such as Anonymous to disrupt government websites and security protocols. Facebook and Twitter became the go-to social media for receiving and spreading information about street protests. And foreign bloggers, journalists, and news agencies (Al Jazeera, Russia Today, BBC) served as significant sources for the latest news and analysis, as did the whistle-blowing site Wikileaks for revealing the extent of corruption and nepotism by the Ben Ali–Trabelsi clan (Breuer, Landman, and Farquhar 2015, 782; El-Khawas 2012, 10; Honwana 2011, 9).

Ben Ali's regime responded by trying to brutally repress the protests, calling in the army, declaring a national emergency, and imposing dusk-to-dawn curfews across the country. But despite the threats, and the arrest, murder, and torture of protestors and opposition leaders, the wave of unrest mounted from mid-December 2010 to mid-January 2011. Soon, Ben Ali offered a series of economic and political concessions (see below), even making two desperate television addresses to help quell the unrest. But finally, with no sign of backing down from the protestors, he fled the country to Saudi Arabia on January 14, family in tow.

The overthrow of the regime was an undeniable victory, ending twenty-three years of Ben Ali's despotic rule. But the political struggle was not over as a new political order was waiting to be created. Once again, the UGTT played a key role, helping to broker a deal among rival factions for the establishment of a constituent assembly, to be elected by proportional representation and tasked with drafting a new constitution. In the ensuing October election, it was the Islamic Ennahda party that won the most seats, and despite tensions among assembly members, it successfully worked with other secular parties to promulgate a new constitution. Indeed, Ennahda had been banned under Ben Ali, but gained prominence in the wake of the revolution, ditching several planks of its religious platform to appeal to the more moderate Muslim democratic sections of the population.

Since that time, Ennahda and Nidaa Tounes have each held power in succession, with the two parties governing together in partnership between 2015 and 2018. Nidaa Tounes, it should be specified, is a loose coalition of Bourguibists and former Ben Ali loyalists, for the most part committed to the continuation of Ben Ali's socioeconomic policies. Together with Ennahda, it has pursued a mostly neoliberal program, implementing strict austerity measures to comply with the Deauville Partnership/IMF[3] loans, taken out to service the large debt accumulated under and after Ben Ali.

To be sure, in 2010 the country's foreign public debt amounted to 41 percent of GDP, ballooning to 71 percent of GDP in 2018 and taking up 22 percent of the country's budget for debt service payments (Chandoul 2018). IMF structural adjustment conditions have meant a devaluation of the dinar, soaring import bills, public-sector wage and hiring freezes, and increases in consumption taxes and food prices. The hardest hit have been the poorest sections of the population, leading to food riots and another wave of popular protests across the country, especially since 2016.

## Perversion and Hysteria

How then to interpret the Tunisian revolution and its aftermath in psychoanalytic terms? I want to turn to two key notions—perversion and hysteria—for help in this regard. Freud gives both a distinctly sexual connotation: sexual perversion is behavior that falls outside the (heterosexual) norm, while hysteria is about an anxious reaction and resistance to (sexual) trauma (1977, 15; 1993).[4] Lacan retains the meaning of both notions, but he differs from Freud in detaching them from their sexual stereotypes, making them (so to speak) "technical" concepts. That is, he defines both terms in relation to social norms, not natural/biological aberration (Lacan 1988, 221). Thus, perversion and hysteria refer not to the subject's identity or behavior (e.g., as homosexuals or women); they are character structures describing how the subject relates to the Law (i.e., the "big Other," the realm of social and institutional authority). As a consequence, anyone can be a pervert or a hysteric.

What matters to Lacan is the dialectical relationship between Law and desire. As human animals, our entry into the Symbolic-qua-Law results in limiting access to biological drives (Lacan 1977, 697–698; 1998, 84). The function of the Law is thus to regulate our *jouissance*, that is, to protect the subject from unbridled and unbearable enjoyment. In this sense, Law manages pleasure, stabilizing and reassuring the subject, enabling her to desire within the ambit of its prescriptions. Desire, in contrast, "is the reverse of the law" (Lacan 1977, 787): it emerges only because of the imposition of the Law, in response to the establishment of limits and restrictions. As Evans puts it, "Desire is essentially the desire to transgress, and for there to be transgression it is first necessary for there to be prohibition" (2006, 102). In this sense, the Law does not only generate but needs transgression in order to assert itself as Law, while desire is not only elicited by but also needs the Law in order to be able to transgress it.

But there is also a murky, enjoyable side to the Law. This is what Žižek denotes by "obscene superego supplement" (2006, 80–81), stressing that the Law is always split between its public face and its obscene superegoic additive. The latter is evident, for example, in the way that the global North's development has been enabled by (neo)colonial plunder, a regime's stability is secured by emergency laws, or a new political regime is inaugurated by violent repression: in each case, for the Law to be instituted, its defenders must disavow its dirty underside (i.e., its violent, racist, or criminal founding).

There is, moreover, a crucial enjoyment factor to add, and this is where the superego enters the picture: for Lacanians, the superego is not the Freudian moral conscience that keeps the ego in check but the unconscious command to enjoy that accompanies the Law. It is the obscene superego supplement to the Law that enjoins the subject (or pervert/hysteric) to take pleasure in complying with or trespassing against the Law. The superego helps mitigate the anxiety or guilt the subject may experience through her/his compliance or challenge to the Law, thereby increasing the Law's hold over her/him. The

Law may well allow a degree of deviation and defiance, but submission is most often ensured through its libidinal complement. To illustrate (see Žižek 2006, 22ff.), one thinks here of: the ascetic who renounces worldly desires, but engages in strict ritual practices that themselves become a source of pleasure; the civil servant who publicly scorns red tape but covertly revels in it, delighting in his/her power to apply rules and procedures (see chapters 2, 7, and 12); or the academic who feels the pressure to "publish or perish" that many of us dislike and forever feel guilty about, but who is thereby libidinally bound to the university and the (corporate) academic publishing machine. To be sure, not only is doing one's duty or complying with the Law pleasurable, but even resisting or perverting the Law brings feelings of enjoyment and guilt that oblige the subject to the Law. The Law is thus asserted and maintained through quasi transgressions that provide people with secret pleasures; and subjects comply with or defy this Law not necessarily because it is morally right and good, but because it is libidinally charged.

For Lacan, perversion and hysteria are failed attempts at resolving the impasse between Law and desire/enjoyment.[5] Since, as just underlined, simply to desire is to defy the Law, everyone is a pervert. We seek enjoyment, but the Law stands in our way, so we transgress it. Yet the problem with perversion is that it is characterized by disavowal: perverts, according to Lacan, are aware that we are all castrated/lacking, but nonetheless deny it. In fact, as stressed in chapter 6, they often resort to the use of a fetish (e.g., a shoe, underwear) as a substitute for the lack, to soothe and cover over the trauma of castration. In other words, perverts know well that the Law stands in the way, but when it comes down to it—orienting their desire toward challenging the Law—they opt for a reflective and distant position (this is what we referred to in chapters 2 and 6 as "fetishistic disavowal"). Their knowledge becomes extraneous and inoperative when they act. They may well outwardly criticize and expose the dirty power games of the master/Law, but by not carrying through with their desire to transgress, they effectively become a complicit partner in the master's fantasy. In fact, according to Lacan, they make themselves the instrument of the master's pleasure, enjoying such self-instrumentalization (1977, 320). Their propensity toward disavowal allows them to evacuate any nagging questions, to relish assuming the position of the object, and to find in that a relief to their torment: "the pervert has no doubt that his acts serve the *jouissance* of the Other" (Evans 2006, 142).

In this scheme of things, the pervert turns out to be a political conservative, defender of the status quo. This is because s/he can only enjoy within the purview of the Law. S/he may well critique the status quo, but this is merely an ironic acting out that ultimately sides, and takes enjoyment in siding, with the Law (Žižek 1999, 247ff.). Through processes of pleasure and guilt, the Law's obscene superego supplement may well incite her/him to transgress, but it does so only within the political and libidinal limits prescribed by the Law, that is, "in a completely non-dangerous way" (Kotsko 2008, 49).

But if perversion is ultimately about refraining from challenging the Law, hysteria is about constantly questioning it. For Lacan, hysteria is a form of neurosis, wherein the subject struggles against being integrated into the symbolic order/Law (1993, 70–78). The master can go about issuing authoritative orders or symbolic mandates, but the hysteric doubts them, interrogates them, contests them. Unlike the pervert, she dreads rather than relishes becoming the tool of the Other. And the more she resists and dreads, the more she gleans that the Other is an impostor with no legitimate authority over her. Lacan champions such a questioning attitude, seeing it not as a neurosis to be cured (à la Freud) but a subject position to come to terms with.

One can easily discern the subversive political dimensions of such a character structure. The hysteric approaches and responds to authority with radical doubt and uncertainty, yielding a more provocative, albeit unrehearsed and unpredictable, politics. As Žižek suggests, hysteria is about being out of joint in the face of the Law: "what is hysteria if not precisely the effect . . . of a failed interpellation; what is the hysterical question if not the articulation of the incapacity of the subject to fulfil the symbolic identification, to assume fully and without restraint the symbolic mandate?" (1989, 113; see also Dolar 1993, 78). The hysteric recognizes the hail/call of the master but is not sure it is meant for her. "What does he want from me? Who is he to hail me? And why is he hailing *me*?," she asks. A kind of dialogue of the deaf ensues, with the hysteric resisting and challenging her putative master (Kay 2003, 164). She may provisionally accept his role as master, but may just as quickly decide that he is neither appealing nor masterful enough for her. She is, in a way, in search of a master, secretly wishing he will help unlock the deadlock of her desire, yet ultimately finding it impossible to locate anyone who quite fits the bill.

The hysteric's questioning attitude means that she is constantly trying to find out what the Other wants, yet never identifies with the Other's desire, always aspiring to something different (Žižek 1997, xvi, 44). In this sense, she resists the superego supplement, forever postponing satisfaction and refusing to be the object of the Other's enjoyment. This postponement, this constantly unsatisfied desire, translates into a demand for something else, outside the bounds of what is on offer by the Law. Hence the possibility of a deviant politics.

Thus, in contrast to the pervert, the false transgressor who refrains from making any threatening demands, the hysteric is the perpetual doubter who bombards the master with questions and impossible demands. The pervert protests, cynically resigned to the fact that only that change will happen that is tolerated by the Law, while the hysteric insists on change that exceeds the limits of the Law. The pervert knows what the master wants and enjoys delivering it; the hysteric questions the master's desires, postponing enjoyment in favor of other possibilities. The pervert is, in this sense, confident and ready to act but more unconscious of the deadlock of desire, whereas the hysteric is circumspect but more psychoanalytically aware of the ultimate impossibility of enjoyment.

The problem though is that the hysteric can so easily succumb to the trap of perversion. Rather than opting for an alternate politics, the hysteric may warily give in to the superego command to enjoy, seduced by what the Law has to offer (e.g., capitalist consumerism, liberal democracy). Perversion after all is much easier—you get to cut to the chase by adopting the master at hand and promptly enjoying. While hysteria is comparatively much harder: you have to postpone your enjoyment and bear the burden of being your own master. Hysterical politics can thus all too frequently get diverted, stopped in its tracks by the lure, comfort, and authority of the status quo.

The successfully hystericized subject, then, is not one who is just questioning, but one more conscious of the machinations of *jouissance*. It is the realization that *jouissance* is in fact not possible, that there is no enjoyment beyond the Law, that enables the hysteric to see that mere transgression/perversion of the Law is not necessarily a path to liberation (Wells 2014, 28). Hence understanding that what is on offer by the master is suspect and fraudulent, that his authority is incomplete and illegitimate, is what makes the obscene superego supplement obsolete and inoperative.

Wells stresses the important point that, ultimately, the hysteric needs to grasp that the "obstacle to the realization of desire is not beyond the Law, but internal to desire itself. The obstacle to desire's fulfilment beyond the Law is precisely its secret reliance on the Law to sustain itself" (2014, 29). So it seems, as a consequence, that only after being able to suspend the obscene libidinal attachments to the Law, to make the "radically negative gesture of 'unplugging' from the symbolic order" (Kotsko 2008, 47), can one begin transforming into a self-legislating subject.

## The Politics of Perversion and Hysteria in the Jasmine Revolution and Its Aftermath

In order to examine how the politics of perversion and hysteria have played out in Tunisia during and after the revolution, it is important to specify what

I mean by the Law (as symbolic authority or big Other), since both perversion and hysteria make sense only in relation to it. In the Tunisian case, I take the Law to mean the authority of the state (its institutional, political, and economic power) and the broader cultural and political economy (e.g., global capitalism, the forces of Westernization, other powerful actors/states such as the IMF).

Both Nidaa Tounes and Ennahda—the one largely representing the Bourguibist and Ben Ali political and economic elites, the other a modernist democratic Islam—appear to have engaged in a politics of perversion. Leading up to the revolution, these parties' putative supporters had increasingly strayed from the Ben Ali regime. The elites' ties to the regime had strained, faced with a severe economic recession, rising state authoritarianism, and the growing economic threat posed by the clientelism and dominance of the Ben Ali–Trabelsi clan. For their part, the religious sections of the population bore growing resentment toward the regime after decades of state persecution of religious leaders under the guise of "secularism" and antiterror measures and the ban of Ennahda. So when the putative supporters and leaders of Nidaa and Ennahda broke with their political master (Ben Ali) and sided with the protestors in late 2010 and early 2011, they were perverting/transgressing the Law. The state had become an obstacle to their enjoyment (of political-economic-religious power and autonomy); hence the superegoic incitement to violate the Law.

But in the wake of the revolution, Nidaa and Ennahda have increasingly reconciled to the Law, if not in some cases *become* the master/Law, and in this lies their perversion.[6] While Ben Ali's former party (Rassemblement Constitutionnel Démocratique, RCD) was banned, Nidaa and Ennahda helped pass legislation to rehabilitate the erstwhile Ben Ali establishment, granting many of them amnesty and allowing them to continue to be active in the state apparatus. This has meant a certain continuity and attachment to "Ben Ali as master," despite his formal overthrow and the creation of a "new" political order.

But nowhere is such reconciliation to the Law more apparent than when it comes to the economy. Nidaa and Ennahda leaders may well have supported the revolution, including demands for alleviating poverty and improving youth employment, but to date they have done little to address these problems, preferring instead to advance the country's integration into the global economy. As underlined earlier, both parties have maintained many of Ben Ali's economic policies, continuing to implement IMF-imposed austerity measures and service the country's external debt. This includes economic liberalization policies (in particular, opening up the country's natural resource sector), freezing or cutting public-sector employment and wages, and increasing prices of basic commodities and food items (Allahoum 2019; Legrand 2018). Of late, faced with renewed popular protests against austerity, and unable to adequately meet its crushing external debt obligations without compromising human rights, the Nidaa Tounes government has resorted to muzzling dissent and arresting protestors (Mahmoud 2018).

Typical of the pervert-fetishist, then, Nidaa and Ennahda have made themselves the instruments of both global capital and the Tunisian ruling elites, helping to create a somewhat stable political environment and an open and safe economy for trade and investment. They appear to have forsaken the revolution's main goals of social justice and equality in favor of continuing global capitalist integration. Such fetishistic disavowal, to be sure, is the stamp of perversion, and in the Tunisian case it applies both politically and economically ("we repudiate Ben Ali, but support what he stood for anyway"). The upshot is that Ben Ali's RCD cadres continue to operate at the level of the state, and his economic policies continue to flourish. Nidaa and Ennahda's recent trajectory—from violating the Law and supporting revolution to becoming status quo neoliberals—underlines once again Lacan's important point that the pervert's (false) transgression becomes the very condition of the Law's operation and that, all said and done, the pervert-as-putative-transgressor actually longs for the Law. To wit, before the revolution, Tunisia's political-economic status quo *needed* a transgressive event to move beyond the contradictions created by Ben Ali and reassert itself as Law. And after the revolution, Nidaa and Ennahda have been only too willing to serve this new-fangled Law in a way that perpetuates the Ben Ali regime, minus Ben Ali himself. *Plus ça change, plus c'est (pratiquement) la même chose!*

But Nidaa's and Ennahda's politics of perversion stands in contrast to the politics of hysteria of the protestors. As pointed out earlier, the demonstrations were made up of a wide cross-section of Tunisian society, with youth leaders and the UGTT at the forefront of the movement. Their defiance had been unthinkable until then, given the atmosphere of brutal repression and fear created under Ben Ali. But they had had enough of years of authoritarian rule, unemployment, and socioeconomic and geographic marginalization, and so began to doubt, interrogate, and increasingly contest the Ben Ali regime, sparked and emboldened by Mohamed Bouazizi's self-immolation.

As the revolution progressed, the protestors steadfastly stood their ground. They demanded not only Ben Ali's departure and the dissolution of his party, but also better economic opportunities, political freedom, and self-dignity, reflected in such popular slogans as "Ben Ali Dégage!," "The Game is Over," and "Work, Freedom, Dignity" (Ayeb 2011, 475–76; Beissinger, Jamal, and Mazur 2019, 19; Falk 2016, 2325; Saidin 2018, 70, 72). The protests continued even as the military was deployed on the streets, curfews were imposed, and police repeatedly arrested, tortured, and opened fire on protestors, killing over 200 (Saidin 2018, 71). So determined were the demonstrators that they rebuffed repeated offers from Ben Ali to create more employment, release arrested protestors, and step down after his term finished in 2014.

It would have been easier for the protestors to give in to the obscene superego supplement to the Law, to secretly take comfort in what the status quo offered them, but they resisted. Despite the threats and concessions, they decided to postpone immediate gratification for better sociopolitical possibilities. In this sense, they refused to become the tool of the Ben Ali regime (as the pervert would), realizing that the more they resisted, the more the master stood as increasingly desperate impostor with no legitimate authority. The protestors' unsatisfied desire and postponement of enjoyment translated not only into a refusal to dialogue or compromise with the Law but to make demands that fell outside the limits of the Law. As hysterics, they bombarded the master with impossible demands (work, freedom, dignity) as if to say, "prove your worth to us!": in effect they were demanding a "true" master, one to which the Ben Ali regime did not, and could not, measure up.

The departure of Ben Ali and the overthrow of his regime was a ground-breaking event, but once victory had been achieved and the master deposed, significant dangers loomed. The demonstrators' hysterical politics, their political and psychoanalytic resolve, was to be further challenged by new putative masters. The first crucial test came during the "constitutional phase," during which a new political order was to be created. The interim government, led by Ennahda's Rached Ghannouchi, began by resisting popular calls for dissolving Ben Ali's former RCD party and establishing an elected constituent assembly to draft a new constitution. It relented only after repeated public "Caravans of Freedom" were organized across the country and in Tunis, and agreed to disband and outlaw the RCD and lend support for the election for a constituent assembly based on proportional representation (see Zemni 2015).[7]

The ensuing October 2011 elections saw Ennahda win the most seats, followed by Nidaa Tounes. There was fierce debate among constituent assembly members about whether to opt for a modern liberal democratic, Islamic republican, or a secular socialist framework, but the liberal democratic one mostly prevailed. Despite moves by a few Ennahda members to uphold Sharia law, decisive victories were won for the protection of human and women's rights, gender equality, and freedom of speech, association, and assembly (Hitman 2018, 178). Opting for a liberal democratic republican framework meant, however, the de facto acceptance of a market economy, which laid the ground for the second key test for the protestors.

Indeed, as highlighted earlier, successive post-2011 governments headed by Nidaa and Ennahda have chosen to pursue neoliberal austerity measures rather than prioritize the main socioeconomic demands of the revolution. Inequality continues unabated, food prices have risen, and unemployment remains high (15 percent), especially for the country's youth (30 percent) (Allahoum 2019; Legrand 2018). Moreover, while a commitment to alleviating regional disparity is enshrined in the new constitution, nothing meaningful has materialized on that front, with successive governments simply postponing action for another day (Allahoum 2019). The result, as outlined earlier, has been a renewal of popular protests, especially since 2016. Although civil servants and youth groups have been at the forefront of these protests, demanding an end to state neoliberal austerity programs, a good deal of social unrest has taken place in the country's interior. This is particularly the case in the southern region of Tataouine, where workers have been fighting job layoffs by foreign multinational oil and gas companies, calling on the government to nationalize the sector.

But although this new wave of protests is politically significant, it is not nearly as widespread or broad-based as that of 2010–2011, and is hence unlikely to destabilize the current regime. There appears to be no group willing to assume the mantle of the UGTT to lead and coordinate the protests. The UGTT has proceeded to play a more pragmatic and less insurgent role in the postrevolutionary era, focusing on immediate issues such as securing contracts for temporary workers and better wages for teachers and farm workers (Yousfi 2018). Meanwhile, several youth groups have splintered, many of their members disenchanted with mainstream politics and secular elites, and turning instead to (what they see as) the more radical Islamist/Salafist movements (Mahmoud 2018; Zemni 2015, 9–10, 13).

We glean here how the protestors' politics of hysteria has, for all intents and purposes, mutated into a politics of perversion. That is, they began by carrying through on their initial desire for political change, successfully toppling Ben Ali. This was a crucial milestone in Tunisia's political landscape. But then, equally crucially, they compromised their desire, settling for new but ultimately unsatisfactory masters (Ennahda, Nidaa Tounes, the IMF). One set of inadequate masters replaced (and was allowed to replace) another, the latter undoubtedly less authoritarian, but still failing to deliver on meaningful economic equality. The protestors', and the country's, democratic acquiescence to a market-based liberal democracy, resulted in the new political state imposing further neoliberalization of the economy.

Tunisia's revolutionary movement thus appears to have engaged in a certain disavowal: wanting revolution, yet supporting (willingly or grudgingly) a postrevolutionary state unlikely to bring it about. The protestors' revolutionary fervor was perverted by allowing itself to be seduced by what the Law seemingly had to offer (a return to political stability, the promise of freedom and democracy, a market economy). So rather than postponing their enjoyment and bearing the burden of searching for a worthy master,[8] the bulk of protestors settled for the masters at hand (i.e., the continued hegemony of Bourguibist and Ben Ali political and economic elites and bureaucratic cadres) and the prospect of imminent *jouissance*. True, significant civil and political rights were won under the new constitutional order, but key socioeconomic demands (jobs, socioeconomic and regional equality) were sacrificed. In this lies the compromise of desire.

The broader implication here is that toppling a political regime, while rare and extraordinary, is still nothing compared to toppling a capitalist regime (and its accompanying socioeconomic elites). The seductions of market capitalism and a return to relative political stability appear so very difficult to overcome. No wonder that, alienated by politics as usual, some Tunisian youth have turned to (seemingly) more radical Islamist movements instead to satisfy their revolutionary fervor.[9]

But in addition to this libidinal-political trap, it is also the Tunisian Left's failure to adequately mobilize and tap into people's postrevolutionary potential that has meant that the comfort and authority of the status quo has won over a more unpredictable and out-of-joint hysterical politics. As mentioned above, revolutionary zeal is not enough; after the initial revolution, it must continue to be mobilized, articulated, and deftly deployed to have lasting impact. No UGTT-like organization has stepped in to lead, coordinate, and organize the after-revolution. Hence, Žižek states, "this is the fatal weakness of recent protests: they express an authentic rage which is not able to transform into a [long-term] positive programme for sociopolitical change. They express a spirit of revolt without revolution" (2011). The challenge of revolutionary movements such as that of Tunisia is finding the political, organizational, and psychoanalytic resources to *sustain* the revolt, most especially in the aftermath of the initial victory. It is as if Ben Ali served as *point de capiton* for disparate social groups in Tunisia—an anchoring point or ideological screen onto which people projected their varying socioeconomic frustrations and rage. But once Ben Ali fled, there was no replacement *point de capiton* to help focus and unify people's political hopes and fantasies, thereby scattering people's revolutionary fervor.

Before concluding this section, let me briefly compare and contrast the Tunisian case with the other significant Arab Spring revolution—the Egyptian one. I have examined the 2011 Egyptian revolution elsewhere (Kapoor 2018), claiming that there, too, a politics of hysteria has morphed into a politics of perversion: protestors ousted Mubarak, but have settled on a regime—led by Abdel Fattah el-Sisi—that has turned out to be even more brutal than before, continuing to serve the country's military and socioeconomic elites at the expense of the poor and marginalized, and furthering the country's neoliberal integration into the world economy.

The Tunisian revolution thus appears comparatively more "successful," but only at the level of political form: postrevolutionary Tunisia "enjoys" a liberal democratic framework, while post-2011 Egypt suffers an authoritarian one, yet both countries continue to abide by the Law of the market. Perhaps what makes this difference is each country's particular sociohistorical context, with the Egyptian case complicated by the presence of a powerful army (which has significant interests not just in national security but also the country's economy) and a now retreating political Islam (led by the Muslim Brotherhood, which has been significantly repressed by the el-Sisi regime). But I would also claim that the Egyptian revolution's failure relative to Tunisia's lies in two other factors: (1) The much-lauded "leaderlessness" of the Egyptian revolution likely turned out to be its Achilles's heel, since the lack of a coordinating organization and political vision allowed el-Sisi to divide and rule, ensuring that the protestors posed no threat to, and in fact ended up supporting, the army. In contrast, it is the leadership of Tunisia's UGTT and youth activists during the revolution and its immediate aftermath that helped secure an elected constituent assembly and the establishment of liberal democracy; and the absence of such leadership in the longer term that has facilitated the ruling elites' backing of austerity and economic liberalization, despite the current renewal of social unrest. And (2) the relative class composition of the protestors perhaps helps explain the comparative "economy of desire" of both revolutions: new research suggests that the Tunisian revolution was much more socially diverse than the Egyptian one (Beissinger, Jamal, and Mazur 2019). In the former case, participants were younger, more secular, and more socially diverse (in terms of class, gender, and geography), including a mix of middle- and working-class, and rural and urban, people, as well as students, union members, and the unemployed; while in the latter case, participants were mostly urban and middle-class youth and professionals (Beissinger, Jamal, and Mazur 2019, 4, 14, 17). Thus, the Egyptian revolution appears to have been a primarily middle-class revolution, lacking adequate participation by disenfranchised peasants and workers, whereas the Tunisian revolution was more broad-based, managing to include the dispossessed and unemployed. This difference in social base would explain the difference in the two cases of the political resolve (and socioeconomic alienation) of the protestors and the extent of their willingness to compromise on such key goals as freedom, democracy, and social and regional equality. The desire not to compromise has been stronger in the Tunisian case, but not so strong as to overcome the interests and seductions of global capitalism.

## Conclusion

I have attempted, in this chapter, to highlight the libidinal underpinnings of popular uprisings. What a Lacanian psychoanalytic lens helps emphasize is that critiquing or challenging the Law is only seemingly rebellious: by way of the obscene superego supplement to the Law, not only is our violation needed for the Law to function, but such violation binds us to the Law, keeping our rebellion within the (unthreatening) bounds that the Law itself defines and tolerates. "Perversion" is the name given to such quiescent defiance, and "hysteria" to a more thoroughgoing transgression that enables the rebel to uncompromisingly hold on to his/her desire for radical change.[10]

What the Tunisian case underlines is not only how perversion and hysteria can play out (and have played out) in a specific power constellation, but also how hysteria can mutate into perversion. Doubting authority, always maintaining a questioning attitude toward it, is so very difficult when the stability of the status quo and the prospect of immediate (capitalist) *jouissance* seem comparatively easier and more compelling. In the Tunisian case, to be more politically effective, a hysterical politics would have required not just greater and more sustained political mobilization and articulation by the Left (no easy task), but also tremendous psychoanalytic resources, it seems.

The revolutionary subject would need, then, to be able to stick obstinately to his/her desire, to be so attuned to the machinations of *jouissance* as to suspend the commands of the obscene superego supplement. Žižek calls this the "ethical Act": "'falling into some kind of death' . . . there is no ethical act proper without taking the risk of such a momentary suspension of the big Other" (Žižek 1999, 263). This means not just violating the Law but reconstituting its parameters, not just refusing to play the master's game, but restructuring the nature of the game itself and one's position within it (see chapters 8, 10, and 12).

## Notes

1. It is significant, in fact, that even though this wave of discontent came to be known as the Jasmine Revolution, it began not in the rich jasmine-growing areas of the country

but in the impoverished alfa-grass regions, which led some to suggest that it should more aptly be named the Alfa-Grass Revolution to better reflect the uprising's "grassroots" sociospatial origins (Ayeb 2011, 470).

2. In 2015, the UGTT was one of four Tunisian organizations to receive the Nobel Peace Prize.

3. These loans result from the Deauville Partnership created in 2011 to support Arab Spring countries, bringing together a host of creditors led by the International Monetary Fund (IMF) and including the World Bank, G8 countries (Group of Eight Industrialized Nations), Turkey, and the Gulf States.

4. Freud's studies on hysteria were based in good measure on the case of Dora (his pseudonym for a female patient he treated for hysteria; see Freud 1993) concerning Dora's suspicion that her father, involved in an unhappy marriage with her mother, is underhandedly trying to palm her off to his friend, Herr K, in return for having an illicit affair with Frau K, Herr K's wife. Dora ends up abruptly terminating her psychoanalytic treatment, with Freud seeing the case largely as a therapeutic failure, although a pioneering one from which he learned (he blames himself for, among other things, not adequately considering Dora's attachment to Frau K).

5. Lacan (1993) posits three main character structures—perversion, neurosis (subdivided into hysteria and obsessionality), and psychosis—all of which he sees as failed attempts at resolving the impasse between desire and Law.

6. Ennahda, it should be pointed out, is increasingly akin to Turkey's Justice and Development Party (AKP), to which Ennahda leaders readily make comparisons. Not only did Ennahda move toward a more moderate and democratic form of Islamic politics after the revolution, but in 2016 it even decided to split into a civil political party and a religious movement (McCarthy 2016), to make itself more electable. This split reflects the two camps of the party: those who embrace liberal notions of democratic citizenship based on rights (religious and gender equality, protection of human rights, etc.), and those who lean more heavily on the side of Sharia law (e.g., banning alcohol consumption, instituting blasphemy laws, etc.). The modernist wing now effectively controls the party, focusing on issues of internal security and economic development (see Lewis 2011). Anne Wolf (2017, 166ff.) suggests that, given the repression of the party under both Bourguiba and Ben Ali, this pragmatic political approach, in addition to being an election strategy, is also a kind of insurance policy against further repression by the regime.

7. The Ghannouchi government had first proposed that the new constitution be drafted by a panel of "eminent jurists," but subsequent to pressure from the Caravans of Freedom, it agreed in March 2011 to set up a High Authority (made up of mainly secular and leftist political leaders and intellectuals) charged with organizing elections for the constituent assembly. To ensure that no one party dominated the assembly, the High Authority opted for proportional representation on the constituent assembly (Zemni 2015, 8).

8. The only worthy master would presumably be the self-legislating subject.

9. I have argued elsewhere (Kapoor 2018, 274–275) that the radicalism of such Islamic movements as the Muslim Brotherhood is compromised by their lack of critique (and reproduction) of global capitalism: they are scathing of Western political meddling and neocolonial cultural deracination in the Muslim world (e.g., secularism, etc.),

but fail to link these to capitalist globalization (which has often been the chief cause of such deracination, through the commodification of culture, for example). In fact, the Muslim Brotherhood's extensive welfare services often incorporate neoliberal practices (e.g., job training), and help let the state off the hook by filling in the many gaps of the latter's welfare responsibilities.

10. I see Left reformism (as opposed to Left radicalism) as a form of perversion: it compromises its desire for meaningful change by settling for patchwork reforms (e.g., liberal human rights, welfare/charity for the poor and marginalized, etc.) that are unthreatening to, and in fact supportive of, liberal democratic capitalism. This stands in contrast to today's notable *hysterical* Right populism (e.g., the politics of Trump, Modi, or Berlusconi), which refuses to compromise its desires (e.g., for a flourishing capitalism) in the face of what it sees as a threatening Left secularism/multiculturalism—to the point of unapologetic racism, xenophobia, homophobia, and sexism that targets Muslims, Latinos, immigrants, LGBT people, women, and so on.

# References

Allahoum, Ramy. 2019. "Tunisia: Socioeconomic Injustice Persists 8 Years after Uprising," January 14. https://www.aljazeera.com/news/2019/01/tunisia-socioeconomic-injustice-persists-8-years-uprising-190111105510482.html.

Ayeb, Habib. 2011. "Briefing: Social and Political Geography of the Tunisian Revolution: The Alfa Grass Revolution." *Review of African Political Economy* 38 (129): 467–479.

Beissinger, Mark R, Amaney Jamal, and Kevin Mazur. 2019. "Who Participated in the Arab Spring? A Comparison of Egyptian and Tunisian Revolutions." Princeton University, Department of Political Science. https://pdfs.semanticscholar.org/bf96/ad6d9ce044ee0dd1865ded7dcaae75f198eb.pdf.

Breuer, Anita, Todd Landman, and Dorothea Farquhar. 2015. "Social Media and Protest Mobilization: Evidence from the Tunisian Revolution." *Democratization* 22 (4): 764–792.

Chandoul, Jihen. 2018. "The IMF Has Choked Tunisia. No Wonder the People Are Protesting." *The Guardian*, January 17. https://www.theguardian.com/commentisfree/2018/jan/17/imf-tunisia-people-rioting-2011-economic-reforms.

Dolar, Mladen. 1993. "Beyond Interpellation." *Qui Parle* 6 (2): 75–96.

El-Khawas, Mohamed A. 2012. "Tunisia's Jasmine Revolution: Causes and Impact." *Mediterranean Quarterly* 23 (4): 1–23.

Evans, Dylan. 2006. *An Introductory Dictionary of Lacanian Psychoanalysis.* London: Routledge.

Falk, Richard. 2016. "Rethinking the Arab Spring: Uprisings, Counterrevolution, Chaos and Global Reverberations." *Third World Quarterly* 37 (12): 2322–2334.

Freud, Sigmund. 1977. *On Sexuality: Three Essays on the Theory of Sexuality and Other Works.* Edited by James Strachey. Harmondsworth: Penguin.

———. 1993. *Dora: An Analysis of a Case of Hysteria*. Edited by Philip Rieff. New York: Collier.

Hitman, Gadi. 2018. "Arab Spring Era: Winds of Change in the Direction of Gender Equality for Tunisian Women: Arab Spring Era." *Digest of Middle East Studies* 27 (2): 168–184.

Honwana, Alcinda. 2011. "Youth and the Tunisian Revolution." Social Science Research Council, Conflict Prevention and Peace Forum. http://webarchive.ssrc.org/pdfs/Alcinda_Honwana%2C_Youth_and_the_Tunisian_Revolution%2C_September_2011-CPPF_policy%20paper.pdf.

Kapoor, Ilan. 2018. "The Pervert versus the Hysteric: Politics at Tahrir Square." In *Psychoanalysis and the GlObal*, edited by Ilan Kapoor, 257–282. Lincoln: University of Nebraska Press.

Kay, Sarah. 2003. *Žižek: A Critical Introduction*. Cambridge: Polity.

Kotsko, Adam. 2008. "Politics and Perversion: Situating Žižek's Paul." *Journal for Cultural and Religious Theory* 9 (2): 43–52.

Lacan, Jacques. 1977. *Écrits: A Selection*. Translated by Alan Sheridan. New York: Norton.

———. 1988. *Freud's Papers on Technique, 1953–1954: The Seminar of Jacques Lacan, Book I*. Edited by Jacques-Alain Miller. New York: Norton.

———. 1993. *The Psychoses: The Seminar of Jacques Lacan, Book III*. Edited by Jacques-Alain Miller. New York: Norton.

———. 1998. *The Ego in Freud's Theory and in the Technique of Psychoanalysis, 1954–1955: The Seminar of Jacques Lacan, Book II*. Edited by Jacques-Alain Miller. New York: Norton.

Legrand, Nathan. 2018. "The Fate of the Revolution." *Jacobin*, February 17. http://jacobinmag.com/2018/02/tunisia-revolution-ben-ali-austerity.

Lewis, Aidan. 2011. "Profile: Tunisia's Ennahda Party." BBC News, Africa, October 25. https://www.bbc.com/news/world-africa-15442859.

Mahmoud, Ines. 2018. "Tunisia's Next Revolution." *Jacobin*, February 17. http://jacobinmag.com/2018/02/tunisias-next-revolution.

McCarthy, Rory. 2016. "How Tunisia's Ennahda Party Turned from Its Islamist Roots." *Washington Post*, May 23. https://www.washingtonpost.com/news/monkey-cage/wp/2016/05/23/how-tunisias-ennahda-party-turned-from-their-islamist-roots/.

Saidin, Mohd Irwan Syazli. 2018. "Rethinking the 'Arab Spring': The Root Causes of the Tunisian Jasmine Revolution and Egyptian January 25 Revolution." *International Journal of Islamic Thought* 13 (1): 69–79.

Wells, Charles. 2014. *The Subject of Liberation: Žižek, Politics, Psychoanalysis*. London: Bloomsbury.

Wolf, Anne. 2017. *Political Islam in Tunisia: The History of Ennahda*. New York: Oxford University Press.

Yousfi, Hèla. 2018. *Trade Unions and Arab Revolutions: The Tunisian Case of UGTT*. New York: Routledge.

Zemni, Sami. 2015. "The Extraordinary Politics of the Tunisian Revolution: The Process of Constitution Making." *Mediterranean Politics* 20 (1): 1–17.

Žižek, Slavoj. 1989. *The Sublime Object of Ideology*. London: Verso.

——. 1997. *The Plague of Fantasies*. London: Verso.
——. 1999. *The Ticklish Subject: The Absent Centre of Political Ontology*. London: Verso.
——. 2006. *How to Read Lacan*. London: Granta.
——. 2011. "For Egypt, This Is the Miracle of Tahrir Square." *The Guardian*,
    February 10. https://www.theguardian.com/global/2011/feb/10/egypt
    -miracle-tahrir-square.

CHAPTER 10

# The Queer Third World

KEYWORD: *Queerness*

## Introduction

There is more than a certain affinity between "queer" and "Third World." Indeed, the derogatory epithet "queer" was reclaimed by gay and lesbian activists during the North American AIDS crisis of the 1980s and 1990s to frame a new politics of gay liberation. As a result, in contrast to mainstream LGBTI politics, which has most often centered on a liberal politics of identity and rights, queer politics has come to signify a more radical politics—an interrogation and disruption of social norms. For its part, the term "Third World," despite its current pejorative connotations about poverty, instability, and the "third rate," possesses notably principled origins: it was coined by French demographer Alfred Sauvy and became popular after the 1955 Bandung Conference, at which the leaders of newly independent states (Nasser, Nehru, U Nu, Sukarno) articulated a program of political nonalignment. The intent was to chart a new global arrangement (subsequently called the New International Economic Order) that steered clear of either capitalist or communist-bloc rivalries.

What "queer" and "Third World" thus have in common is a politics of nonconformity and dissidence. Both arise from a history of subjugation, attempting to resist and destabilize domination and the power of the status quo. Both operate from the margins, questioning normalizing power mechanisms and social order, while upholding a deviant, nonconformist, and nonassimilation-ist politics. And both are associated with equally negative and disparaging discursive connotations—the one attempting to reclaim such meanings in favor of a radical politics, the other stemming from a (failed) progressive politics of development that now awaits recuperation. My aim, in this chapter, is to try and align the two concepts—that is, group them in their common inheritance of subjugation and disparagement and their shared allegiance precisely to nonalignment and a radical politics (of development).

In assembling both terms, in fact, one is struck by how, in the mainstream discourse of international development, the Third World comes off looking remarkably queer: under Western eyes, it has often been constructed as perverse, abnormal, and passive. Its sociocultural values and institutions are seen as deviantly strange—backward, effete, even effeminate. Its economic development is depicted as abnormal, always needing to emulate the West, yet never living up to the mark ("emerging" perhaps, but never quite arriving). For their part, despite the inheritance of Bandung, post-colonial Third World nation-states[1] have tended to disown and purge such queering—by denying their queerness and, in fact, often characterizing it as a "Western import"—yet at the same time imitating the West, modernizing or Westernizing sociocultural institutions, and pursuing neoliberal capitalist growth. I want not only to make the claim that the Western and Third World stances are two sides of the same discourse but, drawing on Lacanian queer theory, also to suggest that a "queer Third World" would better transgress this discourse by embracing queerness as the site of structural negativity and destabilizing politics.

Before teasing out these arguments, a clarificatory note on my use of the word "queer": it is often employed as an umbrella term for lesbian, gay, bisexual, transgender, and intersex (LGBTI); and while I, too, will use it in that sense to an extent, in this chapter I am more interested in its political sense of deviant, perverse, or resistant to normalizing practices. In many ways, the latter meaning is incompatible with the former, since queerness is precisely a questioning of fixed identity, no matter whether gay or straight. Moreover, to the extent that queerness is about deviancy from social norms, it is not restricted to issues of sexuality, but can apply equally to categories of "race," economy, nation, or gender (hence my attempt at grouping it with "Third World" as metaphor for "nonaligned"). Nonetheless, the notion of queerness has grown out of the particular historical experience of marginalization of queers as a sexual minority, which has shed light not just on questions of sexual perversity, but a range of normalizing practices that my analysis will attempt to highlight.

## Queerness and the West

According to Foucault (1979), homosexuality is a Western construct of the nineteenth century, at which time it became a site for systematic legal, religious, and medical investigation. Prior to that period, "sodomy" and same-sex relations did of course happen, but although considered "sinful" and always under risk of being suppressed and harshly punished, such sexually "deviant" practices also had a certain degree of social acceptance, with even a few instances of its flourishing in urban subcultures. It was only in the late nineteenth century that "sexual perversion" began to be scrutinized, classified, and pathologized (as a disease), giving way to the modern notion of homosexuality. "The sodomite had been a temporary aberration; the homosexual was now a species," writes Foucault (1979, 43).

But whether in premodern or modern times, queerness has a history of marginalization and oppression. Heteronormativity—the social ordering that privileges heterosexuality and accepts as normal and natural the complementarity between the sexes—has meant the simultaneous production of sexual minorities as "queer," abnormal, unnatural, defective. Lee Edelman calls this "reproductive futurism": Western society sustains itself on the promise of a harmonious future by upholding the image of the innocent child to buttress social reproduction and the "absolute privilege of heteronormativity" (2004, 2). Generational succession is ensured, then, through a forward-looking reproductive politics of hope. And, according to such a politics, to the extent that queers do not procreate (at least they did not until the advent of in vitro fertilization), they do not reproduce the social. Indeed, they are often seen as threatening key social institutions: their lack of family orientation compromises such things as community and civil society, while their "sterile" and nonreproductive "lifestyle" endangers capitalism, which so depends on labor and wealth accumulation.

No wonder, as a consequence, that queers in the West have been subjected to torment through the ages. One thinks here of the castration of "effeminate" young boys in the Middle Ages, the vilification and persecution of homosexuals (as well as women, witches, Muslims, Jews, and the poor) during the Crusades and Inquisition, and the execution of "sodomites" under the sixteenth-century English Buggery Act (Crompton 2006).[2] More recent, often right-wing and conservative attacks against queers include the Nazi persecution of gay men (as well as Jews and Gypsies), antihomosexual discrimination during McCarthy's anticommunist purge, and the Anita Bryant "Save Our Children" crusade against gay rights in the late 1970s. All speak to attempts at preserving the social fabric, and hence reforming or eliminating queers as an embodiment of the threat to reproductive futurism.

Of late, a much more liberal approach to queerness has taken hold in the West (and other parts of the world, too). Contemporary liberalism now treats homosexuality as a sexual expression, lifestyle, and identity, and grants sexual minorities legal rights and protections, including gay marriage. This mainstreaming of LGBTI identities is reflected in liberal political economy as well, with queers targeted by mass-media and lifestyle marketing. "Out Is In," or so the slogan goes. Rather than being treated as a limit or threat to the social, the queer nonreproductive lifestyle is now a marketing and consumer opportunity.

But as several queer theorists have been quick to point out (Edelman 2004; Halberstam 2011; Hennessy 1994; Warner 1999), such "queer liberalism" tends to leave heteronormativity intact. It deals with sex as a personal or civil rights issue, thus avoiding broader structural change. In fact, far from posing a threat to the social order, queer liberalism helps reinforce it: it continues to uphold reproductive futurism by buttressing the institutions of marriage, family, domesticity, and nation, while also strengthening and promoting heteropatriarchal global capitalism through niche marketing and consumerism.

## Queering the Third World

It should come as no surprise that, prior to decolonization, the discursive representations of queerness in the West found their way into European colonial representations of the Third World. Indeed, as several postcolonial analysts have argued (e.g., McClintock 2013; Philips 2006; Stoler 1995), colonial domination was often justified and exercised through various forms of homophobia (as well as sexism and racism). Queering the Third World enabled the colonizer to distinguish himself from the colonized, buttressing his masculinity and social respectability, and as a result, rationalizing both his "civilizing mission" and denigration of local culture.

Thus, early colonial reports represented Amerindians in Colombia as sexual deviants and degenerates, engaging in "bestiality, sodomy, incest, and other unnatural practices" (Jara and Spadaccini, quoted in Kempadoo 2004, 30). Similarly, sixteenth- and seventeenth-century European travel journals referred to Africans as "hot-tempered" and "lascivious" (Jordan 2000, 44), with historian and colonial administrator Edward Long describing African women as "libidinous . . . monkeys" (quoted in Young 1995, 151; see also Gosine 2009). Black men and women were frequently reduced to their bodies (or to animality), lacking cognitive abilities or self-control, and invariably depicted as unintelligible, deceptive, and dishonest (Fanon 1963, 221; Gosine 2006, 32; 2009, 27). In this regard, Eve Sedgwick (1990, 4–5, 73), writing about the "closet" in modern Western culture, claims that the hetero/homo binary was often intertwined with the knowledge/ignorance binary, so that secrecy, opacity, and deceitfulness were associated with homosexuality. Such associations, it seems, circulated well in the racialized colonial context, too.

It was not uncommon for the sexualization of the Third World to resort to various forms of misogyny (as evidenced by the Edward Long quote above). Anne McClintock (2013, 21ff.) coins the term "porno-tropics" to describe how colonized lands were labelled "virgin territories" to rationalize their takeover (or their "penetration" or "rape"), while at the same time representing their inhabitants, and especially native women, as sexually promiscuous and voracious. Native men, for their part, if they were not being directly portrayed as "sodomites," were often symbolically castrated by being labeled "effeminate."[3] Mrinalini Sinha (1995) shows, in this regard, how the stereotype of the effeminate Bengali helped secure the British self-image of masculinity and justify continued British presence in India in the late nineteenth century, for example by helping rebuff (emasculate?) Indian demands for greater access to power.

The theme of sexual perversity and the myth of the "erotic East" are repeated in a plethora of writings about the Orient by European adventurers, travelers, geographers, anthropologists, and administrators (Kabbani 1994, 26, 66). Often, it is Arab and Muslim cultures that are depicted as sexually promiscuous, with much of the writing presenting them as tolerating and even propagating such "aberrant" practices as sodomy (Kabbani 1994, 65; Zavala 1989, 330). Of particular note is the work of late nineteenth-century adventurer-explorer Richard Burton, who hypothesized that there is a "Sotadic Zone" stretching from Southern Europe, the Middle East, and Africa to Asia-Pacific and the Southern "New World," where sexual perversion is endemic due to the warm climate. He claimed that this Sotadic Zone is rife with "debaucherie" and "erotic perversion," and that pederasty (referred to as "Le Vice contre nature") is practiced alongside bestiality, cannibalism, infanticide, and prostitution (Burton 1885, 10:206–207, 209, 222, 240; see also Kabbani 1994, 66).

Of course, representations such as Burton's amounted to more than simply naïve orientalist exoticism; as suggested above, their homophobia, misogyny, and racism served as important technologies to support and advance colonial power. In this connection, Ann Stoler (1995) talks about racialized sexual hierarchies established in the Dutch Indies between colonialists and natives—how strict laws were constructed to distinguish all-white from mixed couples, and "pure breeds" from the progeny of mixed marriages or cohabitation. According to Richard Philips (2006, 5), such sexual control was also present in the British Empire during the Victorian period, with carefully thought-out rules regulating sexual relationships among and between Britishers and locals. These covered everything from marriage, cohabitation, and consensual sex to prostitution, "buggery," and sexual diseases, all aimed at ensuring "moral" and social order. In a similar vein, Glen Elder (1995) argues in the South African context that colonial domination reflected pervasive anxieties about homosexual relations among and between whites and Blacks. Such anxieties were visible, for example, in the geographic ordering of apartheid, with clearly demarcated and strictly enforced spatial/discursive divisions (e.g., between Black miners' dormitories and white family residential estates, or between the ethnicized Bantustans or Black township ghettos and the white inner-city neighborhoods).

The sexualization and queering of the Third World thus helped discursively construct the Third World. This is what Edward Said famously called Orientalism. On the one hand, as Said points out, such a construction had "less to do with the Orient than it [did] with 'our' [Western] world" (1979, 12). To be sure, the colonizers were acting out their own European homophobic (and other) prejudices and representations in the colonies. The Third World served, in this sense, as a screen onto which Western colonial sexual fantasies, desires, and anxieties were being projected or transferred (see Kapoor 2008, 64–66; Nyongo'o 2012, 53). But on the other hand, these were not neutral prejudices and representations; they had material and institutional consequences. Racist homophobia resulted in physical violence against the colonized (Epprecht 2008, 58), while colonial sexual control, as we saw above, yielded enforceable laws, social hierarchies, and geographic demarcations. The Third World was thus produced as queer: not in the sense of the West imposing homosexuality on the colonies (quite the opposite), but in the Saidian sense of Orientalism as the "enormously systematic discipline by which European culture was able to manage—and even produce—the Orient" (Said 1979, 3). Regardless of whether the Third World actually was "queer," it was represented, regulated, and disciplined as such.

Given these material and institutional impacts, no wonder that the colonial queering of the Third World has had enduring legacies. This is evident perhaps nowhere more than in the field of international development. For example, the very notion of development stages "traditional" societies as pathological—that is, deviating from what is taken as the natural progression toward (Western) capitalist modernity. What is remarkable about the "trad-mod" binary that undergirds this discourse is how queer the Third World is made out to be—unnatural, abnormal, effete, passive (read: effeminate), strange, backward, underdeveloped, threatening. This is particularly true in relation to economic performance, assessments of which tend to be nothing less than emasculating: growth is invariably shown to be limping, if not falling short, the result of incompetence, corruption, and weak entrepreneurialism, which render the typical Third World economy incapable of competing against aggressive, win-or-die global business. The solution to such feebleness and failure is usually structural adjustment and debt relief, which as we know, many countries, especially in sub-Saharan Africa, have been coerced into accepting. These frequently entail severe "austerity" measures (fiscal "discipline," budget slashing, privatization, market liberalization) and a heavy dose of browbeating (the need for economic "correctness" and sound policy, "good" governance, and greater transparency and anticorruption rules; see chapter 5). Through a queer lens, this all looks like an exercise in economic *straight*-ening, aimed at disciplining, punishing, and exorcising the "Third World as queer."

And the recent global security discourse continues in this vein. As Mark Duffield (2007, ix, 24) contends,[4] this discourse constructs the "borderlands" (i.e., the Third World) as an imagined geographic space of instability, excess, and social breakdown, thus posing as a threat to the West. The Third World is typically seen as violent and unpredictable, or at least a potential danger; it is the source of many of the problems seen to plague global security, including drug trafficking, terrorism, rapid population growth, refugee flows, weak/corrupt/rogue states, and, more recently, infectious disease.

To be sure, the global spread of infectious diseases has been used to aid and abet, if not the queering of the Third World, certainly its continued sexualization, while also buttressing the global security discourse. With regard to the HIV/AIDS pandemic, Black African men and women, in particular, have tended to be portrayed as dangerous and irresponsible in their sexual behavior, with the colonial stereotype of the sexually voracious African commonly reproduced in Western donor and international health agency policy documents as the main explanation for the spread of AIDS (Gosine 2006, 32; Wilson 2012, 97ff.; see also chapter 1). Other infectious diseases (SARS, bird flu, swine flu, Ebola), while not sexually transmitted, have nonetheless retained a racialized sexual dimension in media and development/security discourses (see Lavin and Russill 2010): they are seen as originating in "overpopulated" places (i.e., China, Mexico, West Africa), where people apparently reproduce too much and live in close proximity both to billions of animals (i.e., poultry, swine, bats, and other wild animals) and to one another, which propagates the exchange of bodily fluids and disease. Reminiscent of colonial technologies of power, this pitting of "normal" against "abnormal" populations—healthy versus unhealthy, peopled versus overpopulated/teeming, sexually conventional versus licentious/queer, clean versus infected/lascivious/beastly—helps construct and justify the policies that we have now come to associate with global security: the profiling, detention, deportation, quarantining, or indeed elimination, of threatening groups.

It is also important to note the West's newfound championing of gay rights globally, in the wake of queer liberalism. Colonial homophobia toward the Third World has been replaced by a high-mindedness, which now sees the West judging Third World (and Eastern European) states as either homo-friendly or homophobic, frequently hectoring them when they fail to protect LGBTI rights, to the point of withholding aid (as was the case under the Obama regime's U.S. aid program in Uganda, for example). Yet, despite appearances, this latest Western stand is also a form of queering: the colonial maneuver may well have hinged on homophobia, which the West now conveniently condemns; but the current Western strategy nonetheless pivots on a manipulative "homorighteousness," as it were. Both are equally orientalist technologies of power aimed at estranging the Third World, belittling it, putting it in its place.

## "Unqueering" the Third World

But while there has been continuity from colonial to contemporary times in the Western representation of the "Third World as queer," there have also been moves in the opposite direction on the part of post-colonial Third World countries—attempts at "unqueering" themselves, at purging the queer from their midst. In some measure, this is a reaction to the humiliation and inferiority wrought by (neo)colonialism and Orientalism: the desire to be equal to one's (former) master, perhaps even to imitate him; and hence the desire *not* to be different or queer. Maureen Sioh (2014) takes a psychoanalytic view of this phenomenon, showing how the anxieties of humiliation and the desire for dignity are played out in East Asian economies. For her, these countries' striving for economic growth is equally a straining to command the same degree of respect globally as does the West.

But to a great measure, such unqueering is specifically geared toward purging the homosexual. A sure sign of this is the continued criminalization of homosexuality in much of the Third World (most of the Middle East, North Africa, sub-Saharan Africa and South Asia, and parts of Latin America and East Asia). Several countries (e.g., Iran, Yemen, Saudi Arabia, Mauritania, parts of Nigeria and Sudan) even make same-sex relationships punishable by death. Of late, it is sub-Saharan Africa that has seen particularly virulent forms of homophobia, exemplified by Uganda's "Kill the Gays" bill, Nigeria's "Jail the Gays" law, Gambia's "Aggravated Homosexuality" legislation, Tanzania's "morality crusade," and Robert Mugabe's repeated statements about homosexuals as offending "the law of nature and the morals and religious beliefs espoused by our society" (*The Star* 1995). Several African leaders, including Mugabe, have characterized homosexuality as "un-African," denouncing it as a dangerous and perverted Western import (see Rukweza 2006). And this in spite of numerous findings of same-sex practices across Africa before colonial rule.[5]

These legal prohibitions and homophobic outbursts appear to have several causes. First, we should recall that many of the sodomy laws criminalizing homosexuality are carry-overs from British, Portuguese, and French colonial rule (see Alexander 2005; Stychin and Herman 2001). Most often, these laws have made sexual practices that were previously socially acceptable into abnormal ones, thus creating an enabling environment for intolerance against queers. Second, homophobia is often used by Third World leaders for political purposes, for example to whip up public sentiment as a diversion from important socioeconomic problems. Mugabe leaps to mind here, given that his repeated homophobic (and anti-West) rants often ran alongside his country's political and social instabilities. And finally, right-wing U.S. evangelical and pentecostal missionizing, particularly in post-colonial sub-Saharan Africa, has played an important part in promoting assaults against homosexuality (and abortion). The prominent role of American religious groups in fanning homophobia in Uganda in recent years is now well acknowledged, but there is also growing evidence of these groups lobbying for conservative policies and laws in such countries as Tanzania, Zambia, Zimbabwe, Malawi, and Kenya (see Kaoma 2012; Williams 2014).

Over the years, all of this has undoubtedly contributed to homophobic violence and prejudice. LGBTI people have been the victims of beatings, detention, torture, purges, murder, and death across the Third World. They have been denied access to health care and other social services and benefits (see Weiss and Bosia 2013). And they have often suffered in silence for fear of being "outed" or reported to the authorities. In relation to present-day Uganda, for example, Sylvia Tamale (2007, 176) underscores how the state's "regime of compulsory heterosexuality" creates a climate of fear among LGBTI people and women, and severely limits public discourse on such key issues as marriage, sex, and gender.

Of course, this process of unqueering does not apply uniformly across the Third World. There are several exceptions worth noting of countries that have embraced a queer liberalism: constitutional protections for LGBTI people in

South Africa, Fiji, and Ecuador; and same-sex marriage/union recognition in Argentina, Uruguay, Brazil, Ecuador, and some states in Mexico (although they are under threat these days, notably in Jair Bolsonaro's Brazil). Yet, while there is no doubt that these places are relatively more progressive on queer issues, there remain nonetheless, in these as in other parts of the Third World, some deep-seated homophobic prejudices and practices (as is the case in many parts of the West as well). A large part of the reason has to do with continuing forms of heteronormativity embedded in development processes.

Indeed, for the most part, development assumes heterosexuality. Hetero-sexual marriage is taken as the basis of the family unit and the building block of social reproduction. Yet this has often meant the de facto legitimation of patriarchal and capitalist relations of power: as head of the household, the hus-band/father wields authority not only over all family members (especially women) but also over the labor of each member. A gendered division of labor ensues: men typically work outside the home for a wage, while women en-gage in unpaid household labor (food preparation, child rearing, cleaning); and if the latter do work outside, they are remunerated less than men. Most of-ten, women carry a double load (homework and professional work), and to that extent, are ensuring the health, well-being, and labor supply of both family and workforce (Hennessy 1994, 102).

So when development programming assumes heterosexuality or takes the "household" for granted, as it customarily does, it is validating and reinforc-ing these heteropatriarchal capitalist relationships. As Susie Jolly points out, land reform programs, antipoverty strategies, and rural planning alike, because they treat the nuclear family and male heads of households as the norm, not only end up favoring men over women but also result in "more pressure on people to . . . stay within heterosexual family set-ups" (2011, 24; 2000, 86).

The consequences for queer people are numerous and generally dire. The social (i.e., heteropatriarchal and capitalist) pressures to marry, along with the socioeconomic benefits of marriage (dowries, inheritance, the prospect of in-creased social status and standard of living) mean that gay and lesbian people are inclined to get and stay married. Such compulsory heterosexuality discour-ages women, in particular, from leaving unhappy, abusive, or violent mar-riages. Lesbians (wives, mothers, daughters) frequently suffer in silence, with suicide rates among their ranks, and the ranks of LGBTI people more gener-ally, tending to be high (see Weiss and Bosia 2013).[6] Should queers dare to "come out," they usually suffer severe social injunctions, including family or community sanctioned rape (Jolly 2000, 80–81). The loss of family, in turn, means the loss of social capital (e.g., family, kinship, and/or caste networks), which threatens their very livelihoods and survival. The result is socioeconomic marginalization, with many LGBTI people being forced into either the informal sector or prostitution and the global sex trade (Altman 2000; Drucker 2009, 827; Jolly 2011, 21–22).

Of late, usually at the behest of international or Western aid agencies, there have been a few attempts at targeting state programs toward "disadvantaged" groups. But these, too, have not escaped heteronormative biases.[7] Gender programming, for example, has generally taken straight women as the norm, thus invisibilizing queer or nontraditional heterosexual women (Jolly 2011, 26). The same appears to be true, at least to a degree, of HIV/AIDS programming, which has tended to assume the disease is transmitted only heterosexually, thus neglecting gay men (see Gosine 2009). As for interventions specifically directed toward LGBTI communities, these are few and far between, and most often not made without reproach. In his assessment of programming for "men who have sex with men" (MSM), for example, Andil Gosine concludes that their representations of gay men tend to mirror those of the colonial era: the queer is seen as "uncivilized, unwieldy, threatening and requiring management to save him from himself, as well as the world. . . . In other words, health care interventions directed at MSM are justified toward protection and preservation of the heterosexual nation" (2009, 30).[8]

The unqueering of the Third World manifests itself, therefore, through homophobic laws, policies, and prejudices that repress and closet homosexuals; and through heteronormative structures that normalize sexual behavior and perpetuate gender and capitalist hierarchies. As for development programming, to the large extent that it incorporates and reflects these underlying structures and prejudices, it can often contribute to the marginalization of queers, sometimes even when it intends to help them.

## The Queer Third World

How, then, to interpret the paradoxical attempts by the West to queer the Third World and the Third World to "unqueer" itself? While seemingly contradictory, I want to suggest that the moves are two sides of the same coin. That is, both result from the same orientalist heteronormative discourse founded on the normal/abnormal or the straight/queer binary. As the historically dominant power, the West is here casting itself in a positive light by othering the Third World; and as the historically subordinate power, the Third World is compensating for its othering and humiliation by shedding and purging its abnormality/queerness. The Third World is thus buying into and reproducing (symbolically and materially) its oppressor's binary structure of signification. It may well characterize homosexuality as a Western "import," yet such characterization is nothing but a continuation of the very colonial technologies of power (homophobia, racism, sexism) that it has purportedly fought against. It may well posture as anti-West, yet such posturing is belied, for the most part, by its de facto imitation of the West—its embrace of Westernization and neoliberal growth strategies, for example.

It is the fact that both the West and the Third World are shot through with the same forces of global capitalism, moreover, that helps explain why they are locked into, and reproduce, the same heteronormative discourse. They are equally beholden to a socioeconomic system that, as we have seen, thrives on a gendered division of labor and the marginalization of queers. Thus, even the recent advent of queer liberalism in (most of) the West and (parts of) Third World can only ensure the tolerant incorporation of LGBTI rights into liberal capitalism, leaving mostly untouched the deeper hierarchic and heteropatriarchal structures.

The irony is that, strive as it may to be equal to the West, the Third World will never be equal to the task. This is because the orientalist heteronormative discourse it consents to already sets it up as a failure, ensuring that it can never be fully "developed"—an "emerging economy" perhaps, but never one that has surfaced.

So how might one avert reproducing this orientalist heteronormative discourse? Is queer/Third World liberation possible without acquiescing to (neo) colonial and homophobic technologies of power? I would like to draw on the work of queer theorist Lee Edelman (2004) to offer some tentative answers. Rather than countering the homophobic stereotypes and practices that result from heteronormative discourses, Edelman argues for embracing, not the stereotypes/practices themselves, but the social antagonisms to which they point (e.g., the impossibility of the "normal"). He thus advocates a relentless politics of negativity as a way of short-circuiting heteronormativity.

Edelman is of course drawing on Lacan here. As we have seen (chapters 1 and 3), for Lacan, reality is precarious, always fractured by gaps and contradictions, which he refers to as the Real. The Real is the limit—the horizon of negativity—of any signifying/discursive system; it punctures meaning and identity, making them forever lacking and unstable. And it is this emphasis on the instability of identity that aligns Lacanian psychoanalysis with queer theory, prompting Tim Dean to state that "Lacan makes psychoanalysis look rather queer" (2003, 238). Lacan and queer theory (of the type espoused by Edelman) share in the radical questioning of social norms. They dispute the very idea of the "normal," upon which heterosexuality is founded. For example, according to Lacan, there is nothing natural or normal about sex (hence his famous one-liner "There is no sexual relation"; see chapter 8). This is because people connect, not through some primordial attraction, but through language, which for Lacan is always incomplete, imprecise, opaque. Thus, far from being tied to biology or the identity or sexual orientation of the Other, desire is tied to language (i.e., it is a surplus to language, reflecting the gaps/ Real in language; see chapter 1). And heteronormativity, by affirming a stable identity and notions of the natural and the normal, conceals or disavows such instability.

Like Lacan (and Žižek), Edelman sees negativity as constitutive of the social.[9] He approaches queerness as an embodiment of such negativity, yielding to a relentless disruption of social norms: queerness "can never define an identity; it can only ever disturb one," he declares (2004, 17). This closely mirrors the feminist psychoanalytic arguments (by Zupančič, Copjec) we encountered in chapter 8. As highlighted earlier, Edelman's book *No Future* (2004) is a critique of "reproductive futurism"; it exposes heteronormativity's nostalgic treatment of childhood innocence and promise for what it is—a strategy to buttress the future, that is, to maintain and further biological, social, and capitalist reproduction. To the extent that queerness is nonreproductive, then, it represents the failure of heteronormativity. Indeed, it threatens and fractures the social, and in that sense—to echo Lacan—tends toward a politics of the Real (Edelman 2004, 5, 9).

Edelman coins the term *"sinthom*osexual" to describe the protagonist of such a politics, a figure who, while created by reproductive futurism, transgresses and dislocates it (2004, 38, 47).[10] What drives the *sinthom*osexual, according to Edelman, is *jouissance*. His idea here is to put queer nonreproductive eros, so often disparaged by straight society as sterile[11] and excessive, to use for political purposes—to make the excessive transgressive, as it were.[12] The *sinthom*osexual thus relishes the thrill derived from a politics of the Real: challenging authority, defying patriarchy, or undoing homophobia and heteronormativity is (or can be) joyful, if not ecstatic (2004, 85). Consequently, it is this paradoxical pleasure—a *jouissance* that delights in the pain or danger of the radical political act—that motivates, nourishes, and sustains a queer politics of the Real. In a sense, Edelman is queering the (feminist) politics of the Real that we highlighted in chapter 8 by insisting on its ecstatic character: it is the queerness of the Real, its unpredictable drive and excess, that makes it politically efficacious.

What are the implications of all of this for the Third World, given the challenge of trying to negotiate orientalist heteronormative discourse without reproducing its binary structure? Clearly, the idea is not to imitate the West since, as we have seen, that merely normalizes both the West's domination and the Third World's subordination. Nor should one simply oppose the hegemon by criticizing homophobia and orientalism or valorizing a non-Western nativist/nationalist authenticity (e.g., "homosexuality is 'un-African'"), since those, too, are an acceptance of, and entrapment within, the given binary logic. At most, the latter yields, as we have seen, to a tolerance of queers (i.e., a queer liberalism) or a virulent and homophobic parochialism, without addressing underlying questions of heteronormativity or neocolonialism. The idea, rather, is for the Third World to embrace its queerness-as-negativity. Indeed, to the extent that it represents (or has been made to represent) the failure of global modernity, the Third World threatens and fractures globalization. Thus, by firmly inhabiting this position of structural negativity, it can help destabilize normalizing practices, be they neocolonial, orientalist, heteronormative, patriarchal, or racist. By revisiting its political roots in nonalignment, it can attempt to trouble the increasing naturalization of global neoliberal capitalism. And by engaging in a relentless queer politics of the Real, it can seek to mess up fixed binaries, identities, or hierarchies, whether political, gendered, or sexual.

This would mean, for example, cultivating queer affect as a political strategy: rather than directly criticizing homophobic, misogynist, or orientalist stereotypes, showing a certain fatigue, indifference, or boredom toward them; rather than taking the hegemon seriously, responding with incredulity, disorderliness, or awkwardness; and rather than conforming to the master's rules, willfully forgetting or ignoring them, improvising with them, or overidentifying with them (i.e., taking them so seriously to the point of absurdity; see chapter 11). Using stereotypical queer affect in this way—whim, insincerity, camp, nonsense, over-the-top emotion, unregenerate sexuality, silliness, goofiness[13]—interrupts and stupefies hegemonic power by declining to address it directly, thereby delegitimizing it. In this regard, Judith/Jack Halberstam suggests the deployment of more explicitly negative queer political emotions—from rage, anger, mania, and spite to incivility, dyke anger, anticolonial despair, and punk pugilism. He[14] states:

> we must be willing to turn away from the comfort zone of polite exchange to embrace a truly political negativity, one that promises, this time, to fail, to make a mess, to fuck shit up, to be loud, unruly, impolite, to breed resentment, to bash back, to speak up and out, to disrupt, assassinate, shock, and annihilate, and to abandon the neat, clever, [and] chiasmatic. (2006, 824; see also 2011, 110)[15]

Queer affect can thus help produce an uncivil politics that no state or sociopolitical regime can easily discipline or regulate.

The effectiveness of any queer Third World politics will hinge crucially on its ability to disrupt (heteronormative) capitalism. This will involve rethinking and reworking institutions as much as cultures: reordering labor relations and the sexual/gender division of labor; moving away from legal regimes that privilege private and civil/political rights toward ones that also favor collective and socioeconomic rights (e.g., land rights, housing rights, indigenous rights, gender and queer rights); undoing capitalist discourses centered on wealth accumulation, entrepreneurialism, market competition, and patriarchal/masculinist codes; and so on. But it will also involve creating spaces for nonconforming and noncapitalist practices. In this regard, echoing queer theorist Eve Sedgwick, J. K. Gibson-Graham ask: "What if we were to depict social existence at loose ends with itself. . . . What if we were to 'queer' capitalist hegemony and break apart some of its consolidating associations?" (1999, 81, 83; see also 1996, 138; Oswin 2007). They have in mind "post-capitalist" social economies such as cooperatives (e.g., the Mondragon Basque Cooperative), local economic trading systems, and remittance-based community projects (e.g., in the Philippines) (Gibson-Graham 1999, 2006), but we could add worker self-management enterprises, social housing, participatory budgeting, and community forestry.[16] In the Third World context, the recuperation and reinvention of highly diverse subjugated, buried, or subaltern socioeconomic institutions, ranging from handicraft ateliers and small animal husbandry to contemporary indigenous medicinal and health clinics and small-scale textile workshops, will also be pertinent and important.

Given its nonconformist bent, a queer Third World politics of the type I am gesturing toward would appear to cater more to nonstate than state actors (the state being a normalizing set of institutions par excellence). Yet, given the state's continuing (albeit changing) significance in both domestic and global politics, queering the state—pressuring it to institute noncapitalist practices such as those described above, for example—will be vital. In this regard, Bolivia's erstwhile Morales regime appears as one of the queerest globally: it purposefully remained *nonaligned* to either the (Western) neoliberal democratic model (adopted by most of the contemporary world) or the authoritarian capitalist model (adopted by the likes of China, Russia, Singapore, etc.). Instead, pursuing a unique communitarian Andean model of "living well," it was one of the very few that put the country's subalterns first (indigenous groups and the socioeconomically most poor and marginalized), while confronting domestic and international economic elites and defying the free-market proposals of the IMF and World Bank (which likely contributed to Morales's ouster).

While certainly not without reproach,[17] it was a better illustration of how to socioeconomically restructure (including how to effectively regulate powerful mining multinationals) than the vast majority of Third World states committed to nonalignment and the New International Economic Order.[18]

Finally, we must ask what a queer Third World politics means for Third World queers. Although it is, of course, a politics that defies normalizing/heteronormative practices and hence robustly defends sexual minority and gender rights, its structural negativity also implies that LGBTI activism settle, not on identity issues (e.g., queer liberalism), but on the intersection of queer politics with other key socioeconomic problems. This is illustrated by the difference between, say, a gay rights activist and a queer socialist revolutionary, or a pro-gay-marriage LGBTI association and LGBTI people fighting for subaltern land rights. So, when Third World HIV/AIDS politics concerns itself not just with discovering new and more effective retroviral drugs—thereby narrowly focusing on science and funding issues—but also with ensuring cheaper and equal access to those drugs for all, thereby bringing the state and multinational pharmaceuticals to account, we have a queer Third World politics truer to its name. Eng, Halberstam, and Muñoz (2005, 7–10) point, in a similar vein, to the emergence of global queer diasporas that are increasingly denaturalizing such institutions as home, nation, marriage, and citizenship on the basis, not of origin, ethnicity, or "race," but destination, sexuality, and sociopolitical commitment. It is such nonconforming, intersectional, and politically messy engagements that yield a queer Third World politics of the Real.

## Conclusion

I have argued that the Third World's attempts at "unqueering" itself are a knee-jerk response to the West's attempts at queering it, thus reproducing the West's binary structure of signification. Instead of allowing it to be nonaligned, such unqueering causes the Third World, on the contrary, to continue to perpetuate orientalism and capitalist heteronormativity, thereby confirming the West as the "best" and the Third Word as too queer to ever quite reach the mark. As a consequence, rather than suppress or disavow its queerness, I have suggested the Third World embrace it. By occupying its (de facto constructed) position of queerness-as-structural negativity, the Third World can dismantle normalizing practices—including orientalism, homophobia, and capitalist heteronormativity—while at the same time search for counterhegemonic and non- or post-capitalist alternatives.

**CHAPTER 10**

But of course none of this is easily done. Many difficult obstacles lie in the way, and there are no guarantees of reaching one's goals. A radical and deviant politics always risks resistance, compromise, and co-optation as a result of, say, elite opposition, state repression, or neoliberal commodification (think of how Che, Gandhi, and feminism have been commoditized of late). And, against these odds, even were a queer counterhegemony to be achieved, there is always the risk of its becoming a new normativity. Contemporary LGBTI politics are a case in point: not only is there nothing intrinsic to LGBTI groups that predisposes them to a radical politics, but as mentioned earlier, Third World queer liberalism has done little to move beyond civil rights and same-sex marriage recognition, the latter tending to reinforce rather than dismantle heteronormativity. Moreover, where Third World LGBTI rights have been won, global capital has not hesitated to use this cultural-political shift as an opportunity for niche marketing and consumerism, thus seducing LGBTI communities and blunting their political resistance.

But then one must ask: what are the conditions of a possibile queer Third World politics? Is it not pie in the sky to suggest that such a radical alternative can be practiced when so much stands in its way? I want to return to the question of *jouissance*, highlighted earlier, to provide (the beginnings of) an answer. The great challenge for the Third World Left will be, not merely to come up with a queer alternative, but to ensure it is a *seductive* one—one that people will enjoy. It is not enough to draw people at the level of the intellect; they/we must also be seduced at the level of the passions. And a Left queer alternative will need to be at least as enjoyable as that put forward by heteronormative neoliberal capitalism—as pleasurable as the power that male patriarchs derive from patriarchy, entrepreneurs from profit making, or consumers from shopping. It is *jouissance*, then, that can create the conditions of possibility of a dissident queer alternative, one from which citizens and queer revolutionaries alike are moved and enlivened—why not?—by the pain and peril of radical political acts or the transgressive pleasures of working toward more just, but always contested, societies.

## Notes

1. "Third World" denotes for me, then, both the promise of nonalignment (as articulated in Bandung) *and* its betrayal, as evidenced by the alignment of most post-colonial Third World states with westernized neoliberal capitalism.

2. In contrast, see Najmabadi (2005), who argues that women and queers played a positive role in the shaping of modern Iranian politics and culture.

3. Homi Bhabha (1994, 82) points out the often contradictory nature of stereotyping: For example, the Third World is stereotyped as weak or effeminate when it comes to economic management but as hypersexed and macho when it comes to questions of "overpopulation." Despite the contradiction, each construction queers the Third World, helping to justify First World superiority and power. But, as chapters 1, 6, and 11 also underline, the contradictions are proof that ideology is at work, meaning that the pull and power of unconscious desires (to dominate the queer Other) outweigh any rational logic or clarity.

4. See also Jasbir Puar (2007) on the deployment of "homonationalism" to distinguish Westerners from racialized and sexualized "terrorists."

5. Same-sex practices have been shown to have occurred across Africa before colonial rule: for example, among the Nuba in Sudan, where men dressed and lived as women; among the Azande in Northern Congo, where warriors habitually married boys, who functioned as temporary wives; in the pastoral communities of Madagascar and Ethiopia, where transvestism was (and is) not uncommon; and among the Khoikhoi in South Africa, where lesbianism was practiced in polygamous households. See Epprecht (2008), Evans-Pritchard (1970), Murray and Roscoe (2001), and Nadel (1947).

6. Note that in the Middle East, low levels of participation by women in the labor force have meant lesbian invisibility. See Drucker (2009, 827), Khayatt (2006), and Lind and Share (2003).

7. In the context of international and Western donor agencies, Robert Mizzi (2013) coins the term "heteroprofessionalism" to describe homophobic and heterosexist behaviors in the workplace that screen out homosexuality and privilege heterosexuality.

8. There is also the risk of "homonormativity" in development programming geared toward LGBTI people, especially by Western donors: that is, taking the white, Western gay man as the standard, and assuming, for instance, that gay rights protection is a key objective when, in the development context, better access to health services or retroviral drugs might be much more significant. See Lind (2010).

9. Along with Leo Bersani (1995) and Judith Halberstam (2011), Edelman is often considered a proponent of the "antisocial" thesis in queer theory, that is, an exponent of queer political negativity, unbelonging, and social alienation.

10. Edelman is here drawing on the Lacanian concept of the *sinthome*, which as we will see in chapter 12, is the particular and unique form that *jouissance* takes when the subject becomes attached to its symptom.

11. The issue of "sterility" applies contradictorily in the Third World context. Just as Edelman argues is the case in the West, LGBTI people in the Third World will tend to be characterized as "sterile" because they threaten reproductive capitalism; but in Western orientalist discourse, the "Third World as queer" will often be depicted as the far opposite of sterile—not just reproductive, but hyperreproductive and "overpopulated," to the point of threatening global sustainability. As underlined in note 3 above, while contradictory, each construction is a way of exercising and justifying domination of an Other (whether LGBTI people or the "Third World as queer") by estranging it.

12. Edelman is, in fact, very hostile to politics, at least of the mainstream kind—one that is always looking toward a future good ("reproductive futurism"). Instead,

he identifies with a queer politics of the Real or the death drive, oriented toward transgression and rupture (see chapters 4 and 8).

13. See Halberstam (2011, 109–110). See also Cvetkovich (2003), which shows how sexual trauma and queer affect can catalyze political activism and communities.

14. Judith Halberstam tends to employ the masculine pronoun to refer to himself, and often goes by the name "Jack."

15. Here, Halberstam is being critical of Edelman. He criticizes *No Future* for relying on examples mainly from "white gay male culture" (Edelman illustrates *sinthomosexuality* drawing on Charles Dickens's Ebenezer Scrooge, George Eliot's Silas Marner, Leonard in Hitchcock's *North by Northwest*, and the birds in Hitchcock's *The Birds*). While I agree to some extent with this criticism, and draw on Halberstam (and Edelman) on the use of queer affect for political purposes, I tend not to endorse Halberstam's main argument in *The Queer Art of Failure*. Indeed, in championing failure as a queer "art," Halberstam ends up essentializing queerness-as-failure. Rather than averting and dismantling the success-failure binary promoted by capitalist heteronormativity, Halberstam reproduces it by seeing failure as success (and characterizing failure as some kind of authentic queer political art). It seems to me that, by living up to "failure," the queer (or in our case, the Third World) is buying into the capitalist logic of success rather than disrupting it. The challenge, to follow Edelman, is not to oppose the discourse of success by valorizing its opposite (i.e., failure as essence), but to see failure as structural negativity (i.e., as the Real, which disrupts every attempt at success, including failure-as-success).

16. None of these are necessarily "post-capitalist," of course; much depends on how they are done. Peck and Theodore (2015) show, for example, how participatory budgeting has been taken up by the World Bank and European Union to serve neoliberal, rather than radical democratic, objectives.

17. A weak judiciary (jeopardizing the country's democratic system), budding state authoritarian tendencies, a growing cult of personality centered on Morales (including his obstinate decision to run for a fourth term as president), are some of the main criticisms directed against the former Bolivian state. Of course, institutionalized heteronormativity (and homophobia) remained, and continues to remain, a big challenge with this state, as with all states. See Fontana (2013).

18. The Bolivian example also suggests that queer states are more likely to emerge in the Third World than the West, given the latter's mostly uncritical championing of neoliberal capitalism and liberal democracy over the last three decades, and at least pockets of resistance to these throughout the Third World during the same period (e.g., Chavez's Venezuela, Castro's Cuba, Allende's Chile, Kerala's democratic communism, etc.).

## References

Alexander, Jacqui. 2005. *Pedagogies of Crossing: Meditations on Feminism, Sexual Politics, Memory and the Sacred*. Durham, NC: Duke University Press.

Altman, Dennis. 2000. "The Emergence of Gay Identities in Southeast Asia." In *Different Rainbows*, edited by Peter Drucker, 137–156. London: Gay Men's Press.

Bersani, Leo. 1995. *Homos*. Cambridge, MA: Harvard University Press.

Bhabha, Homi K. 1994. *The Location of Culture*. London: Routledge.

Burton, Richard. 1885. "Terminal Essay: Pederasty." In *Book of a Thousand Nights and a Night*, 10:205–254. Benares: Kama Shastra Society.

Crompton, Louis. 2006. *Homosexuality and Civilization*. Cambridge, MA: Harvard University Press.

Cvetkovich, Ann. 2003. *An Archive of Feelings: Trauma, Sexuality, and Lesbian Public Cultures*. Durham, NC: Duke University Press.

Dean, Tim. 2003. "Lacan and Queer Theory." In *The Cambridge Companion to Lacan*, edited by Jean-Michel Rabat, 238–252. Cambridge: Cambridge University Press.

Drucker, Peter. 2009. "Changing Families and Communities: An LGBT Contribution to an Alternative Development Path." *Development in Practice* 19 (7): 825–836.

Duffield, Mark. 2007. *Development, Security and Unending War: Governing the World of Peoples*. Cambridge: Polity.

Edelman, Lee. 2004. *No Future: Queer Theory and the Death Drive*. Durham, NC: Duke University Press.

Elder, Glen. 1995. "Of Moffies, Kaffirs and Perverts: Male Homosexuality and the Discourse of Moral Order in the Apartheid State." In *Mapping Desire: Geographies of Sexualities*, edited by David Bell and Gill Valentine, 50–58. New York: Routledge.

Eng, David, Judith Halberstam, and José Esteban Muñoz. 2005. "Introduction: What's Queer about Queer Studies Now?" *Social Text* 23 (3–4): 1–17.

Epprecht, Marc. 2008. *Heterosexual Africa? The History of an Idea from the Age of Exploration to the Age of AIDS*. Athens: Ohio University Press.

Evans-Pritchard, Edward. 1970. "Sexual Inversion among the Azande." *American Anthropologist* 72: 1428–1434.

Fanon, Frantz. 1963. *The Wretched of the Earth*. Translated by Richard Philcox. New York: Grove.

Fontana, Lorenza B. 2013. "On the Perils and Potentialities of Revolution: Conflict and Collective Action in Contemporary Bolivia." *Latin American Perspectives* 40 (3): 26–42.

Foucault, Michel. 1979. *The History of Sexuality*. Vol. 1: *An Introduction*. New York: Allen Lane.

Gibson-Graham, J. K. 1996. *The End of Capitalism (As We Knew It): A Feminist Critique of Political Economy*. Cambridge, MA: Blackwell.

——. 1999. "Queer(y)Ing Capitalism In and Out of the Classroom." In *Journal of Geography in Higher Education* 23 (1): 80–85.

——. 2006. *A Post-Capitalist Politics*. Minneapolis: University of Minnesota Press.

Gosine, Andil. 2006. "'Race', Culture, Power, Sex, Desire, Love: Writing in 'Men Who Have Sex with Men.'" *IDS Bulletin* 37 (5): 27–33.

——. 2009. "Monster, Womb, MSM: The Work of Sex in International Development." *Development* 52 (1): 25–33.

Halberstam, Judith. 2006. "The Politics of Negativity in Recent Queer Theory. In 'Forum: Conference Debates: The Antisocial Thesis in Queer Theory.'" *PMLA* 131 (3): 823–824.

———. 2011. *The Queer Art of Failure*. Durham, NC: Duke University Press.

Hennessy, Rosemary. 1994. "Queer Theory, Left Politics." In *Rethinking Marxism* 7 (3): 85–111.

Jolly, Susie. 2000. "'Queering' Development: Exploring the Links between Same-Sex Sexualities, Gender, and Development." In *Gender and Development* 8: 78–88. 2.

———. 2011. "Why Is Development Work so Straight? Heteronormativity in the International Development Industry." *Development in Practice* 21 (1): 18–28.

Jordan, Winthrop. 2000. "First Impressions." In *Theories of Race and Racism: A Reader*, edited by Les Back and John Solomos, 33–50. London: Routledge.

Kabbani, Rana Imperial. 1994. *Fictions: Europe's Myths of the Orient*. London: Pandora.

Kaoma, Kapya John. 2012. *How the U.S. Christian Right Is Transforming Sexual Politics in Africa*. Somerville, MA: Political Research Associates.

Kapoor, Ilan. 2008. *The Postcolonial Politics of Development*. London: Routledge.

Kempadoo, Kamala. 2004. *Sexing the Caribbean: Gender, Race, and Sexual Labor*. New York: Routledge.

Khayatt, Didi. 2006. "The Place of Desire: Where Are the Lesbians in Egypt?" Unpublished paper presented at the Faculty of Education, York University.

Lavin, Chad, and Chris Russill. 2010. "The Ideology of the Epidemic." *New Political Science* 32 (1): 65–82.

Lind, Amy, ed. 2010. *Development, Sexual Rights and Global Governance*. London: Routledge.

Lind, Amy, and Jessica Share. 2003. "Queering Development: Institutionalized Heterosexuality in Development Theory, Practice and Politics in Latin America." In *Feminist Futures: Reimagining Women, Culture and Development*, edited by Kum-Kum Bhavnani, John Foran, Priya A. Kurian, and Debashish Munshi, 55–73. London: Zed.

McClintock, Anne. 2013. *Imperial Leather: Race, Gender, and Sexuality in the Colonial Contest*. New York: Routledge.

Mizzi, Robert C. 2013. "'There Aren't Any Gays Here': Encountering Heteroprofessionalism in an International Development Workplace." In *Journal of Homosexuality* 60: 1602–1624.

Murray, Stephen O., and Will Roscoe. 2001. *Boy-Wives and Female Husbands: Studies in African-American Homosexualities*. New York: St: Martin's.

Nadel, Siegfried. 1947. *The Nuba*. Oxford: Oxford University Press.

Najmabadi, Afsaneh. 2005. *Women with Mustaches and Men without Beards: Gender and Sexual Anxieties of Iranian Modernity*. Berkeley: University of California Press.

Nyongo'o, Tavia. 2012. "Queer Africa and the Fantasy of Virtual Participation." *Women's Studies Quarterly* 40 (1–2): 40–63.

Oswin, Natalie. 2007. "The End of Queer (as We Knew It): Globalization and the Making of a Gay-Friendly South Africa." *Gender, Place & Culture: Journal of Feminist Geography* 14 (1): 93–110.

Peck, Jamie, and Nikolas Theodore. 2015. *Fast Policy: Experimental Statecraft at the Thresholds of Neoliberalism*. Minneapolis: University of Minnesota Press.

Philips, Richard. 2006. *Sex, Politics and Empire: A Postcolonial Geography*. Manchester: Manchester University Press.

Puar, Jasbir. 2007. *Terrorist Assemblages: Homonationalism in Queer Times*. Durham, NC: Duke University Press.

Rukweza, Jacob. 2006. "Is Homosexuality Really 'UnAfrican'?" In *Pambazuka News*, no. 247 (March). http://www.pambazuka.net/en/category/comment/32974.

Said, Edward W. 1979. *Orientalism*. New York: Vintage.

Sedgwick, Eve Kosofsky. 1990. *Epistemology of the Closet*. Berkeley: University of California Press.

Sinha, Mrinalini. 1995. *Colonial Masculinity: The "Manly Englishman" and the "Effeminate Bengali" in the Late Nineteenth Century*. Manchester: Manchester University Press.

Sioh, Maureen. 2014. "Manicheism Delirium: Desire and Disavowal in the Libidinal Economy of an Emerging Economy." *Third World Quarterly* 35 (7): 1162–1178.

*The Star* (Johannesburg). 1995. "Furious Mugabe Lays into Gays in Address at Fair." August 2, 1995.

Stoler, Ann Laura. 1995. *Race and the Education of Desire: Foucault's "History of Sexuality" and the Colonial Order of Things*. Durham, NC: Duke University Press.

Stychin, Carl F., and Didi Herman, eds. 2001. *Law and Sexuality: The Global Arena*. Minneapolis: University of Minnesota Press.

Tamale, Sylvia. 2007. *Homosexuality: Perspectives from Uganda*. Kampala: Sexual Minorities Uganda (SMUG).

Warner, Michael. 1999. *The Trouble with Normal: Sex, Politics and the Ethics of Queer Life*. New York: Free Press.

Weiss, Meredith L., and Michael J. Bosia, eds. 2013. *Global Homophobia: States, Movements, and the Politics of Oppression*. Urbana: University of Illinois Press.

Williams, Roger Ross, dir. 2014. *God Loves Uganda*. New York: First Run Features. DVD.

Wilson, Kalpana. 2012. *Racism and Development: Interrogating History, Discourse and Practice*. London: Zed.

Young, Robert J. C. 1995. *Colonial Desire: Hybridity in Theory, Culture and Race*. London: Routledge.

Zavala, Iris M. 1989. "Representing the Colonial Subject." In *1492–1992: Re/Discovering Colonial Writing*, edited by René Jara and Nicholas Spadaccini, 323–348. Minneapolis: University of Minnesota Press.

## CHAPTER 11

# The Racist Enjoyments and Fantasies of International Development

KEYWORD: *Racism*

## Silence That Nonetheless Speaks = The Unconscious

In carrying out research for this chapter, I was struck by two things: the small size of the literature on racism in international development, with the emergence of only a few, comparatively recent, sources on the topic (Goudge 2003; Kothari 2006b; Persaud and Walker 2001; White 2002; Wilson 2012), revealing of the relative silence on the issue in this field; and the repeated exclamation in this same literature about such silence, yet with nary a reference to the unconscious. Kothari and White claim, for example, that ideas of "race" are a "taboo" in development circles, "rarely spoken about" overtly or publicly (Kothari 2006a, 2–3; 2006b, 9; White 2002, 407), while Persaud and Walker declare that "race has been given the epistemological status of silence" (Persaud and Walker 2001, 374; see also Wilson 2012, 3, 5). Without taking away from such pioneering arguments (which I readily endorse), what appears to be missing is precisely a psychoanalytic understanding of this silence.

Although these scholars underline a general reticence in talking about racism in development, they proceed to speak about it even so, pointing out the many ways in which it manifests.[1] Sarah White notes, for instance, that despite the public taboo, many in the development field admit to racism "privately" (2002, 407). Yet it seems difficult to understand how racism can be both denied and furtively confessed without recourse to the notion of the unconscious. In fact, "a silence that nonetheless speaks" is the very psychoanalytic definition of the unconscious. Moreover, what remains unexplained is why such racism cannot be publicly or "officially" uttered (at least not without undesirable consequence). Could it be because the racism that supports development is obscene? Is it because development is sustained, willy-nilly, by alluring (unconscious) fantasies of domination and white supremacy, with the result that people actually enjoy racism? And so *this* is why racism cannot be easily admitted (or eliminated)?

## The (Racist) Unconscious of Development Speaks!

In psychoanalysis, gaps, pauses, empty spaces are redolent with meaning: they reveal processes of resistance, repression, disavowal—all aimed at protecting the subject from exposure, at shielding power from crisis. Yet, such resistance inevitably fails, unable to continuously safeguard against the deadlocks or excesses of desire. Which is to say again that international development's silence on racism is never complete: despite efforts to hide it, the (racist) unconscious inexorably speaks.[2] I therefore want to draw attention to some "informal" racist remarks and practices in development, as well as inadvertent racist outbursts or scandals, both of which I take as symptomatic of development's unconscious.

First, the bigoted private remarks made by Western expatriates (recorded in the recent literature):[3] These often impugn local cultural values (e.g., "Nepalis are friendly but lazy," "Muslims are anti-women"), malign people's behavior (e.g., Nigerians/Afghans/Venezuelans are "corrupt"; Nicaraguan NGOs swarm around foreign NGOs such as Oxfam "like *bees around a honey pot*"), or denigrate people's intelligence (e.g., local NGO officials are not working at a high enough "analytical level"; "I am so tired of dealing with 'grassroots' organisations here in Haiti. Unfortunately, 'grassroots' means no brains and no money"). Such "informal" prejudice is frequently mirrored in the segregated socialization patterns of expatriates working in the global South. For example, White writes about how "the disparagement of Bangladesh and things Bangladeshi was the common currency of talk in the bar at expatriate clubs" (2002, 409), while Crewe and Fernando describe the manner in which expatriates "congregate in bars, invite each other for dinner, toddler groups or to 'ladies lunches', hold book swaps or sports events, celebrate (predominantly) Christian festivals, encourage their children to play or even set their own social club with exclusive membership" (2006, 48)

And then there are the unwitting or accidental racist gaffs and outbursts. These sometimes manifest as slips of the tongue by senior officials: for instance, the head of the U.S. Agency for International Development, Andrew Natsios, declared to the *Boston Globe* that many Africans are unable to successfully take HIV/AIDS treatment because they "don't know what Western time is," never having "seen a clock or a watch their entire lives" (quoted in Herbert 2001); and the director of the World Bank's Loan Department opined that he does not recruit Black professionals because "Blacks make poor accountants and the department could not hire too many blacks as the department would look like a ghetto" (quoted in Chiles 2012).

But sometimes, these racist indiscretions manifest as full-on institutional "scandals." One of the most recent is the 2018 Oxfam "sex scandal," in which it has emerged that the Haiti country director organized "sex parties," sexually abusing and exploiting women and possibly minors (see Ratcliffe 2018). In light of the ongoing #MeToo movement, this scandal is likely the tip of the iceberg: already in 2002, aid workers in forty aid agencies in West Africa, including UNHCR and Save the Children, were accused of the sexual exploitation of refugee children (Gillan and Moszynski 2002). Now, there are allegations of widespread use of sex workers and "temporary girlfriends" by Western development staff, as well as sexual exploitation of "vulnerable" women (e.g., migrants, refugees) (Beaumont and Ratcliffe 2018; Waldie 2018). Needless to say, despite being labelled "sexual," these scandals imbricate sex, gender, "race," and class, involving as they do mostly white men abusing women and children of color across North-South and elite-subaltern divides (see Bruce-Raeburn 2018). Such domination happens, then, through multilayered processes of sexual, racial, gendered, and socioeconomic objectification.

What is psychoanalytically significant is that these are all reluctant utterances or outbursts: they would rather not reveal themselves, and to the extent that they do, show themselves only privately, informally, unofficially, or accidentally. It is such reticence that points to the unconscious (see chapter 1), and in particular to processes of racist disavowal: people know well that racism happens in development, that they themselves might be racist, but they would rather it not be known publicly for fear of embarrassment or exposure. Yet they nonetheless admit to it, sometimes "informally," and sometimes in the form of unintentional (read: unconscious) outbursts or slips of the tongue. Racist disavowal, in this sense, is the denial of racism that is simultaneously accompanied by an (allergic) acknowledgment of it.

## Racism as the Obscene Supplement
to (the Law of) Development

But I want to suggest that such unconscious processes of racist disavowal are not just occasional or haphazard but *integral* to development. That is, the informal and intermittent character of the above racist utterances and scandals shows not that development goes awry every so often—because of ignorance or a few "rotten apples"—but that development is already rotten because racism is unconsciously written into it.

One way to understand this, as pointed out in chapter 9, is through what Žižek calls the "obscene superego supplement to the law" (Žižek 1997, 11; 2005, 57): regimes of power sustain themselves not only with explicit rules and norms regulating people's interactions (social values and goals, institutional discipline and hierarchy), but also with an obscene underside—a shadowy realm of quasi-legal transgressions. These are precisely the "informal" racist utterances and segregated, if not "scandalous," social behaviors of expatriates referenced above. They are development's "institutional dirty secrets," not unlike the often racist, sexist, and homophobic gym "locker-room" talk or initiation rituals in the armed forces or university frat houses. They are a supplement to "official" development assistance, but must remain in the shadows, unmentionable in public. In fact, as underlined in the above examples, it is significant that the racist utterances are "private," the segregated social behaviors by expatriates "unofficial" (i.e., they happen outside people's official work places), and the outbursts/scandals "accidental," all indicative of the gray zone in which they operate. People know about them, secretly whisper them, indulge in them, so that they end up being unofficially tolerated, if not condoned.

What is going on psychoanalytically here, to restate what we said in chapter 9, is that a power regime's explicit rules are always accompanied by an implicit superegoic command to gleefully transgress these rules—hence the reference to the "obscene superego supplement to the law" (Žižek 1999, 268).[4] The "law" of development thus both prescribes prohibition and encourages defiance;[5] it is infused with an unconscious solicitation to enjoy violation and illegality: as Lacan puts it, without "transgression, there is no access to *jouissance* [enjoyment]" (1997, 177). Accordingly, the allure of development's institutional dirty secrets is enjoyment, which as we know refers to excessive/orgasmic pleasure, to the point of being counterproductive or morally wrong. The superego imperative to enjoy flouting the law mitigates the subject's anxiety or guilt about doing so, enabling her/him to escape punishment (as long as the illegality remains a secret).

It is perhaps not so surprising, then, that several of development's racist scandals, like the ones mentioned above, are highly sexualized and violent. The combination of (1) the suspension of the official law, (2) enjoyment's libidinal *excess*, and (3) the secrecy of the racist act (i.e., the presumption that "no one is watching") is often a lethal one resulting in sadomasochistic abuse, rape, or even torture, reaching its apogee in such cases as the 2003 sexual humiliation and torture of Iraqis at Abu Ghraib prison at the hands of U.S. soldiers, or the Catholic Church's ongoing implication in the sexual abuse of children—many of them indigenous—across the global South and North (see Razack 2005; West 2017).[6] In these examples, the power of development is supplemented by an unconscious message to do the *extreme* opposite, to the point of racialized sexual violence.

But whether in such extreme cases of racism or not, the implication is that what binds communities such as expatriate development ones is not simply what their members share (common values, norms, etc.) but what they transgress. It is the underbelly of the law—the racist remarks/jokes at expatriate clubs, the segregated socialization patterns, the prejudicial hiring practices, the unpublicized "sex parties"—that helps build and sustain their group cohesion and discipline (see Žižek and Daly 2004, 128). The "private" racist utterings and practices thereby become a kind of initiation ritual, constructing social ties within development circles. And it is not just engaging in the racist banter or behavior that is enjoyable but also the fact that it is a shared "dirty secret"— the common knowledge that what "we" are doing is illicit or obscene. In fact, often the worst betrayal is not so much when group members speak publicly about development's operational weaknesses or failures (i.e., its explicit power) but when they divulge its implicit membership codes and practices—"our club rules are racist," "X's jokes are misogynist," "Y organizes sex parties"—the latter revelations sometimes resulting in embarrassing public "scandals." Development's unspoken (racist) rules thereby stand as codes of honor, helping buttress credibility, loyalty, and order.

This notion of having to "keep up appearances" brings out well development's dual (schizophrenic?) character, betraying the gap between its outward image of benevolence and its unacknowledged obscene supplement. My point, of course, is that the two sides are intimately connected, with each enabling the other. There is a direct relationship between what development says we should not do ("we are here to help, not belittle or dominate, the Other") and the perverse thrill we get from doing it nonetheless (Hook 2017, 609). In fact, the injunction to help becomes a license to transgress: the (not so) guilty pleasure of dominating the Other is the well-earned reward for our ostensible beneficence and humanitarianism. Racism is, in this sense, a kind of recompense for our hard work, sacrifice, and loyalty to (the law of) our group/organization, and the more we obey such a law, the more we are entitled (by the superego) to deviate from it. Thus, the shadowy realm of racism, far from undermining the civilized and respectable semblance of the power of development, serves as its inherent support.

This, in short, is why racism is not an aberration but intrinsic to development. It may well remain under the cover of night, revealing itself informally and sporadically, but this underlines only its enduring unconscious character, not its rarity.[7] Indeed, racism is to be apprehended psychoanalytically as the clandestine supplement to the law of development, the latter making transgression into an obligation and enjoyment a libidinal profit. It is this double-sidedness of the law of development—the fact that it must seek support in an illegal enjoyment—that shows why bigotry can thrive alongside aid and humanitarianism, respectable aid workers can be racist sexual predators, and helping the Other can involve dominating the Other.

## The Discourse of Development: White Supremacy, Fantasy, and Enjoyment

We have examined the dirty (superegoic) underside of development discourse, which can result in the domination of the Third World. It is this unconscious process that helps us understand informal or accidental acts of bigotry as integral, not incidental, to development. Yet what remains unexplained is why such domination is necessarily racist. The underbelly of the development may well incline subjects to enjoyably transgress the injunction to "help" the Third World Other, it may well aid in forging community through libidinal ties (i.e., shared dirty secrets), but there is no compelling reason such deviance take the form of racism. To wit, as we have seen, the domination of the Third World includes many interconnected dimensions of power—sexual, class, gender, and so on. But I want to suggest that racism is an abiding supplement to development discourse because the latter is accompanied by broader racialized power dynamics. That is, development discourse is armed with an (unconscious) ideological apparatus premised on white supremacy and fantasies of Third World subordination, which predispose it toward racist domination of the Other. Superegoic commands thus work with ideological fantasy to enact an obscene enjoyment-producing racism.

## White Supremacy and Development

According to Žižek (1989, 87), ideology—racist or otherwise—draws on a multitude of "floating signifiers," which are structured into a unified field by means of a "master signifier" that "quilts them" and "fixes their meaning." Thus, master signifiers such as "Beauty," "Freedom," "Democracy," or "Jesus Christ" provide a (temporary) point of fixity, helping anchor people's beliefs and practices (aesthetic, political, religious, etc.).

Such is the case with racist ideology, which, as Kalpana Seshadri-Crooks (2000) explains, is a significant way of organizing human difference and social activity. She focuses, in particular, on "whiteness" as master signifier. For her, the "fixing" of whiteness in racist discourse coincides with the rise of European colonialism, serving as a modern system of social categorization and control (Seshadri-Crooks 1998, 354; see also Bonilla-Silva 1997, 471).[8] White supremacy helped support Europe's "civilizing mission" as much as its imperialist designs: it fostered the circulation of racial stereotypes (e.g., "lazy natives," "savage Africans," "dirty Indians"), constructed colonized lands as "dark continents," and rationalized such institutions as slavery, forced labor, and the eviction and "resettlement" of indigenous peoples (Bhabha 1994, 94ff.; Fanon 1963; Parry 1972; Ross 1982). Whiteness, in this sense, came to pervade not just colonialism's cultural practices, but also its political and socioeconomic institutions—from education, work, and marriage (antimiscegenation) to taxation, property laws, and voting regulations. In places such as the Caribbean, for instance, Black and brown women tended to be relegated to domestic service, while Indian and Chinese men could find employment only in specified sectors (e.g., building railroads, managing laundries, working as indentured laborers on sugar plantations) (Damir-Geilsdorf et al. 2016; Page and Sonnenburg 2003, 492; Watson 2001). Meanwhile, white men (and to a lesser extent, white women) epitomized culture, civilization, and moral virtue, enjoying the relative opportunity and legal entitlements to engage in all manner of socioeconomic and political advancements, especially in the colonies.

The implication is that whiteness is a lie, made true (i.e., "fixed" as master signifier) only through colonial rule/power. Indeed, despite eighteenth- and nineteenth-century theories advocating "scientific racism," there is no credible scientific basis for "race,"[9] with recent DNA studies showing, ironically, that we all have African ancestors (Bonilla-Silva 1997; Kolbert 2018). Racial discourse is thus a modern ideological construction aimed at dominating the Other by assigning social difference on the basis primarily of physical characteristics (skin color, hair, facial or bodily features, etc.), with whiteness as a significant "structuring principle of racial meaning" (Seshadri-Crooks 1998, 355; see also Mbembe 2017, 32).

The psychoanalytic peculiarity of whiteness though is that it is socially authoritative and determining, yet invisible. On the one hand, it serves as standard: the white subject is the universal subject "coterminous with being human" (Seshadri-Crooks 1998, 369; 2000), while the nonwhite subject is constructed and evaluated only in terms of whiteness, which functions as ideal and norm. Whiteness thus becomes associated with fullness, virtue, and infinite possibility, in contrast to nonwhiteness, which is equated with the exotic, strange, and abnormal. In the colonial context, blackness in particular is linked with evil, filth, sin, bestiality—a negrophobia that helped justify a slew of social institutions, including slavery, strict antimiscegenation laws, and the creation of Bantustans under apartheid (see Doty 1996; McClintock 2013; Nast 2000; Pieterse 1992).

Yet on the other hand, whiteness is disavowed. Race becomes a primary form of identification for the white subject, so much so that whiteness is (unconsciously) assumed as a default position: it becomes an "ontologically neutral category that advances [the white] subject as raceless and unmarked . . . [with the result that] white identification disavows crucial knowledge about difference" (Seshadri-Crooks 1998, 354, 370). The ruse of white supremacist ideology, in other words, is to abject whiteness, denying it as master signifier, treating it as either invisible or just one among many colors. This is certainly the subterfuge of such current multicultural labels as "people of color" or "visible minority," which assume that whiteness is neither a color nor visible, thereby further naturalizing it. There is, in short, an unconscious ground to the racialized authority of whiteness, which consists of inferiorizing the nonwhite subject, while disavowing whiteness and the ways in which it advantages the white subject (see Alcoff 2006).

These unconscious dynamics play out on the side of the racialized Other, too. The legacy of colonial domination, coupled with the fact that whiteness-as-master-signifier has come to pervade the (globalized) symbolic order, has meant that nonwhite bodies are not easily able to register in the Symbolic. They are constructed, as we have seen, as incomplete and abject, defined not on their own terms, but only in relation to whiteness (Zevnik 2017, 625). This ineluctable difference between whiteness and nonwhiteness signifies that racialized subjects are positioned as misfits, always out of place. That is what Fanon had in mind when he spoke of the intense racial anxiety and alienation experienced by Black subjects: unable to represent themselves, they are defined only on the basis of their skin color, imprisoned by it, held responsible for it (Fanon 1967, 110, 112, 134; see also hooks 1997). While the white subject comes to accept her whiteness "naturally," the identification process for the Black subject is traumatic: racial epidermalization implies s/he is immediately hailed, and only culturally recognizable, in terms of her/his physical appearance.

One way to escape such estrangement is by donning a white mask (see chapter 1). Fanon describes this as the internalization of whiteness, as a result of which the Black subject attempts to be recognized by presenting himself in the image of the white dominant (1967, 112; see also MacCannell 1996). It implies not only a certain dependency complex (an acceptance of white supremacy and the inferiority of nonwhiteness), but also a yearning to become white, to live up to the image of whiteness, indeed to aspire to white supremacy.[10] This is what some have called "whiteliness"—an ingrained racialized (whitely) way of being in the world so that you could be racist even if you are nonwhite: "the connection between whiteliness and light-colored skin is a contingent connection: this character could be manifested by persons who are not 'white'; it can be absent in persons who are" (Frye 2001, 87). It reveals a certain triumph of whiteness-as-master-signifier: whiteness "quilts" the symbolic order to the extent that subjects, regardless of their skin color, desire it (and nonwhites may even be racist against "their own"). It means that interpellation happens unconsciously, regardless of the subject's will or identity (Sedinger 2002, 47).

So how does all this translate in international development? To the extent that whiteness permeates the global Symbolic (as a result of the West's colonial past and continuing global hegemony, as underlined above), it also suffuses the field of development (see chapter 1). This is all the more the case given that this is a field that centers on (neocolonial) power dynamics between the West and Third World and involves relationships across elite-subaltern and color (i.e., white/nonwhite) lines. Whiteness/whiteliness, in this sense, is not just development's inheritance, it is deeply ingrained symbolically and materially. And it manifests in the way that knowledge is constructed, authority is exercised, and activities are organized. As Sarah White argues, "advantage and disadvantage" in development "are patterned by race" (2002, 409).

Whiteness taints development discourse in multiple ways: what terminology is used (e.g., "expert," "consultant," "facilitator" are often code words for white and Western), what counts as knowledge (if it comes from the West it is best, and if it spoken by a white Westerner it is more credible), who the funder is, who makes key decisions, who trains whom, and so forth. In each case, it matters whether the "privilege of whiteness" is involved or not (Goudge 2003, 188; see also Crewe and Fernando 2006, 44, 50–51). Goudge (2003, 163) sees the presence of technology, for example, as a marker of whiteness (the provision of computers, flat-screen televisions, or chauffeured transportation

on a project signifies superiority and progress), while Kothari (2006b) underlines how whiteness reflects not necessarily the content of the information being imparted but who is imparting it, and where it comes from. In the latter
regard, this declaration by a Zimbabwean NGO staff member is revealing: "If
you want your organization's plans to be approved quickly or you need to raise
funds, you are better off appointing a white director" (quoted in Kothari 2006a,
16). Here again, whiteness equates with greater clout, closer access to power
and resources, more respect, better expertise.

The implication is that white expatriates, whether or not they subscribe to
white supremacy, "benefit from the historically ascribed privilege of whiteness"
(Watson 2001, 450). Whiteness may well be a cultural-ideological construction, not a phenotype, but it nonetheless yields material advantages for white
subjects. This comes through in the following reflection by Sarah White on
fieldwork she carried out in Bangladesh: "my whiteness opened me doors,
jumped me queues, filled me plates, and invited me to speak. . . . Just as pounds
sterling could buy far more in Bangladesh than in Britain, so quite an ordinary
individual could suddenly find him or herself in command of a handsome salary and benefits package, a mansion and a domestic staff—and come to believe it theirs by right" (2002, 409; see also Crewe and Fernando 2006, 46).[11]
What is revealing here is not just that whiteness is socially determining, be-
stowing racial privilege and social advantage, but also, as stressed earlier, that
it is taken for granted, disavowed (the clause "come to believe it theirs by right"
is significant in this regard). And it is this dual character of whiteness that makes
it ideological in the Žižekian sense: it is a form of domination that masks its
very form through unconscious dynamics (disavowal). This is why whiteness/
racism is barely acknowledged or spoken about in development; its effectivity
in ensuring supremacy depends on it being naturalized, assumed.

The other side of the coin is the positioning of "locals" in relation to whiteness. To be sure, it means their relative denigration: local knowledge is devalued, often seen as suspect and unscientific, if not simply ignored in favor of
rational "Western" expertise.[12] Petersen and Lentfer (2017) contend that
"people of colour are assumed to be less qualified and have lower credentials
than they do, and are passed over for jobs, promotions, or pay rises." In this
regard, a white Western NGO worker reveals how, barely a year out of university, he was able to "leapfrog" over a dozen equally if not more qualified
national staff at an NGO in Sudan, in effect because of the color of his skin,
and he reports frequently attending meetings in his new role, with "white
people in management seated at the front and Africans around the edges in
junior roles" (*The Guardian* 2015). This is a scene witnessed all too often in the
literature (e.g., Crewe and Fernando 2006; Goudge 2003), but it speaks once

again to how whiteness helps produce hierarchical social structures, placing nonwhite subjects in subordinate and disadvantaged positions. It also confirms that, although the coercive-legal enforcements of colonialism may not pertain any more, development nonetheless reproduces forms of social and work-related apartheid like the ones mentioned above, at least to some extent.

Given the symbolic and material advantages of whiteness, it is not surprising that "locals"—NGO staff, consultants, government officials, project "beneficiaries"—should also aspire to it. This is the internalized racism, the "whiteliness," we referred to above. It means not just that locals may look up to all things Western/white, but also that they may themselves engage in bigotry: Kothari describes, for example, how local counterparts were "visibly disappointed when they realize[d] that their expatriate consultant [was] not white" (2006a, 15–16), while Crewe and Fernando (2006, 42) reflect on how non-Western development staff working in Africa can be racist toward Africans. Of course, the important difference between such internalized racism and white racism, as we have stressed above and Crewe and Fernando (2006, 42) are right to point out, is that the latter is more historically ingrained and can have "more pervasive consequences." Nonwhite bigotry, in fact, is not a deviation from, but a confirmation and strengthening, of the discourse of whiteness.

White supremacy is thus a key ideological dimension of development discourse. It has deep historical roots and social impacts, affecting the ways in which knowledge is constructed, authority is exercised, and social inequalities are produced. Significantly, its effectivity relies on the unconscious normalization of the privileges and techniques of domination in order to make whiteness neutral and invisible. The obscene evidence of the latter is internalized racism, which, as Fanon underlines, inures the objects of white racism not simply to accept but to desire—indeed to help reproduce—the very system that oppresses them.

## Development's Racist Fantasy and Enjoyments

However, development discourse is supported by not just whiteness but also fantasy. In fact, the fantasmatic dimension of development helps underwrite whiteness-as-master-signifier, providing it with a broader mythical frame (e.g., notions of growth, progress, power, supremacy). To be sure, the stories of development are nothing less than fables—of quest and fate, triumph and failure, heroes and villains. They motivate and inspire people to work toward "development," but they also rationalize and naturalize social and racial division. Most importantly, they direct people to secretly enjoy racism: to take obscene pleasure in lording it over racialized others, denigrating and dominating them. Thus, as I suggest below, the power of development is "animated by fantasy" and "infused with enjoyment" (Hook 2017, 619; see also Stavrakakis 2002, 81).

As we have seen in chapters 1 and 3, in the Žižekian scheme of things (1989, 114; see also Fanon 1967, 157), fantasy is what supports an ideological edifice, helping to cover up or obfuscate the "Real" (i.e., social antagonisms such as alienation, inequality, etc.). Ideologies are thus constructed to fill the gaps and contradictions of the social; they escape the traumatic Real by promising a pristine, harmonious, reconciled social order. This is indeed what international development does: it pledges to make the Third World more wholesome and prosperous, drawing on the West as model.

Like all fantasies, development's dominant fantasy bears an idealized, positive side and a darker, negative side.[13] The West, as we know all too well, is conjured as the space of wealth and fortune, virtue and civilization, unity and harmony, while in contrast the Third World is portrayed as the space of poverty and underdevelopment, superstition and servility, fragmentation and disorder. Not only is this fantasy evolutionist—it posits the West as the goal toward which the Third World must aspire and move—but it also justifies the mission of development—to develop the Third World and make it in the West's image. This dream of development is an unmistakably supremacist one, mirroring at least to an extent the colonial civilizing mission and mapping onto the earlier-mentioned white fantasy of mastery and domination. The (white) Westerner is cast as the hero of the story—expert, consultant-adviser, humanitarian—ready to provide aid and assistance, while the Third World subject is depicted as the damsel in distress, helpless, out of joint, child-like. The one construction, hero / victim, justifies the other, mastery / rescue (see chapter 10).

Granted, this fantasy of development is not outwardly racist. Our multicultural times mean that colonial-era characterizations of the racialized Other as "uncivilized" or "primitive" tend to be shunned. Yet, racial imagery and terminology are still very present, often in veiled forms. Witness the infantilization of the Third World Other through the pervasive use of child imagery by development NGOs (Manzo 2008); the frequent resort to animal imagery, for example when referring to the sexual habits of African men in the context of the HIV / AIDS crisis as we underlined in chapter 1 (Wilson 2012, 97ff.), or the "swarms" or "hordes" of people in relation to the refugee or population "crisis" (Fletcher, Breitling, and Puleo 2014; Goudge 2003, 166); and the reference to Third World states as spaces of instability, excess, and social breakdown in mainstream security discourse (Duffield 2001, 2006, 2007). Analysts also point out how the domain of culture, indeed reference to the very term "culture," is often racially coded (Kothari 2006a, 13; Narayan 1997, x, 84; White 2002, 408; 2006, 62): words such as "tribalism," "ethnicity," "tradition," "religion," "local," "indigenous," "corruption," are frequently stand-ins for the primitive and inferior customs, beliefs, and practices of the (racially marked) Other. Cultural difference, in this sense, signals "race."

Given that, as underlined earlier, the positive fantasmatic construction of the West as a space of order and harmony depends on a negative presentation of the Third World, the result is that the racialized Other is often portrayed as strange, dark, uncanny—menacing to (global) order and harmony. There is always something about the Other that bothers "us"—their exotic clothes or accents, the smell of their food, their religious beliefs, their body odor, their loud laughter or music, their peculiar ("cultural") ways of thinking (hence the earlier-mentioned disparagement of "Bangladesh and things Bangladeshi" at expatriate clubs). Frequently, the fantasmatic Other is identified as the culprit for development's woes, a blockage whose elimination will surely restore balance and cohesion: dishonest and corrupt officials who threaten good governance, fundamentalist terrorists who endanger political stability, superstitious and "traditional" beliefs that undermine modernity, hypersexed men and women who cause over-population, poverty and insecurity that endanger the West. . . . The negative construction of the Other is thus crucial to development's fantasy of harmony, as a consequence of which the (racialized) Other is constructed precisely in a way that makes it responsible for failure and disorder.

The fantasmatic dimension of racism here is significant, since the pathology of development's racism is seeing the Other not as a person, but only as an embodiment of Third World-ness, Muslim-ness, Black-ness, and so forth. In other words, it is not so much the immediate presence of the Other that bothers us, but the *depiction* or *figure* of the Other, the stories and images that circulate and that overdetermine what we understand about the Other. As Žižek (2006) puts it, "Reality in itself, in its stupid facticity, is never intolerable: it is language, its symbolization, which makes it such." Racist discourse constructs the Other as a fiction, so that the very non-existence of the Other functions as the main argument for racism: racist discourse uses the gap between the "fictional Other" and the reality of actually existing Others as the ultimate argument against the Other (Žižek 1996, 25).

The related implication is that if the racialized Third World Other did not exist, it would have to be invented in order to sustain the idea of a harmonious West (or stable global order). This is to say that the only function of the fantasy figure of the Other is to make people believe that a harmonious West exists, covering up that it is impossible, that (capitalist) society—Western or Third World—is always already riven with antagonisms and disorder (social inequalities, ecological disintegration, dispossession of the poor, war and conflict, crises of democracy, etc.). Thus, the West is precisely not the ideal or exemplar it is made out to be, and racism is its symptom. Not only is the Other/ Third World constructed to cover up this fact, but it also serves as an object onto which the West projects or displaces its flaws and contradictions. As Fanon suggests, the white man often soothes his trauma by ascribing the flaws "to someone else" (1967, 190): blaming refugees (rather than a homemade economic downturn) for taking "our" jobs, condemning corrupt officials (rather than global or local inequality) for failures in governance, holding poor people (rather than the overconsumption of elites) responsible for deforestation, pinning political instability in Afghanistan on "ethnic" rivalry (rather than on years of Western interference), and so on. One's prejudice against the Other says more about oneself: it is because one's house is in disorder that one has to displace it onto the (Third World) Other. And this is precisely what makes racism pathological—that it is needed to assert one's identity and power.

What makes racism even more pathological though is its enjoyment dimension, which goes hand in hand with fantasy. To be sure, fantasy is what explains the subject's *lack* of total enjoyment (the fundamental lack that the subject is always in search of), so that, for example, a nationalist narrative (or indeed a racist one) is constructed to identify "enemies" and heal the subject's ontological wound, promising a restoration of full enjoyment. Fantasy thus helps organize and direct the affective elements of the subject, how s/he desires or enjoys (Žižek 1989, 44). The predominant fantasy of development does just that, identifying poverty and underdevelopment as the problem and staging the West as best. In its less malignant form, enjoyment here is to be derived from the presumed superiority of the Western subject, her/his humanitarianism in "rescuing" the Other, or indeed her/his idealization of this Other, whose exotic clothes, music, and food s/he can avidly consume (as lifestyle choice).

But in its more malignant form, such enjoyment can take on sadomasochistic guises. The latter educes from the dream of world mastery that is integral to development's racism (i.e., being on "top," in both its sexual and political senses). For, as suggested earlier, the demand to "develop" is an impossible (superegoic) one: it is an imperative that the West (unconsciously) knows the Third World cannot achieve, which becomes a source of obscene glee. It enables the West to "help," assess, judge, discipline, correct, impose conditionalities—all of which procures *jouissance*. It is because the racialized Other is backward, the story goes, that we must treat him like a child and are forced to sometimes do unpleasant things (structural adjustment, armed intervention, torture and rape by military personnel, etc.). We secretly count on the Other failing, never being able to live up to the mark; and by the same token, we secretly fear that the Other will succeed by catching up with the West, which would mean the demise of the development "industry," depriving us of a valuable wellspring of enjoyment.[14] (There is at least an element of this in the current atmosphere of sinophobia, propagated by the likes of the European Union and Trump's America.)

A similar obscene dynamics is at play in the sex scandals, such as those mentioned at the start of this chapter, which have seen the sexual abuse of Black women and minors by privileged white male development workers. Here, sadomasochistic enjoyment derives from multiple sources (in conjunction with the sex act itself): from abusing "lesser" humans (i.e., being dominant, asserting patriarchy), from "teaching them a lesson" (as sexual abusers often claim), from the shared "dirty secret" that enables a community bond, and from the superego imperative to flout the law—all of which, as stressed earlier, help both rationalize the abuse and allay the abusers' anxiety about so doing.

While racism may take on more or less malignant forms of enjoyment, there are two basic racist fantasies that elicit racist enjoyment (Žižek 1993, 203). Since the role of fantasy is to explain to us our lack of total enjoyment, in the first type of racist fantasy, the cause of the lack of enjoyment is attributed to someone else, who we believe has stolen it from us (see chapters 1 and 5). This "theft of enjoyment" is evident in such (earlier mentioned) slurs as "refugees are invading our lands / stealing our jobs / burdening our welfare programs," "poor people are polluting our global environment / overpopulating the planet," "corruption is threatening investment climates," and so forth. The narrative here is that, by stealing our *jouissance*, the Other is ruining our way of life, preventing us from really enjoying. Exactly what is stolen remains a mystery, of course, since it is a fantasmatic object (what Lacanians call *objet a*), a *je ne sais quoi* "thing" that we (mistakenly) think we possessed and which once recaptured will restore our unity and happiness (see chapter 7).

The second type of racist fantasy centers on the strangeness of Others, more precisely their access to an unfamiliar, if not intemperate, enjoyment, something which bothers us: their sexual potency or promiscuity, loud parties, odd manners, wily business acumen, exotic food, smelly body odor, unhygienic habits, ardent work ethic, laziness, vulgarity, dishonesty, and so on. The story here is that the Other has a peculiar manner of organizing their enjoyment, which "really gets on our nerves" (Žižek 1991, 165). What we can't stand is not just that the way they enjoy is alien to us, but also that it is exces-sive, meaning that they are enjoying more or better than us. Racism in this case is the product of both an incompatibility of modes of *jouissance* and a large dose of envy (of their *plus-de-jouir*) (Fanon 1967, 170; Miller 1994, 79–80; see also chapter 5). And so it is because Others are enjoying eccentrically and immoderately that they need to be disciplined, punished, perhaps even exter-minated (think of the Holocaust, the genocides in Armenia and Rwanda, eth-nic cleansing in Bosnia, etc.).

Ultimately, as Žižek points out, the reason the Other's enjoyment is intol-erable is because I can't relate to my own: it is excessive, intrusive, mysteri-ous, unmanageable, and so, "to resolve this deadlock . . . the subject projects its *jouissance* onto an Other, attributing to this Other full access to a consis-tent *jouissance*" (Žižek 2015). This only underlines once again that the West's racist fantasy of the Third World is meant to cloak the social antagonisms of the West itself, with racist enjoyment following suit through processes of pro-jection, displacement, envy, and so forth.

One can thus better comprehend the libidinal underpinnings of racism in development. It is because such racism is obscenely enjoyable—to the point of sadomasochistic excess—that people indulge in it, despite knowing better. While we may not publicly admit to it, there is an (unconscious) attraction to the perverse pleasures of feeling superior, dominating/exoticizing/disciplining the Other or watching them fail. It is such *jouissance* that explains why racism persists and remains pervasive in development (even racialized Others engage in it, as stressed earlier), and this in spite of decolonization and decades of anti-racist education (more on the latter below). The pull of racist enjoyment lies precisely in its excess, its fantasmatic promise of fullness and deliverance.

This libidinal pull also helps explain why racist ideologies/fantasies can be contradictory. Notice indeed the incongruities of several of the racist stereo-types enumerated above: Others are lazy yet too hard-working, strange yet entirely knowable/visible, job stealers yet welfare abusers . . . Clearly, what matters in this case is not logic or reason but libidinal enjoyment; absent the enjoyment, the incongruities would stand out, causing the racist fantasy to lose its grip. (No wonder that populist regimes such as those of Trump, Erdoğan, Duterte, or Modi can dispense with history or "facts" by character-izing them as "fake news." What works politically for them is not rationality but the lure of their nationalist-populist ideologies, no matter if these are in-consistent or senseless; see Kapoor 2018).[15]

It is worth noting as well the particularity of the subject's fantasy-enjoyment. This is what makes everyone—the Western(ized) subject in this case—unique. Every subject has some "thing" they prize (i.e., growth, wealth, security, etc.)

and are menaced by (i.e., stagnation, poverty, disorder, etc.). Fantasies are therefore extremely sensitive to the intrusion of others, but even though one is protective of one's own fantasy-enjoyment, the latter always becomes imbricated with an Other's. This means that one can never enjoy on one's own; one always ends up fantasizing about the Other's enjoyment, and so envying or loathing it (Bhabha 1994, 112). This identification of the Other's intrusive or excessive enjoyment, in fact, is what helps hold groups together. Indeed what tethers development workers, as we have seen, is not necessarily or just a substantive bond based on cultural identity or shared occupational interests, but a libidinal bond (disavowed enjoyment) centered on a racialized Third Word Other.

A final note about changing fantasies and modes of enjoyment. While the overall unequal West–Third World power relationship that forms the basis of international development is a constant (without such inequality, development would cease to exist), this does not necessarily mean that the fantasies that structure this relationship remain the same. To wit, as the global political economy has restructured over time, so has our symbolic and imaginary order (and hence our Western fantasy worlds).

To illustrate, let's start with Edward Said's important point in *Orientalism* (1979) about how the Arab world has, since the nineteenth century at least, been portrayed as a space of eroticism: "the Orient was a place where one could look for sexual experience unobtainable in Europe," he writes (1979, 190). Here the Arab man is portrayed as hypersexualized, a frequenter of harems and a seducer of (Western) women.

But Todd McGowan (2009) claims that, of late, this Western fantasy has largely disappeared, morphing into its opposite. Whereas the Arab man used to be represented as sexually powerful, he is now made out to be "a naïf when it comes to the question of sexual enjoyment" (McGowan 2009, 3). This shift, according to McGowan, is due not simply to the rise of the "War on Terror" and the consequent equation of Muslims with terrorists but to a significant change in the Western subject's relationship to enjoyment. Whereas early to mid-twentieth-century capitalism used to restrain enjoyment (in favor of working hard, saving, investing prudently), post-Fordist capitalism encourages enjoyment to ensure that people consume irrepressibly, thus securing capitalist growth and accumulation (see chapters 1 and 5). But this shift from prohibition to a superegoic imperative to enjoy makes enjoyment all the more difficult and unsatisfying: the more we are commanded to enjoy, the less we are able to. The easy availability of sex (porn, "rent" girls/boys, etc.) makes sex less arousing. But the "fantasy of the naïve Arab has come to the rescue. . . . By fantasizing the [fundamentalist] Arab as a sexual naïf, [the Western subject finds] a way to re-eroticize [Western sexual] images that have become commonplace and [hence] recreate the possibility of a scandal" (McGowan 2009, 4). McGowan makes his case by drawing on several examples of popular culture (cartoons, Hollywood blockbusters, etc.), his point being that the construction of sexual innocence renders the Arab fundamentalist "capable of enjoying where the Western subject no longer can. . . . The Arab of Western fantasies [today] must be naïve enough to find the banality of Western inducements arousing" (McGowan 2009, 10–11).

What is significant for us is that the Western relationship to the Third World Other remains Orientalist / racist, but the ideological fantasy has changed: the desexualization of Arab men coincides with late capitalism's imperative to enjoy. One can perhaps see parallels here with, among other things, the rise of celebrity humanitarianism: the spectacularization and excess of gift giving by celebrities and corporate philanthropists in our mediatic age can be viewed as a way of reeroticizing aid (i.e., obeying the late capitalist command to enjoy). Accordingly, "humanitainment" helps revision and reinvigorate charity work by rendering it more "arousing," but it continues to center the West as best, with the Third World still being infantilized and serving as backdrop for the benefit and enjoyment of "white saviors" (see Kapoor 2013).

# Conclusion: The Pitfalls and Opportunities of Anti-Racism

The discourse of development therefore functions with the help of an ideological apparatus that relies on both white supremacy-as-master-signifier and fantasies of mastery. Both are mutually reinforcing, aimed at naturalizing Western supremacy, while covering up the instability and disharmony of the West. Both result, through such unconscious processes as displacement, projection, and superegoic commands, in the domination of the Third World, providing the Western(ized) subject with significant symbolic and material privileges. While both depend for their effectivity on disavowal and naturalization, operating in the shadowy realm of institutional secrets, they show up nonetheless in the form of private utterances, informal practices, and involuntary outbursts. Significantly, what makes the racism at their core so alluring and pervasive is enjoyment—the perverse pleasures of dominating, inferiorizing, and disciplining the Other. It is such enjoyment that allows international development to be "humanitarian" and bigoted at the same time, blind to its own shortcomings and inconsistencies.

But then how is the structural racism of development to be tackled? What approaches are there to attend to it? Let me briefly identify four, only the last of which addresses the specifically psychoanalytic dynamics that I have claimed lie at the basis of such racism. The first three are mainstream approaches, which I suggest are inadequate, if not counterproductive.

## Tolerance

The dominant approach to challenging racial discrimination is the liberal multicultural one, which relies on the notion of tolerance. Here, people's cultural identities and practices are to be respected, which in development translates into such activities as diversity training, multicultural curriculum development, promotion of minority/cultural rights, local participation in service delivery, and so forth (see Marc 2009; UNDP 2004).

But multicultural tolerance often amounts to a patronizing disrespect for the Other, something implied in the very notion of "tolerating" the Other: one deigns to respect the Other, but only at a distance and to a point. Racialized others/minorities are welcome to preserve their customs and traditions, as long as they keep to themselves. This results not in genuine sociocultural interaction and exchange, but in ghettoization and social apartheid, where cultural identities are fixed and questions of "race" and racial inequality are left unproblematized.

There are also definite limits to such tolerance. As Žižek avers, multiculturalism "tolerates the Other [only] insofar as it is not the *real* Other, but the aseptic Other of premodern ecological wisdom, fascinating rites, and so on—the moment one is dealing with the *real* Other [e.g., cooking smells, business acumen, work ethic, etc.] . . . with the way the Other regulates the specificity of its *jouissance*, tolerance stops" and full-out bigotry begins (1999, 219).

Liberal tolerance is therefore a myth, in effect spelling the continued subordination and disciplining of the Other at the hands of the white Westerner: "the practice of tolerance means that other cultures are scrutinized, labeled and assessed by dominant norms and values" (Essed 1991, 211). Thus, "their" education curriculum can be diversified, as long as "our" Western notions of education remain preeminent. Local participation can happen, as long as we continue to be in control (see chapter 7). We can "respect" other cultures and recognize their rights, but ultimately they need to be kept at a distance because we can't bear their idiosyncratic enjoyment (i.e., precisely what makes them different).

## Color Blindness

Another common approach is that of color blindness, also typical of liberal multicultural societies and Western donor agencies (especially from the United

States). The notion here is not to valorize racial identity but disregard it so as to implement social programs that are blind to "race" (e.g., color-blind censuses/surveys, employment policies, antidrug enforcement, education curriculum development, etc.) (Loury 2004, 29ff.; Loveman 2014, 290). The implied fantasy is that we live in "postracial" global societies, that we have moved beyond racial identification (Zevnik 2017).

The problem is that this assumes a "level playing field," conveniently ignoring (or wishing away) the historical and structural discrimination that disadvantages racialized people. It also once again assumes whiteness as neutral, naturalizing white privilege and domination. Kelly Oliver calls such an approach a "hysterical symptom," through which "race has become subject to fetishism . . . what we don't dare mention for fear of being rude, racist, or sued" (2001, 164). Color blindness is thus racist by default; it disavows racial inequalities so it can continue to enjoy the advantages of whiteness: "[It] denies racial difference in order to protect whites from a type of symbolic castration that would undermine their power and normalcy" (167; see also Mbembe 2017, 173).[16] What color blindness is really blind to, in other words, is racial injustice and white privilege.

## Anti-Racist Education

A third approach is antiracist education. The idea here is to curb prejudice through consciousness raising and rational argumentation. Better communication and cross-cultural awareness, it is believed, can help decrease hostility and misunderstanding. Thus, for example, although they admit that antiracism requires broader structural change, Crewe and Fernando suggest the need for "candid debate" to confront the taboo of addressing racism in development (2006, 52).

But the difficulty with such an approach is that it assumes that racism is the product of ignorance or "false consciousness," neglecting its significant "irrational" libidinal moorings. A psychoanalytic take on racism underlines, as we have seen, how knowledge/understanding can be overwhelmed by the excesses of desire: despite knowing better, the subject often gets attached to her perverse fantasy-enjoyment of prejudice and domination. Addressing bigotry rationally is inadequate, since it misses the intensity and endurance of disavowed desire.

There is also the added issue that talk and debate—upon which the goal of better or undistorted communication depends—can themselves be the objects of enjoyment (see chapter 7): the thrill of chatting, discussing, participating, winning/losing a debate, can become an end in itself, as a result of which the objective of anti-racist education gets lost. As Jodi Dean puts it, "The problem is not consensus [or debate]—it is the endless discursive loop, the way that discussion itself is the source of satisfaction instead of the norms it is supposed to justify" (2006, 91).

## Tackling Fantasy and Enjoyment

Finally, there is the psychoanalytic approach to antiracism. If bigotry is rooted in the libidinal, as I have claimed, then addressing it means having to come to terms with its unconscious dynamics, notably fantasy and enjoyment. But there are no quick, easy, or ready solutions here, especially since the psychoanalytic terrain involves painstaking and sometimes slow cultural and political transformation, with more guarantees of failure than success. This likely means that palpable change, if it is to happen, would need to take place in a much broader ambit than "international development": it would mean changing socioeconomic and cultural power structures on a global scale—a daunting task.

As it most often does, the most meaningful change is likely to happen from the bottom, and would need to take place in both the global South and North to help alter the global Symbolic. I have in mind here such (radical?) subaltern and indigenous movements as the Confederation of Indigenous Nationalities of Ecuador (CONAIE), Comité Cívico de Organizaciones Populares e Indíginas in Honduras, Black Lives Matter (BLM), the Palestinian International Solidarity Movement, Idle No More, Standing Rock (North Dakota), Dalit and *adivasi* protest groups across India, and so forth. The radicality of many such movements lies in their refusal to accept the master/Law, helping to break the chain of subjugation. This is what enables the racialized Other to start to "traverse the (dominant supremacist) fantasy" that "structures [the Other's] jouissance in a way that keeps [it] attached to the master, that makes [it] accept the framework of the social relationship of domination" (Žižek 1998, 156).

Žižek frequently points to the strategy of "overidentification" as a way of intervening in the superego supplement to the Law: bringing to light—publicly staging—the obscene racist underside of power (Žižek 1995, 936–938; 1998, 171–172). This could mean, for example, taking the ruling ideology at its word by naïvely demanding that the master fulfill his promises (e.g., employment equality, antiracist "training" of staff) or imitating the master to the point of absurdity (e.g., performing in gory detail scenes of racist brutality or sadomasochistic/sexual abuse). In different ways, this is what groups like BLM, Wikileaks, Idle No More, Pussy Riot, and Yes Men have been doing: laying bare the excesses and deviations of power, its hidden and unwritten (racist) codes and practices. The idea is neither to glorify nor necessarily directly criticize the Law but to expose its shadowy underbelly by publicly imitating it, identifying and overconforming with it, or pushing it to live up to its half-hearted and ill-conceived public commitments. Such disidentification has the effect of undermining the hold of the racist fantasy and enjoyment, thereby suspending the efficiency and authority of the Law, unmasking and unmooring its nonsensical libidinal support.

A good part of the struggle is to try and reconfigure the Symbolic (and hence racist master-signifiers and fantasies). In a way this is what civil rights and anti-racist groups like BLM or CONAIE have been fighting for—to confront white supremacy and racist categories, as well as their accompanying practices of citizenship, employment, law and order, land tenure, and so forth (Zevnik 2017, 631–632). It *is* a kind of antiracist public education, although the point is not simply to increase awareness but to undercut and rework dominant fantasies. Part of the challenge is to reconstruct such ideas as equality and liberty by reading them against the grain: "appropriating key elements of the 'white' egalitarian emancipatory tradition, [thereby redefining] *that very tradition*, transforming it not so much in terms of what it says as what it *does not say*—that is, obliterating the implicit qualifications which have *de facto* excluded Blacks from the egalitarian space . . . [while also depriving] whites of the monopoly on defining *their own* tradition " (Žižek 2009, 120, emphasis in original; see also Fanon 1963, 237; Vogt 2013, 153–154).

There are of course many dangers to such a psychoanalytic antiracist politics (including the always present exposure by political movements to such factors as co-optation to the state/market, lack of adequate resources, etc.). Of particular note is the risk that antiracist groups resort back to identity politics: they confront dominant power not by agonistically reconfiguring it but by asserting a putatively "authentic" alternative identity. The peril of identitarian counterclaims such as these is that they are an implicit acceptance of racist discourse, merely inverting the dominant racist binary (whiteness/blackness, modernity/tradition) and often creating new supremacist fantasies (e.g., "real" Blacks/Hindus/Malaysians versus inauthentic ones). There is also the danger of the all-too-frequent and powerful backlash from dominant (right-wing and populist) groups, who lament the fall of their dearly held fantasies (and white privilege) and for whom antiracism amounts to catering to "special" interests.

The onus for antiracist change though lies not just with grassroots groups, but also with the state. The state can help support subalterns/minorities in refashioning dominant racist fantasies (the big challenge is whether it can do so without co-opting, dominating, or disciplining these groups). It can help protect these groups' rights and mitigate racist prejudice through laws and protections. Intrinsic to this contest, as Žižek suggests, is for the state to act as a buffer against the fantasies of civil society (Myers 2004, 106–108): to keep them in check, but also to keep them apart to some extent so they don't get in each other's way.

Implied here is the notion that, because the Other is a traumatic intruder, impossible to really understand or accept (at least at the level of fantasy-enjoyment), it is important not to intrude on their fantasy space where possible. This is precisely the mistake of multiculturalism, as we have seen, since it pretends to encounter the Other, but does so only superficially (e.g., at the level of exotic culture and food), in the end denigrating the traumatic Real of the Other, depriving it of its difference. The "attitude of 'understanding each-other' has to be supplemented by the attitude of 'getting-out-of-each-other's-way', by maintaining an appropriate distance, by implementing a new 'code of discretion'. . . . Perhaps the lesson to be learned is that sometimes a dose of alienation is indispensable for peaceful coexistence" (Žižek 2008, 59). For, ultimately, the problem of intersubjectivity is how to accept the Other in the "ugly" enjoyment of their existence—with their annoying idiosyncrasies, smells, tics, vanities. Or to put it the other way around, as Lacan does, "Leaving this Other to [their] own mode of *jouissance*, that would only be possible by not imposing our own on [them], by not thinking of [them] as underdeveloped" (1990, 32; see also Žižek 1998, 167–168).

## Notes

1. Given their premise that there is general silence on racism in the field of global development, these analysts tend (ironically) to be silent on their own position: what enables them (or for that matter anyone) to speak out against racism if it is taboo? Psychoanalysis can help here, since it consists of detecting the symptoms of racism (e.g., private racist remarks, outburst/scandals, etc.) and trying to decipher their underlying causes (i.e., traumas, desires, enjoyments, fantasies). This is precisely my approach in this chapter, and it differs markedly from those who assume that anti-racism can be conducted only through rational critique. As I will claim later in this chapter, the problem with racism is that it is anchored in nonrational processes (i.e., unconscious desire), which rational critique can neither adequately explain nor address.

2. In this sense, I readily agree with Uma Kothari's statement that "the use of private conversations, anecdotes and personal experience . . . reflects the public silence about 'race'" (2006b, 5), but I interpret such silence psychoanalytically.

3. These quotes are from expatriate development workers, as reported by Crewe and Harrison (1998, 132ff.), Goudge (2003, 166), Petersen and Lentfer (2017), and Crewe and Fernando (2006, 45). The quote about corruption is based on my own experience in the field, one that is all too common.

4. As chapter 9 stresses, unlike Freud, who sees the superego as a kind of conscience, advocating restraint and prohibition, for Lacan (1966, 773), the superego commands the subject to enjoy, advocating transgression (i.e., the opposite of restraint).

5. In Lacanianese, there is overlap between language, law, and discourse/power. This is because the symbolic order is made up of not just linguistic communication but also ideological/discursive conventions and the Law (referred to as the "big Other"). Being a subject of language means being subjected to its dictates or laws, implying an acceptance of its rules and restrictions, which orient the subject's desires.

6. The Abu Ghraib and the Catholic Church sex scandals might not fall entirely within the ambit of "development," but they certainly each have development-related dimensions: the former because it took place in the context of a military invasion that involved "bringing [Western] freedom and democracy" to Iraq, and the latter because one of the Church's key justifications for its continuing presence in the global South has been its mission to "help the poor."

7. As White puts it (2002, 408), "silence on race is a determining silence that both masks and marks its centrality to the development project." But of course, once again, I am interpreting this statement psychoanalytically.

8. Note that "Afro-pessimists" (Sexton 2008; Wilderson 2010; Wilderson et al. 2017) claim that it is not white supremacy that is the problem but anti-Blackness: modernity is founded on slavery, resulting in the fundamental and intractable exclusion of Blacks, so that the main social antagonism is not between white and nonwhite but Black and non-Black. The problem with their claim, however, is that it tends towards a certain authenticity and purity of position, making it virtually impossible for cross-racial or anti-racist politics and coalition-building. See Zahi Zalloua's insightful analysis and critique (2020, chap. 5).

9. It is because "race" is a lie (but made true ideologically) that I tend to use scare quotes. Note that I disagree with Anthony Appiah (1986), who claims that, because "race" is a sociohistorical construction, it is merely an illusion. He misses that it is an ideological fetish (i.e., it is infused with enjoyment), and hence is not only a powerful means of social control but able to endure despite our knowledge that it is a "lie" or a construction.

10. Of course, this yearning to become white remains an impossible one. As Homi Bhabha argues, the colonial civilizing mission contains the ambivalence of creating "mimic men"—colonial subjects who are to be civilized in the image of the colonizer, yet who can never live up to the mark (see chapter 7): *almost the same, but not quite* as he puts it (Bhabha 1994, 86). Or, to twist it for our purposes, "almost the same, but not white"! Or "almost white, but not quite"!

11. It is significant that White is able to access these privileges despite her gender. She says as much when she declares that she was often treated as an "honorary man" in Bangladesh (White 2006, 64), implying that race trumps gender, at least in this case.

12. Sarah White suggests an instructive thought experiment in this regard: "Imagine for a moment that a twenty-two-year-old Bangladeshi who speaks a smattering of English could stay eighteen months in Britain and then return to write a PhD in Bengali on people in Britain. Which is subsequently used as a teaching resource on British society in British universities. The idea is laughable. And yet that is exactly what I did in reverse. The whole situation is structured in and through racial advantage" (2002, 409).

13. Let me try and clarify the ambiguity created by my use of "fantasies" (plural) in the overall title of this chapter and "fantasy" (singular) in this subsection title. There

are, of course, multiple development fantasies—social, ecological, technological, etc. But I would argue that, to the extent that they are *development* fantasies, what they share is a vision centered on key binaries (development/underdevelopment, modernity/tradition, wealth/poverty, white/nonwhite, etc.), hence my reference to a *predominant* development fantasy. Moreover, my claim is that whiteness, a master signifier supported by its own supremacist fantasy, and the dominant development fantasy are mutually reinforcing. So here again, there are two fantasies, but what they share is a notion of Western superiority and an aspiration toward domination/mastery.

14. This is what I have referred to as "institutional enjoyment" in chapters 2, 7, and 12.

15. For example, Pankaj Mishra (2019) sees Modi's 2019 election victory as premised on *ressentiment* and vengeance, successfully scapegoating Muslims, leftists, secular liberals, and English-speaking elites, thereby deftly diverting public scrutiny away from his socioeconomic record.

16. Achille Mbembe is similarly critical of postracialism, advocating instead for a "post-Césairian era [in which] we embrace and retain the signifier 'Black' not with the goal of finding solace within it but rather as a way of clouding the term in order to gain distance from it" (2017, 173).

# References

Alcoff, Linda. 2006. *Visible Identities: Race, Gender, and the Self.* New York: Oxford University Press.

Appiah, Anthony. 1986. "The Uncompleted Argument: Du Bois and the Illusions of Race." In *"Race," Writing, and Difference*, edited by Henry Louis Gates, 21–37. Chicago: University of Chicago Press.

Beaumont, Peter, and Rebecca Ratcliffe. 2018. "#MeToo Strikes Aid Sector as Sexual Exploitation Allegations Proliferate." *The Guardian*, February 12. http://www.theguardian.com/global-development/2018/feb/12/metoo-strikes-aid-sector-as-sexual-exploitation-allegations-proliferate.

Bhabha, Homi K. 1994. *The Location of Culture.* London: Routledge.

Bonilla-Silva, Eduardo. 1997. "Rethinking Racism: Toward a Structural Interpretation." *American Sociological Review* 62 (3): 465–480.

Bruce-Raeburn, Angela. 2018. "Opinion: Why We Can't Separate Sexism from Racism in the Humanitarian and Development Sector." Devex, March 6. https://www.devex.com/news/sponsored/opinion-why-we-can-t-separate-sexism-from-racism-in-the-humanitarian-and-development-sector-92271.

Chiles, Nick. 2012. "Report Details Shocking Racism at the World Bank." *Atlanta Black Star*, December 3. http://atlantablackstar.com/2012/12/03/report-details-shocking-racism-at-the-world-bank/.

Crewe, Emma, and Priyanthi Fernando. 2006. "The Elephant in the Room: Racism in Representations, Relationships and Rituals." *Progress in Development Studies* 6 (1): 40–54.

Crewe, Emma, and Elizabeth Harrison. 1998. *Whose Development? An Ethnography of Aid.* London: Zed.

Damir-Geilsdorf, Sabine, Ulrike Lindner, Gesine Müller, Oliver Tappe, and Michael Zeuske, eds. 2016. *Bonded Labour: Global and Comparative Perspectives (18th–21st Century)*. Bielfeld: Transcript-Verlag.

Dean, Jodi. 2006. "Secrets and Drive." In *Sex, Breath, and Force: Sexual Difference in a Post-Feminist Era*, edited by Ellen Mortensen, 81–96. Oxford: Lexington.

Doty, Roxanne Lynn. 1996. *Imperial Encounters: The Politics of Representation in North-South Relations*. Minneapolis: University of Minnesota Press.

Duffield, Mark. 2001. "Governing the Borderlands: Decoding the Power of Aid." *Disasters* 25 (4): 308–320.

——. 2006. "Racism, Migration and Development: The Foundations of Planetary Order." *Progress in Development Studies* 6 (1): 68–79.

——. 2007. *Development, Security and Unending War: Governing the World of Peoples*. Cambridge: Polity.

Essed, Philomena. 1991. *Understanding Everyday Racism: An Interdisciplinary Theory*. Sage Series on Race and Ethnic Relations, vol. 2. Newbury Park, CA: Sage.

Fanon, Frantz. 1963. *The Wretched of the Earth*. Translated by Richard Philcox. New York: Grove.

——. 1967. *Black Skin, White Masks*. Translated by Charles Markmann. New York: Grove.

Fletcher, Robert, Jan Breitling, and Valerie Puleo. 2014. "Barbarian Hordes: The Overpopulation Scapegoat in International Development Discourse." *Third World Quarterly* 35 (7): 1195–1215.

Frye, Marylin. 2001. "White Woman Feminist 1983–1992." In *Race and Racism*, edited by Bernard R. Boxill, 83–100. Oxford: Oxford University Press.

Gillan, Audrey, and Peter Moszynski. 2002. "Aid Workers in Food for Child Sex Scandal." *The Guardian*, February 27. http://www.theguardian.com/society/2002/feb/27/voluntarysector.

Goudge, Paulette. 2003. *The Power of Whiteness: Racism in Third World Development and Aid*. London: Lawrence and Wishart.

*The Guardian*. 2015. "Secret Aid Worker: There Is Still Racism within Humanitarian Work," August 18. http://www.theguardian.com/global-development-professionals-network/2015/aug/18/secret-aid-worker-racism-humanitarian-work.

Herbert, Bob. 2001. "In America; Refusing To Save Africans." *New York Times*, June 11. https://www.nytimes.com/2001/06/11/opinion/in-america-refusing-to-save-africans.html.

Hook, Derek. 2017. "What Is 'Enjoyment as a Political Factor'?" *Political Psychology* 38 (4): 605–620.

hooks, bell. 1997. "Representing Whiteness in the Black Imagination." In *Displacing Whiteness*, edited by Ruth Frankenberg, 165–179. Durham, NC: Duke University Press.

Kapoor, Ilan. 2013. *Celebrity Humanitarianism: The Ideology of Global Charity*. London: Routledge.

——. 2018. "Epilogue: Affect and the Global Rise of Populism." In *Psychoanalysis and the GlObal*, edited by Ilan Kapoor, 283–291. Lincoln: University of Nebraska Press.

Kolbert, Elizabeth. 2018. "There's No Scientific Basis for Race—It's a Made-Up Label." *National Geographic*, March 12. https://www.nationalgeographic.com/magazine/2018/04/race-genetics-science-africa/.

Kothari, Uma. 2006a. "An Agenda for Thinking about 'Race' in Development." *Progress in Development Studies* 6 (1): 9–23.

——. 2006b. "Critiquing 'Race' and Racism in Development Discourse and Practice." *Progress in Development Studies* 6 (1): 1–7.

Lacan, Jacques. 1966. *Écrits*. Paris: Seuil.

——. 1990. *Television*. Edited by Joan Copjec. New York: Norton.

——. 1997. *The Ethics of Psychoanalysis: The Seminar of Jacques Lacan, Book VII*. Edited by Jacques-Alain Miller. New York: Norton.

Loury, Glenn C. 2004. "The Superficial Morality of Colour-Blindness in the United States." Identities, Conflict and Cohesion Programme Paper No. 5. Geneva: United Nations Research Institute for Social Development (UNRISD).

Loveman, Mara. 2014. *National Colors: Racial Classification and the State in Latin America*. Oxford: Oxford University Press.

MacCannell, Juliet Flower. 1996. "The Postcolonial Unconscious, or The White Man's Thing." *Journal for the Psychoanalysis of Culture and Society* 1 (1): 27–42.

Manzo, Kate. 2008. "Imaging Humanitarianism: NGO Identity and the Iconography of Childhood." *Antipode* 40 (4): 632–657.

Marc, Alexandre. 2009. *Delivering Services in Multicultural Societies*. Washington, DC: World Bank Publications.

Mbembe, Achille. 2017. *Critique of Black Reason*. Translated by Laurent Dubois. Durham, NC: Duke University Press.

McClintock, Anne. 2013. *Imperial Leather: Race, Gender, and Sexuality in the Colonial Contest*. New York: Routledge.

McGowan, Todd. 2009. "Fantasies of the Unsexualized Other, or, the Naiveté of the Arab Mind." *Culture Critique* 1 (2): 1–12.

Miller, Jacques-Alain. 1994. "Extimité." In *Lacanian Theory of Discourse: Subject, Structure, and Society*, edited by Mark Bracher, Marshall W. Alcorn Jr., Ronald J. Corthell, and Françoise Massardier-Kenney, 74–87. New York: New York University Press.

Mishra, Pankaj. 2019. "How Narendra Modi Seduced India with Envy and Hate." *New York Times*, May 28. https://www.nytimes.com/2019/05/23/opinion/modi-india-election.html.

Myers, Tony. 2004. *Slavoj Žižek*. New York: Routledge.

Narayan, Uma. 1997. *Dislocating Cultures: Identities, Traditions, and Third-World Feminism*. New York: Routledge.

Nast, Heidi J. 2000. "Mapping the 'Unconscious': Racism and the Oedipal Family." *Annals of the Association of American Geographers* 90 (2): 215–255.

Oliver, Kelly. 2001. *Witnessing: Beyond Recognition*. Minneapolis: University Of Minnesota Press.

Page, Melvin Eugene, and Penny M. Sonnenburg, eds. 2003. *Colonialism: An International, Social, Cultural, and Political Encyclopedia*. Santa Barbara, CA: ABC-CLIO.

Parry, Benita. 1972. *Delusions and Discoveries: Studies on India in the British Imagination, 1880–1930*. London: Allen Lane.

Persaud, Randolph B., and R. B. J. Walker. 2001. "*Apertura*: Race in International Relations." *Alternatives: Global, Local, Political* 26 (4): 373–376.

Petersen, Rashida, and Jennifer Lentfer. 2017. "'Grassroots Means No Brains": How to Tackle Racism in the Aid Sector.'" *The Guardian*, August 4. http://www .theguardian.com/global-development-professionals-network/2017/aug/04 /grassroots-means-no-brains-how-to-tackle-racism-in-the-aid-sector.

Pieterse, Jan Nederveen. 1992. *White on Black: Images of Africa and Blacks in Western Popular Culture*. New Haven, CT: Yale University Press.

Ratcliffe, Rebecca. 2018. "Oxfam's Disgraced Haiti Official Left Earlier Post over 'Sex Parties.'" *The Guardian*, February 13. http://www.theguardian.com/global -development/2018/feb/13/oxfam-disgraced-haiti-official-liberia-post-roland -van-hauwermeiren.

Razack, Sherene. 2005. "How Is White Supremacy Embodied? Sexualized Racial Violence at Abu Ghraib." *Canadian Journal of Women and the Law* 17 (2): 341–63.

Ross, Robert, ed. 1982. *Racism and Colonialism: Essays on Ideology and Social Structure*. Comparative Studies in Overseas History, vol. 4. The Hague: Martinus Nijhoff.

Said, Edward W. 1979. *Orientalism*. New York: Vintage.

Sedinger, Tracey. 2002. "Nation and Identification: Psychoanalysis, Race, and Sexual Difference." *Cultural Critique* 50 (1): 40–73.

Seshadri-Crooks, Kalpana. 1998. "The Comedy of Domination: Psychoanalysis and the Conceit of Whiteness." In *The Psychoanalysis of Race*, edited by Christopher Lane, 353–379. New York: Columbia University Press.

——. 2000. *Desiring Whiteness: A Lacanian Analysis of Race*. London: Routledge.

Sexton, Jared. 2008. *Amalgamation Schemes: Antiblackness and the Critique of Multiracialism*. Minneapolis: University Of Minnesota Press.

Stavrakakis, Yannis. 2002. *Lacan and the Political*. London: Routledge.

United Nations Development Programme (UNDP). 2004. *Human Development Report 2004: Cultural Liberty in Today's Diverse World*. New York: United Nations Development Programme.

Vogt, Erik. 2013. "Žižek and Fanon: On Violence and Related Matters." In *Žižek Now: Current Perspectives in Žižek Studies*, edited by Jamil Khader and Molly Anne Rothenberg. Cambridge: Polity.

Waldie, Paul. 2018. "Sexual Misconduct 'Endemic' among International Aid Agencies, U.K. Report Finds." *Globe and Mail*, July 31. https://www .theglobeandmail.com/world/article-sexual-misconduct-endemic-among -international-aid-agencies-uk/.

Watson, Hilbourne. 2001. "Theorizing the Racialization of Global Politics and the Caribbean Experience." *Alternatives: Global, Local, Political* 26 (4): 449–483.

West, Andrew. 2017. "Worst of Catholic Sexual Abuse Scandal Still to Come in Developing World: Report." ABC News, September 13, 2017. http://www .abc.net.au/news/2017-09-13/worst-catholic-sexual-abuse-scandal-developing -world/8900616.

White, Sarah C. 2002. "Thinking Race, Thinking Development." *Third World Quarterly* 23 (3): 407–419.

——. 2006. "The 'Gender Lens': A Racial Blinder?" *Progress in Development Studies* 6 (1): 55–67.

Wilderson, Frank B., III. 2010. *Red, White & Black: Cinema and the Structure of U.S. Antagonisms*. Durham, NC: Duke University Press.

Wilderson, Frank B., III, Saidiya Hartman, Steve Martinot, Jared Sexton, and Hortense J. Spillers. 2017. *Afro-Pessimism: An Introduction*. Minneapolis, MN: Racked & Dispatched. https://rackedanddispatched.noblogs.org/files/2017/01/Afro-pessimism2_imposed.pdf.

Wilson, Kalpana. 2012. *Racism and Development: Interrogating History, Discourse and Practice*. London: Zed.

Zalloua, Zahi. 2020. *Žižek on Race: Toward and Anti-Racist Future*. London: Bloomsbury.

Zevnik, Andreja. 2017. "Postracial Society as Social Fantasy: Black Communities Trapped Between Racism and a Struggle for Political Recognition." *Political Psychology* 38 (4): 621–635.

Žižek, Slavoj. 1989. *The Sublime Object of Ideology*. London: Verso.

——. 1991. *Looking Awry: An Introduction to Jacques Lacan through Popular Culture*. Cambridge, MA: MIT Press.

——. 1993. *Tarrying with the Negative: Kant, Hegel, and the Critique of Ideology*. Durham, NC: Duke University Press.

——. 1995. "Superego by Default." *Cardozo Law Review* 16 (3–4): 925–942.

——. 1996. "Invisible Ideology: Political Violence between Fiction and Fantasy." *Journal of Political Ideologies* 1 (1): 15–32.

——. 1997. *The Plague of Fantasies*. London: Verso.

——. 1998. "Love Thy Neighbor? No, Thanks!" In *The Psychoanalysis of Race*, edited by Christopher Lane, 154–175. New York: Columbia University Press.

——. 1999. *The Ticklish Subject: The Absent Centre of Political Ontology*. London: Verso.

——. 2005. *The Metastases of Enjoyment: Six Essays on Women and Causality*. London: Verso.

——. 2006. "The Antinomies of Tolerant Reason: A Blood-Dimmed Tide Is Loosed." Lacan.com. http://www.lacan.com/zizantinomies.htm.

——. 2008. *Violence: Six Sideways Reflections*. New York: Picador.

——. 2009. *First as Tragedy, Then as Farce*. London: Verso.

——. 2015. "The Need to Traverse the Fantasy." In These Times, December 28. http://inthesetimes.com/article/18722/Slavoj-Zizek-on-Syria-refugees-Eurocentrism-Western-Values-Lacan-Islam.

Žižek, Slavoj, and Glyn Daly. 2004. *Conversations with Žižek*. Cambridge: Polity.

CHAPTER 12

# Development and the Poor

Enjoy Your Symptom!

KEYWORD: *Symptom*

## Introduction

The field of international development is premised on addressing poverty, particularly the needs of the poorest of the poor (the underclass, indigenous communities, subaltern women, racialized minorities, migrants, "untouchables," slum dwellers, etc.). A massive institutional apparatus exists—aid agencies, NGOs, government departments, financial institutions—to cater to these needs. I want to draw on Lacanian psychoanalysis to zero in on the kernel of enjoyment involved in regulating the poor. Here, not only are the poor seen as symptoms of capitalist development—its rejects and disposables—but a significant economy of enjoyment is produced wherein the development industry, as well as the poor themselves, enjoy the(ir) symptom.[1] The poor, in this sense, are what Lacan would call the *sinthome* of development, whose presence is what binds the massive institutional machinery together, serving as its very *raison d'être*, yet whose absence would cause it to fall apart. The poor so conceived are the potentially disruptive limit point (what Žižek terms the "concrete universal") of the global capitalist order.

My Lacanian analysis of poverty contrasts with both a Marxist political economy approach, which tends to interrogate poverty regulation in the context of global capital accumulation, and a Foucauldian one, which tends to accentuate issues of governmentality (i.e., the disciplining and self-regulation of states or the poor). An instance of the former approach is Paul Cammack's (2009), claiming that, in the current milieu of advancing global capitalism, poverty reduction strategies center on spreading capitalist competitiveness: they help create a cheap labor force by consolidating Third World states as agents of accumulation (see also Frank 1967; Harriss-White and Heyer 2010). An instance of the latter is Jonathan Joseph's (2010a),[2] which, while sympathetic to Cammack, criticizes him (correctly, in my view) for inadequately considering how neoliberal discourse takes root globally. Accordingly, Joseph draws on Foucault to argue for a "global governmentality" that institutionally embeds disciplines of capitalist competitiveness. He contends that international organizations such as the World Bank use poverty reduction schemes not necessarily to improve the material conditions of people but to better regulate states (see also Ilcan and Lacey 2011; Tan 2011).

Yet Joseph does not himself go far enough in considering how capitalist governmentality germinates: he submits that neoliberal ideology only takes hold institutionally at the level of the state, leaving aside Commack's important point that it penetrates widely and globally, including within local populations. In what follows, I want to suggest that it is the notion of *jouissance* (enjoyment) which better helps explain how capitalist ideology can psychoanalytically (and materially) embed itself at the level of the state as much as local citizens, and in the development apparatus as much as the ranks of the poor-as-symptom.

## From Symptom to Sinthome

In psychoanalysis, the symptom refers to a veiled message from the unconscious. It manifests psychosomatically as a bodily ailment (e.g., pain, numbness), for which a medical cause cannot be found; or as dreams, bungled actions, slips of the tongue, or verbal and physical tics, to be interpreted and cured by the analyst. Freud (2013) emphasizes that the symptom is not important in itself but should be seen as pointing to a broader disorder that analysis can help decipher.

Initially, Lacan (2007, 223) follows the same logic, characterizing the symptom as a metaphor betraying the subject's neurosis and prescribing therapy aimed at its symbolic dissolution. But later he realizes that his patients' symptoms often persist despite interpretation: therapy may well identify the causes of their symptomatic ills, but this does not mean it is able to make their neuroses disappear (Lacan 2016, 1–19). He therefore concludes that the symptom is a real kernel of enjoyment and hence cannot be interpreted away. In other words, the symptom is simultaneously an indication of an underlying disorder *and* that which subjects cling on to for their very life. It is this latter characteristic that Lacan names the *sinthome*. As Žižek puts it, the sinthome is "a way for the subject to organize his enjoyment" so much so that he ends up "lov[ing] his symptom more than himself" (1989, 74).

By organizing our *jouissance*, the sinthome gives us consistency, constituting our psychosocial existence. Echoing Lacan, Žižek aptly refers to it as a "bearer of *jouis-sense*," underlining how it gives meaning to the subject, defining the particular modality of her enjoyment. He insists, in fact, that the sinthome is not simply what holds us together—our only positive substance as human beings—but is also what we cannot give up: without it we'd fall apart, go mad, or commit suicide (Žižek 1989, 75; see also Evans 2006, 191). This is why we end up choosing something (the symptom-formation) instead of nothing (psychosis).

What is not to be missed here is the sinthome's traumatic dimension. It may well be a nexus of enjoyment, giving the subject meaning, but it is nonetheless pathological. That is, it procures "enjoy-meant," which, for all that, remains an "idiotic enjoyment," feckless and only sought out for its own sake (Žižek 1991, 128; see also Thurston 2002). This is why Lacan sees it as indecipherable, irresolvable, and for that matter ineradicable. Unlike the symptom, which is addressed to the analyst (or the big Other) as a coded message to be unraveled, the sinthome is not addressed to anyone. Instead, it releases itself from the signifying chain, being there—present—but meaning nothing. This is the clear import of Lacan's *Seminar XXIII* (2016, 20–31), where the sinthome is associated, not with the register of the Symbolic like the symptom, but the Real. As stupid or disgusting enjoyment, it is a pathological stain, resisting interpretation and always threatening to erupt, disrupt, or bankrupt. It may well hold the subject together, but it is equally a traumatic formation that can lead the very same subject astray—to uncertainty, perverse excess, or even danger.

## The Poor as Symptom of Development

> "One death is a tragedy, a million deaths a statistic."
>
> Attributed to Stalin (quoted in Gupta 2012, 14)

In *The Sublime Object of Ideology* (1989, 11ff.), Žižek focuses on Lacan's assertion that "Marx invented the symptom" (Lacan 2006, 50), arguing that Marx was the first to see how every socioeconomic system fails at some historical conjuncture—these failures being its symptom. For Žižek, one of Marx's greatest contributions was showing how such malfunctions are integral to the system even as they threaten it: they are the "necessary products of the system itself—the points at which the 'truth', the immanent antagonistic character of the system, erupts" (Žižek 1989, 128). Unsurprisingly, then, Marx identified the proletariat as capitalism's symptom, the site where the rationality of the social order encounters its irrationality.

Just as the proletariat are symptomatic of capitalism, so the poor are symptomatic of capitalist development.[3] The poor are development's internal limit point—those whom the system needs but must ultimately forsake. They are, in this view, the embodiment of the contradictions, failures, and gaps of development. Such a view is consistent with the work of Marxist development theory. Dependency and World-Systems analysis, as I have already underlined (see chapters 1 and 5), have long argued that poverty is the result of the unevenness and inequality intrinsic to global capitalism: the development of the core is made possible only by the underdevelopment of the periphery through a process of surplus extraction (Cardoso and Faletto 1979; Frank 1989; Wallerstein 2004).

This is why, globally, the gap between rich and poor has risen dramatically over time, in spite of a massive expansion of overall global wealth: in 1820, the ratio of per capita incomes of Western countries versus countries in Latin America, Africa, and Asia was in the order of 2:1, whereas now it stands closer to 68:1 (Szirmai 2005, 26). This is also why, today, China, India, and Brazil can figure among the top ten global economies, yet still rank comparatively low in the UNDP Human Development Index (90th, 131st, and 79th, respectively, among 188 countries). All three countries have witnessed rapid economic growth in recent years (averaging over 7 percent annually in China between 2012 and 2016, for example), yet Brazil places among the highest globally in terms of (income) inequality, China among the highest in terms of rural poverty, and India among the highest in terms of infant mortality (Tobin 2011; UNDP 2016, 199–200, 207–208). While rates of poverty in India have certainly improved of late[4]—from 55 percent in 1973–1974 to 29.8 percent in 2009–2010—poverty is still pervasive across the country, especially in rural areas and among farm workers, casual workers, women, indigenous people, Dalits (untouchables), and Muslims (Biswas 2012). The same is true, for instance, of Senegal and Rwanda: although they have stood out as some of the world's fastest-growing economies in the last decade, both countries remain among the most unequal in sub-Saharan Africa, with almost half of their citizens facing shortages of food, clean water, medicine, and health services (Nossiter 2013; Sindayigaya 2015).

What such data confirms is not simply that under a system of (capitalist) development, wealth and capital accumulation stand alongside poverty, but that impoverishment is integral to wealth creation. This explains why poverty has persisted even as market economies have continued to "develop," and why rapid economic growth has resulted not in less but more inequality (as illustrated above). So it is not simply that deprivation (or scarcity) is socially constructed—a truism these days—but that impoverishment is constitutive of global capitalism—it holds the system together. The thesis that "poverty is the symptom of development" registers the fact that development exists only in so far as the poor confer consistency upon it.

Marxist political economists are spot on, then, in emphasizing that the very instance of the poor (as symptom) reveals the truth about the global capitalist system. (What they miss, as I argue below, are the unconscious desires/enjoyment that are part and parcel of this process.) Cammack writes for instance that capitalism "depends on the existence of a multitudinous poor" (2009, 50). The crux for analysts like him, as it was for Marx, is that such poverty is closely linked to iniquitous social relations (relative class positioning, the division between those who control/own the means of production and those who do not) which results in socioeconomic domination and exploitation of labor (and the subaltern more generally—see below). For instance, as highlighted earlier, he points out that since the 1990s, international financial institutions (IFIs) such as the World Bank and IMF have pursued a neoliberal antipoverty strategy that ensures the hegemony of capital over labor: under the pretext of skills training, education, and health programs, they end up making workers available to global capital, proletarianizing the latter by incorporating them into the international division of labor (34). Note here though that it is not just sweatshop and semi-skilled labor (on which Cammack tends to focus) that supports the system, but the reserve army of un- or underemployed workers who, precisely because they are in excess, make possible the continuation of sweatshop conditions and the "efficient" functioning of contemporary global capitalism.

But it is important not to equate "the poor" with just the proletariat, at least not in the classical Marxist sense of working class. Under late global capitalist conditions especially, the marginalization and impoverishment of people happens as a consequence not simply of their socioeconomic status, but *also* of their gendered, sexual, epistemic, ethnoracialized, or environmental positioning. This means that it is not only the capitalist/corporate bourgeoisie that dominates the poor, it is also the state (e.g., by colluding with elites to dispossess people from their land or cultural heritage; see Harvey 2003, 145), patriarchal elites (e.g., by enabling a gendered/sexual division of labor; see Mies

1998), and development agencies and the university sector (e.g., by producing a politics of representation that silences the subaltern; see Kapoor 2004). This means as well that poverty cannot be reduced to economic categories, but rather, under our global *capitalist* regime, needs to be broadened to include the socioeconomic as it intersects with the political, cultural, sexual, environmental, and so forth.

It is not just classical Marxist political economy that is guilty of such narrowing, but also (and perhaps especially) neoclassical economics, which has so dominated the field of development. By reducing poverty to economic measures (read: capitalistic or market-oriented measures), it has tended to ignore poverty that is not market-related (i.e., poverty that is not quantifiable or cannot be monetized). Many analysts have pointed out, for example, the disproportionate number of women, minorities, migrants, and indigenous groups living in poverty—what is often referred to as the feminization, securitization, and racialization of poverty (see for example Hall and Patrinos 2014; Kaur 2008; Saha and Lima 2003). As a result, not only are several subcategories of the poor missed or underrepresented in poverty statistics, but antipoverty interventions by the state or international development agencies can often exclude large groups of the poor.

But the problem with a broad list of the poor is that it is *ever*-broadening (over time and space) and thereby never complete. Here for example is a general list of the types of groups that make up "the poor" today (it contains intersectional and overlapping categories): casualized and part-time labor, farmworkers, indentured labor, sweatshop workers, the poor working class, ethnoracialized minorities, migrants and the *sans papiers*, slum dwellers (of the *favelas* and inner cities), indigenous groups, informal-sector workers, subaltern women and queers, the homeless, the disabled, Dalits (see for example Davies and Ryner 2006; Harriss-White 2006). Yet, no definitive categorization or enumeration of the poor is possible since, under today's dynamic global capitalist system, there is always some new excluded group that will occupy the position of the poor.[5] This is why, in my estimation, it makes sense to equate the poor with Rancière's more evocative notion of the "part that has no part" (1999, 11; see also Koster and de Vries 2012, 86), which refers to those who have no properly defined place in society. The notion is a reminder not to lose the forest for the trees, not to get bogged down in lists and categories but rather to understand the poor as *part* of a capitalist system with *no part* in it. Following Rancière, Žižek appropriately coins the terms "the Excluded" (2009, 98),[6] emphasizing those who are marginalized or do not fit. The poor/Excluded/part-that-has-no-part are thus not simply to be posited as a long list; they are more importantly to be seen as symptomatic of—that is, inherent to—the system's internal failures, gaps, elisions.

Losing the forest for the trees though is exactly what mainstream development does, and wants us to do, when it comes to poverty, and I would like to suggest that this is a typically ideological move. Ideology, as we saw in earlier chapters, is indeed an attempt to cover over the symptom (i.e., antagonism, gap, failure): "the self-consistency of a symbolic construction of reality depends on the harmony instituted by fantasy . . . [which] can only be sustained by the neutralisation of the symptom" (Stavrakakis 2002, 65; see also Žižek 1989, 33). Accordingly, the discourse of development, while centered on addressing poverty, operates by denying *poverty-as-symptom*. It presents (capitalist) growth as a positive and smooth entity, in which all blemishes can be removed. This is evident, for instance, in such dominant global institutions as the World Bank, whose well-known slogans are "Working for a World Free of Poverty" and "Our Dream Is a World Free of Poverty" (see Cammack 2009, 37). It is also evident in Modernization theory and neoclassical economics, which tend to sanitize the history of development/ poverty by omitting analysis of Western imperialism (see chapter 1, and Kapoor 2014, 1126–1127). Such sanitization enables modernity and progress to be constructed as pure and slick. Even the more liberal economists such as Amartya Sen, Joseph Stiglitz, and Jeffrey Sachs, while primarily concerned about the problem of poverty, take for granted a capitalist political economy as the solution. As Blaney and Inayatullah point out, "what such narrow readings [by the likes of Sachs and Sen] ignore is that . . . *poverty might be intrinsic to wealth creation* . . . additional wealth creation, rather than solving poverty, only exacerbates the pathology of the wealth/poverty nexus" (2010, 2, italics in original). The result of such ideological contrivance is that not only is global capitalism naturalized, but so is poverty. We take for granted wealth creation alongside inequality, high poverty rates in "Third World" countries, and the immiseration of indigenous communities or, say, Afro-Brazilians. Thus, Akhil Gupta asks: "Could it be that . . . programs to care for the poor are in place in order to inoculate us from the political possibility that their death should constitute a scandal?" (2012, 38).

It must be underlined that fantasy does not eliminate the symptom (which inevitably shows up sometime, somewhere) but can only help tame or subdue it.[7] So let me point out some of the ideological tactics involved in gentrifying poverty-as-symptom. One is to isolate the symptom, to disconnect it from the underlying disorder. As implied above, this is the procedure that mainstream development is premised upon—treating poverty as a separate issue by delinking it from the global capitalist system. Consequently, pauperization is detached from inequality, underdevelopment from development, the informal sector from the formal sector, "tradition" from modernity, dispossession and "primitive accumulation" from neoliberal governance, and so on—all obscuring that the former condition in each binary opposition is not only tied to but produced by the latter. Isolating the symptom thus allows development "experts" and policy makers to situate themselves above or outside the problem in order to study and address it in "neutral" and "objective" ways. It also allows celebrities and political and corporate elites to act as moral and compassionate agents, doing charity work one day, while engaging in poverty-creating activities the next (e.g., financial speculation, investments).[8] These fantasmatic ploys permit poverty to be constructed not as a systemic failure, but as an insular and curable defect.

A related ideological strategy is to externalize the symptom, displacing it onto uncontrollable outside factors. For instance, as we saw in chapter 5, one of the most pervasive beliefs today is that corruption is the source of the problem of "underdevelopment"/poverty; corrupt politicians, police, civil servants are all seen as "bad apples" who pervert the efficient functioning of the state. But this obviates that it is primarily inequality that breeds corruption, enabling and empowering state officials and intermediaries to use their position to extract bribes (sometimes just to eke out a living by supplementing their meager wages, sometimes to enrich themselves). Similarly, poverty is often blamed on fate ("accept your social station," "she is successful because she has good genes") and character (people are poor because they are ignorant, uneducated, idle, submissive, crooked, ill-natured). Ideological beliefs such as these work once again to disavow the systemic cause of poverty by pinning it on an individual trait (personal character) or outside or pathological source (nature, destiny, a "culture of corruption").

A final ideological maneuver is to transform the symptom into an opportunity. Here, the critique of capitalist development is turned into an opening for more intervention. There is for example the neoliberal sleight of hand, whereby antipoverty programming is seen as requiring not less but more market mechanisms (hence the call to privatize education, health, water, housing, etc.). A similar tack is taken by development bureaucracies: not only is their programming premised on addressing poverty (i.e., their operations are founded on making poverty into an opportunity), but as we shall see below, failures in programming are converted into prospects for not less but more administrative involvement. Mainstream development discourse thus constructs both the market and development not as obstacle but solution, providing the opportunity for reproducing more of the same. Poverty-as-symptom becomes a site of enjoyment, a way for the development machine to gratify itself from the very problem it was set up to address (more on this below).

We see, then, the intimate relationship between poverty-as-symptom and the ideology of development. Poverty arises because capitalist development engages in a series of exclusions, and the role of development discourse is to mask said exclusions by constructing a harmonious fantasy (of progress, wealth creation, opportunity, etc.). It is not that the symptom disappears—poverty *is* recognized as an impediment that needs tackling; in fact a massive institutional machine is established for this purpose. But now poverty is treated as an ancillary and manageable issue. Yet as Žižek is quick to remind us, "Symptoms are never just secondary failures or distortions of the basically sound System— they are indicators that there is something 'rotten' (antagonistic, inconsistent) in the very heart of the System" (2013, 523).

# Enjoying Poverty-as-Symptom

If development denies poverty as the symptom of a fundamental disorder, it certainly does not ignore it as an isolated problem; on the contrary, as suggested above, it is premised on making poverty into an opportunity. I would like to argue in what follows that development transforms poverty into a particular type of opportunity—*the opportunity to enjoy*. Here, poverty-as-symptom becomes not only a question worthy of being deciphered, studied, and addressed, but a way for the development machine to organize its enjoyment. It is enjoyment that explains why development institutions and personnel fail to work themselves out of a job, and why the poor themselves are ill-prepared to renounce the(ir) symptom. Development thus persists (and expands) institutionally because of an underlying economy of enjoyment. To echo Žižek, rather than getting rid of poverty-as-symptom, development ends up enjoying its symptom more than itself.

## Institutional Enjoyment

Since the Second World War and the onset of decolonization in the Third World, there has been a massive expansion of development institutions devoted to addressing poverty—state bureaucracies, civil society organizations, and international aid and financial agencies. Faced with the unprecedented socioeconomic dislocation and immiseration caused by colonialism (and its concomitant spread of capitalism), development had to address mass starvation and poverty as pressing issues. As a consequence, as Escobar and other

Post-Development analysts have persuasively argued (see Escobar 1995, 21ff.; Ferguson 1990; Mitchell 1991), poverty was "problematized," giving way to new approaches to social intervention. The poor became objects of knowledge: they were associated with such phenomena/traits as crime, vagrancy, sexual promiscuity, or laziness, justifying interventions in a vast (and growing) number of areas ranging from education, health, and housing to employment, gender, and even moral and sexual conduct (i.e., population "control," HIV/ AIDS treatment).

The poor may well have been produced by an evolving capitalist system, but they were increasingly represented discursively and institutionally through their enumeration, classification, and study. The specification of a poverty line, for example, helped construct a hierarchical relationship between the poor and an institutional authority now charged with collecting data, carrying out poverty assessments, and designing antipoverty programming. Along with the establishment of a development bureaucracy came a panoply of bureaucratic rules and procedures, as well as an array of "experts" (economists, statisticians, health and nutrition specialists, gender advisers, etc.). The production of these experts implied the need for universities, which have in turn acquired their own interests in the study of poverty (the creation and persistence of such departments as anthropology, health, agriculture, forestry, nutrition, political science, women's studies, sociology, development studies, and area studies can be traced, at least in part, to international development work; see Dixon, Humble, and Counihan 2015).

Initially, during the period from 1945 to the late 1960s, the problem of poverty was mainly dealt with by the international community through localized and short-term emergency relief operations (to address famines, health crises, etc.). Then, more long-term interventions against poverty were devised (e.g., by the likes of the World Bank, World Food Programme, UNDP, and UNICEF). But since the 1980s, international development has taken a more advanced liberal orientation, linking poverty reduction to (neoliberal) market-based "solutions" through globalized operations that have brought together an assemblage of organizations—international aid and financial agencies, national governments, businesses, NGOs, and the poor themselves (see Ilcan and Lacey 2011, 19ff.). This neoliberalization of poverty programming has resulted in a leaner national state, but it has thereby been accompanied by a proliferation of civil society organizations that have filled some of the gaps left by the hollowed state. Not to be forgotten as well is the rise of what Barbara Harriss-White (2004) calls a "shadow state" made up of intermediaries, brokers, crooks, contractors, and consultants, many of whom are themselves government personnel, draining the state of resources for private benefit.

Poverty-as-symptom has thus become the grist for national and global institutions to justify, maintain, and substantially expand their antipoverty operations since 1945. By serving as an organizing concept for the development machine, poverty has enabled what Post-Development analysts refer to as the "governmentalization" of development, intensifying the relationship between instruments of knowledge and instruments of rule in relation to the poor (see chapter 2). But what I want to draw attention to presently is the enjoyment factor in such governmentalization.

### Enjoying (Neoliberal) Capitalism

Let me underline here again that enjoyment (*jouissance*) for Lacanians is intimately tied to culture: it is the unconscious libidinal surplus produced when we, as human animals, enter the symbolic order. This surplus—a mix of pleasure and pain that overwhelms us to the point of irrationality and excess—is what drives yet troubles human pursuits (see Lacan 2006, 50–51). Now given the growing hegemony of capitalist globalization, capitalism has become central to the construction of our present-day symbolic order—and hence of *jouissance*. As Samo Tomšič claims, the structure of today's unconscious is closely tied to the structure of capitalism (Tomšič 2015; see also Kapoor 2018; Žižek 1999a, 222, 276). This means that the unconscious surplus produced under a global capitalist order is increasingly oriented toward the reproduction of that order: capitalism has colonized not just culture, but also desire.

These unconscious capitalist proclivities are reinforced by the fact that, psychoanalytically speaking, *jouissance* is closely aligned with the superego. Unlike Freud, who sees the superego as an ethical conscience keeping the id/enjoyment in check, Lacan conceptualizes the superego as inciting enjoyment: its senseless injunction is for us to "Enjoy!" (Lacan 1998a, 10). Such a command to enjoy feeds very well into the logic of the market and capital's continuous need to reproduce itself, a point Lacanian commentators often underscore (see Dean 2006, 31; McGowan 2004; Žižek 2006, 297). As chapter 5 points out, we are duly urged to obey our superego's injunction to "express" ourselves, have satisfying sexual lives or careers, or seek out products that promise instant gratification or excess.

And this culture of capitalist enjoyment is one in which the massive development machinery in both the global North and South is immersed—economic and political elites, civil servants, NGO staff, policy makers, program officers, activists. It is hardly surprising, then, that states and international aid and financial organizations alike are inclined toward, if not actively promoting, market-friendly goals. The neoliberal fantasy that poverty can be solved through market-induced wealth accumulation ("trickle-down growth") is a widely shared, and largely unchallenged, one. It is supported by corporate elites who pressure the state because they stand to directly benefit from such neoliberal policies as privatization or tax and investment incentives. It is advantageous to those brokers/intermediaries who inhabit the "shadow state" (see above), providing a rationale for them to further their private accumulative projects. It is propped up by such "progressive" NGOs as Oxfam, which champion social justice, yet endorse campaigns for trade liberalization as a tool for poverty reduction (Ilcan and Lacey 2011, 14, 97–104). And it is upheld by the many development administrators and workers who help deliver antipoverty programming under the umbrella of (neoliberal) structural adjustment.

We should note, in this regard, the political shift that has occurred in relation to structural adjustment-related antipoverty programming. During the 1980s and 1990s, adjustment used to be a blatantly neocolonial tool imposed by the IFIs on states. But faced with resistance from recipient countries and a barrage of criticism about coercive conditionalities, the IFIs have now moved toward a more (outwardly) consensual approach. This involves the elaboration of poverty reduction strategy papers (PRSPs) that work through "partnerships" between IFIs, governments, businesses, and civil society organizations. PRSPs seek to "responsibilize" each stakeholder, encouraging "local ownership," "private-public partnerships," healthy "competition," "self-reliance," and "empowerment" (see Klugman 2002). As Ilcan and Lacey outline (2011, 64, 67), typical projects include the education of girls, training youth as self-employed entrepreneurs, and ubiquitous microfinance and microcredit programs targeting the poor.

Marxist commentators such as Cammack are correct, then, to claim that the IFI's structural adjustment strategy is to pressure states and their civil society "partners" to secure the hegemony of capital (2009; see also 2003; Jessop 2007, 29). Neoliberal projects supporting the education, health, and microfinancing of the poor are indeed aimed at incorporating the latter into global capitalism. But as pointed out earlier, Foucauldian-inspired analysts such as Joseph are equally correct to press the likes of Cammack on the mechanics of this process. What is missing in Cammack's analysis of neocolonialism, according to Joseph, are the "social and cultural conditions necessary for [the neoliberal free market idea] to enter our social practices. . . . [C]apitalism does not reproduce itself automatically—hence, the importance of focusing on forms of social regulation through the state and other institutional regimes" (Joseph 2010a, 42, 45). Joseph turns to the notion of governmentality, arguing that it works toward the self-regulation of states, institutionally embedding disciplines of neoliberal capitalism, thereby allowing the IFIs to govern at a distance. Foucauldian analysts, Ilcan and Lacey (2011)—mentioned above— make a similar argument, claiming that neoliberal governmentalization "responsibilizes" governments and their partners for promoting market solutions to poverty alleviation.

But Joseph, as well as Ilcan and Lacey, are themselves missing out: by ignoring culture's libidinal underpinnings, they underappreciate its importance in helping to institutionally embed neoliberal capitalism. Like Foucault, they equate culture/discourse with knowledge, whose structuring/framing brings about relations of rule. Yet, as Žižek (1989) has underscored, we live in times when neoliberal ideology grips us not so much at the level of knowledge but unconscious desire. This is why, as I have stressed several times (see chapters 2, 6, 8, and 11), the critique of knowledge systems is inadequate—irony, sarcasm, or other forms of distancing are tolerated, taken into account in advance, by liberal capitalist ideology: they are ultimately unthreatening to the global capitalist order. No wonder that Oxfam can stand for social justice, yet still favor the liberalization of trade. And no wonder that the IFIs can neutralize the criticisms of neocolonial structural adjustment by replacing it with more consensual "partnerships" that nonetheless continue to make the poor available to global capital. What Joseph and Ilcan/Lacey are missing out on is the unconscious dimension of culture, which ensures adherence to the prevailing ideology *despite critique*. As a consequence, they miscalculate the hold that neoliberal culture has on governmentality. Knowledge may well be laced with power, but it is knowledge's libidinal lining that one needs to heed to better appreciate how neoliberalism seduces us all, even the naysayers, thus reproducing itself culturally and institutionally.

*Jouissance* is a cultural surplus, the little extra that comes with today's hegemony of capitalist ideology. Its effect is to mesmerize state actors and international development administrators so that they buy into the fantasy of progress, markets, and wealth. Yet it also has a crucial material dimension, since it libidinally binds us to capitalist political economy: people do not just buy into development-as-ideological-fantasy, they live their lives and build their worlds on the basis of it. Neoliberal ideology activates their desires/enjoyment, inuring them to become investors, shoppers, entrepreneurs, and so forth. In other words, ideological fantasy is not just a kind of escapism or dream, it is externalized and materialized in the form of social practices, policies, or resource allocations; and it relies on enjoyment to grip us, thereby confirming we create and reproduce social reality in its image.

## The Enjoyment of Administering
## and Delivering Development

Of course, enjoyment comes in varying forms and is directed toward differ-ent pursuits; hence my reference to an "economy of *jouissance*" when it comes to regulating poverty. For the moment, let me focus on *jouissance* as it relates to administering and delivering programs. Now perhaps this is an impossible task, given the range of organizations that make up the development indus-try, each with its own agenda, functions, projects, and many with overlapping and sometimes contradictory activities, but I want to suggest that there are certain unifying features among this complex amalgam, from which it may be possible to retrieve a kernel of enjoyment. For example, there is, at least to a degree, a certain bureaucratic logic and rationality in the operations of the development apparatus, which is characteristic of modernity more generally (see Weber 2006). Thus, an NGO might operate somewhat differently from the civil service (e.g., the former is typically, although not necessarily, less hi-erarchical than the latter), yet the two still share a certain bureaucratic/or-ganizational behavior (e.g., red tape), all the more so in the case of larger, transnational NGOs such as Oxfam, Médecins Sans Frontières (MSF), or Care International. Moreover, as emphasized in the previous section, the develop-ment industry shares a symbolic world, which in the current global conjunc-ture means not only that it tends to be biased toward neoliberal capitalism, but also that it inevitably partakes in the "society of the spectacle" (Debord 2012) that our information age has ushered in. As we shall see, this has impli-cations for the manner in which poverty programs are delivered.

Let me begin though with the idea of institutional enjoyment. For, despite the inevitable complaints about red tape, there is an unmistakable reassurance and stability to be derived from it. As chapters 2 and 5 have intimated, like re-ligious rituals, bureaucratic rules and procedures provide people with a cer-tain regularity, routine, discipline and structure that is satisfying and comforting. Routine may be boring sometimes, but there is a repetitive and habit-forming dimension to it that is sobering, especially given the busy and complex lives that administrators must negotiate both at work and home. Structure may solidify and tend toward the inflexible, but it also helps organize time and make difficult tasks more manageable. And red tape may threaten administra-tive efficiency, but it can also become a gratifying ritual: applying rules, fol-lowing procedures, and attending endless meetings take on a certain ceremonial quality, connecting one to an office community or larger international devel-opment circle.

From a Lacanian perspective, the comfort obtained from these administrative tasks speaks to our ontological condition as human beings: after all, enjoyment is the libidinal response to original loss and trauma, which we are forever trying to soothe and cover up. So it is not surprising that, in this case, bureaucrats seek out stability, structure, and community through red tape; these supply contentment even as they alleviate deep anxiety (which underscores why *jouissance* is not just about pleasure, but always about pleasure *and/in* pain).

Yet the more immediate implication is that the question of poverty gets lost in this melee. The enjoyment of red tape hijacks, obstructs, or trumps the putative goal of poverty alleviation. Bureaucratic rituals take on a life, logic, and pleasurable economy of their own, working to gratify administrators to the detriment of the poor. Presumably, the more the pleasure drawn from red tape the more the urge for more red tape and the less the effort or resources spent on the poor. There is an irrationality to administering development, then, and it lies not just in the bureaucracy's "iron cage" rigidity (Weber), panopticism (Foucault), or authoritarianism (Orwell), but also in the excess and stupidity of enjoyment.

In addition to administrative enjoyment, there is the enjoyment of delivering aid and development to the "needy." What is striking here is the often frenetic activity in which many development organizations are engaged, particularly NGOs involved in the humanitarian sector (e.g., MSF, CARE, International Committee of the Red Cross, etc.). The latter's main purpose is to respond to short-term global emergencies, ranging from armed conflicts and epidemics to earthquakes and famines. Mark Duffield sees in this shifting from crisis to crisis the making of a "permanent emergency regime" (2013, 25, 47–49, 219), which serves as both rationale for and description of the feverish NGO activity.

Added to this feverishness is the spectacle of it all (see Kapoor 2013a, 84ff.). Our digital/media age thrives on the sensational, and covering global emergencies fits the bill well: it allows the humanitarian NGO to draw public attention to the crisis, parade the victims, and foreground the heroic work being done to "rescue" them. Frenetic activity and spectacle come together to provide a veritable "reality show." Witness the extensive recent media coverage of such disasters as earthquakes (Haiti 2010, Pakistan 2013, China 2014, Nepal 2015), tsunamis (the 2004 Asian tsunami), hurricanes (Nicaragua and Honduras 2007, Caribbean and Puerto Rico 2017), and famines (Ethiopia 1998, South Sudan 2017, Yemen 2016–2019).

There is a nugget of enjoyment in the frenzied actions of these NGOs, as well as in the showcasing of their actions. Psychoanalytically speaking, it is hard to understand their hyperactivity as anything but a *drive* to enjoy, the drive in Lacanian thought being conceived as a pleasurable but never-ending circular and repetitive movement around an object of desire (see chapter 4, and Johnston 2005). My claim is that NGOs—or rather, their staff—"get off" on the constant sensory-motor activity, intense experiences, crisis management, and quick decision-making that are integral to the scene of an emergency. While they may well be "saving" lives, there is a not-to-be-missed mix of buzz and anxiety (i.e., *jouissance*) in their work. In this sense, the permanent emergency regime is premised on the enjoyment-producing drive of incessant engagement and intervention.

Added to this hyperactivity is the enjoyment-inducing spectacle of humanitarian work. Here, NGOs are enacting a key characteristic of our current mediated world: the necessity and thrill of always being watched. It is not enough to live a life or do one's work anymore; one has to exhibit all of it in all its detail (on the Internet, social media, television, etc.). Accordingly, most NGOs (and most development organizations for that matter) actively seek out the media to publicize their frontline work, accomplishments, celebrity endorsements, and so forth. Partly, this is done for outreach and fundraising, but I am suggesting that partly it is also done for public recognition, for the glitz and glam of it all. It is as if, today, (the thrill of) being gazed at is an ontological validation of one's being, so much so that *not* being gazed at becomes anxiety-producing (see chapters 5 and 7).

The conundrum once again though is that instead of working themselves out of a job, NGOs depend (and count) on more and more enjoyment-inducing crises. They have every interest in global capitalism's continued production of emergencies, which enables and legitimizes their spectacular humanitarianism. In this sense, today's NGO-ization of humanitarianism (and development) may well center on finding *affective*, rather than effective, solutions to poverty. The enjoyment of crisis management may be a way of keeping the humanitarian business in business.

Moreover, if NGOs intervene to save the "vulnerable" mainly for the enjoyment of being *seen* to be saving them, then it is the performance, much more than the content of the performance that matters. If what mostly counts is the joy of exhibitionism, then NGOs do not really need to do too much, as long as they *look* like they are. Their activity really becomes a pseudo-activity. The threat today, as Žižek claims "is not passivity, but pseudo-activity, the urge to 'be active', to 'participate', to mask the nothingness of what goes on" (2008, 217). NGOs (and other development organizations as well) appear to have internalized and institutionalized a perpetual mode of pseudo-activity, which aims not at dealing with the long-term, underlying causes of poverty/crises, but at addressing only the short-term, spectacular symptoms.

## Enjoying One's Status (Quo)

There is no doubt that, on the whole, civil servants and NGO staff dispense their functions with earnestness and care, and rarely with indifference (see Gupta 2012, 13, 23–24). Nonetheless it would be a mistake to deny that their posts come with notable social status, which can also be a source of enjoyment. For a start, belonging to an "official" organization—governmental, nongovernmental, multilateral—positions the bureaucrat as the Master in relation to the poor, bringing with it a certain hubris and prestige. But this hierarchical positioning is amplified in the field of development, which has a history of paternalism and *noblesse oblige*, all the more so across the North-South divide, where "whiteness" signifies superiority (see Baaz 2008). There is, in addition, the distinction of the development officer's qualifications and socioeconomic position, the seniority of her rank within the bureaucratic hierarchy, or the benevolence of her profession (seemingly inherent to the fields of development and humanitarianism)—all of which can be a source of comfort, pride, even entitlement.

This hierarchical aspect of bureaucracy, coupled with the patron-client relationships integral to development, are conducive to sadomasochistic practices as well, whether within and among organizations or between them and the subaltern. Red tape, as emphasized in chapter 2, lends itself to a variety of unspoken perverse delights: ensuring compliance, monitoring performance, auditing accounts, extracting bribes, threatening withdrawal (of support, resources), delaying or expediting decisions, adding or removing obstacles, concealing or revealing information (gatekeeping), inventing "facts" or forging data, circulating rumors, and so forth. There is undoubted relish to be had in seeing clients, colleagues, or competitors succeed or fail, or be put through hoops and denied or granted funding. The enjoyment factor in governmentality is thus rife with examples and possibilities, and Foucauldians ignore it to their peril.

## Enjoying Scapegoating the Poor

Development may be premised on "helping" the poor, but it also has a history of blaming the poor. This points up once again the sadomasochistic dimensions of enjoyment, accentuating how the development establishment can tend toward the irrational, counterproductive, and "necropolitical" (see Mbembe 2008).

While there is a long tradition of impugning the poor that stretches back to colonialism (e.g., depicting the colonized as "primitive" and "barbarous"; see Fanon 1967, 170–171), some of its most recent manifestation along West–Third World lines are evident in neo-Malthusian and security discourses. The former makes the argument that it is exploding population growth in the developing world that is the main cause of poverty and environmental destruction (see Ehrlich 1971; Hardin 1968). The specific target here tends to be the Third World poor—their high fertility rates, their degradation of the environment, their overutilization of grazing and agricultural lands, and so forth. The security discourse, for its part, tends to equate poverty with peril. Duffield argues that the discourse is constructed on the basis of the metaphor of the "borderlands" (i.e. the Third World), an imagined geographic space of instability, excess, and social breakdown, which is seen as posing a threat to the metropolitan areas (2001, 309). The borderlands are portrayed as violent, dangerous, unpredictable; they are the source of the problems plaguing global security—drug trafficking, terrorism, refugee flows, and corrupt/weak/"rogue" states. Here, poverty is to be feared much more than alleviated. As a consequence, development and humanitarianism center not so much on reducing inequality or protecting the most vulnerable but on technologies of security aimed at managing instability and disorder. Hence the need to intervene in the Third World under the guise of the "responsibility to protect," even if it means ignoring international law and yields to (Western) military intervention (think of the recent military intrusions in Iraq, Afghanistan, Somalia, Haiti, Bosnia, East Timor, Sierra Leone, Liberia, the Democratic Republic of Congo, Sudan, Côte d'Ivoire, etc.).

In the Third World, discourses such as these have translated into palpable harm to the poor. For example, neo-Malthusian notions of poverty as the obstacle to development have fueled forced sterilization programs in such countries as India (an astonishing 6.2 million poor men were forcibly sterilized during Indira Gandhi's 1975 emergency) and China (forced tubectomies were carried out on peasant women in the 1980s) (Biswas 2014). A variation on this necropolitical theme is the frequent demolition of slums and the relocation of the poor, under the pretext of urban renewal or infrastructure development (e.g., dam construction). Local authorities sometimes recruit NGOs to convince slum dwellers or rural indigenous communities of the benefits of such relocation or, failing that, resort to forcibly evicting particular groups (e.g., poor Muslims) by characterizing them as security threats (Jha, Shajahan, and Vyas 2013, 56).

Similarly, environmental policy managers across the developing world have used the overpopulation bogeyman to frequently accuse the poor of inefficiency and overexploitation of resources, thereby justifying a clampdown on "traditional" peasant ecological practices (e.g., community forestry, shifting cultivation) in favor of "modern" conservation and agricultural methods (e.g., "scientific" forestry, "green revolution" technologies) (see Meffe, Ehrlich, and Ehrenfeld 1993). As if echoing such thinking, the World Bank has characterized shifting cultivation in the Sudano-Sahelian region as resulting in a "downward spiral of extensive land degradation and fuelwood shortage" (quoted in Bernstein 2005, 81), advocating for its curtailment.

The scapegoating of the poor in these multiple ways is indicative of the need to stigmatize, if not eliminate, the Other in order to produce a harmonious ideological fantasy of development (see Fletcher, Breitling, and Puleo 2014). Rather than seeing capitalist development as being blocked by its own internal antagonisms (inequality, unevenness, exploitation, environmental destruction), the blockages are projected (by the West/Third World state) onto the figure of the poor. Accordingly, the poor are portrayed as preventing "us" from fully enjoying. They are stealing "our" enjoyment, and in fact enjoying more than us (by engaging in their "traditional" practices, as opposed to our "modern" scientific ones). Therefore, the logic goes, only by constraining or eliminating them can we recapture our lost enjoyment. But of course, what is concealed by attributing to the poor such theft of enjoyment is that we never possessed what is allegedly robbed from us in the first place: enjoyment is only conceived as stolen because of a mythological originary castration/lack (Stavrakakis 2007, 197–198; Žižek 1993, 203–204).

The effect of scapegoating the poor, as implied above, is that it allows the development apparatus to consolidate itself, although in paradoxical ways. While the poor are the supposed "clients" of development, they are at the same time constructed as a threat, conferring a stronger unity among development administrators/institutions. Indeed, for Lacanians, enjoyment is what binds people together (as groups, nations, communities), often taking on a pernicious character (i.e., targeting and victimizing outsiders, migrants, people of color, etc.); but it is also full of ambiguity: we may well enjoy catering to the poor, but we nonetheless find them threatening; our enjoyment is inaccessible to the poor (this inaccessibility is what makes us / the state / the West unique), while at the same time being threatened by them. Yet it is precisely this ambiguity that is the defining characteristic of *jouissance*—you are condemned to enjoying your suffering and suffering your enjoyment.

## Enjoying Institutional Failure

One of the fantasies of development administration, particularly in this neo-liberal era of performance measurement, is that success brings rewards and failure penalties. But what this obscures is that bureaucracies sometimes also reward failures. That is, institutional expansion—a key measure of *bureaucratic success*—can happen despite (or because) of failure. This is certainly the import of James Ferguson's work (1990) on institutional politics in Lesotho, as we stressed in chapter 2, which claims that project failures help deepen the intrusion of the state into the Lesotho countryside: "again and again development projects . . . are launched, and again and again they fail; but no matter how many times this happens there always seems to be someone ready to try again with yet another project. For the 'development' industry . . . failure appears to be the norm" (8). So institutional failure, rather than deterring the reproduction of the administrative machinery, seems to operate to ensure it (Ferguson calls this "etatization"). The implication, once again, is that what matters is bureaucratic expansion, not poverty reduction.

But such an institutional politics is the description itself of drive, which, as mentioned earlier, is associated with compulsion, repetition, and failure. In distinction to desire, for which gratification always remains elusive (i.e., no object quite satisfies), drive derives enjoyment from relentless and repetitive failure (i.e., from desire's constant disappointment) (see chapter 4 and Kapoor 2015c). Institutional drive, in this sense, is premised on a strange enjoyment through repeated failure: it does not matter if projects fail, if poverty is not addressed, as long as more projects can be devised and "new" kinds development interventions can be operationalized. This is not to say that the bureaucracy operates only through failure, but rather that the enjoyment of failure is a key ingredient of governmentality; it puts paid to the myth of a "rational" bureaucracy and the neoliberal fantasy of only rewarding success. There is an excess inherent to institutional politics for the sake of which bureaucrats do what might otherwise seem irrational.

Such an argument runs counter to that of James Scott, whose *Seeing Like a State* (2008) is often considered an authority on bureaucracy gone wrong. Scott's view of Nyerere's villagization program in the 1970s, for example, is that it was a classic case of bureaucratic authoritarianism: it violently forced peasants to settle in villages as a way of bringing the rural economy under state control (223ff.). Scott sees this case as one of many examples of modernist hubris, of systematic plans for human improvement that are based on the oversimplification of complex problems (81, 184, 309ff.). But the accusation that state bureaucrats oversimplify assumes that success is necessarily their goal. What Scott ignores is the human/bureaucratic enjoyment of failure. He overlooks that excess (and indeed violence) might be inherent to the life of institutions, and that administrators might actually be attached to that which derails their plans.

## Enjoyment as Institutional Raison d'Être?

So is enjoyment the institutional *raison d'être* when it comes to poverty reduction? Well, it may not be "the" *raison d'être* but I am suggesting that it is certainly "a key" *raison d'être*. I have examined some of the many ways in which institutional enjoyment plays out in development: how administrators are seduced by capitalism, derive satisfaction from red tape and frenzied action, and perversely relish failure, hierarchy, and scapegoating. Enjoyment thus helps support the system, becoming an essential institutional factor, so much so that administrators may seek out thrill rather than effectiveness in their poverty alleviation activities. Poverty-as-symptom transforms into poverty-as-sinthome—a way for the development machinery to gratify itself from the very problem it is set up to address.

Two important implications follow. First, if poverty is what maintains the consistency of the development industry, eliminating the problem of poverty is not an option, since that would mean relinquishing the industry's capacity to enjoy its symptom. Development cannot do without the poor, in the same way that the alcoholic cannot survive without liquor or anorexics cannot budge on their refusal to eat—all of them "love their symptom more than themselves." Development is therefore deeply invested in the perpetuation of poverty.

And second, the passage from symptom to sinthome means that what used to be the exception that troubled the system has now become generalized: the system not only needs poverty but literally thrives on it. The violence and "pathology" of poverty is normalized, laying the background on which development rests. Poverty, in this sense, becomes unexceptional; it is what is required for the "normal" functioning and routine administration of development (Gupta 2012, 22–23; Žižek 2008, 1–2).

## How the Poor Enjoy The(ir) Symptom, Too!

But the poor can love the(ir) symptom, too. That is, they can relish the very system that impoverishes them, thus consenting to their social positioning. This is evident in the way they assert the (hard-won) identity-based rights accorded to them under capitalist liberal democracy—their rights as indigenous people, women, disabled persons, LGBTI people, "backward castes" (the official label in India), and so forth. They have organized politically around these identities as social movements to pressure the state for recognition or as political parties to contest elections, win power, and further their rights. They have fought for, and taken advantage of, identity-based affirmative-action measures ("quota politics") that increase their opportunities to be employed or get school or university admissions. They have mobilized to claim welfare entitlements (ration cards, pension assistance, housing subsidies, etc.) and demand legal enforcement and protection (e.g., enforcement of minimum wage or corruption laws, protection against rape or harassment) (see Corbridge et al. 2005, 7, 19, 82–83). And of course, like all of us, they have participated in the capitalist economy as shoppers, bank creditors, and / or (small) entrepreneurs and investors (to the extent that their subaltern position allows).

My point here is not to deride the daily struggles and political accomplishments of the poor (often achieved at great cost and suffering), but to point out that they, like all of us, are also ideologically interpellated: they, too, enjoy commodity fetishism, claim their rights and "entitlements," and often willingly obey the bureaucracy-as-master (see below). Capitalist development sets them / us up to enjoy only those activities that either help perpetuate the system (shopping, investing) or are unthreatening to it (identity-based rights and welfare entitlements, as opposed to substantive socioeconomic rights such as the right to land and decent wages or worker ownership and self-management). The *jouissance* taken in both claiming and benefitting from these rights gives the poor an interest in reproducing the very system that subalternizes them. By participating in capitalist development, they are consenting to it, even if (and perhaps especially when) they criticize it on the basis of identity politics. In short, the poor end up enjoying their own poverty-as-symptom.

Such *jouissance*, it should be pointed out, is even to be found in the encounter between the poor and bureaucratic authority (of the state / development machinery). Psychoanalytically speaking, the bureaucracy stands as Master or Law, interpellating "the poor" as subject.[9] But there is an unconscious complement to the Law which is the superego, whose role, as stressed earlier (see also chapters 9 and 11), is to incite compliance to the Law—"submit to the Law!" (or "Enjoy capitalism!", "Express yourself!," "Be healthy!"). The superego helps maintain the illusion of symbolic plenitude by bombarding the subject with either guilt (if s/he is moved not to follow the Law) or surplus enjoyment (if s/he willingly submits to the Law) (see McMillan 2008, 13–14). Thus, just as the bureaucrat enjoys applying rules and prescribing procedures, so the poor enjoy submitting to these rules and following these procedures. They may well be skeptical of the Law, despise the arrogance of such and such a civil servant, or complain about having to pay bribes, but most often they end up following the Law nonetheless: they "appear to do the state's work even when they have little respect for the institutions and individuals who represent it" (Garmany 2009, 729).

Let me end by contrasting this argument with that of Jonathan Joseph, who you will recall claims that the IFI's poverty alleviation strategies aim not to improve the conditions of the poor but to regulate states. What is curious about his analysis is that it is critical of Marxists such as Cammack for not considering how regulation is socioculturally embedded, yet when it comes down to it, falls short of doing so itself. Joseph writes that he wants to resist "the reductionist tendency to explain what happens in governmentality by appealing to some lower level" (i.e., showing how the poor discipline themselves), contending that governmentality does not succeed in "responsibilizing the majority of the population" (2010a, 45–46). This is because, for him, neoliberalism originated in the West, and while it can embed itself in the Third World at the top (i.e., in the state), it has little impact or "organic basis" at the bottom (2010a, 47; see also 2010b).

Joseph's Foucauldianism is premised on a cultural analysis, yet as I underlined earlier, he ends up not taking culture seriously enough. Given the globalization of capitalist culture, how does he explain that the *shared* network that is culture reaches only the top but not the bottom? Although Marxists such as Cammack may tend to ignore culture, they are right in seeing capitalism as a *global* order, which materially (and from our perspective, symbolically) scales up as much as down. While the West may have a dominant position in global capitalism relative to the Third World, it is precisely such historical dominance that has ensured the broad reach of the capitalist Symbolic. And as I have suggested earlier, this means psychoanalytically that neoliberal capitalism has been able to rearrange desires in the West as much as the Third World, at the level of the state as much as the poor. Thus, if IFIs can "govern at a distance," it is not only by regulating states, but also by reaching the poor through culture, that is to say, libidinally through an economy of *jouissance*.

I cannot help but suspect that Joseph refrains from speculating about the self-regulation of the poor due to some leftover romanticism (about subaltern or "local" cultures). This gives the impression that subalterns are transparent to themselves, immune to struggle or failure. Yet, as Linda Alcoff suggests, such a move ends up "essializ[ing] the oppressed as nonideologically constructed subjects" (1991, 22; see also Kapoor 2008, 53).

# Conclusion: Politicizing the Symptom: The Poor as Concrete Universal/Point of Disruption

This chapter contends that a massive development industry has been established to address poverty, not as a symptom of capitalism, but as a manageable problem. The industry is supported, on the one hand, by an ideological apparatus that constructs development as a harmonious whole, helping to deny or gentrify poverty-as-symptom, and, on the other hand, by an economy of enjoyment that ensures *affective* rather than effective solutions to poverty. The poor are themselves caught in this economy of enjoyment, as a result of which they end up getting attached to the very system that oppresses them.

A significant implication of the notion of poverty-as-symptom is that poverty is not a mere obstacle standing in the way of capitalist development but rather the very condition of the formation of development, the "outside" that allows the inside to be constructed. The poor-as-symptom, in this sense, is what Žižek would call the "concrete universal" (1999a, 92): it reveals the truth about the universalizing system that is global capitalism, marking its point of failure and impossibility—that which must be excluded for capitalism to constitute itself as a totality. As Todd McGowan conveys it, "though the symptom does not fit within the logic of the system, it expresses the truth of the system that confronts the system in an external form" (2014, 243; see also McMillan 2008, 3). And it is because the poor-as-symptom reveals the truth/failure of the system that development refrains from acknowledging it, at least in its symptomatic abject manifestation, proceeding instead to cover it over in favor of a tractable Other.

The problem though is that the symptom always threatens to break through and reveal itself: it remains a stain, the site of the repressed Other that can return at any moment to trouble the false appearance of development-as-ideology. Thus, while the market economy produces the poor-as-symptom, the existence of the poor represents a danger to development. Or, to put it in more strictly psychoanalytic terms, although poverty-as-symptom is enjoyed (by the development machinery and the poor themselves), it is also "potentially the cause of anxiety and dislocation" (McMillan 2008, 7).

But then how can the poor-as-symptom be politicized? How to move from symptom to point of disruption? There are no easy or ready answers here, all the more so that so many challenges stand in the way. Despite vociferous criticism of development, the seductions of capitalism manage to pull people in the direction of the status quo, dissuading them from following through on their desire for change. Faced with the great difficulty of loosening the grip of capitalist enjoyment or thinking beyond a market frame, Žižek himself suggests that anticapitalist change may *not* be in the cards, at least not in the foreseeable future (1999a, 352; 2018). Now of course the subaltern does have a long history of resistance and political mobilization—from insurrections and popular/social movements to electoral politics and localized resistance (see for example Bebbington et al. 2010; Corbridge et al. 2005, 219ff.; Koster and de Vries 2012). But what appears to be missing is an uncompromising, coordinated attempt at dismantling capitalism itself. As chapter 8 suggests, protest movements tend to be divided and ghettoized, acting locally or sporadically without affecting broader structures; or taking up identity-related issues that, as mentioned above, may well result in reforms but are ultimately unthreatening to the global order.

All I can do then, to conclude, is to sketch a few elements—admittedly tentative and incomplete, but which flow from the logic of my preceding psychoanalytic argument—to move in the direction of radical change. A first element involves recognizing, and being intensely committed to, the possibility of post-capitalist societies. There are plenty of post-capitalist visions (e.g., Bolivia's "Buen Vivir" or the proposals of Albert 2004; Gandhi 1970; Gibson-Graham 2006; Mason 2017; Schumacher 1973); the problem is pursuing them doggedly, without being placated or discouraged (i.e., without compromising one's desire). Part of the challenge here is to avoid seeing the big Other (the authority of the state/development apparatus) as a barrier to one's enjoyment; hence refusing to be beholden to institutional power or to reduce one's politics to that of the existing capitalist order. And part of the challenge is to steer clear of delegating change to an Other: for example, when the subaltern trusts that the development state or big business—the very sources of its oppression—will finally liberate them; or when we, Left intellectuals and elites, rely on others (subaltern groups, progressive movements, Left parties, etc.) to transform the System.[10] Radical change does not happen, it seems, by taking the position of the "beautiful soul," as a consequence of which one avoids dirtying one's hands by outsourcing one's activism or relying on the big Other to fulfill one's desires (see Flemming 2011, 90). The overall challenge, in other words, is to transform the "idiotic enjoyment" that perpetuates the poor-as-symptom into a shared, vibrant enjoyment that revolts against development ideology to open up an anti-/post-capitalist politics of alternate possibilities (see chapter 10).

A second element is fashioning a politics of the symptom. This is important if one is to obviate the above-mentioned problem of a ghettoized, divided, and uncoordinated oppositional politics. The reason for such fragmentation is that group claims are expressed in terms of limited particularities (women's rights, indigenous self-determination, gay marriage, Black or Dalit affirmative action, etc.). What is missing according to Žižek (1999a, 98–103; 2013, 357–358), as underlined in chapter 3, is the articulation of a common universality, which is precisely the function of the poor-as-symptom: it represents the concrete universality expressing the failures of the global capitalist system, for which *all* subaltern groups pay the price. In other words, solidarity among differing groups/movements can be constructed on the basis of a common adversary—capitalist development—*and* by politicizing not particular identities but *shared exclusion*. What brings people together is not some substantive content but a negative condition—their status as the Excluded or "part that has no part"—that results in a collection of misfits and oddballs. As McGowan states, "[r]ather than a politics in which we overcome the obstacles that inhibit completion, Žižek proposes a politics of the symptom in which we identify with these obstacles" (McGowan 2014, 244–245). This is why revolutions—the Haitian or the French, or the more recent Arab Spring—resonate worldwide: they are expressed in terms of broad issues such as freedom, equality, and justice, which transcend particularity so that everyone can identify with them. They mean something specific for each struggle yet express something universal about the global order. Thus, it is by politicizing poverty-as-symptom as a universality that a unity-in-diversity (among multiple transnational movements) can be constructed. In this way, the symptom of the universalizing capitalist system can itself be used against the system, elevating the excluded truth "to the place of the universal" (Stavrakakis 2002, 133).

A final (related) element involves the very difficult task of unplugging from, and reconfiguring, the big Other/Symbolic. Partly, this is a radicalization of the above-mentioned first element: not just distancing oneself from the prevailing ideological apparatus but struggling to isolate the sinthome, wresting it from its seductive power and seeing it as something disgusting and meaningless. Žižek pens it this way: the goal is to view the sinthome "in its utter stupidity, as a meaningless fragment of the Real. In other words we must (as Lacan puts it in *Seminar XI*) 'change the precious gift into a piece of shit'" (1999b, 17; see also 1991, 129). The idea is not to rid oneself of the sinthome (one never can since enjoyment is constitutive of the human subject) but to identify with it, to isolate the kernel of "idiotic enjoyment." By removing its efficacy in the discourse of development, one can better see through that which mesmerizes us and clouds our judgment.

In so doing, one can begin moving from an "acting out" of the symptom/sinthome, where one remains bound to the big Other (qua Symbolic), to what Lacan calls the "Act" (enabled by arduously "traversing the fantasy"), which engenders a break with the Symbolic (1998b, 273–274; 2014, 77). The revolutionary Act is made possible when one suspends the Law, implying a kind of "subjective destitution" (Žižek 1991, 139), a leap into the void. It is this that enables the creation of a new master signifier (post-capitalism?), that is, the refashioning of a symbolic order and the movement toward a more just political economy.

But of course, there are no guarantees, with failure a distinct possibility and "success" nothing short of miraculous. And if the revolutionary act were to help produce a post-capitalist world, it would inevitably be beset by its own antagonisms (e.g., the threat of authoritarianism, the rise of new elites or inequalities, etc.). As McGowan reminds us (2014, 245), the symptom / sinthome remains a barrier to all political projects, post-capitalist or not.

## Notes

1. Note that the subtitle of this chapter, "Enjoy Your Symptom!," is indebted to Žižek's well-known book title of the same name (see 1992). Also, for the sake of further clarity, my argument is that it is poverty and the poor that are the symptom of capitalist development. So when I say "the poor enjoy the(ir) symptom," I of course mean they enjoy, not their personal psychosomatic symptom (which they well might, though that is not my concern here), but the symptom induced by the capitalist System of which they are part (i.e., they enjoy *their* condition as poor, or to put it differently, they enjoy *the* systemically produced symptom). My focus is on systemic processes, not individual traits.

2. Joseph characterizes his analysis as "more Marxist than Foucauldian" (2010a, 30). Yet, given that he centers his article on "global governmentality," I would characterize his work here as a foregrounding of governmentality more than political economy. One of the gaps in his work, as I argue below, is precisely his relative neglect of the material conditions of governmentality (and how to more adequately explain how governmentality itself takes root), which a psychoanalytic framework, through its emphasis on *jouissance*, better helps explain.

3. As I emphasize throughout this chapter, by development I mean *capitalist* development, which in the global South today takes on one of two main political forms: liberal democratic capitalist development (e.g., India, Brazil, Senegal, South Africa, etc.) and authoritarian capitalist development (China, Rwanda, Singapore, Iran, Turkey, etc.). This is mirrored in the global North by the rivalry between the liberal democratic capitalist West (United States, Western Europe, etc.) and the authoritarian capitalist East (Russia). Although the former political-economic system is dominant globally, the latter appears increasingly ascendant, especially given the recent rise of nationalist-populist regimes (Modi, Duterte, Trump, Erdoğan, Kaczynski, Bolsonaro, etc.) and their tendencies toward xenophobia and command neoliberal economic policy. What is not to be missed here, of course, is that *global* capitalism stands as the common, unifying force despite these outward divergences, producing a political arrangement that lies on the liberal democratic-authoritarian continuum. Meanwhile, surrounded by such a sea of capitalism, (present or recently past) regimes such as that

of Morales (Bolivia), Correa (Ecuador), and Chavez (Venezuela) represent possible exceptions, examples of what in chapter 10 I call a "queer Third World," trying to negotiate (with great difficulty and not without many gaps/failures) a nonaligned political economy that puts the poor/Excluded first (see also Kapoor 2015b).

4. There are many reasons for such poverty reduction—the primary one being the state's welfare/development activities from 1947 onward. Note that at India's independence, poverty had reached some of its worst levels ever in the wake of the shock of colonialism and the devastating aftermath of decolonization (i.e., the violent partitioning of the subcontinent); so state/development interventions were bound to improve socioeconomic conditions that had hit close to rock bottom. But the broader point is that much poverty still remains decades later, in India and the rest of the Third World (as much as in the West itself), with inequality within and among countries increasing despite massive wealth creation globally. So state welfare/development activities may well help attenuate such poverty but never eliminate it. And as I argue, attenuating rather than eliminating poverty is precisely what development is premised upon (i.e., poverty is *required* to keep the business of development in business).

5. This is especially the case given the intersectionality involved in poverty, so that at one spatiohistorical conjuncture, it may be the class position of the poor that predominantly determines their pauperization, while at another it may be their gender status (although under the capitalist regime, class will still play an important role). It is likely that the most marginalized in society will be those at the intersection of multiple oppressions (e.g., a trans, disabled, indigenous person), although this may not necessarily be the case (e.g., it is the person's class position that may end up being the most determining factor). As capitalism evolves, moreover, there are always new social antagonisms that play out, giving way to new forms of pauperization (e.g., the onset of neoliberalism and the environmental crisis has produced new technologies of immiseration, notably the ejection of people from communal forests and lands, a phenomenon variously called the "new enclosure movement" or "accumulation by dispossession").

6. The "subaltern" is also a term to be equated with "the poor," since it designates those who are marginalized based on "class, caste, age, gender and office or in any other way" (Guha 1988, 35). Like the term "the Excluded," it points to systemic marginalization.

7. In some ways, subduing poverty-as-symptom, as opposed to eliminating it (repressing it), may be ideologically more nefarious, since it means having to invest a lot of effort, time, and resources politically and institutionally to actively and continuously gentrify it, vilify it, minoritize it.

8. This is what I have elsewhere called "decaf capitalism" (Kapoor 2013a, 80–82; 2013b; 2015a).

9. Žižek points out that the entire functioning of the bureaucracy is based on a tautology: "I obey the master because he is the master" (2013, 424–430). But the mystique of the authority of the state has such psychic power that even when I am confronted "with the choice of 'whom do you believe, my word or your eyes?', I choose the Other's words without hesitation, dismissing the factual testimony of my eyes" (Laine 2014, 20; Žižek 1999a, 394–395). Once registered in the Symbolic/big Other, the state's directives become operative, interpellating the subject, who in turn acts as if s/he believes in the power of the state, thus buying into the latter's own fantasy.

10. My implication is that it is the Excluded (as the "concrete universal") who would need to lead any radical movement for change, with Left intellectuals and elites actively involved as supporters (thereby identifying with the poor-as-symptom). Leadership, vision, and organization would also be essential to such a movement for change.

# References

Albert, Michael. 2004. *Parecon: Life after Capitalism*. London: Verso.

Alcoff, Linda. 1991. "The Problem of Speaking for Others." *Cultural Critique* 20 (Winter): 5–32.

Baaz, Maria Eriksson. 2008. *The Paternalism of Partnership: A Postcolonial Reading of Identity in Development Aid*. London: Zed.

Bebbington, Anthony J., Diana Mitlin, Jan Mogaladi, Martin J. Scurrah, and Claudia Bielich. 2010. "Decentring Poverty, Reworking Government: Social Movements and States in the Government of Poverty." *Journal of Development Studies* 46 (7): 1304–1326.

Bernstein, Henry. 2005. "Rural Land and Conflicts in Sub-Saharan Africa." In *Reclaiming the Land: The Resurgence of Rural Movements in Africa, Asia and Latin America*, edited by Sam Moyo and Paris Yeros, 67–101. London: Zed.

Biswas, Soutik. 2012. "Who Are the Poor in India?" BBC News, India, March 23. http://www.bbc.com/news/world-asia-india-17455646.

——. 2014. "India's Dark History of Sterilisation." BBC News, India, November 14. http://www.bbc.com/news/world-asia-india-30040790.

Blaney, David L., and Naeem Inayatullah, eds. 2010. *Savage Economics: Wealth, Poverty and the Temporal Walls of Capitalism*. London: Routledge.

Cammack, Paul Anthony. 2003. "The Governance of Global Capitalism: A New Materialist Perspective." *Historical Materialism* 11 (2): 37–59.

——. 2009. "Poverty Reduction and Universal Competitiveness." *Labour, Capital and Society* 42 (1/2): 32–54.

Cardoso, Fernando Henrique, and Enzo Faletto. 1979. *Dependency and Development in Latin America*. Berkeley: University of California Press.

Corbridge, Stuart, Glyn Williams, Manoj Srivastava, and Rene Veron. 2005. *Seeing the State: Governance and Governmentality in India*. Cambridge: Cambridge University Press.

Davies, Matt, and Magnus Ryner, eds. 2006. *Poverty and the Production of World Politics*. Basingstoke: Palgrave Macmillan.

Dean, Jodi. 2006. *Žižek's Politics*. New York: Routledge.

Debord, Guy. 2012. *Society of the Spectacle*. London: Bread and Circuses.

Dixon, Pauline, Steve Humble, and Chris Counihan, eds. 2015. *Handbook of International Development and Education*. Cheltenham: Edward Elgar.

Duffield, Mark. 2001. "Governing the Borderlands: Decoding the Power of Aid." *Disasters* 25 (4): 308–320.

——. 2013. *Development, Security and Unending War: Governing the World of Peoples*. John Wiley and Sons.

Ehrlich, Paul R. 1971. *The Population Bomb*. London: Ballantine.

Escobar, Arturo. 1995. *Encountering Development: The Making and Unmaking of the Third World*. Princeton, NJ: Princeton University Press.

Evans, Dylan. 2006. *An Introductory Dictionary of Lacanian Psychoanalysis*. London: Routledge.

Fanon, Frantz. 1967. *Black Skin, White Masks*. Translated by Charles Markmann. New York: Grove.

Ferguson, James. 1990. *The Anti-Politics Machine: "Development," Depoliticization, and Bureaucratic Power in Lesotho*. Minneapolis: University of Minnesota Press.

Flemming, Gregory C. 2011. "Onitsha? It's Always Like This in Onitsha: 3903 and the 'Big Other.'" *Problematique* 13: 73–94.

Fletcher, Robert, Jan Breitling, and Valerie Puleo. 2014. "Barbarian Hordes: The Overpopulation Scapegoat in International Development Discourse." *Third World Quarterly* 35 (7): 1195–1215.

Frank, Andre Gunder. 1967. *Capitalism and Underdevelopment in Latin America*. New York: Monthly Review.

——. 1989. "The Development of Underdevelopment." *Monthly Review* 41 (2): 37–52.

Freud, Sigmund. 2013. *Inhibitions, Symptoms and Anxiety*. Translated by Alix Strachey. Mansfield Centre, CT: Martino.

Gandhi, Mohandas K. 1970. *The Collected Works of Mahatma Gandhi*. New Delhi: Ministry of Information and Broadcasting.

Garmany, Jeff. 2009. "The Embodied State: Governmentality in a Brazilian Favela." *Social and Cultural Geography* 10 (7): 721–739. https://doi.org/10.1080/14649360903205132.

Gibson-Graham, J. K. 2006. *A Post-Capitalist Politics*. Minneapolis: University of Minnesota Press.

Guha, Ranajit. 1988. "Preface." In *Selected Subaltern Studies*, edited by Ranajit Guha and Gayatri Chakravorty Spivak, 35–36. New York: Oxford University Press.

Gupta, Akhil. 2012. *Red Tape: Bureaucracy, Structural Violence and Poverty in India*. Durham, NC: Duke University Press.

Hall, Gillette H., and Harry Anthony Patrinos, eds. 2014. *Indigenous Peoples, Poverty, and Development*. Cambridge: Cambridge University Press.

Hardin, Garrett. 1968. "The Tragedy of the Commons." *Science* 162 (3859): 1243–1248. https://doi.org/10.1126/science.162.3859.1243.

Harriss-White, Barbara. 2004. *India Working: Essays on Society and Economy*. New Delhi: Cambridge University Press.

——. 2006. "Poverty and Capitalism." *Economic and Political Weekly* 41 (13): 1–7.

Harriss-White, Barbara, and Judith Heyer, eds. 2010. *The Comparative Political Economy of Development: Africa and South Asia*. London: Routledge.

Harvey, David. 2003. *The New Imperialism*. Oxford: Oxford University Press.

Ilcan, Suzan, and Anita Lacey. 2011. *Governing the Poor: Exercises of Poverty Reduction, Practices of Global Aid*. Montreal and Kingston: McGill-Queen's University Press.

Jessop, Bob. 2007. *State Power: A Strategic-Relational Approach*. Cambridge: Polity.

Jha, Manish K., P. K. Shajahan, and Mouleshri Vyas. 2013. "Biopolitics and Urban Governmentality in Mumbai." In *The Biopolitics of Development: Reading Michel*

*Foucault in the Postcolonial Present*, edited by Sandro Mezzadra, Julian Reid, and Ranabir Samaddara, 45–66. New Delhi: Springer.

Johnston, Adrian. 2005. *Time Driven: Metapsychology and the Splitting of the Drive*. Evanston, IL: Northwestern University Press.

Joseph, Jonathan. 2010a. "Poverty Reduction and the New Global Governmentality." *Alternatives: Global, Local, Political* 35 (1): 29–51.

——. 2010b. "The Limits of Governmentality: Social Theory and the International." *European Journal of International Relations* 16 (2): 223–246.

Kapoor, Ilan. 2004. "Hyper-Self-Reflexive Development? Spivak on Representing the Third World 'Other.'" *Third World Quarterly* 25 (4): 627–647.

——. 2008. *The Postcolonial Politics of Development*. London: Routledge.

——. 2013a. *Celebrity Humanitarianism: The Ideology of Global Charity*. London: Routledge.

——. 2013b. "Humanitarian Heroes?" In *Age of Icons: Exploring Philanthrocapitalism in the Contemporary World*, edited by Gavin Fridell and Martin Konings, 26–49. Toronto: University of Toronto Press.

——. 2014. "Psychoanalysis and Development: Contributions, Examples, Limits." *Third World Quarterly* 35 (7): 1120–1143.

——. 2015a. "Billionaire Philanthropy: 'Decaf Capitalism.'" In *International Handbook of Wealth and the Super-Rich*, edited by Jonathan Beaverstock and Iain Hay, 113–131. Cheltenham: Edward Elgar.

——. 2015b. "The Queer Third World." *Third World Quarterly* 36 (9): 1611–1628.

——. 2015c. "What 'Drives' Capitalist Development?" *Human Geography* 8 (3): 66–78.

——, ed. 2018. *Psychoanalysis and the GlObal*. Lincoln: University of Nebraska Press.

Kaur, Simran. 2008. *Women and Poverty*. Jaipur: Book Enclave.

Klugman, Jeni, ed. 2002. *A Sourcebook for Poverty Reduction Strategies*. Vol. 1, *Core Techniques and Cross-Cutting Issues*. Washington, DC: World Bank.

Koster, Martijn, and Pieter de Vries. 2012. "Slum Politics: Community Leaders, Everyday Needs, and Utopian Aspirations in Recife, Brazil." *Focaal* 2012 (62): 83–98.

Lacan, Jacques. 1998a. *Encore. On Feminine Sexuality, the Limits of Love and Knowledge: The Seminar of Jacques Lacan, Book XX*. Edited by Jacques-Alain Miller. Translated by Bruce Fink. New York: Norton.

——. 1998b. *The Four Fundamental Concepts of Psychoanalysis: The Seminar of Jacques Lacan, Book XI*. Edited by Jacques-Alain Miller. New York: Norton.

——. 2006. *The Other Side of Psychoanalysis: The Seminar of Jacques Lacan, Book XVII*. Edited by Jacques-Alain Miller. New York: Norton.

——. 2007. *Écrits: The First Complete Edition in English*. Translated by Bruce Fink. New York: Norton.

——. 2014. *Anxiety: The Seminar of Jacques Lacan, Book X*. Edited by Jacques-Alain Miller. Cambridge: Polity.

——. 2016. *The Sinthome: The Seminar of Jacques Lacan, Book XXIII*. Cambridge: Polity.

Laine, Eero. 2014. "Bureaucracy." In *The Žižek Dictionary*, edited by Rex Butler, 19–22. Durham: Acumen.

Mason, Paul. 2017. *Postcapitalism: A Guide to Our Future*. New York: Farrar, Straus and Giroux.

Mbembe, Achille. 2008. "Necropolitics." In *Foucault in an Age of Terror: Essays on Biopolitics and the Defence of Society*, edited by Stephen Morton and Stephen Bygrave, 152–182. Basingstoke: Palgrave Macmillan. http://link.springer.com /chapter/10.1057/9780230584334_9.

McGowan, Todd. 2004. *The End of Dissatisfaction? Jacques Lacan and the Emerging Society of Enjoyment.* Albany: SUNY Press.

———. 2014. "Symptom." In *The Žižek Dictionary*, edited by Rex Butler, 242–245. Durham: Acumen.

McMillan, Chris. 2008. "Symptomatic Readings: Žižekian Theory as a Discursive Strategy." *International Journal of Žižek Studies* 2 (1): 1–22. https://zizekstudies .org/index.php/IJZS/article/view/75/72.

Meffe, Gary K., Anne H. Ehrlich, and David Ehrenfeld. 1993. "Human Population Control: The Missing Agenda." *Conservation Biology* 7 (1): 1–3.

Mies, Maria. 1998. *Patriarchy and Accumulation on a World Scale: Women in the International Division of Labour.* London: Zed.

Mitchell, Tim. 1991. "America's Egypt: Discourse of the Development Industry." *Middle East Report* 169 (March/April): 18–36.

Nossiter, Adam. 2013. "Behind Those Fast Growth Rates, Rising Inequality." *New York Times*, November 5. http://www.nytimes.com/2013/11/06/world /africa/behind-those-fast-growth-rates-rising-inequality.html.

Rancière, Jacques. 1999. *Disagreement: Politics and Philosophy.* Minneapolis: University of Minnesota Press.

Saha, Saranjit Kumar, and Marcos Costa Lima. 2003. "The Dynamics of Chronic Poverty and Social Exclusion in Brazil: Which Way after Lula Victory?" Department for International Development, January 1. https://www.gov.uk /dfid-research-outputs/the-dynamics-of-chronic-poverty-and-social-exclusion -in-brazil-which-way-after-lula-victory.

Schumacher, E. F. 1973. *Small Is Beautiful: Economics as If People Mattered.* London: Blong and Briggs.

Scott, James C. 2008. *Seeing Like a State: How Certain Schemes to Improve the Human Condition Have Failed.* New Haven, CT: Yale University Press.

Sindayigaya, Aime Muligo. 2015. "Rwanda: Looking beyond Economic Growth Numbers (Part One)." Insightful Quotient, February 23. http://insightful quotient.com/rwanda-looking-beyond-economic-growth-numbers-part-one/.

Stavrakakis, Yannis. 2002. *Lacan and the Political.* London: Routledge.

———. 2007. *The Lacanian Left: Essays on Psychoanalysis and Politics.* Albany: SUNY Press.

Szirmai, Adam. 2005. *The Dynamics of Socio-Economic Development: An Introduction.* Cambridge: Cambridge University Press.

Tan, Celine. 2011. *Governance through Development: Poverty Reduction Strategies, International Law and the Disciplining of Third World States.* New York: Routledge.

Thurston, Luke, ed. 2002. *Re-Inventing the Symptom: Essays on the Final Lacan.* New York: Other Press.

Tobin, Damian. 2011. "Inequality in China: Rural Poverty Persists as Urban Wealth Balloons." BBC News, June 29. https://www.bbc.co.uk/news/business -13945072.

Tomšič, Samo. 2015. *The Capitalist Unconscious: Marx and Lacan.* London: Verso.

United Nations Development Programme (UNDP). 2016. *Human Development Report 2016: Human Development for Everyone*. New York: United Nations Development Programme.

Wallerstein, Immanuel Maurice. 2004. *World-Systems Analysis: An Introduction*. Durham, NC: Duke University Press.

Weber, Max. 2006. *Max Weber on Capitalism, Bureaucracy and Religion: A Selection of Texts*. Edited by Stanislav Andreski. London: Routledge.

Žižek, Slavoj. 1989. *The Sublime Object of Ideology*. London: Verso.

——. 1991. *Looking Awry: An Introduction to Jacques Lacan through Popular Culture*. Cambridge, MA: MIT Press.

——. 1992. *Enjoy Your Symptom! Jacques Lacan in Hollywood and Out*. New York: Routledge.

——. 1993. *Tarrying with the Negative: Kant, Hegel, and the Critique of Ideology*. Durham, NC: Duke University Press.

——. 1999a. *The Ticklish Subject: The Absent Centre of Political Ontology*. London: Verso.

——. 1999b. *The Žižek Reader*. Edited by Elizabeth Wright and Edmond Leo Wright. Oxford: Blackwell.

——. 2006. *The Parallax View*. Cambridge, MA: MIT Press.

——. 2008. *Violence: Six Sideways Reflections*. New York: Picador.

——. 2009. *First as Tragedy, Then as Farce*. London: Verso.

——. 2013. *Less than Nothing: Hegel and the Shadow of Dialectical Materialism*. London: Verso.

——. 2018. *The Courage of Hopelessness: Chronicles of a Year of Acting Dangerously*. London: Penguin.

# INDEX

Abu Ghraib, 240, 250n6
Achebe, Chinua, 64
Afro-pessimists, 259n8
AIDS. *See* HIV/AIDS
Alarian, Riad, 61
Alcoff, Linda, 173, 287
Ambani, Mukesh, 104
antagonism, 59–71; Eurocentrism contro-
  versy and, 63–70; gender/sex, as
  fundamental antagonism, 179–82, 184–87;
  ideology critique and, 59–60, 62, 70; the
  Real and, 59, 63, 70; refugee controversy
  and, 60–63, 71n2; universalist dimensions
  of, 59, 60, 65–66, 68–69, 71–72n4
Appiah, Anthony, 259n9
Arab male, change in Western fantasy of,
  252–53
Arab Spring, 115, 140, 187, 194, 290. *See also*
  perversion and hysteria in Tunisian
  Revolution
Asian financial crisis (1997), 81
Augustine, *Confessions*, 95

Bald, Suresht R., 174
Bandung Conference (1955), 214, 215
Basu Thakur, Gautam, 71n4
Baudrillard, Jean, 132
Bayat, Asef, 176–77
Beauvoir, Simone de, 171
Belk, Russell, 105–6, 116n8
Ben Ali, Zine El Abidine, 195–98, 203–7,
  210n6
Bentham, Jeremy, 148
Berani, Leo, 231n9
Berlusconi, Silvio, 109, 211n10
Bhabha, Homi, xi, 130, 143n3, 161, 165n3,
  231n3, 259n10
*Big Brother* (TV show), 158–59
Bishara, Marwan, 64
Blaney, David L., 271
blind spots in development, 11–13, 156, 160

Boko Haram, 101
Bolsonaro, Jair, 17
Bouazizi, Mohamed, 196–97, 204
branding, 157–58
Brazil, income inequality/poverty in, 268
bureaucratic/institutional enjoyment, xiv,
  39, 260n14, 273–75, 278–79
Burton, Richard, 218
Bush, George W., 10, 27n9
Butler, Judith, xii, 64, 170, 174–77, 181, 183,
  184, 185, 190n3

Cammack, Paul Anthony, 266, 269, 276, 287
capitalism: communism and, 69; dispossession, drive to accumulate by, 82–83,
  86–87; as drive to overaccumulate, 78–82;
  economic versus capitalist development,
  76; enjoyment and, 15–16; as envy-
  machine, 95, 96–102; growth fetish and,
  127, 130–32; income inequality, thriving
  on, 97–102, 268–69, 292n4; Islamic
  movements' lack of critique of, 210–11n9;
  master signifier, Capital as, 87; performativity and, 177–78; perversion/hysteria in
  Tunisian Revolution and, 202, 203, 204,
  207; post-development's surrender to,
  40–49; poverty-as-symptom and, 265–66,
  268–71, 274, 275–77, 286, 291–92n3;
  resisting drive of, 88–90; technofetishism
  and, 135, 136, 137–38; universalized
  challenge to, 68; well-functioning system,
  mythology of, 109
Carlson, Shanna, 182, 183
castration/castration anxiety: fetishism and,
  124–25, 128–30, 133–34, 137, 141; gender/
  sex and, 180, 183; in Lacanian psychoanalytic perspective, 5–6; perversion/hysteria
  and, 200; poverty-as-symptom and, 283;
  queerness and, 216, 218; racism and, 255
Catholic Church sex abuse scandal, 240,
  250n6

Lightning Source UK Ltd.
Milton Keynes UK
UKHW010123240621
386004UK00013B/495